STUDENT'S GUIDE TO COLLEGE MUSIC PROGRAMS

SECOND

EDITION

ACKNOWLEDGEMENTS

We proudly acknowledge the following individuals who contributed their expertise in the completion of this publication. Authors Thomas Kikta, Joseph J. Martinkovic, Joanne Monath, Rob Rogers and Mark Thomas. Graphic designers Preeti Jain and Donald McGee. Editor Jennifer H. McInerney for coordinating the editorial effort and Joseph Barbato for his assistance in assembling the database. Melanie A. Prescott for the many hours extended in helping bring this project to print and *SCHOOL BAND AND ORCHESTRA* Group Publisher Sidney Davis and Publisher Richard Kessel for their encouragement and support.

Cover design by Ken Silvia Design Group

Thanks also to Brad Smith and the production staff at Hal Leonard Publishing for their advice and guidance in the production of this publication.

CONTENTS:

Foreword

The Second Edition of the Student's Guide to College Music Programs offers an expanded state-by-state listing of more than 1,300 college and university programs. In addition, the state "home page" features a variety of useful information for the music student, including music programs within the state, state capital and population figures.

We are grateful to the music professional contributors who assisted us in compiling information on financial aid, vocational careers, guidelines for auditions and other topics of interest to the serious music student.

For each of the colleges and universities in this book we present a capsule of information ranging from basic admission contacts to course requirements and music programs. We are grateful to the admissions officers and music departments who supplied the data. Music students are encouraged to contact their school guidance departments and college admissions officers for further information.

The Student's Guide to College Music Programs is affiliated with *School Band and Orchestra*, a magazine for music educators. Readers are encouraged to visit our Web site at www.sbomagazine.com for additional resources.

A. J. Larkin

A J Larkin
President
Larkin Publications

Student's Guide To College Music programs is dedicated to the memory of Alan B. Larkin. He was an ardent supporter of music and the arts, whose encouragement and inspiration made this publication possible.

What's Expected of Incoming Freshmen

BY MARK THOMAS

Most high school juniors and seniors realize that the educational system they have enjoyed for the majority of their young years is nearing an end. Those familiar surroundings that have felt so comfortable are soon going to be replaced by a series of new choices. Gone will be a bell to signal a classroom change, club activities, proms, parent-teacher meetings, school bus rides, Friday night football games, and many other things that have defined the secondary school years.

After high school graduation, some students will enter the job market or decide to serve their country in the armed forces, while the majority will elect to further their education at an institution of higher learning. Students seeking a college education are urged to apply for admission early and send applications to more than one school. Applying to at least three to five institutions with programs that are appealing is quite reasonable, increasing the chances that a suitable school will make an offer.

College is Different

State laws mandate that you must attend secondary schools, whereas colleges and universities select students they wish to accept via the application process. Unlike public schools, colleges and universities – whether public or private – charge tuition to attend. Further, the college/university world is considered an adult world: students are treated accordingly. At the secondary level, it's the "boys' basketball team," or the "girls' tennis team," whereas at the university level, it's the "men's golf team" and the "women's basketball team."

A college student (or undergraduate) who experiences difficulty with a

subject should not expect to arrange a parent-teacher conference to discuss the problem. The professor will discuss the problem with the student, not his or her parents. Students who earn a high grade point average after a semester can expect to be rewarded with a place on the dean's or chancellor's list. Conversely, those who earn a low grade-point average can expect to be on the dean's "other list."

Self Discipline

Failure in too many subjects will soon lead to academic probation and/or expulsion from the college or university. Such failure is frequently the result

of a lack of self-discipline and proper time management. Students often have difficulty accepting personal responsibility for their actions. Young adults away from home for the first time no longer have someone to rouse them in the morning in time for class; indeed, class schedules often seem erratic. The English literature class may meet three times a week for 50 minutes, while a class in biology may meet twice a week for a 50-minute lecture and once a week for a two-and-a-half-hour lab. Also, a student's class schedule is likely to be different from roommates' or hall mates' schedules, since students enrolled in many disciplines room together. Evening classes and ensembles are quite normal. Undergraduates who survive the freshman year learn to use free time during the day for practice and studying.

Freedom is a Double-Edged Sword

Most high schools have enrollments of 1,000 to 2,000, whereas a large university may have 20,000 or more. Consequently, the experience of seeing familiar faces in high school will vary drastically in college. In high school, juniors and seniors represent the upper class; in the university setting, former high school graduates are the youngest age group and freshmen again.

Many college freshmen experience loneliness in their new surroundings and bemoan the loss of their former "upper class" status. The need to find new friends and be accepted is great and can frequently lead to academic problems. Students who learn to balance their social and academic lives in the first year can avoid the disappointment and embarrassment of "flunking out" in college. Students are expected to have class assignments prepared as scheduled; excuses are unacceptable.

Music Courses

At the university level, lesson assignments are more extensive than at the high school level, and all music majors are required to have a one-hour lesson per week on their major instrument. Fundamentals (i.e., all forms of scales and arpeggios) must be mastered; also, professors will assign substantial etude material and repertoire appropriate for freshmen. It is never advisable to inform the private lesson professor that practice time was not available because of a paper or impending test that required extra preparation. Remember that private lessons are a class that can be failed. Private music lessons at the university level should never be considered an easy, automatic "A." Materials should be as carefully prepared for a music lesson as for any other class. Always be on time for your lessons and, should cancellation of a lesson ever be necessary, do so well in advance and only for a very valid reason. Some professors may allow for a make-up lesson. Failure to appear for your lesson will result in a grade of zero for that day.

Practice Habits

Practice sessions for most high school students can vary from one hour or more a day to none, depending on homework or school activities. The majority of private teachers try to accommodate these irregularities if they are not abused. If carried to extremes, of course, many teachers will drop such a student from their schedules.

At the college and university level, each student must find time each week for practice in order to properly prepare the music assigned. Two to four hours or more each day should be sufficient to prepare weekly assignments. Just as a student needs to spend a great deal of time reading literature or studying calculus, he or she must also spend a great deal of time practicing, not only the basics (scales, etudes) but the great literature and orchestral works for that student's instrument. The student who is well prepared in the basics will have more time to learn new things and progress more quickly.

Band, Orchestra and Ensembles

Band, orchestra, and smaller ensembles are an important part of preparing students for musical careers. These various organizations offer artistic challenges not found at the high school level, since personnel is comprised of more advanced, older players. Competition for chair seating arrangements is strong and the directors expect to take students to new musical heights. Exposure to more difficult repertoire will strengthen a sense of phrasing and intonation. As with private lesson assignments, ensemble music must also be well prepared, for numerous section rehearsals are common at the university level. Missed notes, bad intonation, and sloppy phrasing will not be tolerated. Practice time must be allocated for this music as well.

Work and Enjoy

All college and university music professors know that incoming freshmen are not seasoned artists; if they were, they would not be attending an institution of higher learning. By working together with various professors, aspiring musicians can accomplish a great deal during the college years. Students attending a college or university are seeking help in building a life-long career in music; those who enter with an open mind and are ready to learn will be successful.

Music professors have achieved acclaim in their various fields and will gladly share this expertise with students. They were once students themselves – they know what it takes to be successful. By having a positive attitude, students can achieve at this higher level. It is a time of newness and excitement. Freshmen are allowed and encouraged to have fun and enjoyment in college, but must learn to balance social activities and class work wisely. Students who do not allow "Party 101" to become the focus and the dean's "other list" the goal can succeed in music and in life and can enjoy the many benefits and rewards a career in music has to offer. ♪

Mark Thomas is founder and honorary life president of The National Flute Association (NFA). He is professor of flute at the University of North Carolina at Charlotte, where he also directs the university flute choir. A recitalist, soloist, conductor, and clinician, he has appeared in 20 foreign countries and 49 states. He has been on the faculties of The American University, George Washington University, The University of Notre Dame, Indiana University at South Bend, National Music Camp at Interlochen, and Sewanee Summer Music Center, and has lectured at many universities and conservatories. Thomas has numerous published flute works, including the Mark Thomas Flute Method series. He has served as a board member of National Public Radio, board President of the Elkhart County Symphony Association, and as artistic design consultant to several leading flute manufacturers. Thomas can be heard on Golden Crest and Columbia Records.

Financial Aid 101: Making Sense of It All

By Joseph J. Martinkovic

So you're planning to attend college and pursue the program of your dreams. Like most college-bound students, financial aid may be a vital, if not critical, part of your college education plans. There are hundreds of questions running through your mind as you move through the college admissions and financial-aid process. Probably the most troubling question that you may face is, "What if my parents can't afford to send me to college?" Well, that certainly can happen and for a variety of reasons. But my experience in both the college admissions and financial-aid arenas is that most students do have the opportunity to pursue a college education and usually at one of their top-choice institutions.

Before we look at the various aspects of financial aid, let me say this to you: the cost of the colleges, universities, or conservatories that you may be considering should not be your primary consideration as you begin the college search and admissions process. Now I know what you're thinking, "Sure, it's easy for you to say, but my family has to pay for my education." You're right. Just remember that this process can span several months in your senior year of high school. You have to be patient with yourself and let the process work. But you know what? If you do what is asked of you, the process does work, and it can work for you.

The cost of your education may be a determining factor in your choice, but that should occur after you've made application to the col-leges, have been notified of your admission to the colleges, and have received your offers of financial aid from the colleges. At that point, you need to sit down with your family and seriously review your options. Based upon your commitment to what you want to pursue as a potential career (because things can and do change) and your family's financial position and convictions towards your education, getting to one of your top-choice schools may just become a reality for you.

There's a ton of information I'd like to share with you on the subject of financial aid and financing your education. I could probably write a 300-page book on the subject and still forget to include important information. So what I'd like to do here is to highlight some of the key aspects about financial aid and the process. I firmly believe that if you understand the basics and the process of financial aid, then you've got a good shot at cutting through the magic and mystery as you work your way through the financial aid maze.

The Basic Premise

Just what is this magical and mystical thing called financial aid? Well, the easiest way to describe it is that financial aid is money applied against your college's costs to help you obtain your college education. What I do want to emphasize here is that the basic premise of financial aid is that you and your parents are the primary source of funds for your post-secondary education and are expected to contribute to the extent that you and your parents are able. (Did you notice I threw in the word "you"?) I think it's extremely important that you contribute financially toward your education in some way. You could work a part-time job and save to pay for books and supplies, or help with your living expenses if you live in campus housing, or cover your weekly travel expenses if you're commuting from home to a local college. Not only does it help your family out financially, but it also shows your family your commitment and determination (and they just might go that extra mile to help you get to where you want to go.) I've found students who buy into their education tend to benefit more from their education. After all, it is an investment in your future.

One thing's for sure — financial aid is not an entitlement program. Simply stated, there are no guarantees since everything is contingent upon funding. Federal regulations prevail and institutional policies and procedures guide financial aid administrators in their decision-making process. (When you're spending other peoples' money, you always have to play by their rules.) That doesn't mean that there aren't colleges or universities that will offer you a "full ride," because there are. But those institutions are few and far between no matter how talented you may be. You need to know that you and your family will have to contribute something toward your education and perhaps, in some cases, the whole enchilada. But we're here to help you as best we can contingent upon the availability of financial aid funds at our respective institutions.

Types of Financial Aid

There are three types of financial aid: gift aid, loan aid, and work aid. Let's take a brief look at each type.

Gift aid is by far the most popular and sought-after type of financial aid. Gift aid usually takes the form of a grant or scholarship. The best part of this type of award is that it doesn't have to be paid back (I guess that's why they call it a gift.) If you are applying for need-based financial aid, gift aid based on need is usually called a grant. If, for example, you are musically talented and plan to pursue music as a college major or a career, you may be offered a talent scholarship. Scholarships may be based more on your ability, talent, or skills than on your financial need. The same is true if you're an exceptional student scholastically in high school. Some colleges and universities acknowledge students' hard work and efforts and offer academic scholarships. Both talent and academic scholarships can range from a few hundred dollars up to a full tuition scholarship and, in a few cases, may even include room and board (now that's what I call a gift!).

Loan aid is borrowed money that has to be repaid with interest. Again, if you are applying for need-based financial aid, loans are inevitable and will most likely be a part of your financial aid "package." It is also referred to as a "self-help" program. Often, students and parents don't think of loans as financial aid, but they are. This type of financial aid is most readily available and comprises the largest source of funding within federal financial aid programs. If you are offered a loan as part of your financial aid award, you do have the right to decline the loan. Keep in mind, however, that your loan will not be replaced with gift aid. I usually advise students not to be afraid to borrow an educational loan, especially if you're offered a Federal Perkins Loan of a subsidized Federal Stafford Loan. Both of these programs offer low-interest rates with attractive repayment terms (including no payments while you're enrolled in college). The question you have to answer is "Will this loan help me get to a top-choice college, or can it help to reduce the financial burden on my family?" If it does, then I'd like to think of it more as an investment in your future than a financial burden. By borrowing responsibly, the repayment of your loan can be a short-term, manageable debt.

The final type of financial aid is work aid. Work aid is just that — you work, you get paid. Like loan aid, work aid is another self-help program and you can decline a part-time job if it's offered to you. The vast majority of colleges and universities offer some type of work opportunities, either through federally funded programs or their own on-campus programs. For the most part, however, the money you earn is not credited to your account in the business office like gift aid or loan aid would be. It is paid directly to you on a regular basis (weekly, bi-weekly, or monthly.) Some colleges will allow you to have all or a portion of your earnings applied against your college costs. However, if you do opt to work a part-time job while in college, I would advise you to use these funds to help with your weekly support. That could include feeding quarters into your dorm's washer and dryer, buying late-night snacks during exam week, watching an occasional movie or video, or buying a logo sweatshirt from the bookstore for a friend. Keep in mind that if you and your parents need to borrow supplemental educational loans to help offset the cost of your education (other than the two federal loan programs I mentioned above), taking on a part-time job that's based on need can cut into your borrowing potential.

Primary Sources Of Financial Aid

Now that you know the types of financial aid available to you, you're probably wondering who funds these financial aid programs. Well, there are four primary sources of funding: the federal government; your state government; private organizations, businesses and foundations; and, last but certainly not least, the colleges and universities themselves.

By far, the federal government is the biggest player in the financial aid program. Over 70 percent of all sources of financial aid are federally funded. The federal government does provide funds for all three types of financial aid with the loan programs comprising the largest percentage (about 54 percent.) In order for you to be considered for these programs, you have to file the Free Application for Federal Student Aid, commonly known as the FAFSA (an acronym you'll get to know and love.) The FAFSA is the primary "need analysis" document that is used to determine your eligibility for federal funds and to calculate your "demonstrated" financial need. By submitting the FAFSA, you are considered for the Federal Pell Grant Program, the Federal Campus-Based Programs (Federal Supplemental Educational Opportunity Grant, Federal Perkins Loan, and Federal Work-Study), and the Federal Stafford Loan Program. Even if you do not demonstrate a financial need you may be eligible for an unsubsidized Federal Stafford Loan. The major difference between a subsidized and an unsubsidized loan is who pays the interest on the loan while you're in college. If you have a subsidized loan, the federal government pays the interest; for an unsubsidized loan, you are responsible for paying the interest on the loan while enrolled. To get a better understanding of the specifics of the federal programs, you can access information at the U.S. Department of Education's Web site, www.ed.gov.

Your state government is the second source of funding. Most states do offer some form of gift aid based on a student's demonstrated financial need and may also include your scholastic performance (as measured by your class rank or standardized test scores). Since the programs do vary from state to state, it's best that you check on your respective state's program. You do need to find out if your state's grant or scholarship program is "portable," that is, if it can be taken out-of-state. Some states (such as New York and New Jersey) require you to attend a college or university in-state in order to be eligible for the programs. If your state does allow you to apply the grant or scholarship to an out-of-state institution, the amount of the grant or scholarship may be reduced. You also need to know whether the colleges and universities you are considering will reduce any of their own financial aid if you receive a state grant or scholarship.

Although private organizations, businesses, and foundations are the smallest players in the financial aid program, this form of gift aid or loan aid can make a significant contribution to reducing your out-of-pocket college costs. The best place to start is in your own hometown. Your high school's guidance office usually has information available on these local, regional, or national programs. What's best about these scholarship and loan programs is that you don't have to be the class valedictorian or salutatorian in order to be eligible for consideration for these programs. These organizations, businesses, and foundations are willing to invest their dollars in a "few good men and women" just like you. If it took you an hour to complete their application and you win a $500 scholarship, would it not be worth the effort? How many people do you know who earn $500 per hour?

A word of caution about participating in a national scholarship search service: if you have to pay to have someone else find you scholarships, it's probably a scam. There are legitimate scholarship search services that you can do over the Internet that won't cost you a dime. One of the best sites on the Internet is www.finaid.org. It will hyperlink you to free legitimate search services and also provides information on scholarship scams and other important information about financial aid that's worth reading.

Finally, there are the colleges and universities that offer institutional financial aid funds, primarily in the form of gift aid. When financial aid administrators review your financial situation (assuming you submitted the FAFSA), you are usually considered for all possible types of institutional financial aid. Remember two things. First, our job is to help bring you to our respective campuses and help you and your family meet your financial responsibilities once on campus. The operative word is "help." Second, all institutional financial aid is contingent upon the availability of funds. Often, families think that colleges and universities have unlimited resources. It's simply not true. Even nationally renowned institutions with nine-digit endowments have limitations on financial aid availability.

Merit Scholarships

Merit scholarships are a controversial topic. There are institutions that believe financial aid should only be need-based and students should have a demonstrated financial need in order to qualify for aid. Then there are those colleges and universities that adopt the attitude that students who demonstrate outstanding ability or characteristics, or special skills or talent should be acknowledged regardless of their family's financial situation. There appears to be a growing number of institutions (both independent and public colleges and universities) that subscribe to the latter philosophy. That's good news for you. As someone who currently participates in a high school band or orchestra, you have a talent. Colleges and universities who offer degree programs in music or place special emphasis on music as an extra-curricular activity may seek you. Many of these institutions offer merit scholarships. Let your talent pay off for you and help reduce the cost of your college education.

The Application Process

As I noted when discussing federal government funding, you have to file the FAFSA form in order to be considered for federal financial aid programs (with the exception of the Federal PLUS Loan, a supplemental education loan program for parents.) All colleges and universities must use this form for federal financial aid programs. Most states also require you to file the FAFSA in order to be considered for their state grant and scholarship programs. Likewise, the vast majority of institutions also use this form to determine your eligibility for their own need-based financial aid programs. If you plan to apply for financial aid (and I encourage you to do so since it's free), make sure you submit the FAFSA by the deadline dates set by the colleges and universities to which you will be applying. For entering freshmen, most colleges and universities require you to file by early or mid-February of your senior year of high school. Under current federal policies, you cannot file the FAFSA until after January 1st of your senior year. The sooner you file the better, even if it means estimating information about you and your parents' income and assets. You can always update the information once your and your parents' federal tax returns are filed. You can apply via the Internet at www.fafsa.ed.gov. It's the fastest and most accurate way of submitting the FAFSA form.

If you are applying under a college's early admissions' decision program, you'll need to contact the college to find out what need-analysis form you may have to file. Usually, you have to submit your admissions application early in your senior year with an admissions decision sometime by the end of December. Most institutions will provide you with an estimated financial-aid package since you will be required to commit to attending that institution if you are admitted. But in almost all cases, you will still have to submit the FAFSA.

Not all institutions rely solely on the results of the FAFSA when it comes to considering you for institutional financial aid. Another need-analysis form used by about 600 colleges and universities is the College Scholarship Service's (CSS) Profile. CSS charges a nominal fee for processing its need-analysis form for each college you list. The purpose of this form is to supplement information not captured on the FAFSA (such as a family's home equity.) The colleges and universities that require the

Profile factor in the additional information when determining your eligibility for institutional aid. Check with the colleges and universities you're considering as to whether or not they require the Profile or any other need-analysis form (other than the FAFSA, of course.) If they do, you will not be considered for any institutional financial aid programs if you don't submit the form. For further information about the Profile and other pertinent financial aid information, go to www.collegeboard.org.

ACT (which is most popular West of the Mississippi) also offers a free Financial Aid Need Estimator. It doesn't take the place of the FAFSA or any other required need-analysis form, but it can provide you with an idea of what your family's expected financial contribution might be. To access the Estimator, go to www.act.org.

One final comment on the financial aid application process. You have to resubmit the FAFSA (and possibly any other need-analysis form) annually. If your family's financial situation changes, your financial aid can, and most likely will, change. Certainly that's true with the federal or state programs, but that can vary from institution to institution with regard to renewing their own financial aid. It's always best to ask these questions early on in the admissions and financial-aid process to minimize any unforeseen surprises.

About Your Parents

Parental information on the FAFSA or any other need-analysis form is an integral part of determining your demonstrated financial need. If you are currently a high school senior and you're not 24 years of age or older, or not a veteran of the armed services, or do not have a dependent of your own, you are considered a dependent student and information about your parents (and/or step-parent) is required on the FAFSA. If you are a ward of the court or if both of your parents are deceased, you may qualify as an independent student. If you feel there are extenuating circumstances regarding your dependency status, it's always best to contact the financial aid office at the colleges or universities you are considering and explain your situation (preferably in writing with supporting documentation.) The financial-aid office can best advise you as to what you must do to be considered for financial aid at their institution.

If you are a dependent student, there are three scenarios regarding who must provide information on the FAFSA. If you live with both natural (or birthing) parents, information about both parents must provided. If you live in a single-parent family, the custodial parent must provide information on the FAFSA. The custodial parent is the parent with whom you reside the majority of time. If you are a member of a blended family, your natural parent and your parent's spouse (your step-parent) must provide information, even if the step-parent has no legal responsibility for you or your education. Any exceptions to these requirements must be determined by the financial aid administrator in accordance with federal regulations or institutional policies.

Payment Plans and Supplemental Education Loans

Well, you've been accepted at the college of your choice and you've received a great financial-aid package. But it spite of a great package, you and your family may still experience some difficulty in meeting your financial obligations to the college. Does that mean you have to abandon your dreams? Not necessarily. There are alternative financing methods that you can pursue with your family.

Most institutions offer what are known as 10-month payment plans. Here's how it works. Let's say you owe a balance of $5,000 for your freshman year of college. Most institutions will bill you according to their academic schedule (two semesters, three trimesters, or four quarters.) Most institutions operate on a semester schedule, so that means you and your family would have to make two $2,500 payments (one payment for the fall semester; the other payment for the spring semester). For some families, a single $2,500 payment may be difficult. With a 10-month payment plan, your family makes ten $500 payments instead. For most, this is more financially manageable than lump-sum payments. The one benefit of the payment plans that I like is when the last payment of the year is made, you walk away from the plan — you owe nothing. There's no interest, no hidden costs. Companies who manage these programs for colleges and universities charge a nominal annual enrollment fee, usually between $40 and $60. It's a great way to manage your out-of-pocket costs.

Supplemental education loans are another way to help you and your family meet your annual college expenses. These loan programs vary in repayment terms, length of repayment, and interest assessment, to mention a few. If you're considering a supplemental education loan, make sure you understand of all the terms and conditions. For some loan programs, you are the borrower but you may be required to have a co-borrower, especially if you have no credit history or an inadequate income. Other loan programs require the parent to be the borrower. With a few of these programs, a relative (other than your parent) or a friend (a very, very dear friend, I might add) can borrow the loan. Most lenders perform a credit check to determine the borrower's credit-worthiness. For the most part, the borrower can borrow up to the total cost of the education, less any financial aid you're receiving. With a supplemental education loan, repayment can go on for 10 or 15 years or more. That's why financial-aid administrators encourage you to borrow only what you need so that you're not mortgaging your future through educational loans.

You can also combine a payment plan with a supplemental loan. Let's say your family can't make a $500-per-month payment but they can make a $300 payment. Your parents sign up for a $2,000 payment plan and borrow $3,000 through a supplemental education loan program. Now they have a manageable payment each month and have reduced their loan indebtedness — and you're attending the college of your choice. (Sounds like a win-win situation to me.)

Financial-aid offices establish good working relationships with these type of lenders and will gladly provide you with information about these two programs available at their institution. Both the financial aid office and the business office work hand-in-hand to help you to understand what's available and to meet your financial obligations. After all, we have a vested interest in your success as well.

In Conclusion

I hope this information has shed some light on the magical and mystical world of financial aid. If this information made sense to you and you feel more confident about what to expect, then give yourself an "A."

You've just passed Financial Aid 101. Don't let the process intimidate you. It's a necessary evil, but you will survive. As I've said many times, your education is an investment in your future. Make it count; make the investment work for you. Good luck and best wishes in your educational pursuits. ♪

Joseph J. Martinkovic has over 25 years of experience in college admissions and financial aid.

Following a Musical Vocation

BY JOANNE MONATH

Music, "what a beautiful art, but what a wretched profession," said Georges Bizet, the 19th-century composer and pianist. So, if your dream is to become a performing musician, then prepare for part-time schedules, intermittent unemployment, and keen competition for every job. However, there are also plenty of related careers in the music industry that will allow you to be gainfully and steadily employed in your passion, so don't despair.

Music is big business in the United States. NAMM – The International Music Products Association reports that consumer spending on music-related products has nearly doubled in the last decade, with recent sales topping $7 billion. According to the U.S. Department of Labor, overall employment of musicians is expected to grow about as fast as the average for all occupations through the year 2008. Interestingly, the number of people employed in music-related careers is projected to rise even faster. Why? A significant increase is projected in the number of people of all ages who play musical instruments. As the cost of instruments continues to climb and consumers realize the value of keeping

their instruments in good repair, musicians are more likely to contact repair technicians. In addition, the number of ways to make and record music is constantly being developed. All of this is good news for vocational careers in the music industry.

Recording Arts

Consumers spend more money on musical recordings – CDs, tapes, and videos – than on magazines or going to movies. Specialized careers in this field include recording engineers, post-production audio engineers, studio assistants and operators, live sound engineers, lighting technicians, MIDI operators and maintenance technicians.

The recording industry first gained importance in the 1920s, some 40 years after Edison first invented his "talking machine." However, it was the rock 'n roll era of the 1950s that energized the industry. From there, recording has been constantly evolving, using new technology to bring recordings to homes, theatres, live venues and now the Internet. Today, musicians often find themselves dependent upon their mixing consoles and multi-track tape machines, and even more dependent upon technicians and engineers who have mastered recording technology.

Studios have also evolved from the portable, mini-lab-like settings of the early 1900s to the modern studios of today. Now there are private studios, smaller in size and track capability; project studios that are well-equipped and often owned by artists and producers; and commercial studios used by outside clients for making recordings.

In recording arts, the engineer or technician who runs all of the machinery that controls sound has become a key role. In addition to their traditional technical role, recording engineers now create complex sounds, such as orchestral arrangements, from a single musician. Recording engineers must have a solid understanding of electronics, acoustics and sound, a good ear for music, and the ability to work with a wide variety of performers. Because of the sophistication of recording and studio equipment, apprenticeships are seldom adequate training to enter this field (see programs offered at the end of this article).

Film and Video Production

Film and video production careers are closely related to the recording industry. Motion picture companies often own the record labels of music used in their studio's movies. Music has been elevated from merely background sound to becoming a main part of the theme, as in the film "Saturday Night Fever." Today, soundtracks feature several artists, and sometimes songs by popular artists are even introduced through a film.

Film and video production offer careers as production assistants, grips, camera operators, audio engineers, sound designers, lighting technicians, digital video effects operators, etc. Training programs must be supplemented with hands-on experience and state-of-the art equipment to ensure education in the fundamentals as well as specialized knowledge required for a wide variety of recording tasks.

Show Production and Touring

Generating about $1 billion in annual revenues from concert ticket sales, the live entertainment industry is roughly one-tenth the size of the recording industry. Live concerts greatly increase album sales and are important career-builders for the artist.

To qualify for entry-level positions in the field of show production, skills must be developed in staging, sound reinforcement, show lighting and touring. Live event staging experience is also helpful. It is essential to have a fundamental knowledge of sound, multimedia, and computers. Sound systems have become increasingly high tech, so current training in electronics maintenance, computer-aided design and operation of lights must be mastered before taking off on tour.

On the management side, opportunities exist for promoters of live events who obtain talent, locate venues, book concert dates and market tickets. Artists often require concert managers who secure concert engagements and ensure that all live performance needs are met. A career in live event management also requires music business administration knowledge (see next section).

Business of Music: Administration and Management

Careers in the music business require an overall understanding of how the music industry works as well as knowledge of the technical side – administration of recording contracts, record production, publishing, artist management, song writing and copyright law, music on the Internet, concert contracts, etc. On the management side, emphasis is placed on accounting, business law, finance, taxes, retailing and advertising.

Digital and Multimedia

In this career, people design and implement interfaces for digital media products. These presentations may be on CD-ROM, Web sites and digital and analog videos used in education, business, entertainment, interactive presentations, digital video clips and digital audio recordings. After gaining an educational background in digital media, many career paths are possible: graphic artist, interface designer, production manager, design lead, digital image processor, 2D or 3D animator, digital media author and editor, production artist and special effects artist.

In multimedia, computers are used to bring together text, sounds, animation, graphic art and video. Technically, multimedia is the convergence of two or more forms of media – a communication process rather than an industry. Video producers, sound engineers and editors, sound producers and videographers are some of the music-related careers in multimedia.

Digital and multimedia are emerging fields that require formal training and a well-developed portfolio with samples of your work. A career as a sound producer, for example, requires a solid understanding of sound design and processing tools as well as studio recording techniques and an overall understanding of how sound fits into each project. A video producer needs knowledge of traditional video and film production techniques, proper use of lighting and perspective, video cameras, computer hardware and software as well as video recording and editing tools. The occupation of video producer may also require involvement in management activities such as budgeting, scheduling, and planning.

There is an interesting difference between careers in digital and multimedia and other music-related careers: work tends to be project-oriented. Free-lancers often come together to work on a project; their employment terminates at the end of that project and they move on. This is an area where creative and talented people often build initial experience through volunteering and internships that may lead to paid employment opportunities through that company. Be prepared, though, to keep your portfolio updated, to frequently seek employment on new projects and to continually update your knowledge of new tools and techniques.

Musical Instrument Construction, Repair, and Tuning

Because instruments are expensive to buy, the employment outlook for musical instrument repair technicians and tuners is good, especially for those who receive formal training.

Formal training is offered at only a few schools and there are few employers who are willing to take on apprentices or provide training. However, increased numbers of musicians, rental companies, schools and other organizations – which must keep their instruments in good repair – provide plenty of opportunity for those who have been well trained.

A nearly universal requirement in this career is the ability to play any instruments that will be worked on. Through formal training, a student develops an ear for tonal quality and mechanical skills necessary to work on instruments. Usually, the only prerequisite to formal training is a high school diploma or GED certificate. Many programs require coursework in communications and customer service as these occupations require well-developed skills in understanding customer needs and wishes. About two-thirds of workers in this category are self-employed, with the rest working mostly in music store repair shops. Two to five years of training are required to become fully qualified.

Band instrument repair technicians work on woodwind, brass, reed, and percussion instruments that have been damaged or are aging. After a customer describes the problem, the instrument is examined and then restored to established industry specifications. Repair specialists must be familiar with the characteristics and problems of each instrument as well as the tools necessary for repair. In brass and wind instrument repairing, instruments are cleaned and adjusted. Moving parts are adjusted or replaced while worn pads and corks are replaced. Percussion instrument repairers remove tension rods, cut new drumheads from animal skins and replace worn parts on xylophones, among other tasks.

Piano and organ repair technicians and tuners replace worn parts, recondition usable parts, or sometimes completely rebuild upright and grand pianos. Additional service may be provided for pianos with built-in humidity control, recording devices, and automatic player-piano devices. This group keeps up with new developments through trade magazines and organizations, such as The Piano Technicians Guild, which helps members improve upon their skills and become registered as piano technicians.

String instrument repair technicians adjust and repair bowed instruments such as violins, violas, and cellos. Instruments may also need restringing or refinishing. Defects are detected by inspecting and playing the instrument.

Building and restoring instruments is an exacting craft that requires a broad background in the use and care of power and hand tools used for instrument making, the various woods and other materials used in instrument construction, and an ability to make and/or interpret mechanical drawings. For some instruments, such as the violin, students can expect to train for up to three years before entering the field as apprentice repair technicians.

Getting a Job

There is a common thread running through successful music-related careers: formal training. One reason formal training breeds success is that music production and the instruments themselves are becoming more technical and require a greater understanding of electronics and other new technologies. Moreover, schools that offer post-secondary training are often licensed by the state's department of education and offer certificate or degree-training programs to ensure their programs meet state and industry requirements. Employment is more likely when a solid educational foundation has been completed. Additionally, upon program completion, most schools offer some type of job-placement assistance. They may contact potential employers and set up interviews or they may put you in contact with graduates who are already established in the career you are entering. Either way, formal training adds to your credentials and makes you more employable.

Success in finding a job in these careers may also be based upon presentation of a portfolio of your best work in the medium. Further, consider becoming an active member of professional organizations related to these careers, attending professional conferences and meetings, enrolling in continuing education, and networking with other students and faculty. ♪

Joanne Monath is a free-lance writer based in Colorado.

DALLAS SOUND LAB SCHOOL FOR THE RECORDING ARTS

Programs in music business, audio engineering, studio technology.

6305 N. O'CONNOR BLVD. 4,
SUITE 119
IRVING, TX 75039
WWW.DALLASSOUNDLAB.COM

FIVE TOWNS COLLEGE

Programs in music business administration and management, jazz/commercial music.

305 N. SERVICE ROAD
DIX HILLS, NY 11746-6055
516-424-7000
WWW.FIVETOWNS.EDU

FULL SAIL REAL WORLD EDUCATION CENTER

Programs in recording arts, film and video production, digital media, game design, show production and touring.

3300 UNIVERSITY BOULEVARD
WINTER PARK, FL 32792
WWW.FULLSAIL.COM

MUSICIANS INSTITUTE

Programs in commercial music (performance and production), recording arts.

1655 MCCADDEN PLACE
HOLLYWOOD, CA 90028
WWW.MI.EDU

MUSIC TECH

Programs in music performance and production, music business, recording arts.

MUSICIANS TECHNICAL TRAINING CENTER
304 NORTH WASHINGTON AVENUE
MINNEAPOLIS, MN 55401
WWW.MUSICTECH.COM

NORTH BENNET STREET SCHOOL

Programs in piano technology, violin-making and restoration.

39 NORTH BENNET STREET
BOSTON, MA 02113
617-227-0155
WWW.NBSS.ORG

MINNESOTA STATE COLLEGE/ SOUTHEAST TECHNICAL

Programs in band instrument repair, musical string instrument repair and construction.

308 PIONEER ROAD
RED WING, MN 55066
800-657-4849
WWW.SOUTHEASTTECH.MNSCU.EDU

WESTERN IOWA TECH COMMUNITY COLLEGE

Programs in band instrument repair.

4647 STONE AVENUE
SIOUX CITY, IA 51102-5199
712-274-6400
WWW.WITCC.COM

WESTERN VALLEY COLLEGE

Programs in digital media design and production.

14000 FRUITVALE AVENUE
SARATOGA, CA 95070
408-741-2098
WWW.WESTVALLEY.EDU

INDEX BY STATE

ALABAMA *p. 43*

Alabama A&M University
Alabama State University
Arkansas State University at Beebe
Auburn University
Auburn University at Montgomery
Bevill State Community College
Birmingham-Southern College
Bishop State Junior College
Calhoun Community College
Central Alabama Community College
Chattahoochee Valley Community College
Enterprise State Junior College
Faulkner University
G.C. Wallace State Community College
Gadsden State Junior College
Huntingdon College Music
Jacksonville State University
Jefferson State Community College
Judson College
Lurleen B. Wallace State Junior College
Miles College
Northeast Alabama State Junior College
Northwest Alabama State Junior College
Oakwood College
Samford University
Selma College
Shelton State Junior College
Snead State Junior College
Southeastern Bible College
Southern Union State Junior College
Stillman College
Talladega College
Troy State University
Tuskegee University
University of Alabama at Birmingham
University of Alabama at Huntsville
University of Alabama at Tuscaloosa
University of Alabama at Walker College
University of Mobile
University of Montevallo
University of North Alabama
University of South Alabama
University of West Alabama
Wallace State College

ALASKA *p. 51*

Alaska Pacific University
Henderson State University
Hendrix College
University of Alaska at Anchorage
University of Alaska at Fairbanks
University of Arkansas at Fayetteville

ARIZONA *p. 53*

Arizona State University
Arizona Western College
Central Arizona College
Cochise College
Conservatory for Recording Arts and Sciences
Eastern Arizona College
Glendale Community College
Grand Canyon University
Mesa Community College
Northern Arizona University
Northland Pioneer College
Phoenix College
Pima Community College
Scottsdale Community College
University of Arizona
Yavapai College

ARKANSAS *p. 57*

Arkansas State University
Arkansas Tech University
East Arkansas Community College
Harding University
John Brown University
Lyon College
Mississippi County Community College
Ouachita Baptist University
Philander Smith College
University of Arkansas at Little Rock
University of Arkansas at Monticello
University of Arkansas at Pine Bluff
University of Central Alabama
University of Central Arkansas
University of the Ozarks
Westark Community College
Williams Baptist College

CALIFORNIA *p. 61*

Ali Akbar College
Allan Hancock College
American River Community College
American School of Piano Tuning
Antelope Valley College
Azusa Pacific University
Bakersfield College
Bethany College of Assembly of God
Biola University
Cabrillo College
California Baptist University
California Institute of Technology
California Institute of the Arts
California Polytechnic State University at Pomona
California Polytechnic State University at San Luis Obispo
California State University at Bakersfield
California State University at Chico
California State University at Fresno
California State University at Fullerton
California State University at Hayward
California State University at Long Beach
California State University at Long Beach
California State University at Los Angeles
California State University at Northridge
California State University at Sacramento
California State University at San Bernardino
California State University at San Marcos
California State University at Stanislaus
Canada College
Cerritos College
Chabot College
Chaffey College
Chapman University
Christian Heritage College
Citrus College
City College of San Francisco
Claremont Graduate University
Claremont McKenna College
Cogswell Polytechnical College
College of Alameda
College of Marin
College of San Mateo
College of Siskiyous
College of the Canyons
College of the Desert
College of the Redwoods

College of the Sequoias
Colorado Christian University
Columbia College
Community Music School of Temecula
Compton Junior College
Concordia University
Contra Costa College
Cuesta College
Cypress College
De Anza College
Diablo Valley College
Dominican University of California
East Los Angeles College
El Camino College
Evergreen Valley College
Foothill College
Fresno City College
Fresno Pacific College
Fullerton College
Gavilan College
Glendale Community College
Golden Gate Baptist Theology Seminary
Golden West College
Grossmont College
Hartnell College
Harvey Mudd College
Holy Names College
Humboldt State University
Idyllwild School of Music and the Arts
Imperial Valley College
Irvine Valley College
Kings River College
La Sierra University
Lake Tahoe Community College
Laney Community College
Long Beach City College
Los Angeles City College
Los Angeles Harbor College
Los Angeles Mission College
Los Angeles Pierce College
Los Angeles Recording Workshop
Los Angeles Southwest College
Los Angeles Trade Tech College
Los Angeles Valley College
Los Medanos College
Loyola Marymount University
Marymount College
Masters College
Mendocino College
Merced College

Merritt College
Mills College
Miracosta College
Mission College
Modesto Junior College
Monterey Peninsula College
Moorpark College
Mount San Antonio College
Mount St. Mary's College
Music Academy of the West
Musicians Institute
Napa Valley College
Notre Dame de Namur University
Occidental College
Ohlone College
Orange Coast College
Oxnard College
Pacific Union College
Palo Verde Junior College
Palomar College
Pasadena City College
Patten College
Pepperdine University at Malibu
Pitzer College
Point Loma Nazarene University
Pomona College
Porterville College
Rio Hondo College
Riverside Community College
Sacramento City College
San Bernardino Valley College
San Diego City College
San Diego Mesa College
San Diego State University
San Francisco Conservatory of Music
San Francisco State University
San Jose City College
San Jose State University
Santa Barbara City College
Santa Clara University
Santa Monica College
Santa Rosa Junior College
Scripps College
Shasta College
Simpson College
Skyline College
Solano College
Sonoma State University
Southern California Conservatory
Southwestern College

St. John's College
St. Mary's College of California
Stanford University
Taft College
UCLA
University of California at Berkeley
University of California at Davis
University of California at Irvine
University of California at L.A.
University of California at Riverside
University of California at San Diego
University of California at Santa Barbara
University of California at Santa Cruz
University of La Verne
University of Redlands
University of San Diego
University of Southern California
University of the Pacific
Vanguard University
Ventura College
Victor Valley College
Vocal Power School
West Los Angeles College
West Valley College
Westmont College
Whittier College
Yuba College

COLORADO *p. 91*

Adams State College
Arapahoe Community College
Aspen Music Festival and School
Colorado College
Colorado State University
Community College of Aurora
Fort Lewis College
Fort Range Community College
Lamar Community College
Mesa State College
Metropolitan State College of Denver
Naropa University
Northeastern Junior College
Regis University
Trinidad State Junior College
United States Air Force Academy
University of Colorado at Boulder
University of Colorado at Denver
University of Denver
University of Northern Colorado

26

University of Southern Colorado
Western State College of Colorado

CONNECTICUT *p. 97*

Capital Community Technical College
Central Connecticut State University
Connecticut College
Eastern Connecticut State University
Gateway Community Technical College
Hartford College for Women
Housatonic College
National Guitar Workshop
Northwestern Connecticut Community College
Quinnipiac College
Sacred Heart University
Southern Connecticut State University
St. Joseph College
The Hartford Conservatory, The Hartt School
Trinity College
University of Bridgeport
University of Connecticut
University of New Haven
Wesleyan University
Western Connecticut State University
Yale School of Music

DELAWARE *p. 103*

Delaware State College
University of Delaware
Wesley College

FLORIDA *p. 105*

Baptist College of South Florida
Barry University
Bethune-Cookman College
Brenau University
Brevard Community College
Broward Community College
Chipola Junior College
Daytona Beach Community College
Eckerd College
Edison Community College at Collier
Edison Community College at Lee County
Edward Waters College
Flagler College
Florida A&M University

Florida Atlantic University
Florida College
Florida International University
Florida Keys Community College
Florida Southern College
Florida State University
Full Sail Real World Education
Gulf Coast Community College
Harid Conservatory School of Music
Hillsborough Community College
Indian River Community College
Jacksonville University
Jeff Berlin Players School of Music
Lake City Community College
Lake Sumter Community College
Lynn University
Manatee Community College
Miami-Dade Community College at Kendall
Miami-Dade Community College at North
New World School of the Arts
Oskaloosa Walton Community College
Palm Beach Atlantic College
Palm Beach Community College
Pensacola Junior College
Rollins College
Santa Fe Community College
Seminole Community College
South Florida Community College
Southeastern College of Assembly of God
St. John's River Community College
St. Leo University
St. Petersburg College
Stetson University
Tallahassee Community College
University of Central Florida
University of Florida
University of Miami School of Music
University of North Florida
University of South Florida
University of Tampa
University of West Florida
Valencia Community College
Warner Southern College

GEORGIA *p. 115*

Agnes Scott College
Albany State University
Andrew College
Armstrong Atlantic State University

Atlanta Conservatory of Music
Augusta State University
Berry College
Brewton-Parker College
Clark Atlanta University
Clayton College and State University
Columbus State University
Covenant College
Darton College
Emmanuel College
Emory University
Emory University at Oxford College
Floyd College
Fort Valley State University
Georgia College and State University
Georgia Institute of Technology
Georgia Perimeter College
Georgia Southern University
Georgia Southwestern College
Georgia State University
Interdenominational Theological College
Kennesaw State University
LaGrange College
Macon College
Mercer University
Middle Georgia College
Morehouse College
Morris Brown College
North Georgia College and State University
Oglethorpe University
Paine College
Piedmont College
Reinhardt College
Savannah State College
Shorter College
Spelman College
State University of West Georgia
Thomas University
Toccoa Falls College
Truett-McConnel College
University of Georgia
Valdosta State University
Waycross College
Wesleyan College
Young Harris College

HAWAII *p. 123*

Brigham Young University at Hawaii
Chaminade University of Honolulu

Hawaii Loa College
Hawaii Pacific College
Honolulu Community College
Kapiolani Community College
Kauai Community College
Leeward Community College
University of Hawaii at Hilo
University of Hawaii at Manoa
Winward Community College

IDAHO *p. 127*

Albertson College
Boise State University
College of Southern Idaho
Hampton School Of Music
Idaho State University
Lewis and Clark State College
North Idaho College
Northwest Nazarene College
University of Idaho

ILLINOIS *p. 131*

American Conservatory of Music
Augustana College
Aurora University
Black Hawk College
Blackburn College
Bradley University
Carl Sandburg College
Chicago College of Performing Arts
Chicago School of Violin Making
Chicago State University
College of Du Page
College of Lake County
Columbia College
Concordia University
DePaul College of Music
Dominican University
Eastern Illinois University
Elgin Community College
Elmhurst College
Eureka College
Governors State University
Greenville College
Illinois College
Illinois County College
Illinois State University
Illinois Valley Community College

John A. Logan College
John Wood Community College
Joliet Junior College
Judson College
Kankakee Community College
Kishwaukee College
Knox College
Lake Forest College
Lewis and Clark Community College
Lewis University
Lincoln Christian College
Lincoln College
Lincoln Land Community College
Lincoln Trail College
Loyola University Chicago
MacMurray College
McKendree College
Milliken University
Monmouth College
Moody Bible Institute
Moraine Valley Community College
Morton College
National-Louis University
North Central College
North Park University
Northeastern Illinois University
Northern Illinois University
Northwestern University
Olivet Nazarene University
Olney Central College
Parkland College
Principia College
Quincy University
Rend Lake College
Richland Community College
Rock Valley College
Roosevelt University
Saulk Valley Community College
Sherwood Conservatory of Music
South Suburban College
Southeastern Illinois College
Southern Illinois University at Carbondale
Southern Illinois University at Edwardsville
Southwestern Illinois College
Springfield College at Illinois
St. Xavier University
Trinity Christian College
Trinity International University
Triton College
University of Chicago

University of Illinois at Chicago
University of Illinois at Urbana
University of St. Francis
University of St. Mary of the Lake
VanderCook College of Music
Western Illinois University
Wheaton College
William Rainey Harper College

INDIANA *p. 145*

Ancilla College
Anderson University
Associated Mennonite Biblical Seminary
Ball State University
Bethel College
Butler University
Christian Theological Seminary
DePauw University School of Music
Earlham College
Goshen College
Grace College
Hanover College
Huntington College
Illinois Wesleyan University
Indiana State University
Indiana University at Bloomington
Indiana University at Purdue
Indiana University at South Bend
Indiana University at Southeast
Indiana Wesleyan University
Manchester College
Marian College
Oakland City University
Purdue University
St. Joseph's College
St. Mary of the Woods College
St. Mary's College
Taylor University at Upland
The University of Indianapolis
University of Evansville
University of Indianapolis
University of Notre Dame
Valparaiso University
Vincennes University
Wabash College

IOWA *p. 153*

Briar Cliff College
Buena Vista University
Central College
Clarke College
Clinton Community College
Coe College
Cornell College
Drake University
Grinnell College
Iowa State University
Iowa Wesleyan College
Iowa Western College
Kirkwood Community College
Loras College
Luther College
Maharishi University of Management
Morningside College
Mount Mercy College
Mount St. Clare College
North Iowa Area Community College
Northwestern College
Simpson College
Southeastern Community College
St. Ambrose University
University of Dubuque
University of Iowa
University of Northern Iowa
Upper Iowa University
Vennard College
Waldorf College
Wartburg College
Western Iowa Tech Community College
William Penn College

KANSAS *p. 161*

Allen County Community College
Baker University
Barclay College
Benedictine College
Bethany College
Bethel College
Central Christian College
Cloud County Community
Coffeyville Community College
Dodge City Community College
Emporia State University
Fort Hays State University

Fort Scott Community College
Garden City Community College
Hesston College
Hutchinson Community Junior College
Independence Community College
Johnson County Community College
Kansas City Kansas Community College
Kansas State University
Kansas Wesleyan University
Labette Community College
Manhattan Christian College
McPherson College
Neosho County Community College
Newman University
Ottawa University
Pittsburgh State University
Seward County Community College
Southwestern College
Sterling College
Tabor College
University of Kansas
Washburn University
Wichita State University

KENTUCKY *p. 169*

Alice Lloyd College
Asbury College
Asbury Theological Seminary
Ashland Community College
Bellarmine University
Berea College
Boyce College
Brescia University
Campbellsville University
Centre College
Cumberland College
Eastern Kentucky University
Elizabeth Community College
Georgetown College
Kentucky Christian College
Kentucky Mountain Bible College
Kentucky State University
Kentucky Wesleyan College
Lees College
Lindsey Wilson College
Morehead State University
Murray State University
Northern Kentucky University
Paducah Community College

Pikeville College
St. Catherine College
Thomas More College
Transylvania University
Union College
University of Kentucky
University of Kentucky at Louisville
University of Louisville
Western Kentucky University

LOUISIANA *p. 177*

Centenary College of Louisiana
Delgado Community College
Grambling State University
Louisiana College
Louisiana State University
Louisiana Tech University
Loyola University at New Orleans
McNeese State University
New Orleans Baptist Theology Seminary
Nicholls State University
Northwestern State University
Northwestern State University at Louisiana
Our Lady of Holy Cross College
Southeastern Louisiana University
Southern University at Baton Rouge
Southern University at New Orleans
St. Joseph Seminary College
Tulane University
University of Louisiana at Lafayette
University of Louisiana at Monroe
University of New Orleans
Xavier University of Louisiana

MAINE *p. 183*

Bates College
Bowdoin College
Colby College
College of the Atlantic
Delta College
University of Maine
University of Maine at Augusta
University of Maine at Farmington
University of Maine at Fort Kent
University of Maine at Machias
University of Maine at Orono
University of Southern Maine

MARYLAND *p. 187*

Allegany College
Anne Arundel Community College
Baltimore School for the Arts
Chesapeake College
College of Notre Dame of Maryland
Columbia Union College
Community College of Baltimore City
Coppin State College
Frederick Community College
Frostburg State University
Garrett Community College
Goucher College
Hagerstown Community College
Hartford Community College
Hood College
Montgomery College
Morgan State University
Mount St. Mary's College
Peabody Conservatory of Music
Prince Georges Community College
Salisbury University
St. Mary's College of Maryland
The Peabody Institute of Johns Hopkins U.
Towson University
United States Naval Academy
University of Maryland
University of Maryland at Baltimore County
University of Maryland at Eastern Shore
Washington Bible College
Washington College
Washington Conservatory of Music
Western Maryland College

MASSACHUSETTS *p. 193*

American International College
Amherst College
Anna Maria College
Assumption College
Atlantic Union College
Berklee College of Music
Berkshire Community College
Boston College
Boston Conservatory
Boston University
Brandeis University
Bridgewater State College
Cape Cod Community College

Clark University
College of the Holy Cross
Dean College
Eastern Nazarene College
Emerson College
Emmanuel College
Endicott College
Fitchburg State College
Gordon College
Hampshire College
Harvard University
Holyoke Community College
Longy School of Music
Massachusetts College of Liberal Arts
Massachusetts Communications College
Massachusetts Institute of Technology
Mount Holyoke College
New England Conservatory
North Bennet Street School
Northeastern University
Northern Essex Community College
Our Lady of the Elms College
Pine Manor College
Regis College
Salem State College
Simmons College
Smith College
Springfield College
Tufts University
University of Massachusetts at Amherst
University of Massachusetts at Boston
University of Massachusetts at Dartmouth
University of Massachusetts at Lowell
Wellesley College
Westfield State College
Wheaton College
Wheelock College
Williams College
Worcester State College

MICHIGAN *p. 203*

Adrian College
Albion College
Alma College
Andrews University
Aquinas College
Art Center Music School
Bethany Lutheran College
Calvin College

Central Michigan University
Concordia College
Cornerstone University
Eastern Michigan University
Ferris State University
Gogebic Community College
Grace Bible College
Grand Rapids Community College
Grand Valley State University
Great Lakes Christian College
Henry Ford Community College
Hillsdale College
Hope College
Interlochen Center for the Arts
Jackson Community College
Kalamazoo College
Kellogg Community College
Lake Michigan College
Lansing Community College
Macomb Community College Center Campus
Madonna University
Michigan State University
Michigan Technological University
Monroe Community College
Mott Community College
Muskegon Community College
Northern Michigan University
Northwestern Michigan College
Oakland Community College
Oakland University
Olivet College
Rochester College
Saginaw Valley State University
Schoolcraft College
Siena Heights University
Southwestern Michigan
Spring Arbor University
University of Michigan at Ann Arbor
University of Michigan at Dearborn
University of Michigan at Flint
Wayne State University
Western Michigan University
William Tyndale College

MINNESOTA *p. 213*

Anoka Ramsey Community College at Coon
Rapids
Augsburg College
Bemidji State University

Bethel College
Carleton College
College of St. Benedict
College of St. Catherine
College of St. Scholastica
Concordia College at Morehead
Crown College
Fergus Falls Community College
Gustavus Adolphus College
Hamline University
Hibbing Community College
Itasca Community College
Macalester College
Martin Luther College
Minneapolis Community and Technology
College
Minnesota Bible College
Minnesota State College Southeast Technical
Minnesota State University at Mankato
Minnesota State University at Moorhead
Moorhead State University
Musictech College
Normandale Community College
North Central Bible College
North Hennepin Community College
Northland Community and Technology
College
Northwestern College
Red Wing Technical College
Ridgewater College
Riverland Community College
Southwest State University
St. Cloud State University
St. John's University
St. Mary's University of Minnesota
St. Olaf College
University of Minnesota at Crookston
University of Minnesota at Duluth
University of Minnesota at Morris
University of Minnesota at Twin Cities
University of St. Thomas
Vermillion Community College
Winona State University
Worthington Community College

MISSISSIPPI *p. 223*

Alcorn State University
Belhaven College
Blue Mountain College

Copiah-Lincoln Community College
Delta State University
Hinds Community College
Itawamba Community College
Jackson State University
Jones County Junior College
Meridian Community College
Millsaps College
Mississippi College
Mississippi Gulf Coast College
Mississippi State University
Mississippi University for Women
Mississippi Valley State University
Northeast Mississippi Community College
Pearl River Community College
Rust College
Tougaloo College
University of Mississippi
University ofSouthern Mississippi
Wesley College
William Carey College

MISSOURI *p. 229*

Avila College
Calvary Bible College and Theological
Seminary
Central Methodist College
Central Missouri State University
College of the Ozarks
Cottey College
Crowder College
Drury College
Evangel University
Fontbonne College
Hannibal La Grange College
Jefferson College
Lincoln University
Lindenwood University
Maryville University
Mineral Area College
Missouri Southern State College
Missouri Western State College
Northwest Missouri State University
Park University
Rockhurst College
Saint Louis University
Southeast Missouri State University
Southwest Baptist University
Southwest Missouri State University

St. Louis Community College at Forest Park
St. Louis Community College at Meramec
St. Paul School of Theology
Stephens College
Tarkio College
Three Rivers Community College
Truman State University
University of Missouri
University of Missouri at Columbia
University of Missouri at Rolla
University of Missouri at St. Louis
Washington University
Webster University
William Jewell College
William Woods University

MONTANA p. 237

Dawson Community College
Miles Community College
Montana State University at Billings
Montana State University at Bozeman
Northern Montana College
Rocky Mountain College
University of Great Falls
University of Montana
Western Montana College

NEBRASKA p. 241

Central Community College Platte
Chadron State College
College of St. Mary
Concordia College
Creighton University
Dana College
Doane College
Grace University
Hastings College
Midland Lutheran College
Nebraska Wesleyan University
Northeast Community College
Peru State College
Southeast Community College at Beatrice
Union College
University of Nebraska
University of Nebraska at Kearney
University of Nebraska at Omaha
Wayne State College
Western Nebraska Community College
York College

NEVADA p. 245

University of Nevada at Las Vegas
University of Nevada at Reno
Western Nevada Community College

NEW HAMPSHIRE p. 247

Colby-Sawyer College
Dartmouth College
Franklin Pierce College
Keene State College
Notre Dame College
Plymouth State College
Rivier College
St. Anselm College
University of New Hampshire

NEW JERSEY p. 251

Bergen Community College
Brookdale Community College
Caldwell College
Camden County College
College of New Jersey
College of St. Elizabeth
County College of Morris
Drew University
Fairleigh Dickinson University Madison
Felician College
Georgian Court College
Kean University
Mercer County Community College
Monmouth University
Montclair State University
New Jersey City University
Princeton University
Ramapo College of New Jersey
Raritan Valley Community College
Richard Stockton College
Rowan University
Rutgers University
Rutgers University at New Brunswick
Rutgers University at Newark
Seton Hall University
Trenton State College
William Paterson University

NEW MEXICO *p. 257*

College of Sante Fe
Eastern New Mexico University
New Mexico Highlands University
New Mexico Junior College
New Mexico State University
New Mexico Tech
San Juan College
University of New Mexico
Western New Mexico University

NEW YORK *p. 261*

Adelphi University
Alfred University
Bard College
Barnard College
Baruch College
Binghamton University
Borough of Manhattan Community College
Bronx Community College
Brooklyn College
Brooklyn Conservatory of Music
Broome Community College
Canisius College
Cayuga County Community College
Chautauqua School of Music
City College of New York
City University of New York
City University of New York at Brooklyn
City University of New York at City College
City University of New York at Grad Center
City University of New York at Hunter College
City University of New York at Jay College
City University of New York at Lehman
College
City University of New York at Medgar Evers
City University of New York at York University
Colgate University
College of St. Rose
Columbia University
Concordia College
Cornell University
Corning Community College
Crane Institute for Music Business
Daemen College
Dalcroze School of Music
Dutchess Community College
Eastern U.S. Music Camp at Colgate

University
Eastman School of Music of the University of
Rochester
Elmira College
Erie Community College
Erie Community College at North
Erie Community College at South
Finger Lakes Community College
Five Towns College
Fordham University
Hamilton College
Hartwick College
Hebrew Union College
Hobart and William Smith College
Hofstra University
Houghton College
Institute of Audio Research
Ithaca College
Jamestown Community College
Jewish Theological Seminary of America
Julliard School of Music
Keuka College
Kingsborough Community College
LaGuardia Community College
Long Island University at Brooklyn
Long Island University at CW Post
Malloy College
Manhattan School of Music
Manhattanville College
Mannes College of Music
Mercy College
Monroe Community College
Nassau Community College
Nazareth College
New School University
New York Technical College
New York University
Niagara County Community College
Nyack College
Onondaga Community College
Orange County Community College
Packer Collegiate Institute
Queen's College
Queensborough Community College
Rensselaer Polytechnic Institute
Robert Wesleyan College
Rockland Community College
Rockland Summer Institute
Russell Sage College
Sarah Lawrence College

35

Schenectady County Community College
Skidmore College
St. Bonaventure University
St. John's University
St. Lawrence University
Stony Brook University
Suffolk County Community College
SUNY at Binghamton
SUNY at Buffalo
SUNY at Cortland
SUNY at Fredonia
SUNY at Geneseo
SUNY at New Paltz
SUNY at Oneonta
SUNY at Oswego
SUNY at Plattsburgh
SUNY at Potsdam
SUNY at Purchase College
SUNY at Stony Brook
Syracuse University
Teachers College
Tompkins Cortland Community College
Ulster County Community College
Union College
University at Albany
University of Rochester
Utica College of Syracuse
Vassar College
Villa Maria College of Buffalo
Wagner College
Wells College
Westchester Conservatory of Music
Youngstown State University

NORTH CAROLINA *p. 279*

Appalachian State University
Barton College
Bennett College
Blue Ridge Community College at Flat Rock
Brevard College
Campbell University
Catawba College
Chowan College
Coastal Carolina Community College
College of the Albemarle
Davidson College
Duke University
East Carolina University
Eastern Music Festival

Elizabeth City State University
Elon University
Fayetteville State University
Fayetteville Tech Community College
Gardner Webb University
Gaston College
Greensboro College
Guilford College
Guilford Tech Community College
Jamestown College
John Wesley College
Johnson C. Smith University
Lees-McRae College
Lenoir Community College
Lenoir-Rhyne College
Livingstone College
Louisburg College
Mars Hill College
Meredith College
Methodist College
Mitchell Community College
Montreat College
MMount Olive College,North Carolina AandT
State University
North Carolina Central University
North Carolina School of the Arts
North Carolina State University
North Carolina Wesleyan College
Peace College
Pheiffer University
Piedmont Baptist College
Queens College
Rockingham Community College
Salem College
Sandhills Community College
Shaw University
Southeast Baptist Theology Seminary
St. Augustine's College
Surry Community College
University of North Carolina at Asheville
University of North Carolina at Chapel Hill
University of North Carolina at Charlotte
University of North Carolina at Greensboro
University of North Carolina at Pembroke
University of North Carolina at Wilmington
Wake Forest University
Warren Wilson College
Western Carolina University
Wilkes Community College
Wilmington Academy of Music

Wingate University
Winston-Salem State University

NORTH DAKOTA *p. 291*

Bismarck State College
Dickinson State University
Minot State University
North Dakota State University
University of Mary
University of North Dakota Grand Forks
Valley City State University

OHIO *p. 295*

Antioch College
Ashland University
Athenaeum of Ohio
Baldwin-Wallace College
Bluffton College
Bowling Green State University
Capital University
Case Western Reserve University
Cedarville University
Central State University
Cincinnati Bible College and Seminary
Cleveland Institute of Music
Cleveland State University
College of Mount St. Joseph
College of Wooster
Cuyahoga Community College at
Metropolitan
Cuyahoga Community College at West
Dana School of Music
Denison University
Heidelberg College
Hiram College
John Carroll University
Kent State University at Kent
Kent State University at Salem
Kent State University at Tuscarawas
Kenyon College
Lake Erie College
Lorain County Community College
Lourdes College
Malone College
Marietta College
Miami University
Mount Union College
Mount Vernon Nazarene College

Muskingum College
Oberlin Conservatory of Music
Ohio Dominican College
Ohio Northern University
Ohio State University
Ohio State University at Lima
Ohio University
Ohio University at Lancaster
Ohio University at Zanesville
Ohio Wesleyan University
Otterbein College
Recording Workshop
Shawnee State Community College
Shawnee State University
Sinclair Community College
University of Akron
University of Cincinnati
University of Dayton
University of Findlay
University of Toledo
Walsh University
Wilberforce University
Wittenberg University
Wright State University
Xavier University

OKLAHOMA *p. 309*

Bartlesville Wesleyan College
Cameron University
Carl Albert State College
East Central University
Eastern Oklahoma State College
Langston University
Margaret E. Petree School of Music
Northeastern Oklahoma A&M College
Northeastern State University
Northwestern Oklahoma State University
Oakland City University
Oklahoma Baptist University
Oklahoma Christian University
Oklahoma State University
Southwestern Oklahoma State University
University of Oklahoma
University of Science and Arts of Oklahoma
University of Tulsa

OREGON *p. 313*

Britt Institute
Lewis and Clark College
Oregon State University
Portland State University
University of Oregon School of Music
University of Portland
Western Oregon University
Willamette University

PENNSYLVANIA *p. 317*

Albright College
Allegheny College
Bloomsburg University
Bryn Mawr College
California University of Pennsylvania
Carnegie-Mellon University
Clarion University of Pennsylvania
Curtis Institute of Music
Dickinson College
Drexel University
Duquesne University
Edinboro University of Pennsylvania
Franklin and Marshall College
Geneva College
Gettysburg College
Haverford College
Indiana University of Pennsylvania
Lafayette College
LaSalle University
Lebanon Valley College
Lehigh University
Lock Haven University of Pennsylvania
Lycoming College
Mansfield University
Marywood University
Millersville University
Moravian College
Pennsylvania State University
Susquehanna University
Swarthmore College
Technology Institute for Music
Temple University
The Music Academy
University of Pennsylvania
University of Pittsburgh
University of the Arts
Villanova University

West Chester University
Wide World Music
York College

RHODE ISLAND *p. 325*

Brown University
Providence College
University of Rhode Island

SOUTH CAROLINA *p. 327*

Bob Jones University
Clemson University
College of Charleston
Converse College
Furman University
Newberry College
South Carolina State University
University of South Carolina at Aiken
University of South Carolina at Columbia
Winthrop University

SOUTH DAKOTA *p. 331*

Black Hills State University
Dakota State University
Northern State University
South Dakota State University
University of South Dakota

TENNESSEE *p. 335*

Austin Peay State University
Belmont University
Carson-Newman College
Fisk University
Lee University
Lipscomb University
Middle Tennessee State University
Navy Music Program
Rhodes College
Tennessee State University
Tennessee Technological University
Union University
University of Memphis
University of Tennessee at Knoxville
University of Tennessee at Martin
University of the South
Vanderbilt University

TEXAS *p. 341*

Abilene Christian University
Austin College
Baylor University
Del Mar College
East Texas Baptist University
Frank Phillips College
Howard Payne University
International Festival-Institute
Lamar University
Our Lady of the Lake University
Rice University
Sam Houston State University
Southern Methodist University
Southwest Texas State University
Southwestern University
St. Mary College
Stephen F. Austin State University
Texas A&M University
Texas A&M University at Commerce
Texas Christian University
Texas Technological University
Texas Woman's University
Trinity University
University of Houston
University of North Texas
University of Texas at Arlington
University of Texas at Austin
University of Texas at El Paso
University of Texas at Houston
University of Texas at San Antonio
West Texas A&M University

UTAH *p. 347*

Brigham Young University
College of Eastern Utah
Dixie State College
University of Utah
Utah State University

VERMONT *p. 351*

Bennington College
Middlebury College
University of Vermont

VIRGINIA *p. 353*

Armed Forces School of Music
Bridgewater College
College of William and Mary
Ferrum College
George Mason University
Hollins University
James Madison University
Mary Washington College
Norfolk State University
Old Dominion University
Radford University
Randolph-Macon Woman's College
Roanoke College
Shenandoah University
University of Richmond
University of Virginia
Virginia Commonwealth University
Virginia Tech
Virginia Union University
Virginia Wesleyan College
Washington and Lee University

WASHINGTON *p. 359*

Central Washington University
Eastern Washington University
Renton Technical College
Seattle Pacific University
University of Puget Sound
University of Washington School of Music
Washington State University
Western Washington University
Whitman College

WASHINGTON D.C *p. 363*

American University
Benjamin T. Rome School of Music
Catholic University of America
George Washington University
Georgetown University
Howard University
Levine School of Music
Mount Vernon College
Trinity College
University of the District of Columbia

WEST VIRGINIA *p. 367*

Alderson-Broaddus College
Fairmont State College
Marshall University
Shepherd College
University of Charleston
West Virginia University

WISCONSIN *p. 371*

Alverno College
Cardinal Stritch University
Carroll College
International Fine Arts Institute
Lawrence University
Mount Mary College
Ripon College
Silver Lake College
St. Norbert College
University of Wisconsin at Eau Claire
University of Wisconsin at Green Bay
University of Wisconsin at La Crosse
University of Wisconsin at Madison
University of Wisconsin at Milwaukee
University of Wisconsin at Oshkosh
University of Wisconsin at Parkside
University of Wisconsin at Platteville
University of Wisconsin at River Falls
University of Wisconsin at Stevens Point
University of Wisconsin at Superior
University of Wisconsin at Whitewater
Waukesha County Conservatory of Music
Wisconsin Conservatory of Music

WYOMING *p. 377*

Casper College
Central Wyoming College
Eastern Wyoming College
Northwest College
Sheridan College
University of Wyoming

ALABAMA

Population: 4,576,223 (2003 Estimate)

Capital City: Montgomery

Music Colleges and Universities: Alabama A&M University, Alabama State University, Arkansas State University at Beebe, Auburn University, Auburn University at Montgomery, Bevill State Community College, Birmingham-Southern College, Bishop State Junior College, Calhoun Community College, Central Alabama Community College, Chattahoochee Valley Community College, Enterprise State Junior College, Faulkner University, G.C. Wallace State Community College, Gadsden State Junior College, Huntingdon College Music, Jacksonville State University, Jefferson State Community College, Judson College, Lurleen B. Wallace State Junior College, Miles College, Northeast Alabama State Junior College, Northwest Alabama State Junior College, Oakwood College, Samford University, Selma College, Shelton State Junior College, Snead State Junior College, Southeastern Bible College, Southern Union State Junior College, Stillman College, Talladega College, Troy State University, Tuskegee University, University of Alabama at Birmingham, University of Alabama at Huntsville, University of Alabama at Tuscaloosa, University of Alabama at Walker College, University of Mobile, University of Montevallo, University of North Alabama, University of South Alabama, University of West Alabama, Wallace State College

Bird: Yellowhammer

Motto: We Dare Defend Our Rights

Flower: Camellia

Tree: Southern Longleaf Pine

Residents Called: Alabamians

Origin of Name: Means "tribal town" in the Creek Indian language.

Area: 51,781 square miles (29th largest state)

Statehood: December 14, 1899 (22nd state)

Largest Cities: Birmingham, Mobile, Montgomery, Huntsville, Tuscaloosa, Hoover, Dothan, Decatur, Gadsen

College Band Programs: Alabama A&M University, Auburn University, Samford University, Troy State University, Trinity Presbyterian School, University of North Alabama, University of Alabama, University of Alabama-Birmingham, University of Alabama-Tuscaloosa

ALABAMA

ALABAMA A&M UNIVERSITY
DEPARTMENT OF MUSIC
Room 102 Morrison Building
Normal, AL 35762
Dr. Clifton Pearson
256-372-5513
Fax: 205-851-5976
E-mail: cpearson@aamu.edu
www.aamu.edu

ALABAMA STATE UNIVERSITY
SCHOOL OF MUSIC
915 South Jackson St.
Montgomery, AL 36104
Dr. Horace Lamar
334-229-4341
Fax: 334-229-4901
E-mail: hlamar@asunet.alasu.edu
www.alasu.edu
Alabama State University is NASM-accredited.

ARKANSAS STATE UNIVERSITY AT BEEBE
DEPARTMENT OF MUSIC
P.O. Box 1000
Beebe, AL 72012
Lamond Chudomelka
501-882-8268
Fax: 501-882-6452
www.asub.edu

AUBURN UNIVERSITY
DEPARTMENT OF MUSIC
101 Goodwin Music Building
Auburn University, AL 36849-5420
Dr. Thomas R. Smith
334-844-4165
Fax: 334-844-3168
E-mail: smith73@auburn.edu
www.auburn.edu

Auburn University provides quality experiences in music education, performing groups, and music appreciation for students and the community. The Auburn University Department of Music offers Bachelor's Degrees in instrumental and choral music education, as well as a minor in music performance and master's and doctoral degrees in music education.

AUBURN UNIVERSITY AT MONTGOMERY
DEPARTMENT OF FINE ARTS
P.O. Box 244023
Montgomery, AL 36124-4023
Phillip Coley
334-244-3377
Fax: 334-244-3740
E-mail: acoley@edla.aum.edu
www.aum.edu

BEVILL STATE COMMUNITY COLLEGE
DEPARTMENT OF MUSIC
100 State St.
P.O. Box 800
Sumiton, AL 35148
John Stallsmith
205-648-3271

BIRMINGHAM-SOUTHERN COLLEGE
FINE AND PERFORMING ARTS
900 Arkadelphia Rd.
Birmingham, AL 35254
Dee Dee Barnes-Burns
205-226-4600
Fax: 205-226-3058
E-mail: ldburns@bsc.edu
www.bsc.edu

Degrees: B.M., B.A., Bachelor of Music Education, M.M.

Stressing conservatory training in liberal arts environment, the music program at Birmingham-Southern College offers qualified students an exceptional education in performance (piano, voice, organ, guitar, saxophone, orchestral instruments), composition, music history, and church music, leading to the B.M. degree. The Bachelor of Music Education in music education leads to certification at the L-12 level. Students can also elect one of twin tracks in the B.A. degree program with a major in music. The college also offers a selective program leading to the Master of Music degree in the areas of piano, organ, voice, and composition. Facilities in the Hill Music Building include a tracker-action organ by Casavant and Steinway grand pianos in the recital Hall, practice pipe organs by Schantz and Ruhland, an electronic music studio, music technology laboratory, the Taylor Recording Studio, practice rooms with new pianos by Yamaha and Steinway. Graduates include those who go on to find graduate programs, careers in teaching and performing, and professionals in other fields, who nonetheless maintain a lifelong enjoyment of music. Please see our website for information about Fine and Performing Arts Scholarship Day, held annually on a Saturday close to March 1st.

BISHOP STATE JUNIOR COLLEGE
DEPARTMENT OF MUSIC
351 N. Broad St.
Mobile, AL 36603-5833
Helen Campbell
334-690-6416
Fax: 334-432-2290
www.bscc.cc.al.us

CALHOUN COMMUNITY COLLEGE
DEPARTMENT OF FINE ARTS
P.O. Box 2216
Decatur, AL 35609
John Calhoun
256-306-2500
Fax: 256-306-2925
E-mail: jtc@calhoun.cc.al.us
www.calhoun.cc.al.us

CENTRAL ALABAMA COMMUNITY COLLEGE
DEPARTMENT OF MUSIC
P.O. Box 699
Alexander City, AL 35011
Griffin Stephen
256-306-2500
Fax: 256-234-0384
www.cacc.cc.al.us

CHATTAHOOCHEE VALLEY COMMUNITY COLLEGE
DEPARTMENT OF MUSIC AND THEATRE
2602 College Dr.
Phoenix City, AL 36869-7960
Emily Davis
334-291-4988
Fax: 334-291-4980
E-mail: emily.davis@cvcc.cc.al.us
www.cvcc.cc.al.us

ENTERPRISE STATE JUNIOR COLLEGE
P.O. Box 1300
Enterprise, AL 36330
Charles Smith
404-679-4501
www.esjc.cc.al.us

FAULKNER UNIVERSITY

5345 Atlanta Hwy.
Montgomery, AL 36109-3323
Kelly Morris
334-272-5820
Fax: 334-386-3323
E-mail: kmorris@faulkner.edu
www.faulkner.edu

G.C. WALLACE STATE COMMUNITY COLLEGE
DEPARTMENT OF MUSIC

Dothan, AL 36302
Ralph Purvis
334-983-3521
Fax: 334-983-360
www.wcc.cc.al.us

GADSDEN STATE JUNIOR COLLEGE
DEPARTMENT OF MUSIC

1000 George Wallace Dr.
Gadsden, AL 35901
Charles Hill
205-456-0484
E-mail: chill@gadsdenst.cc.al.us
www.gadsdenst.cc.al.us

Huntingdon College Music
Department of Music
1500 East Fairview Ave.
Smith 105
Montgomery, AL 36106
James W. Glass
334-833-4222
Fax: 334-833-4264
E-mail: jwglass@huntingdon.edu
www.huntingdon.edu

JACKSONVILLE STATE UNIVERSITY
DEPARTMENT OF MUSIC

700 Telham Rd. N.
Band Department
304 Mason Hall
Jacksonville, AL 36265
Ken Bodiford
256-782-5896
Fax: 256-833-4264
E-mail: kbodifor@jsucc.jsu.edu
www.jsu.edu

JEFFERSON STATE COMMUNITY COLLEGE
DEPARTMENT OF MUSIC

2601 Carson Rd.
Birmingham, AL 35215
Todd Norton
205-853-1200
E-mail: nortont@jscc.cc.al.us
www.jscc.cc.al.us

JUDSON COLLEGE
DEPARTMENT OF MUSIC

302 Bibb St.
Marion, AL 36756
Charlotte Clemments
334-683-5110
Fax: 334-683-5147
E-mail: admissions@future.judson.edu
www.judson.edu

Degrees: B.A. in Music, and B.S. in Music Education

Judson College is a Christian Liberal Arts and Sciences College for women founded in 1838. At Judson, every resource is focused on our young women, in and out of the classroom. The music department offers degrees in music and music education, and has been accredited by the NASM since 1934. Judson boasts a 1902 Performance Hall with incredible natural acoustics and turn-of-the-century charm. In addition, the department is housed in a state-of-the-art music facility with spacious practice rooms, studios and classrooms, 15 grand pianos, 2 Steinway Model D Concert Grands (1927 and 1938), two organs and an electronic music studio.

This past January, the Judson College Concert Choir was invited to participate in a five-day choral residency program at Carnegie Hall in New York City. On January 20, 2003, Judson's choir combined with other carefully selected choirs from around the country for the invitation-only event as they prepared and presented Mozart's Coronation Mass. In addition to being selected for the residency, the choir was also selected to present a solo recital at Carnegie Hall. In March the choir conducted a fourteen-day tour presenting concerts in Great Britain, including churches in England, Scotland, and Wales as well as performances at Canterbury Cathedral and York Minister Cathedral. The Judson College Concert Choir tours nationally every year and internationally every third year. As a part of previous tour throughout the British Isles, the choir has presented concerts in such historic venues. They have sung at the annual meetings of British Baptist Convention and the Alabama Baptist Convention. They have made four recordings of their music in recent years.

LURLEEN B. WALLACE STATE JUNIOR COLLEGE
P.O. Box 1418
Andalusia, AL 36420
Patrick Jerry Padgett
334-222-6591
Fax: 334-222-6051
http://lbw.edu

MILES COLLEGE
DEPARTMENT OF MUSIC
P.O. Box 3800
Birmingham, AL 35208
Geraldine Kullmann

205-923-2771
www.miles.edu

NORTHEAST ALABAMA STATE JUNIOR COLLEGE
DEPARTMENT OF MUSIC
P.O. Box 159
Rainsville, AL 35986
Daniel Knox
205-228-6001
Fax: 205-228-6861

NORTHWEST ALABAMA STATE JUNIOR COLLEGE
DEPARTMENT OF ART
Phil Campbell, AL 35581
Lenny Mcalistar

OAKWOOD COLLEGE
MUSIC DEPARTMENT
7000 Adventist Blvd.
Huntsville, AL 35896
Dr. Lucile Lacy
256-726-7284
www.oakwood.edu/music

SAMFORD UNIVERSITY
SCHOOL OF PERFORMING ARTS
800 Lakeshore Dr.
Birmingham, AL 35229
Milburn Price
205-726-2778
Fax: 205-726-2165
E-mail: smprice@samford.edu
http://music.samford.edu

Degrees: B.A. in Music; B.S. in Music (for students who wish to combine pre-med studies with music studies); B.M. in Church Music, Music Education, Music Theatre, Performance (instrumental, piano, organ, voice); and Music Theory/Composition; Master of Music in

Church Music; Master of Music Education.

The Samford University Division of Music offers a music program that is large enough to provide diverse academic and ensemble experiences, but small enough to provide personalized attention for each student. Samford music graduates have established distinguished careers in church music (as ministers of music and music missionaries); music education (as successful teachers at both elementary and secondary levels); and performance (including performers at the Metropolitan Opera and other leading opera houses around the world). Several graduates are currently teaching in college and university settings. Samford music faculty members hold advanced degrees from leading American universities and conservatories. Samford performing ensembles have gained recognition for their excellence.

SELMA COLLEGE
DEPARTMENT OF MUSIC

Selma, AL 36701
Curtis Powell
www.concordiaselma.edu

Shelton State Junior College
Department of Music
202 Skyland Blvd.
Tuscaloosa, AL 35405
Glinda Blackshear
205-759-1541
Fax: 205-759-2495
www.sheltonstate.edu

SNEAD STATE JUNIOR COLLEGE
DEPARTMENT OF MUSIC

Boaz, AL 35957
Melinda Brooks
205-593-5120
Fax: 205-593-7180
www.snead.cc.al.us

SOUTHEASTERN BIBLE COLLEGE
DEPARTMENT OF MUSIC

3001 Hwy. 280 S.
Birmingham, AL 35243
Christopher Diffey
205-970-9293
Fax: 205-970-9207
E-mail: cdiffey@sebc.edu
www.sebc.edu

SOUTHERN UNION STATE JUNIOR COLLEGE
DEPARTMENT OF MUSIC

Wadley, AL 36276
Jimmy New
205-395-2211
Fax: 205-970-9207
www.suscc.cc.al.us

STILLMAN COLLEGE
DEPARTMENT OF MUSIC

P.O. Box 1430
Tuscaloosa, AL 35403
Todd Westgate
205-349-4240
Fax: 205-349-4252
www.stillman.edu

TALLADEGA COLLEGE
DEPARTMENT OF FINE ARTS AND MUSIC

Talladega, AL 35160
Hope Davis
205-362-0206
Fax: 205-362-2268

TROY STATE UNIVERSITY
JOHN M. LONG SCHOOL OF MUSIC

University Ave.
Troy, AL 36082
Dr. William Denison

334-670-3322
Fax: 334-670-3858
E-mail: music@trojan.troyst.edu
www.troyst.edu

This active school of music in a small university setting has a wide variety of solo and ensemble opportunities, including "Sound of the South" Marching Band, symphony band, chamber winds, jazz ensembles, collegiate singers, chamber choir, gospel choir, opera ensemble, trumpet ensemble and percussion ensemble.

TUSKEGEE UNIVERSITY
DEPARTMENT OF MUSIC

Tuskegee Institute, AL 36088
Warren Duncan
205-727-8398
www.tusk.edu

UNIVERSITY OF ALABAMA AT BIRMINGHAM
DEPARTMENT OF MUSIC
SCHOOL OF MUSIC

Birmingham, AL 35294-1260
Dr. Jeff Reynolds
205-934-7376
Fax: 205-975-1931
E-mail: jwr@uab.edu
www.music.uab.edu

UNIVERSITY OF ALABAMA AT HUNTSVILLE
DEPARTMENT OF MUSIC
MUSIC DEPARTMENT

Roberts Hall 207
Huntsville, AL 35899
Dr. Don Bowyer
256-824-6436
Fax: 256-824-6411
E-mail: bowyerd@uah.edu
http://info.uah.edu

UNIVERSITY OF ALABAMA AT TUSCALOOSA
DEPARTMENT OF MUSIC

Tuscaloosa, AL 35487-0366
205-348-7110
Fax: 205-348-1473
E-mail: kbarrett@music.ua.edu
http://music.ua.edu

UNIVERSITY OF ALABAMA AT WALKER COLLEGE
DEPARTMENT OF MUSIC

Jasper, AL 35501
Marvin Mccombs
205-387-0511

UNIVERSITY OF MOBILE
DEPARTMENT OF MUSIC

P.O. Box 13220
Mobile, AL 36663
Charles Clark
251-442-2420
Fax: 251-442-2526
E-mail: Charlesclark@free.umobile.edu
www.umobile.edu

UNIVERSITY OF MONTEVALLO
DEPARTMENT OF MUSIC

Station 6670
Montevallo, AL 35115
Robert Adams
205-665-6670
Fax: 205-665-6676
E-mail: adamsr@montevallo.edu
www.montevallo.edu/music

UNIVERSITY OF NORTH ALABAMA
COLLEGE OF ARTS AND SCIENCES

Florence, AL 35632
Donna Howard
256-765-4361
Fax: 256-765-4995
E-mail: jsimpson@unanov.una.edu
www.una.edu

UNIVERSITY OF SOUTH ALABAMA
DEPARTMENT OF MUSIC

LPAC 1151
Mobile, AL 36688
Dr. Greg Gruner
251-460-6695
Fax: 215-460-7328
E-mail: ggruner@jaguar1.usouthal.edu
www.southalabama.edu/music

The University of South Alabama Music
Department is committed to the individual
growth of the music student by offering high
quality programs in all areas with an excellent
faculty and a state-of-the-art facility. All degree
programs are accredited by NASM. The
University of South Alabama serves approximately 12,000 students in nine colleges and
divisions.

UNIVERSITY OF WEST ALABAMA
DEPARTMENT OF FINE ARTS

Station 10
Livingston, AL 35470
Nancy Kudlawiee
205-652-9661
Fax: 205-652-3405
www.uwa.edu

WALLACE STATE COLLEGE
DEPARTMENT OF MUSIC

Hanceville, AL 35077
256-352-8277
Fax: 256-352-8228
www.wallacestatehanceville.edu

ALASKA

Population: 650,830 (2003 Estimate)

Capital City: Juneau

Music Colleges and Universities: Alaska Pacific University, Henderson State University, Hendrix College, University of Alaska at Anchorage, University of Alaska at Fairbanks, University of Arkansas at Fayetteville

Bird: Ptarmigan

Motto: North to the Future

Flower: Forget-Me-Not

Tree: Sitka Spruce

Residents Called: Alaskans

Origin of Name: Based on an Aleut word "alaxsxaq" literally meaning "object toward which the action of the sea is directed" or more simply "the mainland."

Area: 656,425 square miles (the largest state)

Statehood: January 3, 1959 (49th State)

Largest Cities: Anchorage, Juneau, Fairbanks, Sitka, Ketchikan, Kenai, Kodiak, Bethel, Wasilla, Barrow

ALASKA

ALASKA PACIFIC UNIVERSITY
DEPARTMENT OF LIBERAL STUDIES
4101 University Dr.
Anchorage, AK 99508-4625
Eric Redding
907-564-8304
Fax: 907-562-4276
E-mail: eredding@alaskapacific.edu
www.alaskapacific.edu

UNIVERSITY OF ALASKA AT ANCHORAGE
DEPARTMENT OF MUSIC
3211 Providence Dr.
Anchorage, AK 99508
Dr. Timothy C. Smith
907-786-1595
Fax: 907-786-1799
E-mail: aftcs@uaa.alaska.edu
www.uaa.alaska.edu/music

Music is housed in the $25 million arts building, a 10-minute walk from new state-of-the-art residence halls. Student to full-time faculty ratio is approximately 11:1, providing students with much individual attention. Students in music education first finish a four-year undergraduate BM degree. Performance opportunities abound, with many students gaining professional experience with the degree and then applying for a graduate level, one-year teacher certification program. This certification program is a professional development school (PDS) model and is on the cutting edge of teacher education. Music teaching positions in all areas and levels are plentiful in Anchorage and Alaska. Experience life in the "Great Land."

UNIVERSITY OF ALASKA AT FAIRBANKS
DEPARTMENT OF MUSIC
P.O. Box 755660
Fairbanks, AK 99775-5660
Theodore Decorso
907-474-7555
Fax: 907-474-6420
E-mail: fymusic@uaf.edu
www.uaf.edu/music/department

Degrees: B.A. in Music, Music Education, and M.A. in Music

ARIZONA

Population: 5,756,980 (2003 Estimate)

Capital City: Phoenix

Music Colleges and Universities: Arizona State University, Arizona Western College, Central Arizona College, Cochise College, Conservatory for Recording Arts and Sciences, Eastern Arizona College, Glendale Community College, Grand Canyon University, Mesa Community College, Northern Arizona University, Northland Pioneer College, Phoenix College, Pima Community College, Scottsdale Community College, University of Arizona, Yavapai College

Bird: Cactus Wren

Motto: Ditat Deus – God Enriches

Flower: Saguaro Cactus Blossom

Tree: Palo Verde

Residents Called: Arizonans

Origin of Name: The name was probably derived from a native place name that sounded like Aleh-zon or Ali-Shonak which meant small spring or place of the small spring.

Area: 113,909 square miles (6th largest state)

Statehood: February 14, 1912 (48th state)

Largest Cities: Phoenix, Tucson, Mesa, Glendale, Scottsdale, Chandler, Tempe, Gilbert Peoria, Yuma, Flagstaff

College Band Programs: Arizona State University, University of Arizona

ARIZONA

ARIZONA STATE UNIVERSITY
SCHOOL OF MUSIC
P.O. Box 870405
Tempe, AZ 85287
J. Robert Wills
480-727-7700
E-mail: mary.sauve@asu.edu
http://herbergercollege.asu.edu/music

ARIZONA WESTERN COLLEGE
FINE ARTS DEPARTMENT
P.O. Box 929
Yuma, AZ 85366-0929
Chuck Smalley
928-317-6063
E-mail: lupe.fuentes@awc.cc.az.us
www.awc.cc.az.us

CENTRAL ARIZONA COLLEGE
DEPARTMENT OF MUSIC
8470 N. Overfield Rd.
Coolidge, AZ 85228
James Lee
520-426-4399
Fax: 520-426-4234
www.cac.cc.az.us

COCHISE COLLEGE
DEPARTMENT OF MUSIC
901 N. Colombo Ave.
Sierra Vista, AZ 85635-2317
David Meeker
602-458-7110
www.cochise.org

CONSERVATORY OF RECORDING ARTS AND SCIENCES
2300 E. Broadway Rd.
Tempe, AZ 85282-1707
John F. McJunkin
800-562-6383
Fax: 480-829-1332
E-mail: info@cras.org
www.audiorecordingschool.com

Degrees: Diploma-Master Recording Program II

The Conservatory of Recording Arts and Sciences is a world-class private institution for individuals who want to pursue a career in the recording industry. A single program is offered; the 900 clock-hour master recording program II, which is 37 weeks in duration. This comprehensive curriculum covers multi-track music recording, live sound, MIDI and Digital Audio, Troubleshooting, and Music Business. The coursework is taught using world-class state-of-the-art equipment. The conservatory is the only school in the world whose graduates are certified by Digidesign on both ProTools course 135 and 235. Students are required to complete a 280 clock-hour internship at a location of the student's choice in order to graduate. The institution relies on the skills of successful professionals from the industry to develop and teach the curriculum. There are quite a few Gold and Platinum award winners among our instructors. A selective enrollment policy is practiced.

EASTERN ARIZONA COLLEGE
DEPARTMENT OF MUSIC
Thatcher, AZ 85552
David Lunt
602-428-8233
www.easternarizona.com

GLENDALE COMMUNITY COLLEGE
DEPARTMENT OF MUSIC
6000 W. Olive Ave.
Glendale, AZ 85302-3006
Cherrie Watkins
623-845-3720
Fax: 623-845-3754
www.gc.maricopa.edu

GRAND CANYON UNIVERSITY
DEPARTMENT OF MUSIC
P.O. Box 11097
Phoenix, AZ 85061-1097
Sheila Corley
602-589-2482
Fax: 602-589-2459
www.grand-canyon.edu

MESA COMMUNITY COLLEGE
DEPARTMENT OF MUSIC
1833 W. Southern Ave.
Mesa, AZ 85202
Sue Lucius
480-461-7000
Fax: 480-461-7804
www.mc.maricopa.edu

NORTHERN ARIZONA UNIVERSITY
COLLEGE OF FINE ARTS
P.O. Box 6040
Flagstaff, AZ 86011
Dr. John Burton
928-523-8975
E-mail: john.burton@nau.edu
http://www4.nau.edu/cofa

NORTHLAND PIONEER COLLEGE
DEPARTMENT OF MUSIC
1200 Hermosa Dr.
Holbrook, AZ 86025
Steve Dygert
520-536-6247
Fax: 520-524-1997
www.northland.cc.az.us

PHOENIX COLLEGE
DEPARTMENT OF MUSIC
1202 W. Thomas Rd.
Phoenix, AZ 85013
Janet Sessions
602-285-7272
Fax: 602-285-7700
www.phoenix.edu

PIMA COMMUNITY COLLEGE
DEPARTMENT OF MUSIC
2202 W. Anklam Rd.
Tucson, AZ 95709
Mark Nelson
520-206-6826
Fax: 520-206-6719
www.pima.edu

SCOTTSDALE COMMUNITY COLLEGE
DEPARTMENT OF MUSIC
9000 E. Chaparral Rd.
Scottsdale, AZ 85250
John Burley
602-423-6333
Fax: 602-423-6200
www.sc.maricopa.edu

UNIVERSITY OF ARIZONA
Music Department

School of Music and Dance
Music Building, Room 109
Tucson, AZ 85721
Dr. Josef Knott
520-621-1655
Fax: 520-621-8118
E-mail: cuttietta@arizona.edu
http://arizona.edu

The School of Music and Dance is a comprehensive school of 600 majors and a full artist applied faculty. Ensembles include wind ensemble, wind symphony, two campus bands, symphony orchestra, chamber orchestra, opera orchestra, jazz ensembles A & B, chamber music (conducted and non-conducted). Facilities available are the concert hall, recital hall ($500,000 pipe organ), practice rooms, state-of-the-art recording studio, high-tech media arts lab and electronic percussion studio.

YAVAPAI COLLEGE
Music Department

8301 E. Sheldon St.
Prescott, AZ 86301
Dr. Roy Breiling
520-776-2045
Fax: 520-717-2036
E-mail: laura_moore@yavapai.cc.az.us
www.yavapai.cc.az.us/ycmusic.nsf

ARKANSAS

Population: 2,791,803 (2003 Estimate)

Capital City: Little Rock

Music Colleges and Universities: Arkansas State University, Arkansas Tech University, East Arkansas Community College, Harding University, John Brown University, Lyon College, Mississippi County Community College, Ouachita Baptist University, Philander Smith College, University of Arkansas at Little Rock, University of Arkansas at Monticello, University of Arkansas at Pine Bluff, University of Central Alabama, University of Central Arkansas, University of the Ozarks, Westark Community College, Williams Baptist College

Bird: Mockingbird

Motto: Regnat Populus – The People Rule

Flower: Apple Blossom

Tree: Pine

Residents Called: Arkansans

Origin of Name: From the Quapaw Indians, who were called Akansea by certain other tribes. The name means "South Wind." Another possible origin is from the French interpretation of a Sioux word "acansa," meaning "downstream place."

Area: 53,225 square miles (29th largest state)

Statehood: June 15 (25th state)

Largest Cities: Little Rock, Fort Smith, North Little Rock, Fayetteville, Jonesboro, Pine Bluff, Springdale, Conway, Rogers, Hot Springs

College Band Programs: University of Arkansas at Fayetteville, Henderson State University, University of Arkansas, University of Arkansas at Pine Bluff, University of Central Arkansas

ARKANSAS

ARKANSAS STATE UNIVERSITY
DEPARTMENT OF MUSIC

P.O. Box 779
State University, AR 72467
Dr. Tom O'Connor
870-972-2094
Fax: 870-972-3932
E-mail: toconnor@astate.edu
www.astate.edu

Degrees: B.A., B.M., B.M.E., M.M., M.M.E.

Arkansas State University has been a leader in music educator training for decades. Many of the music educators in the mid-south are graduates of the ASU vocal and instrumental programs. Bands and choirs from ASU have performed throughout the world under the direction of Mr. Don Minx and Al Skoog, and current directors are continuing the tradition with an upcoming performance to Carnegie Hall. Students may also gain degrees in solo performance while studying with world-class vocal and instrumental faculty members. Small ensembles and student soloists from the department have recently performed at international conferences such as the International Tuba-Euphonium Conference, International Trombone Society, American Choral Directors Association Convention, and the International Horn Society. The Music Department has 130 music majors, two concert bands, a marching band, three large choirs, concert orchestra, two jazz bands, and several vocal and instrumental small ensembles. Twenty full-time faculty and 6 adjuncts provide instruction.

ARKANSAS TECHNICAL UNIVERSITY
DEPARTMENT OF MUSIC

Forrest City, AR 72801
Debbie Moore
501-968-0368
Fax: 501-968-0467

E-mail: deb.moore@mail.atu.edu
www.atu.edu

EAST ARKANSAS COMMUNITY COLLEGE
DEPARTMENT OF MUSIC

Forrest City, AR 72335
Ruth Vowan
501-633-4480
E-mail: vowan@eacc.cc.ar.us
www.eacc.cc.ar.us

HARDING UNIVERSITY
DEPARTMENT OF MUSIC

P.O. Box 10767
Searcy, AR 72149
Arthur Shearin
501-279-4343
Fax: 501-279-4086
E-mail: mlthomas@harding.edu
www.harding.edu

HENDERSON STATE UNIVERSITY
DEPARTMENT OF MUSIC

P.O. Box 7733
Arkadelphia, AR 71999
David Evens
870-230-5036
Fax: 870-230-5144
www.hsu.edu

HENDRIX COLLEGE
DEPARTMENT OF MUSIC

1600 Washington Ave.
Conway, AR 72032
John Krebs
501-450-1245
Fax: 501-450-1200
E-mail: krebs@hendrix.edu
www.hendrix.edu

JOHN BROWN UNIVERSITY
DEPARTMENT OF MUSIC
2000 W. University
Siloam Springs, AR 72761
Terri Wubbena
501-524-7266
Fax: 501-524-9548
E-mail: twubbena@jbu.edu
www.jbu.edu

LYON COLLEGE
DEPARTMENT OF MUSIC
2300 Highland Rd.
Batesville, AR 72501
Russel Stinson
870-869-4246
Fax: 870-524-9548
E-mail: rstinson@lyon.edu
www.lyon.edu

MISSISSIPPI COUNTY COMMUNITY COLLEGE
DEPARTMENT OF MUSIC
Blytheville, AR 72315
Dennis Hay
501-762-1020
www.mccc.cc.ar.us

OUACHITA BAPTIST UNIVERSITY
JONES SCHOOL OF FINE ARTS-MUSIC DIVISION
Arkadelphia, AR 71998
Charles Wright
501-245-5129
Fax: 501-245-5500
www.obu.edu

PHILANDER SMITH COLLEGE
DEPARTMENT OF MUSIC
812 W. 13th St.
Little Rock, AR 72202
Rosephanye Powell
501-370-5340
Fax: 501-370-5278
www.philander.edu

UNIVERSITY OF ARKANSAS AT FAYETTEVILLE
201 Music Building
Fayetteville, AR 72701
Dr. Steven Gates
501-575-4701
Fax: 501-575-5409
E-mail: sgates@uark.edu
www.uark.edu/depts/uamusic

UNIVERSITY OF ARKANSAS AT LITTLE ROCK
DEPARTMENT OF MUSIC
2801 South University Ave.
Little Rock, AR 72204
Victor Ellsworth
501-569-3294
Fax: 501-569-3559
E-mail: mudept@ualr.edu
www.ualr.edu/~mudept

UNIVERSITY OF ARKANSAS AT MONTICELLO
DIVISION OF MUSIC
P.O. Box 3607
Monticello, AR 71656
Annette Hall
870-460-1160
Fax: 870-460-1260
E-mail: hall@uamont.edu
www.uamont.edu/Music/index.html

UNIVERSITY OF ARKANSAS AT PINE BLUFF
DEPARTMENT OF MUSIC

Mail Slot 4956
Pine Bluff, AR 71601-4956
Josephine Bell
870-575-9905
Fax: 870-575-8108
www.uapb.edu

Degrees: B.S. in Music Teaching/Non-Teaching Instrumental/Vocal Piano and Sound Recording Technology.

UNIVERSITY OF CENTRAL ARKANSAS
MUSIC DEPARTMENT

201 Donaghey Ave.
Conway, AR 72035
Kathy Quinn
501-450-3163
Fax: 501-450-5773
E-mail: kathyo@mail.uca.edu
www.uca.edu

Degrees: B.M. in Performance, B.M. in Music Education, B.A. in Music, M.M. in performance, M.M. in music theory, M.M. in music education, M.M. in conducting

The most extraordinary thing about the UCA music department is its astonishingly well-qualified faculty. The 27 full-time and 9 part-time faculty members carry the credentials from the most prestigious graduate music institutions in the country. In fact, it is probably fair to say that the music faculty at UCA is unique among universities in the south.

These faculty members remain actively and nationally engaged in performing and research, and are dedicated to bringing to their students the benefits of their superb training and broad experience. The acclaimed ensemble and solo performances of UCA music students reflect this faculty dedication.

UNIVERSITY OF THE OZARKS
DEPARTMENT OF MUSIC

415 College Ave.
Clarksville, AR 72830
David Deseguirant
501-979-1349
Fax: 501-979-1349
www.ozarks.edu

WESTARK COMMUNITY COLLEGE
DEPARTMENT OF MUSIC

5210 Grand Ave.
Fort Smith, AR 72913
Joy Beard
501-788-7530
Fax: 501-788-7003
www.westark.edu

WILLIAMS BAPTIST COLLEGE
DEPARTMENT OF MUSIC

P.O. Box 3406
Walnut Ridge, AR 72476
Robert Magee
870-886-6741
Fax: 870-886-3924
E-mail: magee@wbcoll.edu
www.wbcoll.edu

CALIFORNIA

CALIFORNIA REPUBLIC

Population: 35,158,286 (2003 Estimate)

Capital City: Sacramento

Music Colleges and Universities: Ali Akbar College, Allan Hancock College, American River Community College, American School of Piano Tuning, Antelope Valley College, Azusa Pacific University, Bakersfield College, Bethany College of Assembly of God, Biola University, Cabrillo College, California Baptist University, California Institute of Technology, California Institute of the Arts, California Polytechnic State University at Pomona, California Polytechnic State University at San Luis Obispo, California State University at Bakersfield, California State University at Chico, California State University at Fresno, California State University at Fullerton, California State University at Hayward, California State University at Long Beach, California State University at Long Beach, California State University at Los Angeles, California State University at Northridge, California State University at Sacramento, California State University at San Bernardino, California State University at San Marcos, California State University at Stanislaus, Canada College, Cerritos College, Chabot College, Chaffey College, Chapman University, Christian Heritage College, Citrus College, City College of San Francisco, Claremont Graduate University, Claremont McKenna College, Cogswell Polytechnical College, College of Alameda, College of Marin, College of San Mateo, College of Siskiyous, College of the Canyons, College of the Desert, College of the Redwoods, College of the Sequoias, Colorado Christian University, Columbia College, Community Music School of Temecula, Compton Junior College, Concordia University, Contra Costa College, Cuesta College, Cypress College, De Anza College, Diablo Valley College, Dominican University of California, East Los Angeles College, El Camino College, Evergreen Valley College, Foothill College, Fresno City College, Fresno Pacific College, Fullerton College, Gavilan College, Glendale Community College, Golden Gate Baptist Theology Seminary, Golden West College, Grossmont College, Hartnell College, Harvey Mudd College, Holy Names College, Humboldt State University, Idyllwild School of Music and the Arts, Imperial Valley College, Irvine Valley College, Kings River College, La Sierra University, Lake Tahoe Community College, Laney Community College, Long Beach City College, Los Angeles City College, Los Angeles Harbor College, Los Angeles Mission College, Los Angeles Pierce College, Los Angeles Recording Workshop, Los Angeles Southwest College, Los Angeles Trade Tech College, Los Angeles Valley College, Los Medanos College, Loyola Marymount University, Marymount College, Masters College, Mendocino College, Merced College, Merritt College, Mills College, Miracosta College, Mission College, Modesto Junior College, Monterey Peninsula College, Moorpark College, Mount

San Antonio College, Mount St. Mary's College, Music Academy of the West, Musicians Institute, Napa Valley College, Notre Dame de Namur University, Occidental College, Ohlone College, Orange Coast College, Oxnard College, Pacific Union College, Palo Verde Junior College, Palomar College, Pasadena City College, Patten College, Pepperdine University at Malibu, Pitzer College, Point Loma Nazarene University, Pomona College, Porterville College, Rio Hondo College, Riverside Community College, Sacramento City College, San Bernardino Valley College, San Diego City College, San Diego Mesa College, San Diego State University, San Francisco Conservatory of Music, San Francisco State University, San Jose City College, San Jose State University, Santa Barbara City College, Santa Clara University, Santa Monica College, Santa Rosa Junior College, Scripps College, Shasta College, Simpson College, Skyline College, Solano College, Sonoma State University, Southern California Conservatory, Southwestern College, St. John's College, St. Mary's College of California, Stanford University, Taft College, UCLA, University of California at Berkeley, University of California at Davis, University of California at Irvine, University of California at L.A., University of California at Riverside, University of California at San Diego, University of California at Santa Barbara, University of California at Santa Cruz, University of La Verne, University of Redlands, University of San Diego, University of Southern California, University of the Pacific, Vanguard University, Ventura College, Victor Valley College, Vocal Power School, West Los Angeles College, West Valley College, Westmont College, Whittier College, Yuba College

Bird: California Valley Quail

Motto: Eureka: I have found it

Flower: California Poppy

Area: 163,707 square miles

(3rd largest state)

Statehood: September 9, 1850 (31st state)

Largest Cities: Los Angeles, San Diego, San Jose, San Francisco, Long Beach, Fresno, Sacramento, Oakland, Santa Ana, Anaheim

College Band Programs: California Polytechnic State University, California State University, California State University-Fresno, Humboldt State University, Riverside Community College, San Diego State University, San Jose University, Stanford University, University of California-Berkley, University of California-Davis, University of California-Los Angeles, University of Southern California

CALIFORNIA

ALI AKBAR COLLEGE
COLLEGE OF MUSIC
215 W. End Ave.
San Rafael, CA 94901
Ben Kunin
415-454-6264
Fax: 415-454-9396
E-mail: office@aacm.org
www.aacm.org

ALLAN HANCOCK JUNIOR COLLEGE
DEPARTMENT OF FINE ARTS
800 S. College Dr.
Santa Maria, CA 93454
Marcus W. Engelmann
805-922-6966
Fax: 805-928-7905
E-mail: mengelmann@hancock.cc.ca.us
www.hancock.cc.ca.us

AMERICAN RIVER COMMUNITY COLLEGE
DEPARTMENT OF MUSIC
4700 College Oak Dr.
Sacramento, CA 95841
Arthur LaPierre
916-484-8195
Fax: 916-484-8880
E-mail: music@arc.losrios.edu
www.arc.losrios.edu

AMERICAN SCHOOL OF PIANO TUNING
17050 Telfer Dr.
Morgan Hill, CA 95037
Gabrielle Borgnino
800-497-9793
E-mail: director@piano-tuning.com

www.piano-tuning.com
American School of Piano Tuning offers a step-by-step, 10-lesson correspondence course in Piano Tuning and Repair. Tools and parts are included. Free brochure available.

ANTELOPE VALLEY COLLEGE
DEPARTMENT OF MUSIC
3041 W. Ave.
Lancaster, CA 93536-5402
Dr. Davio Nuby
661-722-6385
Fax: 661-722-6390
E-mail: dwhite@avc.edu
www.avc.edu

AZUSA PACIFIC UNIVERSITY
SCHOOL OF MUSIC
901 E. Alosta Ave.
Azusa, CA 91702
Dr. Duane Funderburk
626-815-3848
Fax: 626-969-7419
E-mail: joxley@apu.edu
www.apu.edu/music

BAKERSFIELD COLLEGE
DEPARTMENT OF MUSIC
1801 Panorama Dr.
Bakersfield, CA 93305-1219
John Gerhold
661-395-4404
Fax: 661-395-4078
E-mail: jgerhold@bc.cc.ca.us
www.bc.cc.ca.us

BETHANY COLLEGE OF ASSEMBLY OF GOD
DEPARTMENT OF MUSIC
800 Bethany Dr.
Scott's Valley, CA 95066-2820
Mark Hulse
831-433-800
Fax: 831-438-4517
www.bethany.edu

BIOLA UNIVERSITY
BAND DIVISION
13800 Ave.
Community Programs and Services
La Mirada, CA 90639
Jack Schwarz
562-903-4892
Fax: 562-903-4746
E-mail:
george.boespflug@truth.biola.edu
www.biola.edu

CABRILLO COLLEGE
DEPARTMENT OF MUSIC
6500 Soquel Dr.
Aptos, CA 95003-3119
Micheal Irwin
408-479-6464
Fax: 408-464-8382
www.cabrillo.edu

CALIFORNIA BAPTIST UNIVERSITY
DEPARTMENT OF MUSIC
8432 Magnolia Ave.
Riverside, CA 92504-3206
Dr. Gary Bonner
909-343-4251
Fax: 909-343-4570
E-mail: schoolofmusic@calbaptist.edu
www.calbaptist.edu

Degrees: B.A. in Music

In the school of music at California Baptist University, upholding a higher standard isn't just what we say - it's what we do best. You won't find too many music programs in which students work directly with the dean, but at CBU, you can expect personal guidance from Dr. Gary Bonner. A master teacher, skilled at sparking a fire for perfection in his musicians, Dr. Bonner takes a personal interest in his students' success. Count on his mentoring as one of the most significant experiences in your education, and a set of tools you will carry with you long after you graduate.

Dr. Gary Bonner came to California Baptist University as Dean of the School of Music in 2002, bringing a remarkable background in teaching, conducting and recording music of universal appeal. Emphasizing quality and performance, CBU school of Music offers a conservatory-style education in many respects - intimate, challenging and rigorous. But as part of a comprehensive Christian university, CBU also gives music students exceptional resources that no conservatory can match. Our liberal arts curriculum opens new realms of understanding to students in all majors, and a talented faculty of Christian thinkers challenges CBU students to find their place in the world and to do the most good they can. "When people are around Dr. Bonner, they hold their heads up higher, they stand with better posture, they walk with broader shoulders. Doc brings a higher level of appreciation of who you are, what you can do and what you have to offer. The bar is raised." –Rev. Lance Gaskill, pastor of worship arts at Greeley Wesleyan Church, Greeley, CO.

CALIFORNIA INSTITUTE OF TECHNOLOGY
MUSIC PROGRAM
Pasadena, CA 91125
Daryl Denning
323-395-3295
Fax: 626-585-9284
E-mail: ddenning@caltech.edu
www.music.caltech.edu

CALIFORNIA INSTITUTE OF THE ARTS
School of Music
24700 McBean Pkwy.
Valencia, CA 91355
Eric Barber
661-253-7817
Fax: 661-255-0938
E-mail: info@music.calarts.edu
http://music.calarts.edu

The School of Music at CalArts strives to create a learning environment intended to support creative music-making. Since its founding, the Institute has established an international reputation as a leader in music. Almost every artist at the forefront of new directions has been either a faculty member or visiting artist at CalArts. Our alumni have now taken their places as leaders in the arts and our programs and curriculum continue to set the pace for contemporary music education.

CALIFORNIA POLYTECHNIC STATE UNIVERSITY AT POMONA
3801 West Temple Ave.
Pomona, CA 91768
J. Levine
909-869-3548
Fax: 909-869-4145
E-mail: ilevine@csupomona.edu
www.csupomona.edu

CALIFORNIA POLYTECHNIC STATE UNIVERSITY AT SAN LUIS OBISPO
Music Department
1 Grand Ave.
San Luis Obispo, CA 93407
Music Department
805-756-2406
Fax: 805-756-7464
E-mail: mu@polymail.calpoly.edu
www.calpoly.edu

Cal Poly is one of 23 campuses in California State University, the nation's largest four-year university system. With an enrollment of over 17,000 full-time students, the university is located in San Luis Obispo, midway between San Francisco and Los Angeles. Recently, the university and the community opened a 1,300-seat performing arts center at a cost of more than $32 million. Today, Harman Hall is considered one of the finest concert halls in the nation. The music department has become known for its excellence and for its personal interest in its students. The department serves as a cultural center for both the university and community through a program of public performances by student and faculty groups and through department-sponsored workshops and lectures. The department prides itself on a tradition of musical excellence recognized throughout the state for the past 50 years. The program offers all students an opportunity to participate in a variety of excellent musical organizations, including its internationally known wind orchestra. The BA program in music reflects the qualities for which Cal Poly has become recognized nationally – an intensive major with total involvement of the student and a close relationship between the student and an excellent faculty.

CALIFORNIA STATE UNIVERSITY BAKERSFIELD
9001 Stockdale Hwy.
Bakersfield, CA 93311
Dr. Anita DuPratt
661-664-3093
Fax: 661-665-6901
E-mail: adupratt@csub.edu
www.csub.edu

The Performing Arts Department offers a bachelor of arts degree in music, as well as a minor in music. Serious instrumentalists, singers, composers, and appreciators of music will find performing opportunities and course work that challenges and improves their talent and knowledge. Comprehensive training in performance, theory, music history, pedagogy, music education and composition comprise the curricula. Housed in the new music building, the department offers private studio instruction in voice and various instruments to strengthen the student's technique and performing ability. Musical performance is emphasized, and CSUB offers many opportunities for students to express their musical creativity. Vocal artists may participate in University Singers, Community Singers, Chamber Singers, Jazz Singers, and Opera Workshop. A fully mounted opera is staged every third year, and opera scenes are presented each year. Instrumentalists have opportunities to perform in the jazz Big Band, chamber orchestra, community band, Musica de Camera, and numerous small jazz groups. The jazz students have recorded several CDs of their own compositions, and the choral students have performed at Carnegie Hall and throughout the United States.

CALIFORNIA STATE UNIVERSITY AT CHICO
MUSIC DEPARTMENT

400 W. First
Chico, CA 95929-0805
Dr. James M. Bankhead
530-898-5152
Fax: 530-898-4082
E-mail: jbankhead@csuchico.edu
www.csuchico.edu

Located 90 miles north of Sacramento, Chico State offers excellent musical training in a variety of disciplines. The facilities include three outstanding concert halls, state-of-the-art labs and studios, and ample practice rooms. The faculty is devoted to the education and success of the students.

CALIFORNIA STATE UNIVERSITY AT FRESNO
MUSIC DEPARTMENT

2380 E. Keats Ave. MB77
Fresno, CA 93740
Dr. Kathryn Bumpuss
559-278-7717
Fax: 559-278-6800
E-mail:
kathryn_bumpass@csufresno.edu
www.csufresno.edu/music

A major in music is designed to prepare students for careers in teaching, performance, or music-related fields. It enhances their knowledge of musical art and increases their sensitivity to the musical world around them. The Department of Music provides: Undergraduate instruction in music for those planning professional careers as performers, composers, and studio teachers, as well as those preparing for advanced degrees in performance and composition; state-approved subject matter preparation required for a California teaching credential in music; graduate education for students planning professional and academic careers or seeking professional growth as K-12 teachers or junior college instructors; and broad acquaintance with music for the community and non-music major. Two degree programs accredited by the National Association of Schools of Music are offered: the Bachelor of Arts and the master of arts. The department of music faculty has backgrounds in varied areas of specialization. Many members of the faculty have national and international reputations as performing artists and teachers. Others are well known for their scholarly research, articles, and books. They are all dedicated to providing students with the best music education possible both in their classes and studios. The music building houses recital and concert facilities, rehearsal halls, classrooms, faculty studios, offices, and student practice rooms. The building also contains recording studios, computer labs, MIDI and electronic music labs, and a tracker-action organ.

CALIFORNIA STATE UNIVERSITY AT FULLERTON

DEPARTMENT OF MUSIC

P.O. Box 6850
Fullerton, CA 92834-6850
Gordon Paine
714-278-3511
Fax: 714-278-5956
E-mail: gpaine@fullerton.edu
www.fullerton.edu

CALIFORNIA STATE UNIVERSITY AT HAYWARD

MUSIC DEPARTMENT

25800 Carlos Bee Blvd.
Hayward, CA 94542
Timothy M. Smith
510-885-3285
Fax: 510-885-3461
E-mail: tsmith2@csuhayward.edu
www.isis.csuhayward.edu

The music department's primary interest is to prepare students to be fine musicians. Students benefit greatly from Cal State at Hayward's well-rounded curriculum and wide diversity of performance opportunities. The University's location in the eastern part of the San Francisco Bay Area affords students access to world-class musicians and ensembles, and the music faculty has close associations with the major performing institutions in the Bay Area. The department of music offers an undergraduate program leading to the degree of Bachelor of Arts in music and a graduate program leading to the degree of Master of Arts in music. Both degrees are fully accredited by the National Association of Schools of Music. The curriculum is designed to provide a foundation for a student entering public school or private teaching, a career as a professional performer, or may serve as preparation for further, more specialized study in graduate school.

CALIFORNIA STATE UNIVERSITY AT LONG BEACH

MUSIC DEPARTMENT

1250 Bellflower Blvd.
Long Beach, CA 90840-7101
John Carnahan
562-985-4781
Fax: 562-985-2490
E-mail: music@csulb.edu
www.csulb.edu

The CSULB Department of Music enjoys an outstanding reputation throughout the United States. Such recognition can be achieved only when faculty and students work together toward common goals. Graduates of the department of music have achieved success in the fields of performance, teaching, music composition, music history, and other areas related to the music profession. The faculty of the department of music total more than 40 full-and part-time members who bring practical and academic experience to the classroom. Many of the faculty are highly acclaimed in their respective fields of performance and scholarship. The department of music holds membership in the National Association of Schools of Music; all degrees offered are accredited by NASM. With over 60 practice rooms, 15 classrooms, three rehearsal halls, two theatres, an electronic music studio and a fully automated recording studio, the music department facility is outstanding. In addition, there is the 1,200-seat Richard and Karen Carpenter Performing Arts Center, one of the premier music performance facilities in the university system.

CALIFORNIA STATE UNIVERSITY AT LOS ANGELES

5151 State University Dr.
Los Angeles, CA 90032
Dr. Rene Aravena
323-343-4072
Fax: 323-343-4063
E-mail: raraven@calstatela.edu
www.calstatela.edu

CALIFORNIA STATE UNIVERSITY AT NORTHRIDGE
MUSIC DEPARTMENT
18111 Nordhoff St.
Northridge, CA 91330-3181
Steve Martinez
818-677-3181
Fax: 818-677-5876
E-mail: music@csun.edu
www.csun.edu/music

CALIFORNIA STATE UNIVERSITY AT SACRAMENTO
MUSIC DEPARTMENT
6000 J St.
Sacramento, CA 95819
Dr. Ernie Hills
916-278-5191
Fax: 916-278-7217
E-mail: hills@csus.edu
www.csus.edu

California State University at Sacramento is accredited by NASM.

CALIFORNIA STATE UNIVERSITY AT SAN BERNARDINO
DEPARTMENT OF MUSIC
5500 University Pkwy.
San Bernardino, CA 92407-2397
Robert Dunham
909-880-5859
Fax: 909-880-7016
E-mail: rdunham@csusb.edu
www.csusb.edu

Degrees: B.A. in music

The department of music at California State University, San Bernardino is a vital and growing program, giving students the benefits of a large, full-service, university and the individual attention found in a smaller, conservatory-like setting. The department faculty are highly qualified in their personal areas of expertise, dedicated to continued musical and professional growth, and integrally involved with the development of their students. The Bachelor of Arts in music degree program offers students a solid core of traditional music study, with a variety of emphasis areas tailored to suit individual student interests and needs. A variety of large and small vocal and instrumental ensembles give music students ample opportunities to hone their performance skills and study traditional and modern music repertoire. The CSUSB campus is a refreshing and enlivening environment with open spaces, trees, gardens, and walkways. Campus life is vital, with a variety of ongoing social, cultural, and athletic activities. New, apartment-style residence halls make living on campus easy and enjoyable, and tuition is very reasonable when compared with similar state universities across the country.

CALIFORNIA STATE UNIVERSITY AT SAN MARCOS
VISUAL PERFORMING ARTS DEPARTMENT
San Marcos, CA 95380
William Bradbury
760-750-4174
Fax: 760-750-4111
E-mail: bradbury@csusm.edu
www.csusm.edu/a_s/vpa

CALIFORNIA STATE UNIVERSITY AT STANISLAUS
DEPARTMENT OF MUSIC
801 W. Monte Vista
Turlock, CA 95380
Stephen Thomas
209-667-3421
Fax: 209-647-024
E-mail: music@toto.csustan.edu
www.csustan.edu

CANADA COLLEGE
DEPARTMENT OF MUSIC
4200 Farm Hill Blvd.
Redwood, CA 94061-1030
John Friesen
650-306-3336
Fax: 650-306-3176
http://canadacollege.net

CERRITOS COLLEGE
DEPARTMENT OF MUSIC
11110 Alondra Blvd.
Norwalk, CA 90650-6203
Barry Russel
310-860-2451
Fax: 310-467-5005
E-mail: brussell@cerritos.edu
www.cerritos.edu

CHABOT COLLEGE
DEPARTMENT OF MUSIC
25555 Hesperian Blvd.
Hayward, CA 94545-2447
Sally Fitzgerald
510-786-6829
Fax: 510-782-9315
http://chabotweb.clpccd.cc.ca.us

CHAFFEY COLLEGE
DEPARTMENT OF MUSIC
5885 Haven Ave.
Alta Loma, CA 91737-3002
Gustavo Gil
909-941-2707
Fax: 909-466-2831
www.chaffey.cc.ca.us

CHAPMAN UNIVERSITY
SCHOOL OF MUSIC
Orange, CA 92866
Michael S. Pelly
888-997-6871
Fax: 714-744-7671
E-mail: rickc@chapman.edu
www.chapman.edu

Chapman University, accredited by the National Association of Schools of Music, is the second-oldest private educational institution in California and has a rich tradition in the arts.

CHRISTIAN HERITAGE COLLEGE
DEPARTMENT OF MUSIC
2100 Greenfield Dr.
El Cajon, CA 92019-1161
Donald Ellsworth
619-441-2200
Fax: 619-440-0209
E-mail:
dellsworth@christianheritage.edu
www.christianheritage.edu

CITRUS COLLEGE
DEPARTMENT OF FINE AND PERFORMANCE ARTS
1000 W. Foothill Blvd.
Glendora, CA 91741-1885
Admissions
818-914-8580
Fax: 818-914-8582
E-mail: admissions@citruscollege.edu
www.citrus.cc.ca.us

CITY COLLEGE OF SAN FRANCISCO
DEPARTMENT OF MUSIC
50 Phelan Ave.
San Francisco, CA 94112
Madeline Mueller
415-239-3641
Fax: 415-452-5110
E-mail: mmueller@ccsf.org
www.ccsf.cc.ca.us/departments/liberal_arts

CLAREMONT GRADUATE UNIVERSITY
CENTERS FOR THE ARTS AND HUMANITIES
121 E. 10th St.
Claremont, CA 91711-4405
Dr. Robert Zappulla
909-621-8612
Fax: 909-607-3694
E-mail: Robert.zappulla@cgu.edu
www.cgu.edu/arts/music

Degrees: Master of Arts, Doctor of Church Music, Doctor of Musical Arts, Doctor of Philosophy

The Music Department at Claremont Graduate University offers courses of study leading to the degrees of Master of Arts, Doctor of Church Music, Doctor of Musical Arts, and Doctor of Philosophy. In addition, three professional M.A. degrees are available that combine musicology with sub-specializations in music communications, arts administration, and information management. All programs are designed with special emphasis upon music within its interdisciplinary, cultural and intellectual context. They combine comprehensive training in music literature, historical style analysis, and study of performance practices. The Doctor of Church Music and the Master of Arts degree with a concentration in Church Music are offered in cooperation with the Claremont School of Theology. In addition, the curriculum emphasizes uses of music technology for research, teaching, and creative work. All music students have the opportunity

to receive music technology instruction in several contexts, including notation, composition, performance, and film scoring techniques.

CLAREMONT MCKENNA COLLEGE
DEPARTMENT OF MUSIC
890 Columbia Ave.
Claremont, CA 91711-3901
Micheal Lamkin
909-607-3266
Fax: 909-621-8323
www.scrippscol.edu

COGSWELL POLYTECHNICAL COLLEGE
DIGITAL AUDIO TECHNOLOGY
1175 Bordeaux Dr.
Sunnyvale, CA 94089
Tim Duncan
408-541-0100
Fax: 408-747-0764
www.cogswell.edu

Digital Audio Technology concentrations are available in studio recording, sound design, composing and arranging and Internet audio. The school features three recording studios, two classroom labs, a soundstage, an Iso-booth, MIDI and digital audio, Mac and PC.

COLLEGE OF ALAMEDA
DEPARTMENT OF MUSIC
555 Atlantic Ave.
Alameda, CA 94501-2109
Gunther Puschendorf
415-522-7221
www.peralta.cc.ca.us/coa/coa.htm

COLLEGE OF MARIN
DEPARTMENT OF MUSIC
835 College Ave.
Kentfield, CA 94904
Stanly Kraczek
415-485-9460
Fax: 415-485-0135
www.martin.cc.ca.us

COLLEGE OF SAN MATEO
DEPARTMENT OF MUSIC
1700 W. Hillsdale Blvd.
San Mateo, CA 94402-3757
Grace Sonner
415-574-6161
Fax: 415-574-6680
http://gocsm.net

COLLEGE OF SISKIYOUS
DEPARTMENT OF MUSIC
800 College Ave.
Weed, CA 96094-206
Elaine Schaefer
530-938-5258
Fax: 530-938-5227
E-mail: schaefer@siskiyous.edu
www.siskiyous.edu

COLLEGE OF THE CANYONS
MUSIC DEPARTMENT
26455 North Rockwell Canyon Rd.
Valencia, CA 91355-1803
Bernado Feldman
805-259-7800
Fax: 805-259-8302
E-mail: feldman_b@mail.coc.cc.ca.us
www.coc.cc.ca.us

COLLEGE OF THE DESERT
DEPARTMENT OF MUSIC
43 Monterey Ave.
Palm Desert, CA 92260
John Norman
619-773-2574
Fax: 619-776-7310
www.desert.cc.ca.us

COLLEGE OF THE REDWOODS
DEPARTMENT OF MUSIC
7351 Tomkins Hill Rd.
Eureka, CA 95501-9302
Ed Macan
707-476-4303
Fax: 707-476-4430
E-mail: ed-
macan@eureka.redwoods.cc.ca.us
www.redwoods.cc.ca.us

COLLEGE OF THE SEQUOIAS
DEPARTMENT OF MUSIC
915 S. Mooney Blvd.
Visalia, CA 93277-2214
Jeffery Seward
209-730-3700
Fax: 209-739-3894
www.sequoias.cc.ca.us

COLORADO CHRISTIAN UNIVERSITY
SCHOOL OF MUSIC THEATRE AND ART
180 S. Garrison St.
Lakewood, CA 80226-1053
Steven Taylor
303-963-3135
Fax: 303-963-3131
E-mail: staylor@ccu.edu
www.ccu.edu

Degrees: B.A. in Music with emphases available in Sound Recording Technology and Performance; B.M. in Music Education, B.M. in Music Ministry, Music minor

Colorado Christian University exists to help students pursue a Christ-centered undergraduate and graduate education.

Colorado Christian University is carrying out a commitment to higher education implicit in America's national heritage of Christian faith. The university integrates diverse fields of study with biblical truths. Each academic discipline (e.g., philosophy; drama; art; education; psychology; music; the physical, social, and behavioral sciences) is taught by instructors who have clear biblical presuppositions.

A unique, progressive, and distinctively Christian philosophy guides the music program. Integrated offerings combine all aspects of classical, jazz, folk, contemporary Christian and world music.

The music program provides world-class preparation for life, the opportunity to tour nationally, on- and off-campus production studios, computer-assisted instruction, an emphasis on Christian ministry, and personal attention by an exceptional, creative and caring faculty.

COLUMBIA COLLEGE
MUSIC DEPARTMENT
16000 Columbia College Dr.
Sonora, CA 95370
John Carter
209-588-5214
Fax: 209-588-5104
E-mail: carterj@yosemite.cc.ca.us
www.columbia.yosemite.cc.ca.us

COMMUNITY MUSIC SCHOOL OF TEMECULA
4112 Winchester
Suite B1
Temecula, CA 92592
Diane Gee
909-694-5620

COMPTON JUNIOR COLLEGE
DEPARTMENT OF MUSIC
1111 E. Artesia Blvd.
Compton, CA 90221-5314
David Cobbs
213-635-8081
www.compton.cc.ca.us

CONCORDIA UNIVERSITY
DEPARTMENT OF MUSIC
1530 Concordia W
Irvine, CA 92612-3299
Renee Wacler
949-854-8002
Fax: 949-854-6858
www.cui.edu

CONTRA COSTA COLLEGE
MUSIC DEPARTMENT
2600 Mission Bell Dr.
San Pablo, CA 94806
Wayne Organ
510-235-7800
Fax: 510-236-6768
E-mail: worgan@contracosta.cc.ca.us
www.contracosta.cc.ca.us

CUESTA COLLEGE
DEPARTMENT OF MUSIC
P.O. Box 8106
San Luis Obispo, CA 93403-8106
Robert Evans
805-546-3195
Fax: 805-546-3939
E-mail: banderso@bass.cuesta.cc.ca.us
www.cuesta.cc.ca.us

CYPRESS COLLEGE
DEPARTMENT OF MUSIC
9200 Valley View St.
Cypress, CA 90630-5805
Mark Anderman
714-484-7140
Fax: 714-952-9602
E-mail: manderman@cypress.cc.ca.us
www.cypresscollege.edu

DE ANZA COLLEGE
CREATIVE ARTS
21250 Stevens Creek Blvd.
Cupertino, CA 95014
Nancy J. Canter
408-864-8315
Fax: 408-864-8492
E-mail: canternancy@fhda.edu
www.deanza.fhda.edu

DIABLO VALLEY COLLEGE
DEPARTMENT OF MUSIC
321 Golf Club Rd.
Pleasant Hill, CA 94523-1529
Frederic Johnson
925-685-1230
Fax: 925-685-1551
www.dvc.edu

DOMINICAN UNIVERSITY OF CALIFORNIA
DEPARTMENT OF MUSIC
50 Acacia Ave.
San Rafael, CA 94901-2230
Craig Singleton
415-485-3236
Fax: 415-485-3205
E-mail: singleton@dominican.edu
www.dominican.edu

EAST LOS ANGELES COLLEGE
DEPARTMENT OF MUSIC
1301 Avenida Cesar Chavez
Monterey Park, CA 91754
Barbara Hasty
323-265-8650
www.elac.cc.ca.us

EL CAMINO COLLEGE
DIVISIONS OF FINE ARTS
16007 Crenshaw Blvd.
Torrance, CA 90506-0001
Roger Quadhamer
310-660-3715
Fax: 310-660-3792
www.elcamino.cc.ca.us

EVERGREEN VALLEY COLLEGE
DEPARTMENT OF MUSIC
3095 Yerba Buena Rd.
San Jose, CA 95235-1513
Linda Carbajal
408-274-7900
Fax: 408-223-9291
www.evc.ed

FOOTHILL COLLEGE
MUSIC DEPARTMENT
12345 El Monte Rd.
Los Altos Hills, CA 94022
Music Department
650-949-7262
Fax: 650-949-7375
E-mail: pad3553@discovery.fhda.edu
www.foothill.fhda.edu

FRESNO CITY COLLEGE
DEPARTMENT OF MUSIC
1101 E. University Ave.
Fresno, CA 93704-6219
Michael Dana
559-442-4600
Fax: 559-265-5756
E-mail: mike.dana@scccd.com
www.fresnocitycollege.com

FRESNO PACIFIC COLLEGE
DEPARTMENT OF MUSIC
1717 S. Chestnut Ave.
Fresno, CA 93702-4709
Roy Klassen
559-453-2000
Fax: 559-453-2007
E-mail: rlklasse@fresno.edu
www.fresno.edu

FULLERTON COLLEGE
DEPARTMENT OF MUSIC
321 E. Chapman Ave.
Fullerton, CA 92832-2095
Anita Ward
714-992-7296
Fax: 714-525-8165
E-mail: award@fullcoll.edu
www.fullcoll.edu

GAVILAN COLLEGE
DEPARTMENT OF MUSIC
5055 Santa Teresa Blvd.
Gilroy, CA 95020-9578
Arthur Juncker
408-847-1400
www.gavilan.cc.ca.us

GLENDALE COMMUNITY COLLEGE
DEPARTMENT OF MUSIC
1500 N. Verdrigo Rd.
Glendale, CA 91208-2894
Glenn Delange
818-240-1000
Fax: 818-549-9436
www.glendale.cc.ca.us

GOLDEN GATE BAPTIST THEOLOGY SEMINARY
DIXON SCHOOL OF CHURCH MUSIC
201 Seminary Dr.
P.O. Box 157
Mill Valley, CA 94941-2197
Gary McCoy
415-380-1576
Fax: 415-380-1320
E-mail: garymccoy@ggbts.edu
www.ggbts.edu

GOLDEN WEST COLLEGE
DEPARTMENT OF MUSIC
15744 Golden W. St.
Huntington Beach, CA 92647-2748
Henrietta Carter
714-892-7711
Fax: 714-895-8784
E-mail: hcarter@gwc.cccd.edu
www.gwc.cccd.edu

GROSSMONT COLLEGE
MUSIC DEPARTMENT
8800 Grossmont College Dr.
El Cajon, CA 92020-1799
Steven Baker
619-644-7254
Fax: 619-461-3396
E-mail: steve.baker@gcccd.net
www.grossmont.net/music

The Grossmont College Music Department offers an associate in arts degree in music. It is a traditional two-year music program consisting of four semesters of music theory and ear-training, class piano and performance studies with required recital performance and jury examinations before the music faculty. The music department currently serves more than 50 music majors, plus more than 1,500 general music education students each semester. The school has seven student performance ensembles including the Grossmont Symphony Orchestra, Grossmont College Master Chorale, chamber singers, jazz ensemble, jazz vocal ensemble, concert band and classical guitar ensemble. In addition, the school offers three four-semester courses of classroom instruction in piano, guitar, and voice. Along with the theatre arts department, a transfer degree in musical theatre is offered. Also, the school is currently developing a jazz studies transfer program as well as a music technology program. The facility consists of a two-story complex that includes two large rehearsal rooms, two keyboard/music technology rooms, 11 practice rooms with pianos, and a 240-seat recital hall. In addition, the budget allows for six to 10 yearly concerts in the 1,200-seat East County Performing Arts Center. Scholarships that provide financial support for private lessons for declared full-time music majors are available.

HARTNELL COLLEGE
DEPARTMENT OF MUSIC
156 Homestead Ave.
Salinas, CA 93901
Daniel Ipson
831-755-6905
Fax: 831-755-6751
www.hartnell.cc.ca.us

HARVEY MUDD COLLEGE
DEPARTMENT OF HUMANITIES AND SOCIAL SCIENCES
301 E. Twelfth St.
Claremont, CA 91711
William Alves
909-621-8022
Fax: 909-607-7600
E-mail: alves@hmc.edu
www.hmc.edu

HOLY NAMES COLLEGE
DEPARTMENT OF MUSIC
3500 Mountain Blvd.
Oakland, CA 94619
Elizabeth Adams
510-436-1031
Fax: 510-436-1438
www.hnc.edu

HUMBOLDT STATE UNIVERSITY
DEPARTMENT OF MUSIC
1 Harp St.
Arcata, CA 95521
Ken Ayoob
707-826-3531
Fax: 797-826-3528
E-mail: mus@humboldt.edu
http://humboldt.edu/~mus

IDYLLWILD SCHOOL OF MUSIC AND THE ARTS

52500 Temecula Dr.
P.O. Box 38
Idyllwild, CA 92549
Anne E. Behnke
909-659-2171
Fax: 909-659-4679
E-mail: admission@idyllwildarts.org
www.idyllwildarts.org

IMPERIAL VALLEY COLLEGE
DEPARTMENT OF MUSIC

P.O. Box 158
Imperial, CA 92251-0158
Joel Jacklich
760-352-8320
Fax: 760-355-6398
E-mail: joel@imperial.cc.ca.us
www.imperial.cc.ca.us

IRVINE VALLEY COLLEGE
DEPARTMENT OF MUSIC

5500 Irvine Center Dr.
Irvine, CA 92618
Stephen Rochford
949-451-5453
Fax: 949-451-5775
E-mail: srochford@ivc.cc.ca.us
www.ivc.cc.ca.us

KINGS RIVER COLLEGE
DEPARTMENT OF MUSIC

995 Reed Ave.
Reedley, CA 93654
Shirley Bruegman
209-638-3641
Fax: 209-638-5040

LA SIERRA UNIVERSITY
DEPARTMENT OF MUSIC

4700 Pierce St.
Riverside, CA 92505
Barbara Favorito
909-785-2036
Fax: 909-785-2070
E-mail: bfavorito@lasierra.edu
www.lasierra.edu

LAKE TAHOE COMMUNITY COLLEGE
MUSIC PROGRAM

One College Dr.
South Lake Tahoe, CA 96150
Sharon Susens
530-541-4660
Fax: 530-541-7852
www.ltcc.cc.ca.us

LANEY COMMUNITY COLLEGE
DEPARTMENT OF MUSIC

900 Fallon St.
Oakland, CA 94607
Ernie Strong
415-464-3461
http://laney.peralta.cc.ca.us

LONG BEACH CITY COLLEGE
DEPARTMENT OF MUSIC, RADIO AND TV

4901 E. Carson St.
Long Beach, CA 90808
Priscilla Remeta
562-938-4314
Fax: 562-938-4409
www.lbcc.cc.ca.us

LOS ANGELES CITY COLLEGE
DEPARTMENT OF MUSIC

855 N. Vermont Ave.
Los Angeles, CA 90029
Jane Blomquist
323-953-4377
Fax: 323-953-4294
www.lacc.cc.ca.us

LOS ANGELES HARBOR COLLEGE
DEPARTMENT OF MUSIC

1111 Figueroa Pl
Wilmington, CA 90744
Mark Wood
310-522-8247
Fax: 310-834-1882
www.lahc.cc.ca.us

LOS ANGELES MISSION COLLEGE
MUSIC PROGRAM

13356 Eldridge Ave.
Sylmer, CA 91342
Dudley Foster
818-364-7493
www.lamission.edu

LOS ANGELES PIERCE COLLEGE
DEPARTMENT OF MUSIC

6201 Winnetka Ave.
Woodland Hills, CA 91371
Donna Mae Villanueva
818-719-6476
www.piercecollege.com

LOS ANGELES RECORDING WORKSHOP

5278 Lankershim Blvd.
North Hollywood, CA 91601
Terry Opp
818-763-7400
www.recordingcareer.com

LOS ANGELES SOUTHWEST COLLEGE
DEPARTMENT OF MUSIC

1600 W. Imperial Hwy.
Los Angeles, CA 90047
Roland Jackson
323-241-5320
www.lasc.cc.ca.us

LOS ANGELES TRADE TECH COLLEGE
DEPARTMENT OF MUSIC

400 W. Washington Blvd.
Los Angeles, CA 90015
Felix Hayes
213-744-9404
www.lattc.cc.ca.us

LOS ANGELES VALLEY COLLEGE
DEPARTMENT OF MUSIC

5800 Fulton Ave.
Van Nuys, CA 91401
Dianne Wintrob
818-947-2346
Fax: 818-947-2610
E-mail: maddrecm@lavc.cc.ca.us
www.lavc.cc.ca.us

LOS MEDANOS COLLEGE
DEPARTMENT OF MUSIC AND RECORDING ARTS

2700 E. Leland Rd.
Pittsburgh, CA 94565
R. Paul Ashley
925-439-0200
Fax: 925-427-1599
E-mail: pashley@losmedanos.net
www.losmedanos.net

LOYOLA MARYMOUNT UNIVERSITY
DEPARTMENT OF MUSIC

Burns Fine Arts Center
1 LMU Dr.
MS-8347
Los Angeles, CA 90045
Dr. Mary Braiden
310-338-5154
Fax: 310-338-6046
E-mail: mbreden@lmu.edu
www.lmu.edu/colleges/cfa/music

The purpose of the Department of Music is to provide quality music instruction for students who wish to pursue music as a career and for those who wish to enrich their lives through non-career-oriented study and/or performance. The department is dedicated to providing this training with emphasis on a personal approach, and is committed to conducting and promoting scholarly research and creative musical inquiry and activity. Through the presentation of diverse musical programs, the department also sustains and enriches the educational and cultural vitality of the university as well as its surrounding community. The department of music offers the bachelor of arts in music degree, the requirements of which can serve as an excellent foundation for students undertaking advanced studies in preparation for such careers as musicology, composition, ethnomusicology, music-librarianship, and pedagogy-oriented teaching. In addition to meeting all general university admissions requirements, students who wish to either major or minor in music must meet specific department of music entrance requirements.

MARYMOUNT COLLEGE
DEPARTMENT OF MUSIC

30800 Palos Verdes Dr. E.
Rancho Palos Verdes, CA 90275
Don Marino
310-377-5501
www.marymountpv.edu

MASTERS COLLEGE
DEPARTMENT OF MUSIC

21726 Placerita Canyon Rd. #13
Santa Clarita, CA 91321
Paul Plew
800-568-6248
Fax: 661-253-0783
E-mail: pplew@masters.edu
www.masters.edu

MENDOCINO COLLEGE
MUSIC PROGRAM

1000 Hensley Creek Rd.
Ukiah, CA 95482
Susan Bell
707-468-3002
Fax: 707-468-3120
www.mendocino.cc.ca.us

MERCED COLLEGE
DEPARTMENT OF MUSIC

3600 M St.
Merced, CA 95348
Jamey Brzezinski
209-384-6061
Fax: 209-381-6469
www.merced.cc.ca.us

MERRITT COLLEGE
DEPARTMENT OF MUSIC
12500 Campus Dr.
Oakland, CA 94619
Peggy Pawek
415-531-4911
www.merritt.edu

MILLS COLLEGE
DEPARTMENT OF MUSIC
5000 MacArthur Blvd.
Oakland, CA 94613
David Bernstein
510-430-2171
Fax: 510-430-3228
E-mail: davidb@mills.edu
www.mills.edu

MIRACOSTA COLLEGE
DEPARTMENT OF MUSIC
1 Bernard Dr.
Oceanside, CA 92056
Donald Megill
760-795-6816
Fax: 760-795-6817
E-mail: dmegill@miracosta.cc.ca.us
www.miracosta.cc.ca.us

MISSION COLLEGE
DEPARTMENT OF MUSIC
3000 Mission College Blvd.
Santa Clara, CA 95054
Joseph Ordaz
408-988-2200
Fax: 408-855-5497
E-mail: joseph_ordaz@wvmccd.cc.ca.us
www.missioncollege.org

MODESTO JUNIOR COLLEGE
DEPARTMENT OF MUSIC AND ARTS DIVISION
435 College Ave.
Modesto, CA 95350
Jim Johnson
209-575-6081
Fax: 209-575-6086
www.yosimite.cc.ca.us

MONTEREY PENINSULA COLLEGE
DEPARTMENT OF MUSIC
Monterey, CA 93940
Dan Schamber
408-646-4200
www.mpc.edu

MOORPARK COLLEGE
DEPARTMENT OF MUSIC AND DANCE
7075 Campus Rd.
Moorpark, CA 93021
Dolly Kessner
805-378-1400
Fax: 805-378-1499
E-mail: dkessner@vcccd.net
www.moorparkcollege.net

MOUNT SAN ANTONIO COLLEGE
DEPARTMENT OF MUSIC
1100 N Grand Ave.
Walnut, CA 91789
Katherine Charlton
909-594-5611
Fax: 909-468-4072
E-mail: kcharlto@mtsac.edu
www.mrsac.edu

MOUNT ST. MARY'S COLLEGE
DEPARTMENT OF MUSIC
12001 Chalon Rd.
Los Angeles, CA 90049
Teresita Espinosa
310-954-4266
Fax: 310-954-1709
E-mail: tespinosa@msmc.la.edu
www.msmc.la.edu

MUSIC ACADEMY OF THE WEST
1070 Fairway Rd.
Santa Barbara, CA 93108
Sue Schleifer
805-969-2716
www.musicacademy.org

MUSICIANS INSTITUTE
ADMISSIONS
1655 McCadden Place
Hollywood, CA 90028
Director of Admissions
323-462-1384
Fax: 213-462-6978
E-mail: admissions@mi.edu
www.mi.edu/home.html

NAPA VALLEY COLLEGE
DEPARTMENT OF MUSIC
2277 Napa Vallejo Hwy.
Napa, CA 94558
Richard Rossi
707-253-3111
Fax: 707-253-3018
www.nvc.cc.ca.us

NOTRE DAME DE NAMUR UNIVERSITY
DEPARTMENT OF MUSIC
1500 Ralston Ave.

Belmont, CA 94002
Micheal Schmitz
650-508-3597
Fax: 650-637-3736
E-mail: mschmitz@ndnu.edu
www.music.ndnu.edu

OCCIDENTAL COLLEGE
DEPARTMENT OF MUSIC
Music Department
1600 Campus Rd.
Los Angeles, CA 90041
Dr. Irene Girton
323-259-2785
Fax: 323-341-4983
E-mail: music@oxy.edu
www.oxy.edu

OHLONE COLLEGE
DEPARTMENT OF MUSIC
43600 Mission Blvd.
Fremont, CA 94539
Walter Birkedahl
510-659-6158
Fax: 510-659-6145
www.ohlone.cc.ca.us/inst/music

ORANGE COAST COLLEGE
DEPARTMENT OF MUSIC
2701 Fairview Rd.
Costa Mesa, CA 92626
Dana Wheaton
714-432-5629
Fax: 714-432-5609
E-mail: dwheaton@mail.occ.cccd.edu
www.orangecoastcollege.com

OXNARD COLLEGE
DEPARTMENT OF MUSIC
4000 S. Rose Ave.
Oxnard, CA 93033

James Kenney
805-654-6370
Fax: 805-986-5806
www.oxnardcollege.edu

PACIFIC UNION COLLEGE
DEPARTMENT OF MUSIC
1 Angwin Ave.
Angwin, CA 94508-9797
Charles Lynn Wheeler
707-965-7323
Fax: 707-965-6738
E-mail: lwheeler@puc.edu
www.puc.edu

Degrees: A.S. Music; B.S. Music; B.M.E.;
B.M. of Music Performance

Pacific Union College is located above
California's Napa Valley about 60 miles north
of San Francisco. PUC is a Liberal Arts
Christian College (seventh-day Adventist) set
on a mountaintop main campus of 200 acres
surrounded by 1,800 acres of forested and
agricultural land. The College is accredited by
WASC and is a member of the NASM. The
music department is housed in Paulin Hall, a
quite modern looking facility with 12 teaching
studios, 18 practice rooms, instrumental
rehearsal room, choral rehearsal room, 470
seat-recital hall, 50 pianos, four organs, and
four harpsichords. PUC offers four degrees in
music. A community education program
named Paulin Center for the creative arts is
also housed in the department offering opportunities for college students to teach private
and group lessons to elementary and high
school students.

PALO VERDE JUNIOR COLLEGE
DEPARTMENT OF MUSIC
811 W. Chanslor Way
Blythe, CA 92225
William Davila
714-922-6168
Fax: 714-922-0230
www.paloverde.cc.ca.us

PALOMAR COLLEGE
DEPARTMENT OF PERFORMANCE ARTS AND MUSIC
1140 W. Mission Rd.
San Marcos, CA 92069
Robert Gilson
619-744-1150
Fax: 619-744-8123
E-mail: bgilson@palomar.edu
www.palomar.edu

PASADENA CITY COLLEGE
MUSIC DIVISION
1570 E. Colorado Blvd.
Pasadena, CA 91106
Paul Kilian
626-585-7208
Fax: 626-585-7949
E-mail: pkilian@pasadena.edu
www.pasadena.edu

PATTEN COLLEGE
DEPARTMENT OF MUSIC
2433 Coolidge Ave.
Oakland, CA 94601
Don Benham
510-534-9500
Fax: 510-534-8564
E-mail: admissions@patten.edu
www.patten.edu

PEPPERDINE UNIVERSITY AT MALIBU
DEPARTMENT OF MUSIC
24255 Pacific Coast Hwy.
Malibu, CA 90265
Sonia Sorrell
310-456-4462
Fax: 310-456-4077
E-mail: sonia.sorrell@pepperdine.edu
www.pepperdine.edu

PITZER COLLEGE
MUSIC PROGRAM AT SCRIPPS COLLEGE
1030 Columbia Ave.
Claremont, CA 91711
Anna Demichele
909-607-3266
E-mail: ademiche@scrippscol.edu
www.pitzer.edu

POINT LOMA NAZARENE UNIVERSITY
DEPARTMENT OF MUSIC
3900 Lomaland Dr.
San Diego, CA 92106
Paul Kenyon
619-849-2445
Fax: 619-849-2668
E-mail: pkenyon@ptloma.edu
www.ptloma.edu

Degrees: B.M. in Performance, B.M. in Composition, B.A. in Music Education, B.A. in Music and Ministry, B.A. in Music

Point Loma Nazarene University is a liberal arts institution sponsored by the Church of the Nazarene. Accredited by the Western Association of Schools and Colleges, the University's main campus is located on the Point Loma peninsula between beautiful San Diego bay and the shores of the Pacific Ocean with a student population of approximately 2,900. For many years, the Music Department has been recognized for the quality of its programs. Music faculty members are performing artists who frequently give recitals, serve as guest conductors, clinicians or adjudicators and compose or arrange for publication. The department is housed in the Cooper Music Center which has been acclaimed as a state of the art facility. Most of the department's performances are presented in Crill Performance Hall, which is often described as one of the finest venues of its kind in the southwestern United States.

POMONA COLLEGE
MUSIC DEPARTMENT
340 N. College Ave.
Claremont, CA 91711
Gwendolyn Lytle
909-621-8155
Fax: 909-621-8645
E-mail: music@pomona.edu
www.music.pomona.edu

PORTERVILLE COLLEGE
DEPARTMENT OF MUSIC
100 E. College Ave.
Porterville, CA 93257
David Hensley
559-791-2255
Fax: 559-791-2352
E-mail: dhensley@pc.cc.ca.us
www.pc.cc.ca.us

RIO HONDO COLLEGE
DEPARTMENT OF MUSIC
3600 Workman Mill Rd.
Whittier, CA 90601
Mitjl Capet
562-908-3471
Fax: 562-908-3446
E-mail: mcapet@rh.cc.ca.us
www.rh.cc.ca.us

RIVERSIDE COMMUNITY COLLEGE
DEPARTMENT OF MUSIC
4800 Magnolia Ave.
Riverside, CA 92506
Kevin Mayse
909-222-8395
Fax: 909-328-3535
E-mail: kmayse@rccd.cc.ca.us
www.rccd.cc.ca.us

SACRAMENTO CITY COLLEGE
DEPARTMENT OF MUSIC
3835 Freeport Blvd.
Sacramento, CA 95822
Debra Dyko
805-482-2755
Fax: 805-987-5097
www.scc.losrios.edu

SAN BERNARDINO VALLEY COLLEGE
701 S. Mt. Vernon Ave.
San Bernardino, CA 92410
David Lawrence
909-888-6511
Fax: 909-784-1546
E-mail: dlawrence@sbccd.cc.ca.us
http://sbvc.sbccd.cc.ca.us/music

Degrees: A.A. degree that transfers to most universities

The music department of San Bernardino Valley College has developed into one known throughout the state for not only its musical excellence, but for its personal interest in the individual student. A primary aim of the program is to stimulate musical growth among all students while offering classes leading to a major in music. Performing groups add a necessary dimension to the college, and non-music majors who enjoy the art as an avocation have carried opportunities for expression. The performing groups are the "Wind Ensemble", spring ("Varsity Pep Band" in the fall) "Studio" (day jazz ensemble), "Kicks" (evening jazz ensemble), community concert, saxophone quartet, Percussion Ensemble, Flute Choir, Spectrum Singers, College Singers and Brass Choir.

These performance groups are open to all students, depending upon level of ability. Regular attendance in classes and participation in all scheduled events are important to students' success. Scholarships are available to talented students on an audition basis. Each semester

the department offers two sections in music fundamentals for those with no music background.

Recognizing that the performance before live audiences is essential to developing top quality musicianship, the Valley College instrumental program offers a variety of performance experience for students.

SAN DIEGO CITY COLLEGE
DEPARTMENT OF MUSIC
1425 Russ Blvd.
San Diego, CA 92101
James Dark
619-238-1181
www.city.sdccd.cc.ca.us

SAN DIEGO MESA COLLEGE
DEPARTMENT OF MUSIC-C109
7250 Mesa College Dr.
San Diego, CA 92111
Irvin King
619-627-2809
Fax: 619-388-2968
E-mail: iking@sdccd.net
http://intergate.sdmesa.sdccd.cc.ca.us

SAN DIEGO STATE UNIVERSITY
SCHOOL OF MUSIC
San Diego, CA 92182
Dr. Marian Leibowitz
619-594-6031
Fax: 619-594-1692
www.music.sdsu.edu

SAN FRANCISCO CONSERVATORY OF MUSIC

1201 Ortega St.
San Francisco, CA 94122
Alex Brose
415-759-3430
Fax: 415-759-3405
www.sfcm.edu

SAN FRANCISCO STATE UNIVERSITY
DEPARTMENT OF MUSIC

1600 Holloway Ave.
San Francisco, CA 94132
Patricia Taylor Lee
415-338-1431
Fax: 415-338-3294
E-mail: music@sfsu.edu
www.sfsu.edu/~music

SAN JOSE CITY COLLEGE
DEPARTMENT OF MUSIC

2100 Moorpark Ave.
San Jose, CA 95128
Bahram Behroozi
402-883-7170
Fax: 408-286-2052
www.sjcc.edu

SAN JOSE STATE UNIVERSITY
SCHOOL OF MUSIC AND DANCE

1 Washington Sq.
San José, CA 95193
Edward Harris
408-924-4673
Fax: 408-924-4773
E-mail: music@email.sjsu.edu
www.sjsu.edu

Degrees: B.A., Music, Preparation for Teaching, Music, Concentration in Composition, B.M., Music, Concentration in Electro-Acoustic Music, B.M., Music, Concentration in Performance, Minor, Music M.A., Music.

SANTA BARBARA CITY COLLEGE
DEPARTMENT OF MUSIC

721 Cliff Dr.
Santa Barbara, CA 93109
Dr. Charles Wood
805-965-0581
Fax: 805-963-7222
E-mail: wood@sbcc.net
www.sbcc.cc.ca.us

SANTA CLARA UNIVERSITY
DEPARTMENT OF MUSIC

500 El Camino Real
Santa Clara, CA 95053
Hans C. Boepple
408-554-4428
Fax: 408-554-2171
E-mail: hboepple@scu.edu
www.scu.edu

SANTA MONICA COLLEGE
DEPARTMENT OF MUSIC

1900 Pico Blvd.
Santa Monica, CA 90405
James Smith
310-452-9323
Fax: 310-450-7172
www.wmc.edu

SANTA ROSA JUNIOR COLLEGE
DEPARTMENT OF MUSIC

1501 Mendocino Ave.
Santa Rosa, CA 95401
Jon Nelson
707-527-4249

Fax: 707-527-4816
www.santarosa.edu

SCRIPPS COLLEGE
MUSIC DEPARTMENT
1030 Columbia Ave.
Claremont, CA 91711
Music Department
909-621-8280
Fax: 909-607-8004
www.scrippscol.edu

SHASTA COLLEGE
DEPARTMENT OF MUSIC
P.O. Box 496006
Redding, CA 96049-6006
Dr. Ron Johnson
530-225-4761
Fax: 530-225-4763
E-mail: lgrandy@shastacollege.edu
http://library.shastacollege.edu/music

Degrees: A.A.

The Shasta college Music Department enthusiastically offers a wide variety of music classes and is vibrantly dedicated to serving all student clientele, including music majors, pre-music majors, general college students, and community/adult students. Department enrollment within all music courses is approximately 1,500 per year. The Music Department offers an associate degree in music, a certificate in music, music transfer program, and general studies (humanities) requirements. All interested students are strongly encouraged to participate within the Music Department's activities. The Music Department maintains a supportive and congenial atmosphere.

Facilities include a theater, band room, choir room, central classrooms, practice rooms with pianos, and a computer/electronic laboratory. Performance opportunities are provided by a variety of ensembles including the concert band, symphony orchestra, chorale, concert choir, jazz band, jazz/rock ensemble, and vocal jazz ensemble.

Available full-term classroom courses include a series of six music theory classes, keyboard classes, the history of jazz and rock, music appreciation, general studies, beginning voice, beginning guitar, and a variety of short term courses. Applied music is normally available for declared full-time music majors.

SIMPSON COLLEGE
DEPARTMENT OF MUSIC
2211 College View Dr.
Redding, CA 96003
Paul Thorlakson
530-224-5600
Fax: 530-226-4863
E-mail: pthorlakson@simpsonca.edu
www.simpsonca.edu

SKYLINE COLLEGE
DEPARTMENT OF MUSIC
3300 College Dr.
San Bruno, CA 94066
Donna Bestock
650-738-4100
E-mail: bestock@smccd.net
www.smccd.net

SOLANO COLLEGE
DEPARTMENT OF MUSIC
4000 Suisun Valley Rd.
Suisun City, CA 94585
Delbert Bump
707-864-7000
Fax: 707-864-0361
www.solano.edu

SONOMA STATE UNIVERSITY
DEPARTMENT OF MUSIC
1801 East Cotati Ave.
Ives Hall
Rohnert Park, CA 94928
Dr. Jeffrey Langley
707-664-2324
Fax: 707-664-4332
E-mail: jeff.langley@sonoma.edu
www.sonoma.edu

SOUTHERN CALIFORNIA CONSERVATORY
8711 Sunland Blvd.
Sun Valley, CA 91352
Lurrine Burgess
818-767-6554
Fax: 818-768-6242
E-mail: taeschr@ix.netcom.com

SOUTHWESTERN COLLEGE
DEPARTMENT OF MUSIC
900 Otay Lakes Rd.
Chula Vista, CA 91910
Teresa Russell
619-421-6700
Fax: 619-482-6413
E-mail: trussell@swc.cc.ca.us
www.swc.cc.ca.us

ST. JOHN'S COLLEGE
DEPARTMENT OF MUSIC
Camarillo, CA 93010
Debra Dyko
805-482-2755
Fax: 805-987-5097
www.sjs-sc.org

ST. MARY'S COLLEGE OF CALIFORNIA
DEPARTMENT OF PERFORMING ARTS
Moraga, CA 94575
Sharon Cahill
925-631-4670
Fax: 925-631-4410
E-mail: scahill@stmarys-ca.edu
www.stmarys-ca.edu

STANFORD UNIVERSITY
DEPARTMENT OF MUSIC
BRAUN MUSIC CENTER
541 Lasuen Mall
Stanford, CA 94305
Nette Worthey
650-725-1932
Fax: 650-725-2686
E-mail: nworthey@stanford.edu
http://music.Stanford.edu

Degrees: M.A./M.S.T. (music, science and technology); D.M.A. composition; Ph.D. Musicology or Computer-Based Music Theory and Acoustics

The Stanford University department of music's goals are to provide specialized training for those who plan careers in music as composers, performers, teachers, and research scholars and to promote the understanding and enjoyment of music in the University at large through its courses and abundant performance offerings. Performance and educational opportunities are available for majors and non-majors alike.

Students participating in music at Stanford have access to two theaters, two rehearsal halls, and a small chamber hall; and the Center for Computer Research in Music and Acoustics (CCRMA) houses recording studios and computer labs for those with interests in computer technology, digital audio, signal processing, and acoustic/psycho acoustic foundations of music. Our music library archive of recorded sound has a superb collection of historical recordings of all types. In addition, students have access to practice rooms and rehearsal rooms reserved for chamber music and jazz combos.

TAFT COLLEGE
LIBERAL ARTS DIVISION
29 Emmons Park Dr.
Taft, CA 93268
Ms. Sonja Swenson
805-765-4191
Fax: 805-763-1038
www.taft.cc.ca.us

UCLA
DEPARTMENT OF MUSIC
2539 Schoenberg Hall
P.O. Box 951616
Los Angeles, CA 90095
Music Department
310-825-1839
E-mail: webmaster@cfpa.ucla.edu
www.ucla.edu

UNIVERSITY OF CALIFORNIA AT BERKELEY
PERFORMING ARTS DEPARTMENT
Berkeley, CA 94720-1200
510-642-2678
Fax: 510-642-8480
E-mail: music@uclink.berkeley.edu
www.ls.berkeley.edu/Dept/Music

UNIVERSITY OF CALIFORNIA AT DAVIS
One Shields Ave.
Davis, CA 95616
530-752-5537
Fax: 530-752-0983

E-mail: kmboerner@ucdavis.edu
www.ucdavis.edu

UNIVERSITY OF CALIFORNIA AT IRVINE
SCHOOL OF THE ARTS AND MUSIC
303 Music and Media Bldg.
Irvine, CA 92697
Rae Brown
949-824-6615
Fax: 949-824-4914
E-mail: music@uci.edu
www.arts.uci.edu/music

UNIVERSITY OF CALIFORNIA AT L.A.
DEPARTMENT OF MUSIC
Los Angeles, CA 90095
Ellen Hayes
310-206-3033
Fax: 310-206-4738
E-mail: trice@arts.ucla.edu
www.music.ucla.edu

UNIVERSITY OF CALIFORNIA AT RIVERSIDE
MUSIC DEPARTMENT
Riverside, CA 92521
Cindy Roulette
909-787-3343
Fax: 909-787-4651
E-mail: cindy.roulette@ucr.edu
www.music.ucr.edu

A spectacular new arts building now houses studio art, art history, dance, theatre, and music. Inter-arts endeavors will be fostered by the proximity of departments, faculty and students. Music students enjoy wonderful rehearsal rooms with variable acoustics and the latest sound technology. Music composition is taught in a wide variety of styles and world music ensembles and classes are a growing specialty of the department. Standard ensembles, such as wind ensemble, orchestra, chamber music, early music ensemble, choral society, and jazz ensemble, among others, are enjoying rapid growth in size and quality. The total campus enrollment is projected to increase from 13,000 to 20,000 by 2010 or before.

UNIVERSITY OF CALIFORNIA AT SAN DIEGO
MUSIC DEPARTMENT
La Jolla, CA 92093
Stephanie Ferneyhough
858-534-3230
Fax: 858-534-8502
E-mail: skuhn@ucsd.edu
http://ucsd.edu/music

UNIVERSITY OF CALIFORNIA AT SANTA BARBARA
DEPARTMENT OF MUSIC
Santa Barbara, CA 93106-6070
Donna Saar
805-893-3261
Fax: 805-893-7194
E-mail: rothfarb@mail.lsit.ucsb.edu
http://music.ucsb.edu

UNIVERSITY OF CALIFORNIA AT SANTA CRUZ
DIVISION OF THE ARTS
248 Music Center
Santa Cruz, CA 95064
Music Department Chair
831-459-2292
Fax: 831-459-5584
E-mail: music@cats.ucsc.edu
http://arts.ucsc.edu/music

UNIVERSITY OF LA VERNE
DEPARTMENT OF MUSIC
1950 3rd St.
La Verne, CA 91750
Reed Gratz
909-593-3511
Fax: 909-392-2763
E-mail: gratzr@ulv.edu
www.ulv.edu/music

UNIVERSITY OF REDLANDS
SCHOOL OF MUSIC
1200 E. Colton Ave.
Redlands, CA 92373
Donald Beckie
909-793-2121
Fax: 909-748-6343
E-mail: beckie@uor.edu
www.redlands.edu

UNIVERSITY OF SAN DIEGO
DEPARTMENT OF FINE ARTS
5998 Alcala Park
San Diego, CA 92110
David Smith
619-260-2280
Fax: 619-260-6875
www.ucsd.edu

UNIVERSITY OF SOUTHERN CALIFORNIA
THORNTON SCHOOL OF MUSIC
University Park - UUC 218
Los Angeles, CA 90089
Phillip Placenti
213-740-6835
Fax: 213-740-3217
E-mail: musdean@usc.edu
www.usc.edu

The USC Thornton School of Music provides a comprehensive academic base in virtually all professional and scholarly branches of music. Faculty are solo, chamber, jazz and motion picture/television recording artists, active in the international and local professional music arenas. Facilities include the 1,573-seat Bovard Auditorium, the 300-seat Alfred Newman Recital Hall, the 553-seat Bing Theatre and other various performing venues. The practice and instructional center contains approximately 60 custom-designed practice rooms. Facilities also include extensive computer and multimedia workstations, as well as fully equipped, state-of-the-art recording facilities. Performance opportunities include the USC Thornton Symphony, chamber orchestra, wind symphony, jazz orchestra, percussion ensemble, chamber choir, concert choir, men's chorus, Oriana Choir, opera, early music ensemble, contemporary music ensemble, Afro-Latin jazz ensemble, vocal jazz ensemble, Trojan Marching Band, and a full range of piano, string, woodwind, brass, percussion, guitar, and jazz chamber ensembles.

UNIVERSITY OF THE PACIFIC
CONSERVATORY OF MUSIC
3601 Pacific Ave.
Stockton, CA 95211
Peter Bensen
209-946-2415
Fax: 209-946-2770
E-mail: sanderso@uop.edu
www.uop.edu

VANGUARD UNIVERSITY
DEPARTMENT OF MUSIC
55 Fair Dr.
Costa Mesa, CA 92626
James Melton
714-556-3610
Fax: 714-662-5229
E-mail: jmelton@vangaurd.edu
www.vanguard.edu

VENTURA COLLEGE
DEPARTMENT OF MUSIC
4667 Telegraph Rd.
Ventura, CA 93003
Robert Lawson
805-654-6400
Fax: 805-654-6466
www.venturacollege.edu

VICTOR VALLEY COLLEGE
DEPARTMENT OF MUSIC
18422 Bear Valley Rd.
Victorville, CA 92392
Thomas Miller
760-245-4271
Fax: 760-245-9744
E-mail: tmiller@victor.cc.ca.us
www.vvconline.com

VOCAL POWER SCHOOL
9826 Columbus Ave.
North Hills, CA 91343
Howard Austin
818-895-7464
Fax: 818-893-4270
http://VocalPower.com/vpschool.htm

WEST LOS ANGELES COLLEGE
DEPARTMENT OF MUSIC
4800 Freshman Dr.
Culver City, CA 90230
Alice Taylor
310-287-4209
Fax: 310-841-0396
www.wlac.cc.ca.us

WEST VALLEY COLLEGE
Music Program

14000 Fruitvale Ave.
Saratoga, CA 95070
George Champion
408-867-2200
www.wvmccd.cc.ca.us/wvmccd

WESTMONT COLLEGE
Music Department

955 La Paz Rd.
Santa Barbara, CA 93108
Grey Brothers
805-565-6040
Fax: 805-565-7240
www.westmont.edu

WHITTIER COLLEGE
Music Department

13406 Philadelphia St.
P.O. Box 634
Whittier, CA 90608
Dr. Stephen Gothold
562-907-4865
Fax: 562-907-4237
E-mail: sgothold@whittier.edu
www.whittier.edu/www/catalog/music.ht
ml

Whittier College's primary mission is to educate students in a small college atmosphere where they can learn, acquire skills and form attitudes and values appropriate for leading and serving in a global society. The music department offers instruction in composition, conducting, music education, music literature and materials, music performance and theory. Students may also develop areas of specialization or individual projects under faculty supervision in related fields such as organ and church music, management and music industries, musicology, ethnomusicology, and musical theatre. All students will find in music a varied and enriching program in performance and study. Those with a background in an instrument or in voice are encouraged to consider a major. Exceptional opportunities for both solo and ensemble performance are available, and all students are eligible to audition for membership in the college choir, jazz ensemble, string ensemble or wind ensemble. Individual instruction in voice and instruments is offered at all levels of proficiency by an outstanding artist faculty. Class instruction is also available in piano and voice. The music faculty is active in a wide range of educational, community, and professional activities, including composition, adjudication, performance, musical theatre, jazz and popular music production.

YUBA COLLEGE
Music Program

2088 N. Beale Rd.
Marysville, CA 95901
Allan Miller
916-741-6883
Fax: 916-634-7709
E-mail: amiller@mail2.yuba.cc.ca.us
www.yuba.cc.ca.us

COLORADO

Population: 4,660,420 (2003 Estimate)

Capital City: Denver

Music Colleges and Universities: Adams State College, Arapahoe Community College, Aspen Music Festival and School, Colorado College, Colorado State University, Community College of Aurora, Fort Lewis College, Fort Range Community College, Lamar Community College, Mesa State College, Metropolitan State College of Denver, Naropa University, Northeastern Junior College, Regis University, Trinidad State Junior College, United States Air Force Academy, University of Colorado at Boulder, University of Colorado at Denver, University of Denver, University of Northern Colorado, University of Southern Colorado, Western State College of Colorado

Bird: Lark Bunting

Motto: Nil sine Numine – Nothing without Providence

Flower: Rocky Mountain Columbine

Tree: Colorado Blue Spruce

Residents Called: Coloradans

Origin of Name: Taken from the Spanish for the "color red" and was applied to the Colorado river.

Area: 104,100 square miles (8th largest state)

Statehood: August 1, 1876 (38th state)

Largest Cities: Denver, Colorado Springs, Aurora, Lakewood, Fort Collins, Arvada Pueblo, Westminster, Boulder, Thornton

College Band Programs: Colorado State University, University of Colorado, University of Northern Colorado

COLORADO

ADAMS STATE COLLEGE
MUSIC DEPARTMENT
208 Edgemont Blvd.
Alamosa, CO 81102
Charles Boyer
719-587-7621
Fax: 719-587-7094
E-mail: cgboyer@adams.edu
www.music.adams.edu

AIR FORCE ACADEMY
DEPARTMENT OF PHIL/FINE ARTS-MUSIC
Colorado Springs, CO 80840
Ann Reagan
719-333-2417
Fax: 719-333-2050
www.usafa.af.mil

ARAPAHOE COMMUNITY COLLEGE
DEPARTMENT OF MUSIC
P.O. Box 9002
Littleton, CO 80160-9002
Hidemi Matsushita
303-797-5867
Fax: 303-797-5782
E-mail: jmatsushita@arapahoe
www.arapahoe.edu

ASPEN MUSIC FESTIVAL AND SCHOOL
OFFICE OF STUDENT SERVICES
2 Music School Rd.
Aspen, CO 81611
Joan Gordon
970-925-3254
Fax: 970-920-1643
E-mail: school@aspenmusic.org
www.aspenmusicfestival.com

The Aspen Music Festival and School is a nine-week summer music festival founded in 1949. Formal instruction for the approximately 800 pre-professional students is through private lessons, music-related courses, chamber music studies, master classes, and orchestral experience. During the summer, more than 200 musical events are presented, including symphonic, chamber music, opera, and vocal performances, lectures, and master classes.

COLORADO COLLEGE
MUSIC DEPARTMENT
Colorado Springs, CO 80903
Lyn Doyon
719-389-6545
Fax: 719-389-6862
E-mail: ldoyon@coloradocollege.edu
www.colorado.edu

COLORADO STATE UNIVERSITY
DEPARTMENT OF MUSIC, THEATRE, AND DANCE
Fort Collins, CO 80523-1778
Dr. Michael Thaut
970-491-5529
Fax: 970-491-7541
E-mail: mtdinfo@colostate.edu
www.colostate.edu/Depts/Music
Degrees: M.M., B.M., B.A.

The music degrees at Colorado State University are tailored to meet the needs of students with diverse interests who share a common love of music. A professional Bachelor of Music degree is offered in three different concentrations: Music Performance, Music Education and Music Therapy. The Bachelor of Arts degree with a Music Major allows for a broader liberal arts approach with a secondary emphasis in a supporting area. Master of Music degrees are offered with concentrations in Music Education, Music Therapy, Conducting, and Performance. The department encompasses all three of the major performing arts-music-theatre and dance, which creates special opportunities for inter-disciplinary programs and courses. Music performance opportunities are extensive, with a variety of orchestras, bands, choirs, opera/musical theatre productions, and chamber ensembles open to all Colorado State Students. Groundbreaking ceremonies were held recently for our new, state-of-the-art performance hall, which is expected to be ready in the Fall of 2004.

COMMUNITY COLLEGE OF AURORA
DEPARTMENT OF MUSIC

16000 E. Centre Tech Pkwy
Aurora, CO 80011-9057
Geoffery Hunt
303-361-7425
Fax: 303-361-7374

FORT LEWIS COLLEGE
DEPARTMENT OF MUSIC

1000 Rim Dr.
Durango, CO 81301
John Pennington
970-247-7447
Fax: 970-247-7520
E-mail: pennington_j@fortlewis.edu
www.fortlewis.edu

FORT RANGE COMMUNITY COLLEGE
DEPARTMENT OF MUSIC

3645 W. 112th Ave./East Service Ctr
Westminster, CO 80030-2105
Kevin Garry
303-466-8811
Fax: 303-466-1623
E-mail: kevin.garry@wc.frcc.cccoes.edu
www.frcc.cc.co.us

LAMAR COMMUNITY COLLEGE
MUSIC PROGRAM

2400 S. Main St.
Lamar, CO 81052
Elanor Charvat
719-336-2248
www.lcc.cccoes.edu

MESA STATE COLLEGE
DEPARTMENT OF MUSIC

P.O. Box 2647
Grand Junction, CO 81505
Dr. Calvin Hofer
970-248-1163
Fax: 970-248-1159
E-mail: chofer@mesastate.edu
www.mesastate.edu

METROPOLITAN STATE COLLEGE OF DENVER
DEPARTMENT OF MUSIC

P.O. Box 173362
Denver, CO 80217
Dr. Larry Worster
303-556-3180
Fax: 303-556-2714
E-mail: worster@mscd.edu
www.mscd.edu

NAROPA UNIVERSITY
DEPARTMENT OF MUSIC

2130 Arapahoe Ave.
Boulder, CO 80302
Mark Miller
303-444-0202
Fax: 303-444-0410
E-mail: markm@naropa.edu
www.naropa.edu

NORTHEASTERN JUNIOR COLLEGE
DEPARTMENT OF MUSIC

100 College Dr.
Sterling, CO 80751
Peter Youngers
970-521-6600
Fax: 970-522-4945
www.gonjc.edu

REGIS UNIVERSITY
DEPARTMENT OF FINE ARTS

3333 Regis Blvd.
Denver, CO 80221
Mark Davenport
303-964-3609
Fax: 303-964-5478
E-mail: mdavenpo@regis.edu
www.regis.edu

TRINIDAD STATE JUNIOR COLLEGE
DEPARTMENT OF MUSIC

600 Prospect St.
Trinidad, CO 81082
Robert Pringle
719-846-5652
Fax: 719-846-5667
www.tsjc.cccoes.edu

UNIVERSITY OF COLORADO AT BOULDER
COLLEGE OF MUSIC

Campus P.O. Box 301
Boulder, CO 80309
Daniel Sher
303-492-6352
Fax: 303-492-5619
E-mail: gradmusc@colorado.edu
www.colorado.edu/music

UNIVERSITY OF COLORADO AT DENVER
DEPARTMENT OF MUSIC

P.O. Box 173364
Denver, CO 80217
303-556-2727
Fax: 303-556-2335
E-mail: betsy.ackerman@cudenver.edu
www.cudenver.edu

In Fall of 2002, the Lamont School of Music moved into the newly constructed Robert and Judi Newmand Performing Arts Center. The academic building includes these features: 43 teaching studios; 41 individual and ensemble practice rooms; three large rehearsal spaces for orchestra, choir/opera and jazz; outstanding music library; listening center; and keyboard lab with 21 instructional pianos and a grand disclavier piano; a recording studio wired to each performing space in the center; audio/visual technology in every classroom; an 80-seat recital salon for solo recitals, small chamber concerts, lectures and master classes; administrative offices, comfortable lounges, lockers for instrument storage and other amenities; a 250-seat recital hall for student and faculty concerts and recitals, the center-piece of which is a Schuke Orgelbau Berlin organ with 51 ranks and 2,500 pipes; a 1,000-seat concert/opera hall reminiscent of the Vienna Opera House, with a double-lift orchestra pit, 100-foot fly gallery and appro-priate support space. No seat in the house will be more than 80 feet from the stage apron, and even the highest balcony seat will have a close relationship to the stage. A flexible, 250-seat theatre will serve as the main stage for DU productions. An additional rehearsal space will allow DU theatre faculty and students to stage multiple large shows per quarter for the first time in years. Dressing rooms, scene and cos-tume shops, storage, box office and other spaces will support both the concert/opera hall and flexible theatre. Dramatic public spaces will include a three-story lobby area with sur-rounding colonnade, balcony and barrel-vault-ed ceiling, stone walls and staircases; a meet-the-artist room; and a room for community organizations.

UNIVERSITY OF DENVER
LAMONT SCHOOL OF MUSIC
7111 Montview
Denver, CO 80220
Malcolm Lynn Baker
303-871-6973
Fax: 303-871-6382
E-mail: jdocksey@du.edu
www.du.edu/lamont

UNIVERSITY OF NORTHERN COLORADO
SCHOOL OF MUSIC
501 20th St.
Greeley, CO 80639
Dr. Rob Hallquist
970-351-1924
Fax: 970-351-1923
E-mail: rhallquist@arts.unco.edu
http://arts.unco.edu

UNIVERSITY OF SOUTHERN COLORADO
DEPARTMENT OF MUSIC
2200 Bonforte Blvd.
Pueblo, CO 81001
Mark Hudson
719-549-2552
Fax: 719-549-2120
E-mail: hudsonm@uscolo.edu
www.uscolo.edu

WESTERN STATE COLLEGE OF COLORADO
DEPARTMENT OF ART AND MUSIC
Quigley Hall
Gunnison, CO 81231
Dr. Martha Violett
970-943-3054
Fax: 970-943-2329
E-mail: mviolett@western.edu
www.western.edu

Degrees: B.A. in Music

Western State College of Colorado is a public baccalaureate institution of approximately 2,300 students and is an accredited institutional member of NASM. The long-standing Music Program offers the Bachelor of Arts in Music with three emphases: Comprehensive, Music Education, and Music-Business. The Music Education emphasis works closely with the Teacher Education Program and the local schools to prepare students for Colorado licensure. Students may also pursue a minor in music and all students within the college are welcome to participate in the band, orchestra, choir, and jazz ensembles.

The city of Gunnison is located four hours southwest of Denver and has a population of 7,000. The area's high mountain rural environment at an elevation of 7,000 feet is home to a variety of outdoor activities throughout the year.

CONNECTICUT

Population: 3,408,126 (2003 Estimate)

Capital City: Hartford

Music Colleges and Universities: Capital Community Technical College, Central Connecticut State University, Connecticut College, Eastern Connecticut State University, Gateway Community Technical College, Hartford College for Women, Housatonic College, National Guitar Workshop, Northwestern Connecticut Community College, Quinnipiac College, Sacred Heart University, Southern Connecticut State University, St. Joseph College, The Hartford Conservatory, The Hartt School, Trinity College, University of Bridgeport, University of Connecticut, University of New Haven, Wesleyan University, Western Connecticut State University, Yale School of Music

Bird: Robin

Motto: Qui transtulit sustinet – He who transplanted still sustains

Flower: Mountain Laurel

Tree: White Oak

Residents Called: Nutmeggers

Origin of Name: Based on Mohican and Algonquin Indian words for a "place beside a long river."

Area: 5,544 square miles (48th largest state)

Statehood: January 9, 1788 (5th state)

Largest Cities: Bridgeport, New Haven, Hartford, Stamford, Waterbury, Norwalk, Danbury, New Britain, West Hartford, Greenwich

College Band Programs: Sacred Heart University, University of Connecticut, Yale University

CONNECTICUT

CAPITAL COMMUNITY TECHNICAL COLLEGE
DEPARTMENT OF MUSIC
61 Woodland St.
Hartford, CT 06105-2326
John Christie
203-520-7837
Fax: 203-520-7906
http://webster.commnet.edu

CENTRAL CONNECTICUT STATE UNIVERSITY
MUSIC DEPARTMENT
1615 Stanley St.
New Britain, CT 06050
Pam Perry
860-832-2912
Fax: 860-832-2902
E-mail: perry@ccsu.edu
www.ccsu.edu

CONNECTICUT COLLEGE
DEPARTMENT OF MUSIC
270 Mohegan Ave.
New London, CT 06320-4125
Paul Althouse
860-439-2720
Fax: 860-439-5382
E-mail: Plalt@conncoll.edu
www.camel.conncoll.edu

EASTERN CONNECTICUT STATE UNIVERSITY
MUSIC AND FINE ARTS DEPARTMENT
Shafer Hall, Room 6
83 Windham St.
Willimantic, CT 06226
Dr. Robert Lemon
860-465-5325
www.ecsu.ctstateu.edu

GATEWAY COMMUNITY TECHNICAL COLLEGE
DEPARTMENT OF MUSIC
60 Sergeant Dr.
New Haven, CT 06511-5918
Douglas Salyer
203-789-7053
E-mail: gw_salyer@commnet.edu
www.gwctc.commnet.edu

HARTFORD COLLEGE FOR WOMEN
DEPARTMENT OF MUSIC
1265 Asylum Ave.
Hartford, CT 06105
Peter Harvey
860-768-5657
Fax: 860-768-5693
E-mail: Harvey@mail.hartford.edu
http://uhaweb.hartford.edu/hcw

HOUSATONIC COLLEGE
DEPARTMENT OF MUSIC
900 Lafayette Blvd.
Bridgeport, CT 06604
Charles Haynes
203-332-5100
Fax: 203-332-5250
E-mail: ho_humanitie@commnet.edu
www.htc.commnet.edu

NATIONAL GUITAR WORKSHOP
ADMISSIONS
P.O. Box 222
Lakeside, CT 06758
Emily Flower
800-234-6479
Fax: 800-567-0374
www.guitarworkshop.com

NORTHWESTERN CONNECTICUT COMMUNITY COLLEGE
DEPARTMENT OF MUSIC
Park Pl.
Winstead, CT 06098
Willard Minton
203-738-6373
www.nwc.edu

QUINNIPIAC COLLEGE
DEPARTMENT OF MUSIC
Mount Carmel Ave.
Hamden, CT 06518
Samual Costanzo
203-288-5251
www.quinnipiac.edu

SACRED HEART UNIVERSITY
DEPARTMENT OF MUSIC
5151 Park Ave.
Fairfield, CT 06432
Joseph Carter
203-371-7735
Fax: 203-365-7609
E-mail: carterjoe@sacredheart.edu
www.sacredheart.edu

Degrees: Minor only in Music.

SOUTHERN CONNECTICUT STATE UNIVERSITY
MUSIC DEPARTMENT
501 Crescent St.
New Haven, CT 06515
David Chevan
203-392-6625
Fax: 203-392-6637
E-mail: chevan@southernct.edu
www.southernct.edu

ST. JOSEPH COLLEGE
DEPARTMENT OF FINE AND PERFORMANCE ARTS
1678 Asylum Ave.
W. Hartford, CT 06117
Dorothy Keller
203-232-4571
Fax: 203-233-5695
E-mail: dkeller@sjc.edu
www.sjc.edu

THE HARTFORD CONSERVATORY
834 Asylum. Ave.
Hartford, CT 06154
Lynn Tracey
860-246-2588
Fax: 860-249-6330
E-mail: ltracey@hartfordconservatory.org
www.hartfordconservatory.org

The Hartford Conservatory is a school of performing arts offering programs in music, dance, musical theater and record production. Accredited by the New England Association of Schools and Colleges and licensed by the State of CT Department of Higher Education, the Diploma Division is a two-year performing arts immersion program, culminating in an artist's diploma. The artist's diploma is earned through a planned program offering college-level credit for students 18 years of age and older.

THE HARTT SCHOOL
UNIVERSITY OF HARTFORD
West Hartford, CT 06117
860-768-4465
Fax: 860-768-4441
www.hartford.com

The Hartt School is recognized for the quality of its educational programs in music, dance and theater. Founded in 1920 by Julius Hartt, Moshe Paranov and associated teachers, Hartt became one of three founding institutions of the University of Hartford in 1957. As one of the constituent schools and colleges of the University of Hartford, Hartt is situated on an attractive 320-acre campus approximately two hours from both Boston and New York. Renamed in 1993 with the addition of degree programs in theater and dance, The Hartt School has developed unique programs that combine the high aspirations of professional preparation in the performing arts disciplines with a firm grounding in liberal arts study. It offers internationally acclaimed conservatory training for musicians, dancers and actors, innovative programs for music and dance educators and unique studies in performance management and music technology. The programs at the Hartt School provide superior conservatory training with a faculty of internationally recognized teachers and performers who are the foundation of this training. Students study one-on-one with an experienced member of the faculty committed to helping each student become the best possible musician. Building on each student's prior training and experience, this instruction fosters creativity, enthusiasm and professionalism. The Hartt School, home to the Grammy award-winning Emerson String Quartet and jazz saxophonist Jackie McLean, fosters an environment of the highest artistic caliber. With its low student-to-faculty ratio, Hartt gives individualized attention to all of its students. Performance opportunities abound at The Hartt School. Students may participate in a number of ensembles, including the Hartt Symphony Orchestra, the wind ensemble, contemporary players, the Hartt Chorus, the percussion ensemble and steel band, the bass ensemble, the flute choir, the guitar ensemble, the early music ensemble and various chamber ensembles.

TRINITY COLLEGE
DEPARTMENT OF MUSIC

300 Summit St.
Hartford, CT 06106
Gerald Moshell
860-297-5122
Fax: 860-297-5380

E-mail: gerald.moshell@trincoll.edu
www.trincoll.edu/pub

UNIVERSITY OF BRIDGEPORT
MUSIC DEPARTMENT

126 Park Ave.
Bridgeport, CT 06601
Dr. Jeffrey Johnson
203-576-4407
E-mail: jjohnsonx@aol.com
www.bridgeport.edu

UNIVERSITY OF CONNECTICUT
DEPARTMENT OF MUSIC

876 Coventry Rd.
P.O. Box U-12, Rm. 228
Storrs, CT 06269-1012
Department Head
860-486-3728
Fax: 860-486-3796
E-mail:
contact_musicept@finearts.sfa.uconn.edu
www.music.uconn.edu
Degrees: B.A., B.M., B.S., M.M., M.A., and Ph.D.

UNIVERSITY OF NEW HAVEN
DEPARTMENT OF MUSIC

300 Orange Ave.
West Haven, CT 06516
Michael G. Kaloyanides
203-342-5864
Fax: 203-931-6097
E-mail: mkaloyanides@newhaven.edu
www.newhaven.edu

Degrees: B.A. in Music; B.A, B.S. in Music and Sound Recording; B.A. in Music Industry

The University of New Haven's B.A. in Music Industry and B.A. and B.S. in Music and Sound Recording are among the oldest, most established and respected programs of their kind in the United States. Housed within the

College of Arts and Sciences along with the distinctive B.A. in Music, these innovative programs boast a dedicated faculty and offer the right balance of training in the art of music, the technology of recording and the business of music.

The curricula of all the music programs are offered in the context of a liberal arts education committed to developing critical thinking and learning essential skills in today's rapidly changing world.

WESLEYAN UNIVERSITY
MUSIC DEPARTMENT
Middletown, CT 06459
Hope Hancock
860-685-2950
Fax: 860-685-2651
E-mail: hhancock@wesleyan.edu
www.wesleyan.edu/music/home.html

WESTERN CONNECTICUT STATE UNIVERSITY
DEPARTMENT OF MUSIC
181 White St.
Danbury, CT 06810
Daniel Goble
203-837-8350
Fax: 203-837-8630
www.wcsu.edu

YALE SCHOOL OF MUSIC
OFFICE OF ADMISSIONS
P.O. Box 208246
New Haven, CT 06437
Thomas Masse
203-432-4155
Fax: 203-432-7448
E-mail: gradmusic.admissions@yale.edu
www.yale.edu/music

Degrees: D.M.A., M.M.A., M.M., Artist Diploma, Certificate

DELAWARE

Population: 817,433 (2003 Estimate)

Capital City: Dover

Music Colleges and Universities: Delaware State College, University of Delaware, Wesley College

Bird: Blue Hen Chicken

Motto: Liberty and Independence

Flower: Peach Blossom

Tree: American Holly

Residents Called: Delawareans

Origin of Name: Named after an early Virginia governor, Lord De La Warr.

Area: 2,489 square miles (49th largest)

Statehood: December 7, 1787 (1st state)

Largest Cities: Wilmington, Dover, Newark, Milford, Seaford, Middletown, Elsmere, Smyrna, New Castle, Georgetown

College Band Programs: Delaware State University, University of Delaware

DELAWARE

DELAWARE STATE COLLEGE
DEPARTMENT OF MUSIC
1200 N. Dupont Hwy.
Dover, DE 19901
Davis Lapoint
302-739-4937
Fax: 302-739-4957
www.dsc.edu

UNIVERSITY OF DELAWARE
DEPARTMENT OF MUSIC
Amstel Ave. and Orchard Rd.
Newark, DE 19716
Mary Dunnack
302-831-2577
Fax: 302-831-3589
E-mail: mdunnack@udel.edu
www.music.udel.edu

Degrees: B.M., and B.A.

The University of Delaware Music Department
offers undergraduate and graduate degrees in
music, plus music courses and performance
opportunities for all university students.
Minors are available in applied music, church
music, musical studies, jazz studies and music
management studies. The University of
Delaware is large enough to provide the stimulating atmosphere of a major state university,
yet small enough to retain the convenience and
friendliness of a small college environment.
Music students benefit from a low student to
faculty ratio that provides personalized attention from a distinguished faculty of performers, educators and scholars. The centrally
located Amy E. Dupont music building contains classrooms and teaching studios, rehearsal and practice rooms, a music resource center
and the 400-seat Loudis Recital Hall. The
department is a leader in the development and
implementation of instructional technology. It
is a fully accredited institutional member of
the NASM.

WESLEY COLLEGE
DEPARTMENT OF MUSIC
Dover, DE 19901
Gary Spengler
302-736-2300
Fax: 302-736-2312
www.wesley.edu
Degrees: Minor only in Music.

FLORIDA

Population: 17,098,009 (2003 Estimate)

Capital City: Tallahassee

Music Colleges and Universities: Baptist College of South Florida, Barry University, Bethune-Cookman College, Brenau University, Brevard Community College, Broward Community College, Chipola Junior College, Daytona Beach Community College, Eckerd College, Edison Community College at Collier, Edison Community College at Lee County, Edward Waters College, Flagler College, Florida A&M University, Florida Atlantic University, Florida College, Florida International University, Florida Keys Community College, Florida Southern College, Florida State University, Full Sail Real World Education, Gulf Coast Community College, Harid Conservatory School of Music, Hillsborough Community College, Indian River Community College, Jacksonville University, Jeff Berlin Players School of Music, Lake City Community College, Lake Sumter Community College, Lynn University, Manatee Community College, Miami-Dade Community College at Kendall, Miami-Dade Community College at North, New World School of the Arts, Oskaloosa Walton Community College, Palm Beach Atlantic College, Palm Beach Community College, Pensacola Junior College, Rollins College, Santa Fe Community College, Seminole Community College, South Florida Community College, Southeastern College of Assembly of God, St. John's River Community College, St. Leo University, St. Petersburg College, Stetson University, Tallahassee Community College, University of Central Florida, University of Florida, University of Miami School of Music, University of North Florida, University of South Florida, University of Tampa, University of West Florida, Valencia Community College, Warner Southern College

Bird: Mockingbird

Motto: In God We Trust

Flower: Orange Blossom

Tree: Sabal Palmetto

Residents Called: Floridians

Origin of Name: Named on Easter 1513 by Ponce de Leon for Pascua Florida, meaning "Flowery Easter."

Area: 65,758 square miles (22nd largest state)

Statehood: March 3, 1845 (27th state)

Largest Cities: Jacksonville, Miami, Tampa, Saint Petersburg, Hialeah, Orlando, Fort Lauderdale, Tallahassee, Hollywood, Pembroke, Pines

College Band Programs: Bethune-Cookman College, Florida State University, Jacksonville State University, University of Central Florida, University of Miami, University of South Florida

FLORIDA

BAPTIST COLLEGE OF SOUTH FLORIDA
Music Program
5400 College Dr.
Graceville, FL 32440-3306
Don Odem
850-263-3261
Fax: 850-263-7506
www.sfbc.edu

BARRY UNIVERSITY
School of Arts and Sciences
11300 N.E. 2nd Ave.
Miami, FL 33161
Department of Fine Arts
305-899-3100
Fax: 305-899-1972
E-mail: admissions@mail.barry.edu
www.barry.edu

BETHUNE-COOKMAN COLLEGE
Department of Music
640 Dr. Mary Mcleod Bethune Blvd.
Daytona Beach, FL 32115
Hiram Powell
386-481-2741
Fax: 986-481-2302
E-mail: powellh@cookman.edu
www.cookman.edu

BRENAU UNIVERSITY
Department of Music
1 Centennial Cir.
Gainesville, FL 30501
Michelle Roueche
770-534-6234
Fax: 770-534-6114
E-mail: mroueche@lib.brenau.edu
www.brenau.edu/sfah/music

BREVARD COMMUNITY COLLEGE
Department of Music
Cocoa/Melbourne Campus
Cocoa, FL 32922
James Bishop
407-632-1111
Fax: 407-633-4565
E-mail: bishopj@brevard.cc.fl.us
www.brevard.cc.fl.us

BROWARD COMMUNITY COLLEGE
Department of Music
3501 S.W. Davie
Fort Lauderdale, FL 33314-1694
Loretta Scherperel
954-475-6840
Fax: 954-475-6605
E-mail: lscherpe@broward.cc.fl.us
www.broward.cc.fl.us

CHIPOLA JUNIOR COLLEGE
Department of Music
P.O. Box 3094
Marianna, FL 32446-1701
Joan Stadsklev
850-718-2301
Fax: 850-718-2206
E-mail: stadsklev@chipola.cc.fl.us
www.chipola.cc.fl.us

DAYTONA BEACH COMMUNITY COLLEGE
Department of Music
P.O. Box 1111
Daytona Beach, FL 32446-1779
Fran Perrin
904-255-8131
www.dbcc.cc.fl.us

ECKERD COLLEGE
DEPARTMENT OF MUSIC
P.O. Box 12560
St Petersburg, FL 33733-2560
Joan Epstein
727-864-8471
Fax: 727-864-7890
www.eckerd.edu

EDISON COMMUNITY COLLEGE AT COLLIER
MUSIC PROGRAM
7007 Lely Cultural Pkwy
Naples, FL 34113
James Cain
800-749-2322
Fax: 914-732-8976
www.edison.edu

EDISON COMMUNITY COLLEGE AT LEE COUNTY
DEPARTMENT OF MUSIC
P.O. Box 60210
Fort Myers, FL 33906
Edith Pendleton
941-489-9332
Fax: 941-489-9482
www.edison.edu

EDWARD WATERS COLLEGE
DEPARTMENT OF FINE ARTS
1658 Kings Rd.
Jacksonville, FL 32209
Timothy Hicks
904-366-2527
Fax: 904-366-2544
www.ewc.edu

FLAGLER COLLEGE
MUSIC PROGRAM
P.O. Box 1027
St Augustine, FL 32085-1027
Tom Rahner
904-829-6481
Fax: 904-826-0094
www.flagler.edu

FLORIDA A&M UNIVERSITY
DEPARTMENT OF FINE ARTS
Foster Tanner Music Bldg.
Tallahassee, FL 32307
850-599-3334
Fax: 850-561-2176
www.famu.edu

FLORIDA ATLANTIC UNIVERSITY
DEPARTMENT OF MUSIC
777 Glades Rd.
Boca Raton, FL 33431
Stuart Glazer
561-297-3820
Fax: 561-297-2944
E-mail: sglazer@fau.edu
www.fau.edu

FLORIDA COLLEGE
DEPARTMENT OF MUSIC
119 N. Glen Arven Ave.
Temple Terrace, FL 33617
Doug Barlar
813-988-5131
Fax: 813-899-6772
E-mail: barlard@flcoll.edu
www.flcoll.edu

Ensembles Offered: wind ensemble, jazz ensemble, string ensemble, music theory, music literature, chorus.

FLORIDA INTERNATIONAL UNIVERSITY

WERTHEIM PERFORMING ARTS CENTER

School of Music PAC 14
11100 S.W. 17th St.
Miami, FL 33199
Music Department
305-348-3726
Fax: 305-348-2896
www.fiu.edu

FLORIDA KEYS COMMUNITY COLLEGE

DEPARTMENT OF MUSIC

5901 College Rd.
Key West, FL 33040
Gerald Cash
305-296-9081
Fax: 305-292-5155
E-mail: Cash_g@popmail.firn.edu
www.firn.edu/cc/fkcc

FLORIDA SOUTHERN COLLEGE

DEPARTMENT OF MUSIC

111 Lake Hollingsworth
Lakeland, FL 33801
Music Department
836-680-4229
Fax: 836-680-4395
E-mail: fscmusic@flsouthern.edu
www.flsouthern.edu

FLORIDA STATE UNIVERSITY

SCHOOL OF MUSIC

132 N. Copeland St.
Tallahassee, FL 32306
Dr. James Croft
850-644-3424
Fax: 850-644-2033
E-mail: seaton_d@cmr.fsu.edu
www.music.fsu.edu

FULL SAIL REAL WORLD EDUCATION

MARKETING DEPARTMENT

3300 University Blvd.
Winter Park, FL 32792
Chuck Weiss
800-226-7625
Fax: 407-551-2027
E-mail: cweiss@fullsail.com
www.fullsail.com

Degrees: Recording Arts, Show Production and Touring

Full Sail offers two highly acclaimed Associate of Science Degree Programs preparing students for careers in many aspects of music production.

Our Recording Arts Degree Program takes you on a journey of both analog and digital mixing, editing, and recording. In just 12 months of intense hands-on training in world-class recording studios, MIDI labs and audio post-production suites, students will be ready for exciting entry level careers in music production in any city, in any studio working with anyone.

Our Show Production and Touring Degree Program helps you get your show on the road. In just 13 months our staff of veterans will teach you concert sound, rigging, computerized concert lighting and acoustical measurement for live venues. Everything you'll need to go after a job with a major music tour or backstage on a Broadway Show.

GULF COAST COMMUNITY COLLEGE

DEPARTMENT OF MUSIC

5230 W. Hwy. 98
Panama City, FL 32401
Rusty Gardner
904-872-3887
Fax: 904-872-3836
www.gc.cc.fl.us

HARID CONSERVATORY
SCHOOL OF MUSIC

2285 Potomac Rd.
Boca Raton, FL 33431
Gordon Wright
561-997-2677
Fax: 561-997-8920
E-mail: harid@bellsouth.net
www.harid.edu

The conservatory offers a professional performance degree. Graduates have entered top 10 graduate schools and joined orchestras such as Milwaukee, Pittsburgh, Met Opera Orchestra, Detroit and others.

HILLSBOROUGH COMMUNITY COLLEGE
DEPARTMENT OF MUSIC

P.O. Box 5096
Tampa, FL 33675
James Burge
813-253-7684
Fax: 813-253-7610
E-mail: jburge@hcc.cc.fl.us
www.hcc.cc.fl.us

INDIAN RIVER COMMUNITY COLLEGE
DEPARTMENT OF MUSIC

3209 Virginia Ave.
Fort Pierce, FL 34981-5541
Dale Rieth
561-462-4700
Fax: 561-462-4796
E-mail: drieth@ircc.cc.fl.us
www.ircc.cc.fl.us

JACKSONVILLE UNIVERSITY
MUSIC DEPARTMENT

College of Fine Arts
Jacksonville, FL 32211
Dr. Dennis R. Vincent
904-745-7370
Fax: 904-745-7375
E-mail: jcarlso@ju.edu
www.ju.edu

JEFF BERLIN PLAYERS SCHOOL OF MUSIC

923 McMullen Booth Rd.
Clearwater, FL 33759
Music Department
800-724-4242
E-mail: learnmusic@playerschool.com
www.playerschool.com

LAKE CITY COMMUNITY COLLEGE
DEPARTMENT OF MUSIC

RR 19
P.O. Box 1030
Lake City, FL 32025
Owen Wingate
904-752-1822
Fax: 904-755-1521
E-mail: wingateo@mail.lakecity.cc.fl.us
www.lakecity.cc.fl.us

LAKE SUMTER COMMUNITY COLLEGE
DEPARTMENT OF MUSIC

9501 US Hwy. 441
Leesburg, FL 34788
Peter Arcaro
904-787-3747
Fax: 904-365-3501
www.lscc.cc.fl.us

LYNN UNIVERSITY
CONSERVATORY OF MUSIC
3601 North Military Trail
Boca Raton, FL 33431
Dr. Claudio Jaffe
561-999-4386
Fax: 561-995-0417
E-mail: music@lynn.edu
www.lynn.edu/music

MANATEE COMMUNITY COLLEGE
DEPARTMENT OF FINE ARTS AND PERFORMING ARTS
Music Program
P.O. Box 1849
Bradenton, FL 34206
Charles Turon
941-752-5351
Fax: 941-727-6088
www.mccfl.edu

MIAMI-DADE COMMUNITY COLLEGE AT KENDALL
DEPARTMENT OF MUSIC
11011 S.W. 104th St.
Miami, FL 33176
Vernon Smith
305-237-2282
Fax: 307-237-2411
E-mail: vsmith@mdcc.edu
www.mdcc.edu/kendall

MIAMI-DADE COMMUNITY COLLEGE AT NORTH
DEPARTMENT OF PERFORMING ARTS
11380 N.W. 27th Ave.
Miami, FL 33167
Kenneth Boos
305-323-1450
Fax: 305-237-1850
www.mdcc.edu/north

NEW WORLD SCHOOL OF THE ARTS
DEPARTMENT OF MUSIC
300 N.E. 2nd Ave.
Miami, FL 33132
Dr. Jeffery Hodgson
305-237-3893
Fax: 305-237-3794
E-mail: jhodgson@mdcc.edu
www.mdcc.edu/nwsa/music/index.html

OSKALOOSA WALTON COMMUNITY COLLEGE
DEPARTMENT OF MUSIC
100 College Blvd. E
Niceville, FL 32578
Clifford Herron
850-729-5382
Fax: 850-729-5286
E-mail: bakerm@owcc.net
www.owcc.cc.fl.us

PALM BEACH ATLANTIC COLLEGE
SCHOOL OF MUSIC AND FINE ARTS
901 South Flagler Dr.
P.O. Box 24708
West Palm Beach, FL 33416
Dr. Lloyd Mims
561-803-2400
Fax: 561-803-2424
E-mail: music@pba.edu
www.pba.edu

Degrees: Bachelor of Arts and Bachelor of Music

Palm Beach Atlantic is a Christian liberal arts university located a five-minute walk from the Atlantic Ocean to the east of West Palm Beach's opulent Kravis Center for the Performing Arts to the west. University places a strong emphasis on academic excellence in the context of a non-sectarian Christian environment. The Bachelor of Arts and the Bachelor of Music degrees are awarded through the School of Music and Fine Arts and fully accredited by the National Association of Schools of Music. B.A. degrees are available in music theory and literature, traditional applied music, and popular music (the latter beginning in 2004). The B.M. degree is offered in church music, composition, music education and performance (instrumental, keyboard and vocal). Both degrees stress concentration in performance development as well as academic rigor. The music program is housed in the $10 million state-of-the-art Vera Lea Rinker Hall dedicated in 2002.

PALM BEACH COMMUNITY COLLEGE
DIVISIONS OF HUMANITIES AND MUSIC

4200 S. Congress Ave.
Lake Worth, FL 33461
Allen Webber
561-439-8144
Fax: 561-438-8384
E-mail: webbera@pbcc.cc.fl.us
www.pbcc.cc.fl.us

PENSACOLA JUNIOR COLLEGE
DEPARTMENT OF MUSIC AND THEATRE

1000 College Blvd.
Pensacola, FL 32504
Don Snowden
850-484-1800
Fax: 850-484-1835
E-mail: dsnowden@pjc.cc.fl.us
www.pjc.cc.fl.us

ROLLINS COLLEGE
DEPARTMENT OF MUSIC

1000 Holt Ave. #2731
Winter Park, FL 32789
Joyce Kanavel
407-646-2233
Fax: 407-646-2533
E-mail: jkanavel@rollins.edu
www.rollins.edu

SANTA FE COMMUNITY COLLEGE
DEPARTMENT OF MUSIC

3000 N.W. 83rd St.
Gainesville, FL 32606
Leslie Lambert
352-395-5310
Fax: 352-395-4432
E-mail: leslie.lambert@santafe.cc.fl.us
www.santafe.cc.fl.us

SEMINOLE COMMUNITY COLLEGE
DEPARTMENT OF FINE AND PERFORMANCE ARTS

100 Weldon Blvd.
Sanford, FL 32773
Kimberley Jones
407-328-2039
Fax: 407-328-2354
E-mail: karperp@scc-fl.com
www.seminole.cc.fl.us

SOUTH FLORIDA COMMUNITY COLLEGE
DEPARTMENT OF MUSIC

600 W. College Dr.
Avon Park, FL 33825
Douglas Andrews
863-453-6661
Fax: 863-748-7190
www.sfcc.cc.fl.us

SOUTHEASTERN COLLEGE OF ASSEMBLY OF GOD
MUSIC PROGRAM
1000 Longfellow Blvd.
Lakeland, FL 33801
Danny Tindall
941-667-5000
Fax: 941-667-5200
E-mail: dhtindall@secollege.edu
www.secollege.edu

ST. JOHNS RIVER COMMUNITY COLLEGE
FLORIDA SCHOOL OF THE ARTS
5001 St. Johns Ave.
Palatka, FL 32177
Gary Piazza
904-312-4300
Fax: 904-312-4306
E-mail: piazza_g@firn.edu
www.sjrcc.cc.fl.us

ST. LEO UNIVERSITY
SCHOOL OF ARTS AND SCIENCES
P.O. Box 665 Mc 2127
Saint Leo, FL 33574
June Hammond
352-588-8423
Fax: 352-588-8300
E-mail: june.hammond@saintleo.edu
www.saintleo.edu

ST. PETERSBURG COLLEGE
DEPARTMENT OF MUSIC
P.O. Box 13489
St. Petersburg, FL 33733
Jonathan Stelle
727-341-4360
Fax: 727-341-4744
E-mail: steelej@spcollege.edu
www.spcollege.edu/spg/music

Degrees: A.A. Transfer, Music Emphasis

St. Petersburg College is one of 28 community colleges in the state of Florida offering transfer into the state university system through a state-wide articulation agreement. We offer a comprehensive two-year music program leading toward bachelor's degrees in music performance, music education or other music emphases. A faculty of 33 including 7 full-time and 26 adjunct faculty provide quality instruction in voice, guitar, piano and all orchestral instruments. Students and faculty enjoy the opportunity to perform in an acoustically perfect Music Center, equipped with two Steinway D grand pianos and a new Heissler tracker pipe organ. A modern Music Technology lab provides access to state of the art software for music. Acoustical practice rooms, rehearsal halls for band, chorus and percussion ensemble, and faculty studios are all equipped with the finest instruments. Scholarships for music majors and participants in chorus and band are available.

STETSON UNIVERSITY
SCHOOL OF MUSIC
421 N. Woodland Blvd.
Unit 8399
Deland, FL 33270
Wendy Gabler
904-822-8950
Fax: 904-822-8948
E-mail: kjuusela@stetson.edu
www.stetson.edu

The School of Music at Florida's first private university maintains a 6:1 student to faculty ratio, award-winning ensembles and international faculty. Enrollment consists of 200 music majors with 28 full-time faculty and 17 part-time faculty. Theodore Presser Hall is home to the School of Music with state-of-the-art facilities: Pittman Recital Hall, two ensemble rehearsal halls, 42 practice rooms, computer lab, 26 teaching studios, three computerized voice labs and a music library with 8,000 books, 14,000 scores, 14,000 recordings, and 50 periodical subscriptions. Scholarships are available.

TALLAHASSEE COMMUNITY COLLEGE
DEPARTMENT OF MUSIC
444 Appleyard Dr.
Tallahassee, FL 32304
Marge Banocy-Payne
904-488-9200
Fax: 904-488-2203
www.tcc.cc.fl.us

UNIVERSITY OF CENTRAL FLORIDA
MUSIC DEPARTMENT
P.O. Box 161354
Orlando, FL 32816
407-823-2519
Fax: 407-823-3378
www.ucf.edu

UNIVERSITY OF FLORIDA
SCHOOL OF MUSIC
Gainesville, FL 32611
Linda Black
352-392-0223
Fax: 352-392-0461
www.arts.ufl.edu/music

UNIVERSITY OF MIAMI
SCHOOL OF MUSIC
P.O. Box 248165
Coral Gables, FL 33124
Kenneth J. Moses
305-284-2241
Fax: 305-284-6475
E-mail: whipp@miami.edu
www.music.miami.edu

UNIVERSITY OF NORTH FLORIDA
DEPARTMENT OF MUSIC
4567 St. John's Bluff Rd. S.
Ponte Vedra Beach State, FL 32224
Gordon Brock
904-620-2961
Fax: 904-620-2568
E-mail: gbrock@unf.edu
www.unf.edu/coas/music

Degrees: B.M., B.A., and B.A.E.

Located in its brand new $22 million facility, the UNF Music Department is developing into one of the important music programs in the region. Long known for its top jazz program, the music area offers a complete program for undergraduates interested in the music major. An energetic, talented faculty of artist-teachers and strong ties with the Jacksonville Symphony Orchestra help to make this an exciting place to study.

UNIVERSITY OF SOUTH FLORIDA
SCHOOL OF MUSIC
4202 E. Fowler Ave.
FAH110
Tampa, FL 33620
813-974-2311
Fax: 813-974-8721
E-mail: doane@usf.edu
http://music.arts.usf.edu

UNIVERSITY OF TAMPA
DEPARTMENT OF MUSIC
401 W. Kennedy Blvd.
Tampa, FL 33606
Dr. Jeffery Traster
813-253-3333
Fax: 813-258-7244
E-mail: jtraster@ut.edu
www.utampa.edu

UNIVERSITY OF WEST FLORIDA
DEPARTMENT OF MUSIC

11000 University Pkwy.
Pensacola, FL 32514
Kevin Mobbs
850-474-2147
Fax: 850-474-3247
E-mail: kmobbs@uwf.edu
www.uwf.edu

VALENCIA COMMUNITY COLLEGE
MUSIC PROGRAM

P.O. Box 3028
Orlando, FL 32802
Larry Weed
407-299-5000
Fax: 407-299-5000
http://valencia.cc.fl.us

WARNER SOUTHERN COLLEGE
DEPARTMENT OF MUSIC

Lake Worth, FL 33853
Steven Darr
813-638-7231
Fax: 813-638-1472
www.warner.edu

GEORGIA

Population: 8,851,195 (2003 Estimate)

Capital City: Atlanta

Music Colleges and Universities: Agnes Scott College, Albany State University, Andrew College, Armstrong Atlantic State University, Atlanta Conservatory of Music, Augusta State University, Berry College, Brewton-Parker College, Clark Atlanta University, Clayton College and State University, Columbus State University, Covenant College, Darton College, Emmanuel College, Emory University, Emory University at Oxford College, Floyd College, Fort Valley State University, Georgia College and State University, Georgia Institute of Technology, Georgia Perimeter College, Georgia Southern University, Georgia Southwestern College, Georgia State University, Interdenominational Theological College, Kennesaw State University, LaGrange College, Macon College, Mercer University, Middle Georgia College, Morehouse College, Morris Brown College, North Georgia College and State University, Oglethorpe University, Paine College, Piedmont College, Reinhardt College, Savannah State College, Shorter College, Spelman College, State University of West Georgia, Thomas University, Toccoa Falls College, Truett-McConnel College, University of Georgia, Valdosta State University, Waycross College, Wesleyan College, Young Harris College

Bird: Brown Thrasher

Motto: Wisdom, justice, and moderation

Flower: Cherokee Rose

Tree: Live oak

Residents Called: Georgians

Origin of Name: Named for King George II of England.

Area: 59,441 square miles (24th largest state)

Statehood: January 2, 1788 (4th state)

Largest Cities: Atlanta, Augusta, Columbus, Savannah, Athens, Macon, Roswell, Albany, Marietta, Warner Robins

College Band Programs: Clark Atlanta University, Georgia Southern University, Georgia Institute of Tech, University of Georgia

GEORGIA

AGNES SCOTT COLLEGE
Music Department
141 E. College Ave.
Decatur, GA 30030
Tracey E. W. Laird
404-471-6285
Fax: 404-471-6414
E-mail: tlaird@agnesscott.edu
www.agnesscott.edu

We offer a full complement of applied music instruction on standard orchestral instruments, early instruments, keyboard, and voice. Ensemble opportunities include choir, orchestra, chamber ensembles, jazz ensemble and gospel choir. The college is located in the heart of metro Atlanta with numerous opportunities to participate in Atlanta's rich musical life.

ALBANY STATE UNIVERSITY
Department of Fine Arts
504 College Dr.
Albany, GA 31705
Leroy Bynum
912-430-4849
E-mail: lbynum@asurams.edu
http://asuweb.asurams.edu/asu

ANDREW COLLEGE
Department of Music
413 College St.
Cuthbert, GA 31749-1313
Susan Tusing
229-732-2171
Fax: 229-732-2176
E-mail: susantusing@andrewcollege.edu
www.andrewcollege.edu

ARMSTRONG ATLANTIC STATE UNIVERSITY
Department of Music
11935 Abercorn
Savannah, GA 31419-1909
James Anderson
912-921-5410
Fax: 912-921-5419
E-mail: andersja@mail.armstrong.edu
www.armstrong.edu

ATLANTA CONSERVATORY OF MUSIC
3836-A Stewart Rd.
Atlanta, GA 30340
770-455-8483
Fax: 770-449-6867

AUGUSTA STATE UNIVERSITY
Department of Fine Arts
2500 Walton Way
Augusta, GA 30904-2200
Angela Morgan
706-737-1453
Fax: 706-667-4937
E-mail: finearts@aug.edu
www.aug.edu/finearts

BERRY COLLEGE
Department of Music
P.O. Box 309
Mt. Berry, GA 30149
Dr. Stan Pethel
706-232-5374
Fax: 706-238-7847
E-mail: spethel@berry.edu
www.berry.edu

BREWTON-PARKER COLLEGE
DIVISION OF MUSIC
Hwy 280
P.O. Box 2002
Mount Vernon, GA 30445
Pierce Dickens
800-342-1087
Fax: 912-583-2997
E-mail: dcooper@bpc.edu
www.bpc.edu

CLARK ATLANTA UNIVERSITY
MUSIC DEPARTMENT
Atlanta, GA 30314
Mary Frances Early
404-880-8211
Fax: 404-880-6267
E-mail: mearly@cau.edu
www.cau.edu

CLAYTON COLLEGE AND STATE UNIVERSITY
MUSIC DEPARTMENT
P.O. Box 285
Morrow, GA 30236
Dr. William Graves
770-961-3609
Fax: 770-961-4351
E-mail: williamgraves@mail.clayton.edu
http://a-s.clayton.edu/music

COLUMBUS STATE UNIVERSITY
SCHWAB SCHOOL OF MUSIC
4225 University Ave.
Columbus, GA 31907-5645
Dr. Ning Tien Scialla
706-649-7276
Fax: 706-649-7369
E-mail: scialla_ning@colstate.edu
www.colstate.edu

Established in 1969, the Columbus State University Schwob School of Music is a senior unit of the university system of Georgia. The new $67 million River Center for the Performing Arts is the new home of the Schwob School of Music. This state-of-the-art facility includes three performance halls, a music library/technology center, and a large complement of offices, studios, rehearsal spaces and practice rooms.

COVENANT COLLEGE
DEPARTMENT OF MUSIC
1409 Scenic Hwy.
Lookout Mountain, GA 30750
Timothy Steele
706-820-1560
Fax: 706-820-0893
E-mail: steele@covenant.edu
www.covenant.edu

DARTON COLLEGE
DEPARTMENT OF MUSIC
2400 Gillionville Rd.
Albany, GA 31707-3098
Jeff Kluball
229-430-6856
Fax: 229-420-1106
E-mail:
kluballj@mail.dartnet.peachnet.edu
www.dartnet.peachnet.edu

EMMANUEL COLLEGE
DEPARTMENT OF MUSIC
212 Spring St. P.O. Box 129
Franklin Springs, GA 30639
Mark Goodwin
706-245-7226
Fax: 706-245-4424
E-mail:
mgoodwin@emmanuelcollege.edu
www.emmanuelcollege.edu

EMORY UNIVERSITY
DEPARTMENT OF MUSIC
1804 North Decatur Rd.
Atlanta, GA 30322
Scott A. Stewart
404-727-6445
Fax: 404-727-0074
E-mail: music@emory.edu
www.emory.edu

The Emory University Department of Music offers an outstanding music education at a world-class liberal arts institution. Located in the heart of Atlanta, Emory is home to world-famous scholars, teachers and performers. Over 100 music majors pursue a bachelor of arts in music, and most double-major in performance and an outside liberal arts field or business. Many of the applied faculty are members of the Atlanta Symphony Orchestra and other ensembles, and lessons for majors are free. The department caters to both majors and non-majors in offering a wide array of courses, ensembles and applied study. The Schwartz Center for the Performing Arts, a state-of-the-art facility to house music, dance and theatre, was completed in the fall of 2002.

EMORY UNIVERSITY AT OXFORD
DIVISION OF HUMANITIES
Oxford, GA 30054
Lucus Carpenter
770-784-8888
Fax: 770-784-8364
www.emory.edu

FLOYD COLLEGE
DIVISION OF SOCIAL/CULTURAL STUDIES
P.O. Box 1864
Rome, GA 30162-1864
William Mugleston
709-295-6312
Fax: 709-295-6610

E-mail:
wmugleston@mail.fc.peachnet.edu
www.fc.peachnet.edu

FORT VALLEY STATE UNIVERSITY
DEPARTMENT OF MUSIC
1005 State University Dr.
Fort Valley, GA 31030-4313
William Garcia
912-825-6387
Fax: 912-825-6132
www.fvsu.edu

GEORGIA COLLEGE AND STATE UNIVERSITY
THE MUSIC AND THEATRE DEPARTMENT
Milledgeville, GA 31061
Dr. Richard Greene
912-445-4226
Fax: 912-445-1633
E-mail: rgreene@mail.gcsu.edu
www.gcsu.edu

GEORGIA INSTITUTE OF TECHNOLOGY
DEPARTMENT OF MUSIC
Music Department
Atlanta, GA 30332
Bucky Johnson
404-894-3193
Fax: 404-894-9952
www.gatech.edu

GEORGIA PERIMETER COLLEGE
DEPARTMENT OF FINE ARTS
555 N. Indian Creek Dr.
Clarkston, GA 30021-2361
Tommy Anderson
404-299-4136
Fax: 404-299-4271
E-mail: tanderso@gpc.peachnet.edu
www.gpc.peachnet.edu

GEORGIA SOUTHERN UNIVERSITY
DEPARTMENT OF MUSIC
P.O. Box 8052
Statesboro, GA 30460
Dr. David W. Matthew
912-681-5396
Fax: 912-681-0583
E-mail: music@.gasou.edu
www2.gasou.edu/music

GEORGIA SOUTHWESTERN COLLEGE
Admissions Building, Rm 104
800 Wheatley St.
Americus, GA 31709
Gary Fallis
912-931-2204
Fax: 912-932-9270
E-mail: fallisg@canes.gsw.edu
www.gsw.edu

GEORGIA STATE UNIVERSITY
Public Relations
Department of Music
P.O. Box 4097
Atlanta, GA 30303
Gracie Bergeron
404-651-3676
Fax: 404-651-1583
E-mail: jhaberlen@.gsu.edu
http://music.gsu.edu

INTERDENOMINATIONAL THEOLOGICAL COLLEGE
DEPARTMENT OF MUSIC
700 MLKJ Dr. S.W.
P.O. Box 429
Atlanta, GA 30314
Welva Wilson Costen
404-527-7729
Fax: 404-527-0901
www.itc.edu

KENNESAW STATE UNIVERSITY
DEPARTMENT OF MUSIC
1000 Chastain Rd.
P.O. Box 3201
Kennesaw, GA 30144
Peter Witte
770-423-6151
Fax: 770-423-6368
E-mail: pwitte@kennesaw.edu
www.kennesaw.edu

LAGRANGE COLLEGE
DEPARTMENT OF MUSIC
601 Broad St.
Lagrange, GA 30240
Toni Anderson
706-880-8351
Fax: 706-880-8028
E-mail: tanderson@lgc.edu
www.lgc.peachnet.edu

MACON COLLEGE
DEPARTMENT OF MUSIC
100 College Station Dr.
Macon, GA 31206
Rebecca Lanning
478-471-5773
Fax: 478-757-3624
E-mail: rlanning@mail.maconstate.edu
www.maconstate.edu

MERCER UNIVERSITY
DEPARTMENT OF MUSIC
1400 Coleman Ave.
Macon, GA 31207
Dr. John N. Roberts
912-301-2748
Fax: 912-301-5633
E-mail: Roberts_jn@Mercer.edu
www.mercer.edu/music

MIDDLE GEORGIA COLLEGE
DEPARTMENT OF MUSIC
1100 Second St.
Cochran, GA 30104
Eric Kuhn
478-934-3085
Fax: 478-934-3109
E-mail:
ekuhn@warrior.mgc.peachnet.edu
www.mgc.peachnet.edu

MOREHOUSE COLLEGE
MUSIC DEPARTMENT
830 Westview Dr.
Atlanta, GA 30341
Dr. Uzee Brown, Jr.
404-215-2601
Fax: 404-215-3479
E-mail: ubrown@morehouse.edu
www.morehouse.edu

MORRIS BROWN COLLEGE
DEPARTMENT OF MUSIC
643 Martin Luther King Jr. Dr. N.W.
Atlanta, GA 30314
Sarah West
404-220-0318
www.morrisbrown.edu

NORTH GEORGIA COLLEGE AND STATE UNIVERSITY
DEPARTMENT OF FINE ARTS
Dahlonega, GA 30597
Joe Chapman
706-864-1423
Fax: 706-864-1429
E-mail: estelle@ngcsu.edu
www.ngcsu.edu

OGLETHORPE UNIVERSITY
DIVISION OF MUSIC
4484 Peachtree Rd. N.E.
Atlanta, GA 30319
Irwin Ray
404-261-1441
Fax: 404-364-8442
www.oglethorpe.edu

PAINE COLLEGE
DEPARTMENT OF MUSIC
1235 15th St.
Augusta, GA 30901
George Johnson
706-821-8306
www.paine.edu

PIEDMONT COLLEGE
DEPARTMENT OF MUSIC
165 Central Ave.
Demorest, GA 30535
Wallace Hinson
706-778-3000
Fax: 706-776-2811
E-mail: whinson@piedmont.edu
www.piedmont.edu

REINHARDT COLLEGE
MUSIC PROGRAM
7300 Reinhardt College
Waleska, GA 30183
Judith R. MacMillan
770-720-5600
Fax: 770-720-5602
E-mail: sen@mail.reinhardt.edu
www.reinhardt.edu

SAVANNAH STATE COLLEGE
DEPARTMENT OF FINE ARTS-MUSIC
Savannah, GA 31404
Peggy Blood
912-356-2248
Fax: 912-356-2996
www.savstate.edu/class/finearts

SHORTER COLLEGE
SCHOOL OF THE ARTS AND MUSIC
315 Shorter Ave.
Rome, GA 30165
Alan Wingard
706-233-7247
Fax: 706-236-1517
E-mail: awingard@shorter.edu
www.shorter.edu/academ/soa/index.htm

SPELMAN COLLEGE
DEPARTMENT OF MUSIC
350 Spellman Lane
Atlanta, GA 30314
Dr. Kevin Johnson
404-681-3643
Fax: 404-215-7771
E-mail: johnson@spelman.edu
www.spelman.edu

STATE UNIVERSITY OF WEST GEORGIA
DEPARTMENT OF MUSIC
1600 Maple St.
Carrollton, GA 30118
Scot McBride
770-836-6516
Fax: 770-836-4772
E-mail: musicdpt@westga.edu
www.westga.edu/~musicdpt

THOMAS UNIVERSITY
DEPARTMENT OF MUSIC
1501 Millpond Rd.
Thomasville, GA 31792
Karl Barton
912-226-1621
Fax: 912-226-1653
E-mail: music@thomas.edu
www.thomas.edu

TOCCOA FALLS COLLEGE
SCHOOL OF MUSIC
P.O. Box 847
Toccoa, GA 30598
Phillip Hayner
706-886-6831
Fax: 706-282-6036
E-mail: phayner@tfc.edu
www.tfc.edu

TRUETT-MCCONNEL COLLEGE
DEPARTMENT OF MUSIC
100 Alumni Dr.
Cleveland, GA 30528
Edwin Calloway
706-865-2134
Fax: 706-865-5135
E-mail: Sandy@truett.cc.ga.us
www.truett.cc.ga.us

UNIVERSITY OF GEORGIA
DEPARTMENT OF MUSIC
250 River Rd.
Athens, GA 30677
Suzanne Caruso
706-542-3737
Fax: 706-542-2773
www.uga.edu/~music

VALDOSTA STATE UNIVERSITY

Department of Music
1500 N. Patterson St.
Valdosta, GA 31698
Dr. Tayloe Harding
229-333-5804
Fax: 229-259-5578
E-mail: tharding@valdosta.edu
www.valdosta.edu/music

WAYCROSS COLLEGE
DEPARTMENT OF MUSIC

2001 Francis St.
Waycross, GA 31503
Tommothy Goodwin
912-285-6135
Fax: 912-287-4909
www.waycross.edu

WESLEYAN COLLEGE
DEPARTMENT OF MUSIC

4769 Forsyth Rd.
Macon, GA 31210
Fletcher Anderson
912-757-5259
Fax: 912-757-3268
E-mail: fanderson@wesleyancollege.edu
www.wesleyancollege.edu

YOUNG HARRIS COLLEGE
DEPARTMENT OF MUSIC

Young Harris, GA 30582
Keith Defoor
706-379-4306
Fax: 706-379-4306
E-mail: kdefoor@yhc.edu
www.yhc.edu

HAWAII

Population: 1,241,556 (2003 Estimate)

Capital City: Honolulu

Music Colleges and Universities: Brigham Young University at Hawaii, Chaminade University of Honolulu, Hawaii Loa College, Hawaii Pacific College, Honolulu Community College, Kapiolani Community College, Kauai Community College, Leeward Community College, University of Hawaii at Hilo, University of Hawaii at Manoa, Winward Community College

Bird: Nene

Motto: Ua mau ke ea o ka aina I ka pono – The life of the land is perpetuated in righteousness.

Flower: Hibiscus or Pua Aloalo

Tree: Candlenut or Kukui

Residents Called: Hawaiians

Origin of Name: It could be based on native Hawaiian word for homeland, "Owhyhee."

Area: 10,932 square miles (43rd largest state)

Statehood: August 21, 1959 (50th state)

Largest Cities: Honolulu, Hilo, Kailua, Kaneohe, Waipahu, Pearl City, Waimalu, Mililani, Kahului, Kihe

College Band Programs: Hawaii Pacific University, University of Hawaii-Manoa

HAWAII

BRIGHAM YOUNG UNIVERSITY AT HAWAII
DIVISION OF FINE ARTS AND MUSIC
55-220 Kulanui St.
Laie, HI 96762
Scitt McCarrey
808-293-3892
Fax: 808-293-3900
E-mail: mccarres@byuh.edu
www.byu.edu

CHAMINADE UNIVERSITY OF HONOLULU
DEPARTMENT OF MUSIC
3140 Waialae Ave.
Honolulu, HI 96816-1510
Karen Drozd
808-735-4865
Fax: 808-739-4647
E-mail: kdrozd@chaminade.edu
www.chaminade.edu

HAWAII LOA COLLEGE
DEPARTMENT OF MUSIC
45-045
Kanehameha Hwy.
Kanehameha, HI 96744
Jane Moulin
808-235-3641
Fax: 808-247-8166

HAWAII PACIFIC COLLEGE
DEPARTMENT OF MUSIC
1164 Bishop St.
Honolulu, HI 96813
Richard McKinney
www.hpu.edu
Degrees: Minor only in music.

Honolulu Community College
Department of Music
874 Dillingham Blvd.
Honolulu, HI 96817
Lorna Mount
808-845-9415
Fax: 808-845-9416
E-mail: lmount@hcc.hawaii.edu
www.hcc.hawaii.edu

KAPIOLANI COMMUNITY COLLEGE
DEPARTMENT OF HUMANITIES
4303 Diamond Head
Honolulu, HI 96816
Robert Engle
808-734-9749
Fax: 808-734-9151
E-mail: bengle@hawaii.edu
www.hawaii.edu

KAUAI COMMUNITY COLLEGE
DEPARTMENT OF MUSIC
3-1901 Maumalii Hwy.
Lihue, HI 96766
Gregory Shepherd
908-245-8269
Fax: 908-245-8820
www.kauaicc.hawaii.edu

LEEWARD COMMUNITY COLLEGE
DEPARTMENT OF MUSIC
96-045 Ala Ike St.
Pearl City, HI 96782
Barbara Saromines-Gamne
808-455-0350
Fax: 808-455-0636
www.lcc.hawaii.edu

UNIVERSITY OF HAWAII AT HILO
DEPARTMENT OF PERFORMING ARTS
200 W. Kawili St.
Hilo, HI 96720
John Kusinski
808-974-7352
Fax: 808-974-7736
www.performingarts.net/theatre
Degrees: B. A. in Music Composition,
Music History or Ethnomusicology
Emphasis; Secondary Certification in
Education with the B.A. in Music, Music
Minor, The Performing Arts Certificate.

UNIVERSITY OF HAWAII AT MANOA
MUSIC DEPARTMENT
2411 Dole St.
Honolulu, HI 96822
Lesley A. Wright
808-956-7756
Fax: 808-956-9657
E-mail: wright@hawaii.edu
www.hawaii.edu/uhmmusic
Along with the full range of traditional
western ensembles (bands, choirs,
orchestra, opera, jazz, chamber, contemporary), the University of Hawaii is also
noted for its studies in ethnomusicology,
particularly in the music of Asia and the
Pacific Islands.

WINWARD COMMUNITY COLLEGE
MUSIC PROGRAM
45-720 Keaahala Rd.
Kaneohe, HI 96744
Kahealani Tani
808-235-0077
Fax: 808-235-0077
E-mail: k_taniwccada@wcc.edu
www.hawaii.edu

IDAHO

Population: 1,411,386 (2003 Estimate)

Capital City: Boise

Music Colleges and Universities: Albertson College, Boise State University, College of Southern Idaho, Hampton School Of Music, Idaho State University, Lewis and Clark State College, North Idaho College, Northwest Nazarene College, University of Idaho

Bird: Mountain Bluebird

Motto: Esto perpetual: Let it be perpetual/ It is forever

Flower: Syringa

Tree: Western White Pine

Residents Called: Idahoans

Origin of Name: Idaho is a coined or invented word, and is not a derivation of an Indian phrase "E Dah Hoe (How)" supposedly meaning "gem of the mountains."

Area: 83,574 square miles (14th largest state)

Statehood: July 3, 1890 (43rd state)

Largest Cities: Boise, Nampa, Pocatello, Idaho Falls, Meridian, Coeur d'Alene, Twin Falls, Lewiston, Caldwell, Moscow

College Band Programs: College of Southern Idaho, North Idaho College

IDAHO

ALBERTSON COLLEGE
DEPARTMENT OF MUSIC
2112 Cleveland Blvd.
Caldwell, ID 83605
208-459-5275
Fax: 208-459-5885
E-mail: music@albertson.edu
www.albertson.edu/music

BOISE STATE UNIVERSITY
MUSIC DEPARTMENT
1910 University Dr.
Boise, ID 83725
James Cook
208-385-1772
Fax: 208-426-1771
E-mail: hcalkins@boisestate.edu
www.boisestate.edu/music

The Department of Music at Boise State University has a rich tradition of musical excellence. In support of this excellent heritage, the Idaho State Board of Education has designated BSU as a primary emphasis area in the performing arts. The department has 23 full-time faculty/staff and 19 associate faculty noted for teaching and performing. BSU faculty and students have won state, regional, national and international music awards and competitions. One of the primary strengths of the department is equal opportunity in all areas of musical preparation, as evidenced by the degrees offered.

COLLEGE OF SOUTHERN IDAHO
DEPARTMENT OF MUSIC
315 Falls Ave.
P.O. Box 1238
Twin Falls, ID 83303
Micheal Green
208-733-9554

Fax: 208-736-3015
E-mail: mgreen@csi.edu
www.csi.edu

The Music Department offers a full range of courses to meet the needs of music students. Private instruction is available in voice and all wind, keyboard, and percussion instruments as well as violin and guitar. Students have the opportunity to perform on both solo recitals and in numerous college- and community-based ensembles. Among the performing groups available are the Chamber Choir, Madrigal Ensemble, Magic Valley Chorale, Wind Ensemble, Symphonic Band, Pep Band, Jazz Band, Jazz Combos, and Magic Valley Symphony.

HAMPTON SCHOOL OF MUSIC
UNIVERSITY OF IDAHO
Moscow, ID 83844
208-885-6232
Fax: 208-885-7254
E-mail: music@uidaho.edu
www.uidaho.edu/ls/music

IDAHO STATE UNIVERSITY
DEPARTMENT OF MUSIC
P.O. Box 8099
Pocatello, ID 83209
Dr. Randy Earles
208-282-3636
Fax: 208-282-4884
E-mail: music@isu.edu
www.isu.edu/music

ISU offers a wide array of performing ensembles: four choirs, opera workshop, two concert bands, two jazz bands, marching band and orchestra. A new performing arts center is under construction and is expected to open in Fall 2003.

LEWIS AND CLARK STATE COLLEGE
DIVISION OF FINE AND PERFORMANCE ARTS
500 8th Ave.
Lewiston, ID 83501
Lary Haaoanen
208-792-2297
Fax: 208-792-2324
E-mail: haapanen@lcsc.edu
www.lcsc.edu

Degrees: Minors only in music.

NORTH IDAHO COLLEGE
DEPARTMENT OF MUSIC
1000 W. Garden Ave.
Coeur D Alene, ID 83814
Terry Jones
208-769-3300
E-mail: tjones@nic.edu
www.nic.edu

Degrees: Associate of Arts or Associate of Science degree, and it will provide excellent preparation for you to transfer to a four-year college to obtain a bachelor's degree in music education or music performance.

NORTHWEST NAZARENE COLLEGE
DEPARTMENT OF MUSIC
623 Holly St.
Nampa, ID 83651
Laura Richardson
208-467-8413
Fax: 208-467-8360
www.mnu.edu

Degrees: Bachelor of Arts in Music with emphases in: Applied Music, Music Ministries, Music Theory, General Music, Commercial Music, Worship Leadership, Bachelor of Arts in Music education. Minor emphasis in Music.

UNIVERSITY OF IDAHO
LIONEL HAMPTON SCHOOL OF MUSIC
P.O. Box 444015
Moscow, ID 83844
Susan Hess
208-885-6231
Fax: 208-885-7254
E-mail: music@uidaho.edu
www.uidaho.edu/ls/music

Degrees: B.M. in Performance, Composition, Music Education, Business; Bachelor of Arts in Music, Bachelor of Science in Music; Master of Music with majors in: Performance, Composition, Music Education Piano Pedagogy and Performance Studies, Accompanying, Music History; Ph.D./Ed.D. in Education with Emphasis in Music Education.

ILLINOIS

Population: 12,722,868 (2003 Estimate)

Capital City: Springfield

Music Colleges and Universities: American Conservatory of Music, Augustana College, Aurora University, Black Hawk College, Blackburn College, Bradley University, Carl Sandburg College, Chicago College of Performing Arts, Chicago School of Violin Making, Chicago State University, College of Du Page, College of Lake County, Columbia College, Concordia University, DePaul College of Music, Dominican University, Eastern Illinois University, Elgin Community College, Elmhurst College, Eureka College, Governors State University, Greenville College, Illinois College, Illinois County College, Illinois State University, Illinois Valley Community College, John A. Logan College, John Wood Community College, Joliet Junior College, Judson College, Kankakee Community College, Kishwaukee College, Knox College, Lake Forest College, Lewis and Clark Community College, Lewis University, Lincoln Christian College, Lincoln College, Lincoln Land Community College, Lincoln Trail College, Loyola University Chicago, MacMurray College, McKendree College, Milliken University, Monmouth College, Moody Bible Institute, Moraine Valley Community College, Morton College, National-Louis University, North Central College, North Park University, Northeastern Illinois University, Northern Illinois University, Northwestern University, Olivet Nazarene University, Olney Central College, Parkland College, Principia College, Quincy University, Rend Lake College, Richland Community College, Rock Valley College, Roosevelt University, Saulk Valley Community College, Sherwood Conservatory of Music, South Suburban College, Southeastern Illinois College, Southern Illinois University at Carbondale, Southern Illinois University at Edwardsville, Southwestern Illinois College, Springfield College at Illinois, St. Xavier University, Trinity Christian College, Trinity International University, Triton College, University of Chicago, University of Illinois at Chicago, University of Illinois at Urbana, University of St. Francis, University of St. Mary of the Lake, VanderCook College of Music, Western Illinois University, Wheaton College, William Rainey Harper College

Bird: Cardinal

Motto: State Sovereignty, National Union

Flower: Purple Violet

Tree: White Oak

Residents Called: Illinoisans

Origin of Name: Algonquin Indian for "warriors."

Area: 57,918 square miles (25th largest state)

Statehood: December 3, 1818 (21st state)

Largest Cities: Chicago, Rockford, Aurora, Naperville, Peoria, Springfield, Joliet, Elgin, Waukegan, Cicero

College Band Programs: Eastern Illinois University, Northern Illinois University, Northwestern University, Southern Illinois University- Carbondale, Southern Illinois University-Edwardsville, University of Chicago, University of Illinois

ILLINOIS

AMERICAN CONSERVATORY OF MUSIC
36 South Wabash Ave.
Chicago, IL 60603
Marvin Ziporyn
312-786-1445

AUGUSTANA COLLEGE
DEPARTMENT OF MUSIC
639 38th St.
Rock Island, IL 61201-2296
Rick Jaeschke
309-794-7233
Fax: 309-794-7433
E-mail: mujaeschke@augustana.edu
www.augustana.edu

Several high quality ensembles are available for majors and non-majors.

AURORA UNIVERSITY
DEPARTMENT OF MUSIC
347 S. Gladstone Ave.
Aurora, IL 60506-4877
Valerie Flnn
630-844-6531
Fax: 630-844-5463
E-mail: vflynn@aurora.edu
www.aurora.edu

BLACK HAWK COLLEGE
DEPARTMENT OF MUSIC
6600 34th Ave.
Moline, IL 61265
Jon Palomaki
309-796-5478
Fax: 309-792-3418
E-mail: palomaki@bhc.edu
www.bhc.edu

BLACKBURN COLLEGE
MUSIC DEPARTMENT
600 College Ave.
Carlinville, IL 62626
Elizabeth Zobel
217-854-3232
Fax: 217-854-3713
E-mail: ezobe@mail.blackburn.edu
www.blackburn.edu

BRADLEY UNIVERSITY
CONSTANCE HALL
824 N. Elmwood
Peoria, IL 61625
Dr. David Vroman
309-677-2594
Fax: 309-677-3871
E-mail: dvroman@bradley.edu
www.bradley.edu/cfa/music

The music program at Bradley prepares students for successful careers as teachers or administrators in music, as professional performers, as composers, or as professionals in music-related fields such as music business. The program consists of 75 music majors with 11 full-time and 15 part-time faculty. Strong academics and an active performance program attract students from around the country. Performance opportunities are augmented by participation of some 300 non-music students. At Bradley, full-time students earn credit toward graduation through "tuition-free" ensemble performance. The choral program consists of the Bradley Chorale, women's choir, university chorus and the madrigal singers. The band program consists of the symphonic winds, symphonic band, jazz ensemble, jazz lab band and the basketball band. String students participate in the chamber orchestra with an opportunity to perform with the Peoria Symphony Orchestra or the Knox Galesburg Symphony if audition requirements are met. The curriculum and activities of the department are a blend of tradition and new technologies. The academic facility, Constance

Hall, is being renovated while Dingeldine Music Center continues to offer an outstanding performance venue for solo performers and large ensembles alike. Students interested in Bradley should contact the department directly or the Office of Undergraduate Admissions at (800) 447-6460.

CARL SANDBURG COLLEGE
MUSIC PROGRAM
2400 Tom L. Wilson Blvd.
Galesburg, IL 61401-9574
Tim Pahel
309-341-5317
Fax: 309-341-5441
E-mail: tpahel@csc.cc.il.us
www.csc.cc.il.us

CHICAGO COLLEGE OF PERFORMING ARTS
THE MUSIC CONSERVATORY
430 S. Michigan Ave.
Chicago, IL 60605
Brian J. Wis
312-341-3796
Fax: 312-341-6358
E-mail: bwis@roosevelt.edu
www.roosevelt.edu/ccpa/music/index.htm

CHICAGO SCHOOL OF VIOLIN MAKING
3636 Oakton St.
Skokie, IL 60076
Fred Thompson
847-673-9545
Fax: 847-673-9546

CHICAGO STATE UNIVERSITY
DEPARTMENT OF MUSIC
9501 S. King Dr.
Chicago, IL 60628
Mark Smith

773-995-2155
Fax: 773-995-3767
E-mail: music@csu.edu
www.csu.edu

COLLEGE OF DU PAGE
DEPARTMENT OF MUSIC
425 22nd St.
Glen Ellyn, IL 60137
Lee Kesselman
630-942-3008
Fax: 630-790-9806
E-mail: kesselma@cdnet.cod.edu
www.cod.edu

COLLEGE OF LAKE COUNTY
DEPARTMENT OF MUSIC
19351 W. Washington St.
Grayslake, IL 60030-1148
Bruce Mark
847-543-2040
E-mail: bmack-mus@clc.cc.il.us
www.clc.cc.il.us

COLUMBIA COLLEGE
DEPARTMENT OF MUSIC
72 E. 11th St.
Chicago, IL 60605-2312
William Russo
312-663-9462
Fax: 312-663-0589
www.colum.edu

CONCORDIA UNIVERSITY
DEPARTMENT OF MUSIC
7400 Augusta St.
River Forrest, IL 60305-1402
Steven Wente
708-209-3060
Fax: 708-209-3176
www.curf.edu

DEPAUL COLLEGE
SCHOOL OF MUSIC
804 W. Belden St.
Chicago, IL 60614
Dr. Judy Bundra
773-325-1037
Fax: 773-325-7429
E-mail: jbundra@depaul.edu
http://music.depaul.edu

DePaul University School of Music offers students the unique opportunity to study with professors actively performing at the highest levels of their fields in Chicago, one of the world's great cultural environments. Approximately 390 music majors work toward degrees in performance, jazz studies, music education, composition, sound recording technology and music business with a faculty drawn from members of the Chicago Symphony, Lyric Opera and Chicago's major jazz and chamber musicians. Students perform in symphony orchestra, chamber orchestra, wind ensemble, wind symphony, several choruses, three large jazz ensembles, two annual opera productions and a large number of chamber ensembles. Our music education majors student-teach at the elementary level during their junior year and the middle school and senior high levels during their senior year. SRT majors and music business majors participate in internships with major Chicago-based companies in their chosen field. One hundred percent of our music business, music education and sound recording graduates secure full-time employment in their field of study within a year of graduation, and many of our performance majors have gone on to successful careers. DePaul School of Music Alumni are currently performing with the Chicago Symphony, the Metropolitan Opera, Los Angeles Philharmonic, Berlin Philharmonic, Chicago Opera Theater, Winnipeg Symphony Orchestra, the United States Marine Band, and Grant Park Symphony Orchestra to name a few.

DOMINICAN UNIVERSITY
MUSIC DISCIPLINE
7900 W. Division St.
River Forest, IL 60305
Hugh Mccelwain
708-366-2490
Fax: 708-366-5360
www.dom.edu

EASTERN ILLINOIS UNIVERSITY
MUSIC DEPARTMENT
600 Lincoln Ave.
Charleston, IL 61920
Roger Stoner
217-581-3010
Fax: 217-581-7137
www.eiu.edu

ELGIN COMMUNITY COLLEGE
MUSIC PROGRAM
1700 Spartan Dr.
Elgin, IL 60123-7189
Randall Green
847-697-1000
Fax: 847-931-3921
www.elgin.edu

ELMHURST COLLEGE
190 Prospect Ave.
Elmhurst, IL 60126
Kevin Olsen
630-617-3524
Fax: 630-617-3738
E-mail: kevino@elmhurst.edu
www.elmhurst.edu

EUREKA COLLEGE
DEPARTMENT OF MUSIC
300 E. College Ave.
Eureka, IL 61530

Joseph Henry
309-467-6397
Fax: 309-467-6386
E-mail: Jdhenry@eureka.edu
www.eureka.edu

GOVERNORS STATE UNIVERSITY
DEPARTMENT OF MUSIC
Park Forest, IL 60466
Arthur Bourgeois
708-534-5000
www.govst.edu

GREENVILLE COLLEGE
DEPARTMENT OF MUSIC
315 E. College Ave.
Greenville, IL 62246
Tom Stampfli
618-664-2800
Fax: 618-664-6580
E-mail: Tstampfli@greenville.edu
www.greenville.edu

ILLINOIS COLLEGE
DEPARTMENT OF MUSIC
1101 W. College Ave.
McGaw Room 133
Jacksonville, IL 62650
Garrett Allman
217-245-3384
Fax: 217-245-3470
www.ic.edu

ILLINOIS COUNTY COLLEGE
MUSIC PROGRAM
1 College Dr.
Peoria, IL 61635-0001
Jeffrey Hoover
309-694-5113
Fax: 309-694-8505
E-mail: jhoover@icc.cc.il.us
www.icc.cc.il.us

ILLINOIS STATE UNIVERSITY
SCHOOL OF MUSIC
P.O. Box 5660
Normal, IL 61790
James Major
309-438-8731
Fax: 309-438-5833
E-mail: jmajor@ilstu.edu
www.music.ilstu.edu

ILLINOIS VALLEY COMMUNITY COLLEGE
DEPARTMENT OF MUSIC
815 N. Orlando Smith Ave.
Oglesby, IL 61348
Micheal Peckerek
815-224-2720
www.ivcc.edu

ILLINOIS WESLEYAN UNIVERSITY
SCHOOL OF MUSIC
P.O. Box 2900
Bloomington, IL 61701
Mario Pelusi
309-556-3061
Fax: 309-556-3121
E-mail: mpelusi@titan.iwu.edu
http://sun.iwu.edu/~music

The School of Music at Illinois Wesleyan has enjoyed a tradition of excellence for more than a century, and the future is brighter than ever. A prestigious teaching faculty, admirable facilities and a substantial scholarship program ensure that music will remain a vital force in shaping the lives of Illinois Wesleyan students for years to come.

JOHN A LOGAN COLLEGE
MUSIC PROGRAM
Carterville, IL 62918
Gary Kent
618-985-3741
Fax: 618-985-2248
E-mail: gary.kent@jal.cc.il.us
www.jal.cc.il.us

JOHN WOOD COMMUNITY COLLEGE
DEPARTMENT OF MUSIC
150 S. 48th St.
Quincy, IL 62301-0400
Gary Declue
217-227-6500
www.jwcc.edu

JOLIET JUNIOR COLLEGE
DEPARTMENT OF FINE ARTS AT MUSIC
1215 Houbolt Rd.
Joliet, IL 60431-8938
Thomas Liley
815-280-2232
Fax: 815-280-6729
www.jjc.cc.il.us

JUDSON COLLEGE
MUSIC DEPARTMENT
Elgin, IL 60123
Ernest Gross
847-695-2500
Fax: 847-695-8014
www.judson-il.edu

Judson College has a separate fine arts building, an excellent recital hall with a new Steinway grand piano, music classrooms, practice rooms, faculty teaching studios, and a beautiful chapel with a Steinway concert grand and a large pipe organ. Majors offered include music education, music performance (piano, voice, and orchestral instruments) and music ministry. Music minors and music concentrations are also offered in those areas. Many music graduates hold significant music positions in churches, schools, and the music profession in general. Judson also offers symphonic band, orchestra, jazz ensemble, hand bell choir and chamber singers, all of which perform regularly. The choir tours extensively in the U.S.A. and abroad, including Europe and Brazil in the last four years, and the symphonic band, chamber singers, and hand bell choir also tour. Our 80-acre campus is located in Elgin, Ill. Housing is available. Students find part-time, off-campus employment easily accessible because of its location. Judson is located 30 minutes from O'Hare Airport and one hour from downtown Chicago, the Lyric Opera, the Chicago Symphony Orchestra, the Ravinia Festival, and other performing arts organizations.

KANKAKEE COMMUNITY COLLEGE
DIVISION HUMANITIES AND SOCIAL SCIENCES
P.O. Box 888
Kankakee, IL 60901
Louis Anderson
815-933-0345
Fax: 815-933-0217
www.kcc.cc.il.us

KISHWAUKEE COLLEGE
MUSIC PROGRAM
21193 Malta Rd.
Malta, IL 60150
Rufus Brown
815-825-2086
Fax: 815-825-2072
www.kish.cc.il.us

KNOX COLLEGE
MUSIC DEPARTMENT

2 E. South St.
Galesburg, IL 61401
Bruce Polay
309-341-7208
Fax: 309-341-7090
E-mail: bpolay@knox.edu
www.knox.edu

LAKE FOREST COLLEGE
DEPARTMENT OF MUSIC

555 N. Sheridan Rd.
Lake Forest, IL 60045
Rami Y. Levin
847-735-5170
Fax: 847-735-6192
E-mail: levin@lfc.edu
www.lfc.edu

LEWIS AND CLARK COMMUNITY COLLEGE
DEPARTMENT OF MUSIC

5800 Godfrey Rd.
Godfrey, IL 62035
Harlan Hock
618-467-2233
Fax: 618-467-2240
E-mail: sravers@lc.cc.il.us
www.lc.cc.il.us

LEWIS UNIVERSITY
DEPARTMENT OF MUSIC

1 University Pkwy.
Romeoville, IL 60446
Dr. Lawrence Sisk
815-836-5619
Fax: 815-836-5540
E-mail: siskla@lewisu.edu
www.lewisu.edu

LINCOLN CHRISTIAN COLLEGE
DEPARTMENT OF MUSIC

100 Campus View Dr.
Lincoln, IL 62856
John Sarno
217-732-3168
Fax: 217-732-1729
www.lccs.edu

LINCOLN COLLEGE
MUSIC PROGRAM

5250 Shepherd Rd.
Lincoln, IL 62656
Bill Buffington
217-732-3155
Fax: 217-732-8859
www.llcc.cc.il.us

LINCOLN LAND COMMUNITY COLLEGE
MUSIC PROGRAM

5250 Shepherd Rd.
Springfield, IL 62794
David Laubersheimer
217-786-2240
Fax: 217-786-2340
E-mail: david.laubersheimer@llcc.cc.il.us
www.ll.cc.il.us

LINCOLN TRAIL COLLEGE
DEPARTMENT OF MUSIC

11220 State Hwy. 1
Robinson, IL 62454
Gayle Saunders
618-544-8657
Fax: 618-544-3957

LOYOLA UNIVERSITY CHICAGO
DIVISION OF ARTS AND SCIENCES
6525 N. Sheridan Rd.
Chicago, IL 60626
Eliza Kenney
773-508-2820
Fax: 773-508-8008
E-mail: ekenney@luc.edu
www.luc.edu

MACMURRAY COLLEGE
DEPARTMENT OF MUSIC
East College Ave.
Jacksonville, IL 62650
Jay Peterson
217-479-7000
Fax: 217-479-7078
E-mail: orgpete@mac.edu
www.mac.edu

MCKENDREE COLLEGE
DEPARTMENT OF MUSIC
701 College Rd.
Lebanon, IL 62254
Nancy Ypma
618-537-6922
Fax: 618-537-6259
E-mail: nypma@mckendree.edu
www.mckendree.edu

MILLIKEN UNIVERSITY
SCHOOL OF MUSIC
1184 W. Main St.
Decatur, IL 62522
Mary Ellen Poole
217-424-6300
Fax: 217-420-6652
E-mail: mpoole@mail.millikin.edu
www.millikin.edu

Why study music at Millikin University, the

school for musicians for nearly 100 years? People: 57 gifted, energetic, and dedicated faculty members whose main concern is their students' growth as musicians; lots of individual attention; a student-teacher ratio of 8:1. Facilities: the newly renovated and expanded Perkinson Music Center; 41 new Steinway and Boston pianos. Technology: Millitrax recording studio; a 24-station computer-assisted instruction lab; and a separate MIDI studio for advanced work; Kaeuper Hall for intimate performances and Kirkland Fine Arts Center for grand events. Opportunities: Eight degree programs designed to challenge and prepare students for a life in music; 40 ensembles of all sizes, genres, and media offer multiple performance outlets for every student; cutting-edge curricula in commercial music and music business, and a 100 percent placement rate in music education; young artists awards, the Presser Scholarship, and the Hollis Prize reward superior performance.

MONMOUTH COLLEGE
DEPARTMENT OF MUSIC
700 E. Broadway
Monmouth, IL 61462
Perry White
309-457-2131
Fax: 309-457-2141
E-mail: pwhite@monm.edu
www.monm.edu/academic/music

Degrees: B.A. in Music, Vocal, Music Education

In the first years of this new millennium, the Monmouth College Music Department is well positioned to usher in a new era of quality music education for our students and community. While the Monmouth Chorale continues to be the most prominent music ensemble on our campus, the group has simply paved the way for further developments within the department. Recent renovations to Austin Hall of Music have upgraded teaching and practice spaces, while the $3.3 million renovations to the Dahl Chapel and Auditorium have provided our campus a state of the art rehearsal and performance facility. The resurrection of the Instrumental Music Education Curriculum and the String Ensemble, under the spirited direction of Carolyn Suda, has generated tremendous excitement and forms a portion of our plan to broaden the music curriculum, creating greater visibility for the department and college as a while.

MOODY BIBLE INSTITUTE
DEPARTMENT OF SACRED MUSIC
820 N. La Salle Blvd.
Chicago, IL 60610
Cynthia Uitermarkt
312-329-4080
Fax: 312-329-4098
E-mail: cynthia.uitermarkt@moody.edu
www.moody.edu

MORAINE VALLEY COMMUNITY COLLEGE
DEPARTMENT OF FINE ARTS
10900 S. 88th Ave.
Palos Hills, IL 60465
Robert Reifsnyder
708-974-5215
Fax: 708-974-5366
www.morainevalley.edu

MORTON COLLEGE
DEPARTMENT OF MUSIC
3801 S. Central Ave.
Cicero, IL 60804
Paul Kukec
708-656-8000
www.morton.cc.il.us

NATIONAL-LOUIS UNIVERSITY
DEPARTMENT OF MUSIC
Evanston, IL 60201
Elinor Olin
847-256-5150
Fax: 847-256-1057
www.nl.edu

NORTH CENTRAL COLLEGE
DEPARTMENT OF MUSIC
30 North Braiard St.
Naperville, IL 60540
Larry Van Oyen
630-637-5628
Fax: 630-637-5405
E-mail: lavanoye@noctrl.edu
www.noctrl.edu

NORTH PARK UNIVERSITY
SCHOOL OF MUSIC
3225 W. Foster Ave.
Chicago, IL 60625
Joseph Lill
773-244-5625
Fax: 773-244-5230
E-mail: tshofner-emrich@northpark.edu
www.northpark.edu

NORTHEASTERN ILLINOIS UNIVERSITY
DEPARTMENT OF MUSIC
Chicago, IL 60625
Nelson Mandrell
773-583-2675
Fax: 312-794-6243
E-mail: vc-stifler@neiu.edu
http://neiu.edu

NORTHERN ILLINOIS UNIVERSITY
SCHOOL OF MUSIC

DeKalb, IL 60115
Lynn Slater
815-753-1546
Fax: 815-753-1759
E-mail: lslater@niu.edu
www.niu.edu/music

Degrees: The School of Music at Northern Illinois University offers the Bachelor of Music degree with emphases in performance (including jazz studies), composition, and music education, the Bachelor of Arts, the Master of Music, and the advanced performer's certificate. We also have individualized degree programs for graduate and undergraduate students interested in nontraditional courses of study. The enrollment currently stands at approximately 400 music majors. There are 60 full- and part-time faculty members whose activities are nationally significant. The world-famous Vermeer String Quartet is in residence, and its members teach both graduate and undergraduate string majors.

NIU is the second-largest single-campus university in Illinois, with over 23,000 students. The city of DeKalb, located 65 miles west of Chicago, combines the best urban and rural locales.

NORTHWESTERN UNIVERSITY
SCHOOL OF MUSIC

711 Elgin Rd.
Evanston, IL 60208
Heather Landes
847-491-3141
Fax: 847-467-7440
E-mail: hlandes@northwestern.edu
www.music.northwestern.edu

Degrees: B.A., B.M. and M.M.

Located on the shores of Lake Michigan in Evanston, Illinois, the Northwestern University School of music offers a unique musical education based on tradition, innovation and excellence. The university's 240-acre campus lies just 12 miles north of downtown Chicago and its rich cultural opportunities provide faculty and students with a vibrant educational setting that blends the best of the urban with the suburban.

Established in 1895 as an integral and inseparable part of Northwestern University, the school combines the privileges and resources of an excellent private research university with a nationally ranked music program of conservatory intensity. As one of the oldest degree-granting music schools in the United States, it has been shaped by those dedicated to honoring tradition while pursuing innovation, reflecting an ever-evolving music aesthetic. Its distinguished faculty of musician-scholars, the small and highly qualified student body and the extraordinary breadth of academic programs have brought distinction to the school for more than 100 years, building a foundation for developing the informed musicians, productive scholars and inspired teachers of the 21st century.

OLIVET NAZARENE UNIVERSITY
DEPARTMENT OF MUSIC

One University Ave.
Bourbonnais, IL 60914
Don Reddick
815-939-5110
Fax: 815-939-5112
E-mail: dreddick@olivet.edu
www.olivet.edu/departments/finearts

OLNEY CENTRAL COLLEGE
MUSIC PROGRAM

305 Northwest St.
Olney, IL 62450
Steve Marrs
618-395-7777
Fax: 618-392-3293
E-mail: marrss@iecc.cc.il.us
www.iecc.cc.il.us

PARKLAND COLLEGE
DEPARTMENT OF MUSIC
2400 W. Bradley Ave.
Champaign, IL 61821
David Jones
217-351-2392
Fax: 217-373-3899
www.parkland.edu

PRINCIPIA COLLEGE
DEPARTMENT OF MUSIC
Elsah, IL 62028
Marie Garritson
618-374-5006
Fax: 618-374-5911
E-mail: mbg@prin.edu
ww.prin.edu

QUINCY UNIVERSITY
SCHOOL OF ARTS AND HUMANITIES
1800 College Ave.
Quincy, IL 62301
Dennis Schafer
217-228-5455
Fax: 217-228-5257
www.quincy.edu

REND LAKE COLLEGE
DEPARTMENT OF LIBERAL ARTS
468 N. Key Gray Pkwy.
Ina, IL 62846
Julie Wilkerson
618-437-5321
Fax: 618-437-5677
E-mail: wilkerson@rlc.cc.il.us
www.rlc.cc.il.us

RICHLAND COMMUNITY COLLEGE
DEPARTMENT OF MUSIC
1 College Park
Decatur, IL 62521
Thom Bayuum
217-875-7200
Fax: 217-875-6961
www.richland.cc.il.us

ROCK VALLEY COLLEGE
DIVISION OF HUMANITIES AND FINE ARTS
3301 N. Mulford Rd.
Rockford, IL 61114
Dave Ross
815-639-2570
Fax: 815-654-5359
www.rvc.cc.il.us

ROOSEVELT UNIVERSITY
MUSIC DEPARTMENT
430 South Michigan Ave.
Chicago, IL 60601
Greg MacAyeal
312-341-3648
Fax: 312-341-6394
E-mail: gmacayea@roosevelt.edu
www.roosevelt.edu

SAULK VALLEY COMMUNITY COLLEGE
DEPARTMENT OF MUSIC
173 Illinois Route 2
Dixon, IL 61021
Kris Murray
815-288-5511
Fax: 815-288-1880
www.svcc.edu

SHERWOOD CONSERVATORY OF MUSIC
1312 S. Michigan Ave.

Chicago, IL 60605
Jeff Smith
312-427-6267
Fax: 312-427-6677
www.sherwoodmusic.org

SOUTH SUBURBAN COLLEGE
Department of Music

15800 S. State St.
South Holland, IL 60473
Andrew Hoefle
708-596-2000
Fax: 708-210-5797
E-mail: ahoefle@ssc.cc.il.us
www.ssc.cc.il.us

SOUTHEASTERN ILLINOIS COLLEGE
Department of Music

3575 College Rd.
Harrisburg, IL 62946
Bruce Boone
618-252-5400
Fax: 618-252-3156
E-mail: bboone@sic.cc.il.us
www.sic.il.us/departments/music

SOUTHERN ILLINOIS UNIVERSITY AT CARBONDALE
School of Music

Mailcode 4302
Carbondale, IL 62901
Dr. Robert L. Weiss, Jr.
618-536-8742
Fax: 618-453-5808
E-mail: rweiss@siu.edu
www.siu.edu/~music

SOUTHERN ILLINOIS UNIVERSITY AT EDWARDSVILLE
School of Music

105 Altgeld
Edwardsville, IL 62026
John Korak
618-650-3900
Fax: 618-650-5988
E-mail: jkorak@siue.edu
www.siue.edu/MUSIC/

Degrees: B.A., B.M., M.M.; Undergraduate Specializations: Jazz Performance, Music Education, Music History/Literature, Music Merchandising, Music Performance, Music Theory and Composition; Graduate Specializations: Music Education, Music Performance.

The School of Music offers degrees in performance, music education, piano pedagogy, music business, opera and music theater and theory/composition

SOUTHWESTERN ILLINOIS COLLEGE
Department of Music

2500 Carlyle Ave.
Belleville, IL 62221
Jerry Bolen
618-235-2700
Fax: 618-235-1578
E-mail: bolen@apci.net
www.southwestern.cc.il.us

SPRINGFIELD COLLEGE AT ILLINOIS
Department of Music

1500 North 5th
Springfield, IL 62702
Jeff Garland
217-525-1420
Fax: 217-789-1698
www.sci.edu

ST. XAVIER UNIVERSITY
DEPARTMENT OF MUSIC
3700 W. 103rd St.
Chicago, IL 60655
Dr. Greg Coutts
773-298-3421
Fax: 773-779-9061
E-mail: coutts@sxu.edu
www.sxu.edu

TRINITY CHRISTIAN COLLEGE
DEPARTMENT OF MUSIC
6601 W. College Dr.
Palos Heights, IL 60463
Helen Van Wyck
708-239-4877
Fax: 708-239-4890
E-mail: helen.vanwyck@trnty.edu
www.trnty.edu

TRINITY INTERNATIONAL UNIVERSITY
DEPARTMENT OF MUSIC
2065 Half Day Rd.
Deerfield, IL 60015
Beth Foemmel
847-317-7035
Fax: 847-317-4786
E-mail: bfoemmel@tiu.edu
www.tiu.edu

TRITON COLLEGE
DEPARTMENT OF MUSIC
2000 N. 5th Ave.
River Grove, IL 60171
Shelley Yoelin
708-456-0300
Fax: 708-583-3121
E-mail: syoelin@triton.cc.il.us
www.triton.cc.il.us

UNIVERSITY OF CHICAGO
DEPARTMENT OF MUSIC
Godspeed Hall
1010 E. 59th St.
Chicago, IL 60637
Richard Cohn
773-702-8484
Fax: 773-753-0558
E-mail: music@uchicago.edu
http://music.uchicago.edu

UNIVERSITY OF ILLINOIS AT CHICAGO
DEPARTMENT OF PERFORMING ARTS
1040 W. Harrison St. MC 255
Chicago, IL 60607
Necolia Cade
312-996-2977
Fax: 312-996-0954
E-mail: wmkaplan@uic.edu
www.uic.edu/depts/adpa

This is a smaller program with a low teacher-to-student ratio in an urban setting. A traditional program in theory, history and ear-training or performance track is offered. Private teachers feature outstanding Chicago artist-performers. Ensembles include concert band, jazz ensembles, three choirs, chamber music.

UNIVERSITY OF ILLINOIS AT URBANA
SCHOOL OF MUSIC
1114 W. Nevada
Urbana, IL 61801
Edward Rath
217-333-2620
E-mail: j-rath1@uiuc.edu
www.music.uiuc.edu/music

UNIVERSITY OF ST. FRANCIS
DEPARTMENT OF MUSIC

500 Wilcox St.
Joliet, IL 60435
Patrick Brannon
815-740-3219
Fax: 815-740-4285
E-mail: pbrannon@stfrancis.edu
www.stfrancis.edu

UNIVERSITY OF ST. MARY OF THE LAKE
DEPARTMENT OF MUSIC

1000 E. Maple Ave.
Mundelein, IL 60060
Arlene Michna
847-566-6401
Fax: 847-566-7330
www.vocations.org

VANDERCOOK COLLEGE OF MUSIC

3140 S. Federal St.
Chicago, IL 60616
James P. Malley, Jr.
312-225-6288
Fax: 312-225-5211
E-mail: pberghoff@vandercook.edu
www.vandercook.edu

WESTERN ILLINOIS UNIVERSITY
MUSIC DEPARTMENT

1 University Cir.
Macomb, IL 61455
Dr. Mark Hansen
309-298-1544
Fax: 309-298-1968
www.wiu.edu/music

The Department of Music is an accredited member of the National Association of Schools of Music. It offers a Bachelor of Arts degree in music (with comprehensive options in applied music, music business, music therapy, and teacher certification) and a Master of Arts degree (with options in performance, music education, theory/composition, conducting, and music history/literature). Students may elect study in keyboard, voice, winds, strings, and percussion as well as specialized study in jazz, composition, and conducting. All undergraduate majors and minors must pass entrance performance auditions and placement examinations in music theory, ear-training and piano. Undergraduate scholarships and talent grants are available to students who audition early in the spring semester prior to fall enrollment. All graduate students must meet the general admission requirements of the School of Graduate Studies and must have earned a bachelor's degree or equivalent with a major in music from an accredited institution. Prior to entrance, an advisory examination in music theory and music history/literature is required. Graduate assistantships are available in all areas of study (deadline for applications is April 15 of the year in which fall enrollment is desired).

WHEATON COLLEGE
CONSERVATORY OF MUSIC

Wheaton, IL 60187
Music Department
630-752-5098
www.wheaton.edu/Conservatory

WILLIAM RAINEY HARPER COLLEGE
DEPARTMENT OF MUSIC

1200 W. Algonquin Rd.
Palatine, IL 60067
Cathy Albergo
847-925-6568
Fax: 847-925-6582
E-mail: calbergo@harper.cc.il.us
www.harpercollege.edu

INDIANA

Population: 6,248,801 (2003 Estimate)

Capital City: Indianapolis

Music Colleges and Universities: Ancilla College, Anderson University, Associated Mennonite Biblical Seminary, Ball State University, Bethel College, Butler University, Christian Theological Seminary, DePauw University School of Music, Earlham College, Goshen College, Grace College, Hanover College, Huntington College, Illinois Wesleyan University, Indiana State University, Indiana University at Bloomington, Indiana University at Purdue, Indiana University at South Bend, Indiana University at Southeast, Indiana Wesleyan University, Manchester College, Marian College, Oakland City University, Purdue University, St. Joseph's College, St. Mary of the Woods College, St. Mary's College, Taylor University at Upland, The University of Indianapolis, University of Evansville, University of Indianapolis, University of Notre Dame, Valparaiso University, Vincennes University, Wabash College

Bird: Cardinal

Motto: The Crossroads of America

Flower: Peony

Tree: Tulip tree

Residents Called: Hoosiers

Origin of Name: "Land of the Indians"

Area: 36,420 square miles (38th state)

Statehood: December 11, 1816 (19th state)

Largest Cities: Indianapolis, Fort Wayne, Evansville, South Bend, Gary, Hammond, Bloomington, Muncie, Anderson, Terre Haute

College Band Programs: Ball State University, Indiana University, Purdue University, University of Notre Dame

INDIANA

ANCILLA COLLEGE
DEPARTMENT OF MUSIC
P.O. Box 1
Donaldson, IN 46513
Diann Rasch
E-mail: drasch@ancilla.edu
www.ancilla.edu

ANDERSON UNIVERSITY
DEPARTMENT OF MUSIC
1100 East 5th St.
Anderson, IN 46012
Dr. Jeffery Wright
765-641-4450
Fax: 765-641-3809
E-mail: jwright@anderson.edu
www.anderson.edu

Since its beginning in 1917, music has played a significant role in the life of Anderson University. That tradition continues today. The music department at A.U. is thriving with vibrant students, accomplished faculty, high caliber performances, challenging classes, and satisfying musical experiences. The music department offers four degree programs: music performance, music education, music business and church music. The music performance degree program prepares students with the basic knowledge and skills needed to pursue a career in instrumental or vocal performance. The music education degree program prepares students for a career in teaching instrumental and choral music in elementary and secondary schools. The music business degree program prepares students for a career in one of the many facets of the music industry. The church music degree program prepares students to lead music ministries and assist the church in worship through music. Audition information: all students who want to major in music at Anderson University must complete an audition before registering for music classes. For audition dates, requirements and forms, please contact the music department office at (800) 428-6414, ext. 4450. The department of music at Anderson University is an accredited institutional member of the National Association of Schools of Music.

ASSOCIATED MENNONITE BIBLICAL SEMINARY
DEPARTMENT OF CHURCH AND MINISTRY
3003 Benham Ave.
Elkhart, IN 46517
Rebecca Slough
219-295-3726
Fax: 219-295-0092
E-mail: rslough@ambs.edu
www.ambs.edu

BALL STATE UNIVERSITY
SCHOOL OF MUSIC
Muncie, IN 47306
Erwin Mueller
765-285-5506
Fax: 765-285-5401
E-mail: emueller@bsu.edu
www.bsu.edu/cfa

BETHEL COLLEGE
DEPARTMENT OF MUSIC
1001 W. McKinley Ave.
Mishawaka, IN 46545
Susan Holmes
219-257-3393
Fax: 219-257-3326
E-mail: holmess@bethelcollege.edu
www.bethelcollege.edu

BUTLER UNIVERSITY
JORDAN COLLEGE OF FINE ARTS
4600 Sunset Blvd.
Indianapolis, IN 46208
Suzan Zurbuchen
317-940-9231
Fax: 317-940-9658
E-mail: szurbuch@butler.edu
www.butler.edu

Jordan College of Fine Arts has a distinguished tradition extending from the year 1895, when the Metropolitan School of Music was founded. The name was changed to Jordan College of Fine Arts in 1978. The primary mission of the college is to educate students in the arts as professions by means of its undergraduate and graduate programs. Such an education integrates training in the arts as disciplines while developing a lifetime commitment to creativity and communication, nurturing the view of the arts as interrelated and responsible to society. The college is housed in Lilly Hall, which is being expanded beginning Fall of 2001 with a three-story addition to the building. The new Center for Arts and Culture, scheduled to break ground in 2002-03, will give Butler University a second performance hall, to complement the existing 2,200-seat Clowes Memorial Hall.

CHRISTIAN THEOLOGICAL SEMINARY
PROGRAM IN CHURCH MUSIC
1000 W. 42nd St.
Indianapolis, IN 46208-3301
Frank Brown
317-931-2343
Fax: 317-931-2399
E-mail: jkrauser@cts.edu
www.cts.edu

DE PAUW UNIVERSITY
SCHOOL OF MUSIC
600 S. Locust St.
Greencastle, IN 46135-1944
Verna S. Abe
765-658-4395
Fax: 765-658-4042
E-mail: vabe@depauw.edu
www.depauw.edu

Degrees: B.A., B.M., and M.M.

The DePauw University School of Music has been training talented students for more than one hundred years. With one of the finest undergraduate music programs in the country, set in the midst of one of the nation's greatest liberal arts universities, DePauw students have the unique opportunities to experience the best of both worlds. DePauw University offers a wide range of musical possibilities. In addition to the traditional majors in music performance and music education, students can also major in music/business or pursue a double major curriculum. Students can participate in choirs, university band, symphonic orchestra, jazz ensemble, and combos, chamber music or an opera production. Whether you want to major in music or any of the other forty-two majors offered at DePauw, you will have the luxury of keeping your options open.

DEPAUW UNIVERSITY SCHOOL OF MUSIC
SCHOOL OF MUSIC
701 S. College Ave.
Greencastle, IN 46135-0037
Lisa D. Bruns
765-658-4380
Fax: 765-653-4042
E-mail: ldburns@depauw.edu
www.depauw.edu/music

EARLHAM COLLEGE
DEPARTMENT OF MUSIC
801 National Rd.
Richmond, IN 47374-4095
Daniel Graves
765-983-1200
Fax: 765-983-1247
E-mail: dang@earlham.edu
www.earlham.edu

GOSHEN COLLEGE
DEPARTMENT OF MUSIC
1700 S. Main St.
Goshen, IN 46526
Debra Kauffman
574-535-7361
Fax: 574-535-7609
E-mail: deblk@goshen.edu
www.goshen.edu

GRACE COLLEGE
DEPARTMENT OF MUSIC
Music Department
200 Seminary Dr.
Winona Lake, IN 46590
Dr. Peter Gano
219-372-5100
Fax: 219-372-5138
E-mail: music@grace.edu
www.grace.edu

HANOVER COLLEGE
DEPARTMENT OF MUSIC
P.O. Box 890
Hanover, IN 47243
Kimm Hollis
812-866-7342
Fax: 812-866-7114
E-mail: hollis@hanover.edu
www.hanover.edu

HUNTINGTON COLLEGE
DEPARTMENT OF MUSIC
2303 College Ave.
Huntington, IN 46750
Janice Fulbright
219-359-4266
Fax: 219-359-4249
E-mail: jfulbright@huntington.edu
www.huntington.edu/music

INDIANA STATE UNIVERSITY
DEPARTMENT OF MUSIC
FA 402
Terre Haute, IN 47809
Dr. Todd Sullivan
812-237-2771
Fax: 812-237-3009
E-mail: misulliv@ruby.indstate.edu
www.indstate.edu/music

INDIANA UNIVERSITY AT BLOOMINGTON
ADMISSIONS
School of Music
1201 E. Third St.
Bloomington, IN 47405
Jeff Clanton
812-855-2435
Fax: 812-855-4936
E-mail: musdean@indiana.edu
www.music.indiana.edu

Central to this program is a faculty of 150 teachers and scholars and a select student body. The quality of the School of Music faculty has four times led the deans and faculty members of the country's music schools to rank IU number one in the nation. More than 1,600 students from throughout the United States and from 35 foreign countries attend the School of Music during the school year. The facilities of the School of Music include six buildings housing more than 100 offices and studios, 200 practice rooms, choral and instrumental rehearsal rooms, three recital halls, and a music library with more than 380,000 books, scores, microfilms, and periodicals and nearly 160,000 recordings. The School of Music is highlighted by the Musical Arts Center, a complex featuring an acoustically-refined auditorium and a stage with technical capabilities unequaled by any other U.S. university facility.

INDIANA UNIVERSITY AT PURDUE
SCHOOL OF MUSIC
525 North Blackford
Indianapolis, IN 46202
G. David Peters
317-274-4000
Fax: 317-274-2590
www.iupui.edu

INDIANA UNIVERSITY AT SOUTH BEND
DEPARTMENT OF MUSIC
1700 Mishawaka Ave.
P.O. Box 1700
South Bend, IN 46634-1700
Christine Seitz
219-237-4134
Fax: 219-237-4317
www.iusb.edu

INDIANA UNIVERSITY AT SOUTHEAST
DEPARTMENT OF MUSIC
4201 Grant Line Rd.
New Albany, IN 47150-2158
Kurt Sander
812-941-2655
E-mail: ksander@ius.edu
www.ius.edu/music

INDIANA WESLEYAN UNIVERSITY
DIVISION OF MUSIC
4201 S. Washington St.
Marion, IN 46953
Dr. Todd Guy
765-677-2152
Fax: 765-677-2620
E-mail: tguy@indwes.edu
www.indwes.edu

MANCHESTER COLLEGE
DEPARTMENT OF MUSIC
604 E. College Ave.
North Manchester, IN 46962
Debora DeWitt
219-982-5292
Fax: 219-982-5043
E-mail: dedewiit@manchester.edu
www.manchester.edu

MARIAN COLLEGE
DEPARTMENT OF PERFORMANCE ARTS
3200 Cold Spring Rd.
Indianapolis, IN 46222
Phillip Kern
317-955-6108
Fax: 317-955-6448
E-mail: pkern@marian.edu
www.marian.edu

OAKLAND CITY UNIVERSITY
DEPARTMENT OF MUSIC
143 Lucretia St.
Oakland City, IN 47660
Jean Cox
812-749-4781
Fax: 812-749-1233
E-mail: vjcox40@gibsoncounty.net
www.ocu.edu

PURDUE UNIVERSITY
DEPARTMENT OF UNIVERSITY BANDS
1514 Elliot Hall of Music
West Lafayette, IN 47907
David Leppla
317-494-0770
Fax: 317-496-2822
E-mail: bandsinfo@purdue.edu
www.purdue.edu/bands
Degrees: Elementary Education Majors,
Minor in Music Theory, Music History.
Six of the division's courses fulfill general education requirements in the B.A.
and B.S. degrees in the schools of the liberal arts.

ST. JOSEPH'S COLLEGE
DEPARTMENT OF MUSIC
P.O. Box 932
Rensselaer, IN 47978
John Egan
219-866-6205
Fax: 219-866-4497
E-mail: johne@saintjoe.edu
www.saintjoe.edu

ST. MARY OF THE WOODS COLLEGE
DEPARTMENT OF MUSIC
St. Mary of the Woods, IN 47876
Laurette Bellamy
812-535-5180
Fax: 812-535-4613
E-mail: lbellamy@smwc.edu
www.smwc.edu

ST. MARY'S COLLEGE
DEPARTMENT OF MUSIC
313 Moreau Center for the Arts
Notre Dame, IN 46556
Nancy Menk
219-284-4632
Fax: 219-284-4884
E-mail: nmenk@saintmarys.edu
www.saintmarys.edu/~music

TAYLOR UNIVERSITY AT UPLAND
DEPARTMENT OF MUSIC
236 W. Reade Ave.
Upland, IN 46989
Albert Harrison
765-998-5232
Fax: 765-998-4910
E-mail: alharriso@tayloru.edu
www.tayloru.edu

THE UNIVERSITY OF INDIANAPOLIS
1400 E. HANNA AVE.
Indianapolis, IN 46227
317-788-3255
www.uindy.edu

UNIVERSITY OF EVANSVILLE
DEPARTMENT OF MUSIC
1800 Lincoln Ave.
Evansville, IN 47722
Eva Kay
812-479-2742
Fax: 812-479-2101
E-mail: music@evansville.edu
http://music.evansville.edu

Degrees: B.M., B.S. and B.A.

When you are accepted to the university of Evansville's department of music, you join a community of students and artist-teachers who work together to achieve artistic excellence and professional success. In all degrees, emphasis is placed on your academic, creative and technical development and your career preparation and placement. Faculty mentors will advise you in career choices and offer ongoing support, guidance, and networking in your artistic and scholarly activities.

UNIVERSITY OF INDIANAPOLIS
DEPARTMENT OF MUSIC
1400 E. Hanna Ave.
Indianapolis, IN 46227
Dr. Jo Ann Domb
317-788-3255
Fax: 317-788-6105
E-mail: lessig@uindy.edu
http://music.uindy.edu/~music

UNIVERSITY OF NOTRE DAME
DEPARTMENT OF MUSIC
105 Crowley Hall of Music
Notre Dame, IN 46556
Paul Johnson
219-631-6211
Fax: 219-631-4539
E-mail: music@nd.edu
www.nd.edu/~music

Degrees: B.A., M.M., M.A. minors also offered

The department of music at the University of Notre Dame offers intensive professional training in music to students in performance, musicology, and theory. Students in the department's music programs receive extensive personal attention and close supervision from a faculty that is itself extremely active in the professional musical world. The department's programs provide its majors with the opportunity to receive the essential experiences and background to help prepare them for careers in music. In addition, the department features small class sizes and well-equipped classrooms and studios, all within a university, the proud history of which extends over 150 years.

At Notre Dame, students have an opportunity to work directly with an accomplished faculty active in both performance and scholarship. The faculty performers maintain a busy schedule of recitals on and off campus. The department's musicologists, theorists, and composers are well known for their publications and compositions.

VALPARAISO UNIVERSITY
DEPARTMENT OF MUSIC
VU Center for the Arts
Valparaiso, IN 46383
Katharine Wehling
219-464-5454
Fax: 219-464-5244
www.valpo.edu/music

Valparaiso's department of music, fully accredited by the National Association of Schools of Music, offers liberal and professional degree programs in music, balancing practical training and experiences in music with academic foundations in music and general studies. It occupies the VU Center for the Arts, dedicated in 1995, which functions as a working laboratory for performance, production, presentation, and management of arts events, as well as for academic study. Its dedicated faculty of artist-teachers are committed to helping students develop as musicians and as people. Valparaiso University is a private university associated with the Lutheran church, with 3,500 students drawn from across the U.S. and many foreign countries. Approximately 150 students major in music, and hundreds more take part in music ensembles, studio lessons, and elective studies.

VINCENNES UNIVERSITY
DEPARTMENT OF MUSIC

1002 N. 1st St.
Vinvennes, IN 47591
Scott Mercer
812-888-4175
Fax: 812-888-5531
E-mail: smercer@indian.vinu.edu
www.vinu.edu

WABASH COLLEGE
MUSIC DEPARTMENT

301 W. Wabash Ave.
Crawfordsville, IN 47933
Steve Klein
765-361-6089
Fax: 765-361-6341
E-mail: danbyj@wabash.edu
www.wabash.edu/depart/music

The fine arts have played a large part in the lives of Wabash College students, faculty, and community members since 1841, and they continue to be central to the liberal arts curriculum and to the college community. The Fine Arts Center is home to the department of music, as well as the theater, art and speech departments. The building includes a concert hall, a lecture hall suitable for recitals and multi-media presentations, practice rooms, classrooms, faculty studios, and electronic music studios, a suite of three studios that support a variety of educational and research activities. A wide variety of musical instruments are available for student use, including a Boesendorfer concert piano, grand pianos for practicing, a Dowd harpsichord, a pipe organ (in the college chapel), and wind, brass, string and percussion instruments. The Wabash Music Department has a number of ensembles, including a glee club, orchestra, brass ensemble, brass quintet, jazz big band, jazz improvisation combo, string quartet, and the Wamidan World Music Ensemble. The music department offers a variety of courses in music history, theory, analysis, composition, electronic music, world music and special topics courses in American music, music and technology, and instrument design.

IOWA

Population: 2,962,721 (2003 Estimate)

Capital City: Des Moines

Music Colleges and Universities: Briar Cliff College, Buena Vista University, Central College, Clarke College, Clinton Community College, Coe College, Cornell College, Drake University, Grinnell College, Iowa State University, Iowa Wesleyan College, Iowa Western College, Kirkwood Community College, Loras College, Luther College, Maharishi University of Management, Morningside College, Mount Mercy College, Mount St. Clare College, North Iowa Area Community College, Northwestern College, Simpson College, Southeastern Community College, St. Ambrose University, University of Dubuque, University of Iowa, University of Northern Iowa, Upper Iowa University, Vennard College, Waldorf College, Wartburg College, Western Iowa Tech Community College, William Penn College

Bird: Eastern Goldfinch

Motto: Our liberties we prize and our rights we will maintain

Flower: Wild Prairie Rose

Tree: Oak

Residents Called: Iowans

Origin of Name: The word "Iowa" comes from the American Indian tribe of the same name.

Area: 56,276 square miles (26th largest state)

Statehood: December 28, 1846 (29th state)

Largest Cities: Des Moines, Cedar Rapids, Davenport, Sioux City, Waterloo, Iowa City, Council Bluffs, Dubuque, Ames, Cedar Falls

College Band Programs: Iowa State University, University of Iowa

IOWA

BRIAR CLIFF COLLEGE
DEPARTMENT OF MUSIC
3303 Rebecca St.
Sioux City, IA 51104
Mary Day
712-279-5567
Fax: 712-279-1698
E-mail: daym@briarcliff.edu
www.briarcliff.edu

BUENA VISTA UNIVERSITY
DEPARTMENT OF MUSIC
610 West Fourth St.
Storm Lake, IA 50588
Jerry Bertrand
712-749-2176
Fax: 712-749-2037
E-mail: bertrand@bvu.edu
www.bvu.edu

CENTRAL COLLEGE
DEPARTMENT OF MUSIC
P.O. Box 6100
Pella, IA 50219
Sue Cerwinske
515-628-5236
Fax: 515-628-5316
www.central.edu

CLARKE COLLEGE
DEPARTMENT OF MUSIC
1500 Clarke Dr.
Dubuque, IA 52001
Catherine Hendel
319-588-6412
Fax: 319-588-6789
E-mail: khendel@keller.clarke.edu
www.clarke.edu

CLINTON COMMUNITY COLLEGE
DEPARTMENT OF MUSIC
1000 Lincoln Blvd.
Clinton, IA 52732-6224
Maurice Rogers
319-244-7001
Fax: 319-242-7868
E-mail: mrogers@clintoncc.suny.edu
http://clintoncc.suny.edu

COE COLLEGE
DEPARTMENT OF MUSIC
1220 First Ave. N.E.
Cedar Rapids, IA 52402
Sharon Kay Stang
319-399-8521
Fax: 319-399-8209
E-mail: btiede@coe.edu
www.coe.edu

Coe offers a bachelor of music degree for those interested in studying music at the graduate level, teaching music in the public schools, or preparing for a career in performance or composition. Also available is a Bachelor of Arts degree with a major in music. Coe's music facility, Marquis Hall, includes a music library with an excellent and comprehensive collection, spacious rehearsal areas, an electronic music and recording studio, classrooms, and individual practice rooms. Two concert halls are available for performances. Coe College is a private liberal arts school with an enrollment of 1,300 students representing most states and 20 foreign countries. Coe offers more than 40 areas of study in Bachelor of Arts degrees, plus the Master of Arts in teaching. For admission information, call (800) 332-8404 or visit the web site.

CORNELL COLLEGE
MUSIC DEPARTMENT

600 First St. West
Mount Vernon, IA 52314
Dr. Donald Chamberlain
319-895-4228
Fax: 319-895-5926
E-mail:
dchamberlain@cornellcollege.edu
www.cornellcollege.edu

DRAKE UNIVERSITY
HARMON FINE ARTS CENTER

Des Moines, IA 50311-4505
Dr. Chiu-Ling Lin
515-271-3975
Fax: 515-271-2558
E-mail: Chiu-Ling.Lin@drake.edu
www.drake.edu

GRINNELL COLLEGE
DEPARTMENT OF MUSIC

Grinnell, IA 50112
Roger Vetter
641-269-3067
Fax: 641-269-4420
E-mail: vetter@grinnell.edu
www.grinnell.edu/music

The department of music is in a highly selective, national liberal arts college. Performance ensembles include orchestra, choirs, band, early music, gamelan, jazz, percussion, gospel choir, Latin American ensemble and chamber music. Private lessons offered in 25 areas. All programs are open equally to major and non-majors. Recently built and renovated facilities.

IOWA STATE UNIVERSITY
DEPARTMENT OF MUSIC

157 Music Hall
Ames, IA 50011
Dr. Sue Haug
515-294-5364
Fax: 515-294-6409
E-mail: shaug@iastate.edu
www.music.iastate.edu

The ISU Music Department offers an outstanding program of instruction for music majors as well as a wide variety of opportunities for non-majors including: a four-year professional course of study in music, culminating in one of four undergraduate degree options; many performance opportunities, including participation in one of over 20 large and small ensembles; opportunities to study with a distinguished faculty; many academic courses in music history and theory, some designed especially for the general student; and outstanding cultural offerings in the performing arts.

IOWA WESLEYAN COLLEGE
DEPARTMENT OF MUSIC

601 N. Main
Mount Pleasant, IA 52641
Carl Moehlman
319-385-8021
Fax: 319-385-6286
E-mail: moehlman@iwc.edu
www.iwc.edu

IOWA WESTERN COLLEGE
DEPARTMENT OF MUSIC

2700 College Rd.
Council Bluffs, IA 51503-0567
Viola Bichel
www.iwcc.cc.ia.us

KIRKWOOD COMMUNITY COLLEGE

Music Program
P.O. Box 2068
Cedar Rapids, IA 52406
Rhonda Kekke
319-398-4913
Fax: 319-398-1021
www.kirkwood.cc.ia.us

LORAS COLLEGE
DEPARTMENT OF MUSIC

1450 Alta Vista
Dubuque, IA 52001
Brian Hughes
319-588-7153
Fax: 319-557-4086
E-mail: bhughes@loras.edu
www.loras.edu

LUTHER COLLEGE
DEPARTMENT OF MUSIC

700 College Dr.
Decorah, IA 52101
John Strauss
563-387-1208
Fax: 563-387-1076
www.luther.edu

MAHARISHI UNIVERSITY OF MANAGEMENT
DEPARTMENT OF MUSIC

Fairfield, IA 52556
Paul Fauerso
515-472-7000
www.mum.edu

MORNINGSIDE COLLEGE
MUSIC DEPARTMENT

1501 Morningside Ave.
Sioux City, IA 51106
Lance Lehmberg
712-274-5218
Fax: 712-274-5280
E-mail: lehmberg@morningside.edu
http://music.morningside.edu

Morningside College offers a great deal of large-school and large-city musical opportunities in a close-knit liberal arts environment. Many scholarship opportunities lower the cost to below that of many state universities.

MOUNT MERCY COLLEGE
DEPARTMENT OF MUSIC

1330 Elmhurst Dr. N.E.
Cedar Rapids, IA 52402
Bruce Sternfield
319-363-8213
Fax: 319-363-5270
www.mtmercy.edu

MOUNT ST. CLARE COLLEGE
DEPARTMENT OF MUSIC

400 N. Bluff Blvd.
Clinton, IA 52732
Robert Engelson
319-242-4023
Fax: 319-242-2003
E-mail: robeng@clare.edu
www.clare.edu

NORTH IOWA AREA COMMUNITY COLLEGE
DEPARTMENT OF MUSIC

500 College Dr.
Mason City, IA 50401
James Zirnhelt
515-421-4241
Fax: 515-424-1711
www.niacc.cc.ia.us

NORTHWESTERN COLLEGE
ADMISSIONS
101 College Lane
Orange City, IA 51041
Ron De John
800-747-4757
Fax: 712-737-7164
E-mail: admissions@nwciowa.edu
www.nwciowa.edu

Degrees: B.A.

Among a select group of music programs listed in Rugg's Recommendations on the colleges, Northwestern College's music department is distinguished by its commitment to integrate the Christian faith in all areas. Majors are offered in music, music education and music ministry, with pre-professional programs in music performance and music therapy. Northwestern's faculty are active composers, conductors, clinicians and performers who encourage student collaboration. The department's ensembles—the A capella Choir, Brass Quintet, Heritage Singers (mixed chamber choir), Jazz Band, Percussion Ensemble, String Quartet, Symphonette, Symphonic Band, Women's Chorus and Woodwind Quintet— perform in the award-winning 1,000-seat Christ Chapel/Performing Arts Center. The adjoining DeWitt Music Hall houses rehearsal rooms for ensembles, practice rooms, a music library, classrooms and an electronic music lab. Alumni have performed with the International Youth Wind Orchestra, earned Ph.D. degrees in music, won teaching awards, served as music ministers and provided music therapy. Numerous scholarships are available.

SIMPSON COLLEGE
DEPARTMENT OF MUSIC
701 North C St.
Indianola, IA 50125
Deborah Terry
515-961-1637
Fax: 515-961-1498

E-mail: terry@storm.simpson.edu
www.simspon.edu

SOUTHEASTERN COMMUNITY COLLEGE
DEPARTMENT OF MUSIC
P.O. Box F
West Burlington, IA 52655
Deigh Pirrle
319-752-2731
Fax: 319-752-4957
www.secc.cc.ia.us

SOUTHWESTERN COMMUNITY COLLEGE
SCHOOL FOR MUSIC VOCATION
Creston, IA 50801
Phil Matlson
515-782-7081
Fax: 515-782-3312
www.southwest.cc.nc.us

ST. AMBROSE UNIVERSITY
DEPARTMENT OF MUSIC
Davenport, IA 52803
Keith Haan
563-333-6149
Fax: 563-333-6248
E-mail: HaanKeithA@sau.edu
www.sau.edu/music

UNIVERSITY OF DUBUQUE
DEPARTMENT OF MUSIC
2000 University Ave.
Dubuque, IA 52001
Music Department
319-589-3249
Fax: 319-589-3244
www.dbq.edu

UNIVERSITY OF IOWA
ALL STATE MUSIC CAMP
1064 Voxman Music Bldg
Iowa City, IA 52242
L. Kevin Kastens
319-335-1603
Fax: 319-353-2637
E-mail: music-admissions@uiowa.edu
www.uiowa.edu/~music

UNIVERSITY OF IOWA
BAND DEPARTMENT
Iowa City, IA 52242
Dr. Myron Welch
319-335-1635
Fax: 319-353-2555
E-mail: myron-welch@uiowa.edu
www.uiowa.edu/~music/bands.html

UNIVERSITY OF NORTHERN IOWA
SCHOOL OF MUSIC
131 Russell Hall
Cedar Falls, IA 50614
Alan Schmitz
319-273-7180
E-mail: Alan.Schmitz@uni.edu
www.uni.edu/music/web

UPPER IOWA UNIVERSITY
DIVISION OF LIBERAL ARTS
P.O. Box 1857
Fayette, IA 52142
Music Department
319-425-5244
Fax: 319-425-5379
www.uiu.edu

VENNARD COLLEGE
DEPARTMENT OF MUSIC
P.O. Box 29
University Park, IA 52595
Sally Hart
515-673-8391
www.vennard.edu

WALDORF COLLEGE
DEPARTMENT OF MUSIC
106 S. 6th St.
Forrest City, IA 50436
Brad Creswell
515-582-8177
Fax: 515-582-8194
E-mail: creswellb@waldorf.edu
www.waldorf.edu

WARTBURG COLLEGE
22 9th St. N.W.
Waverly, IA 50677
Ania Meinert
800-772-2300
Fax: 319-352-8501
www.wartburg.edu

WESTERN IOWA TECH COMMUNITY COLLEGE

BAND INSTRUMENT TECHNOLOGY

4647 Stone Ave.
Sioux City, IA 51106
Larry Balanos
712-274-6400
Fax: 712-274-6412
E-mail: siljenr@witcc.com
www.witcc.com

Western Iowa Tech offers a complete course in
the repair and restoration of woodwind and
brass instruments. Design is also available for
those who plan to enter the band instrument
repair profession.

WILLIAM PENN COLLEGE

DEPARTMENT OF FINE ARTS

201 Trueblood Ave.
Oskaloosa, IA 52577
Anita Meinert
515-673-1063
Fax: 505-673-1396
E-mail: meinerta@wmpenn.edu
www.wmpenn.edu

KANSAS

Population: 2,753,245 (2003 Estimate)

Capital City: Topeka

Music Colleges and Universities: Allen County Community College, Baker University, Barclay College, Benedictine College, Bethany College, Bethel College, Central Christian College, Cloud County Community, Coffeyville Community College, Dodge City Community College, Emporia State University, Fort Hays State University, Fort Scott Community College, Garden City Community College, Hesston College, Hutchinson Community Junior College, Independence Community College, Johnson County Community College, Kansas City Kansas Community College, Kansas State University, Kansas Wesleyan University, Labette Community College, Manhattan Christian College, McPherson College, Neosho County Community College, Newman University, Ottawa University, Pittsburgh State University, Seward County Community College, Southwestern College, Sterling College, Tabor College, University of Kansas, Washburn University, Wichita State University

Bird: Western Meadowlark

Motto: Ad astra per aspera – To the stars through difficulties

Flower: Sunflower

Tree: Cottonwood

Residents Called: Kansans

Origin of Name: From the Sioux Indian for "south wind people."

Area: 82,282 square miles (15th largest state)

Statehood: January 29, 1861 (34th state)

Largest Cities: Wichita, Overland Park, Kansas City, Topeka, Olathe, Lawrence, Shawnee, Salina, Manhattan, Hutchinson

College Band Programs: Kansas State University, University of Kansas

KANSAS

ALLEN COUNTY COMMUNITY COLLEGE
DEPARTMENT OF MUSIC
1801 North Cottonwood St.
Iola, KS 66749
Bradley Herdon
316-365-8308
E-mail: herndon@allencc.net
www.allen.cc.ks.us

BAKER UNIVERSITY
MUSIC DEPARTMENT
408 W. Eighth St.
Baldwin City, KS 66006
John Buehler
785-594-5252
Fax: 785-594-4546
E-mail: jbuehler@harvey.bakeru.edu
www.bakeru.edu

Baker music students have all the advantages an intimate, small college environment affords plus the performance opportunities of much larger schools. Baker University music ensembles enjoy major international concert tours every three years and Baker choirs have sung with the Kansas City Symphony during recent terms. The ability to offer serious music students both depth and breadth in the music experience makes Baker's music program truly unique. Baker is regarded as the top private college in Kansas and has been ranked among the top private schools in the nation by Money magazine, one of the "300 Best Buys" in America by "Barron's Best Buys in College Education", and one of the top 35 universities in the Midwest by U.S. News and World Report.

BARCLAY COLLEGE
DEPARTMENT OF MUSIC
607 Kingman Rd.
Haviland, KS 67059
Steven Elmore
316-862-5252
Fax: 316-862-5403
E-mail: elmst@barclaycollege.edu
www.barclaycollege.edu

BENEDICTINE COLLEGE
MUSIC DEPARTMENT
1020 N. 2nd St.
Atchison, KS 66002
Dr. Ruth E. Krusemark
913-360-7598
Fax: 913-367-6324
E-mail: ruthk@benedictine.edu
www.benedictine.edu

The music department at Benedictine College is a comprehensive music program accredited by the National Association of Schools of Music within the context of the Benedictine College Mission: liberal arts, Benedictine, residential, and catholic.

BETHANY COLLEGE
DEPARTMENT OF MUSIC
421 N. First St.
Lindsborg, KS 67456-1897
Paul Tegels
785-227-3311
Fax: 785-227-2004
www.bethanylb.edu

BETHEL COLLEGE
MUSIC DEPARTMENT
300 E. 27th St.
North Newton, KS 67117
Shirley King
316-284-5296
Fax: 316-284-5286
E-mail: kschlab@bethelks.edu
www.bethelks.edu/academics/music

CENTRAL CHRISTIAN COLLEGE
DEPARTMENT OF MUSIC
1200 S. Main St.
P.O. Box 1403
Mc Pherson, KS 67460-5740
Thomas Seaman
316-241-0723
Fax: 316-241-6032
E-mail:
tom.seaman@centralchristian.edu
www.centralchristian.edu

CLOUD COUNTY COMMUNITY
DEPARTMENT OF MUSIC
P.O. Box 1002
Concordia, KS 66901-1002
Everett Miller
785-243-1435
Fax: 785-243-1043
www.cloudccc.cc.ks.us

COFFEYVILLE COMMUNITY COLLEGE
DEPARTMENT OF MUSIC
11th Willow
Coffeyville, KS 67337
Justin Writer
316-251-7700
Fax: 316-251-7798
E-mail: justinw@raven.ccc.cc.ks.us
www.ccc.cc.ks.us

DODGE CITY COMMUNITY COLLEGE
DEPARTMENT OF MUSIC
2501 N. 14th Ave.
Dodge City, KS 67801-2316
Dana Waters
620-225-1321
Fax: 620-227-9200
E-mail: fdurant@dccc.cc.ks.us
www.dccc.cc.ks.us

EMPORIA STATE UNIVERSITY
MUSIC DEPARTMENT
1200 Commercial Rd.
P.O. Box 4029
Emporia, KS 66801
Marie Miller
620-341-5431
Fax: 620-341-5601
E-mail: millerma@emporia.edu
www.emporia.edu

Nationally accredited music program within a Liberal Arts University. Opportunities for advanced studies in all instruments, composition, music theory, music history, and music education. Facilities include the newly renovated Beach Music Hall and the new Shepherd Music Center, constructed in 2000. The facility houses a state-of-the-art music computer laboratory, electronic composition studio, recital hall, and keyboard laboratory. Degree programs prepare students for active careers in music and for graduate and doctoral music studies. The bachelor of music education degree offers a K-12 State of Kansas certification to teach vocal and instrumental music. The Music Department currently has 100 percent placement rate of its music education graduates.

FORT HAYS STATE UNIVERSITY
DEPARTMENT OF MUSIC
600 Park St.
Hays, KS 67601
Dr.Timothy Crowley
785-628-4226
Fax: 785-628-4227
E-mail: tcrowley@fhsu.edu
www.fhsu.edu/music

FORT SCOTT COMMUNITY COLLEGE
DEPARTMENT OF MUSIC
2108 S. Horton St.
Fort Scott, KS 66701-3140
Gregory Turner
620-223-2700
Fax: 620-223-4927
www.ftscott.cc.ks.us

GARDEN CITY COMMUNITY COLLEGE
DEPARTMENT OF MUSIC
801 Campus Dr.
Garden City, KS 67846-6333
Bruce Spiller
316-276-7611
Fax: 316-276-9630
E-mail: bspiller@gccc.cc.ks.us
www.gccc.cc.ks.us

HESSTON COLLEGE
DEPARTMENT OF MUSIC
P.O. Box 3000
Hesston, KS 67062
Karen Unruh
620-327-8143
Fax: 620-327-8300
E-mail: jaker@hesston.edu
www.hesston.edu

HUTCHINSON COMMUNITY JUNIOR COLLEGE
FINE ARTS DEPARTMENT
1300 N. Plum St.
Hutchinson, KS 67501-5831
Bill Brewer
316-665-3500
Fax: 316-665-3310
E-mail: brewerb@hutchcc.edu
www.hutchcc.edu

INDEPENDENCE COMMUNITY COLLEGE
MUSIC PROGRAM
P.O. Box 708
Independence, KS 67301
David Sherlock
316-331-4100
Fax: 316-331-5344
www.indy.cc.ks.us

JOHNSON COUNTY COMMUNITY COLLEGE
DEPARTMENT OF MUSIC
12345 College Blvd.
Overland Park, KS 66210-1283
Ken Gibson
913-469-8500
Fax: 913-469-4409
www.jccc.net

KANSAS CITY KANSAS COMMUNITY COLLEGE
DEPARTMENT OF MUSIC
7520 State Ave.
Kansas City, KS 66112
Amy Lee Fugate
913-288-7634
Fax: 913-288-7638
E-mail: afugate@toto.net
www.kckcc.cc.ks.us/music

KANSAS STATE UNIVERSITY
DEPARTMENT OF MUSIC

109 McCain Auditorium
Manhattan, KS 66506
Dr. Paul Hunt
785-532-5740
Fax: 785-532-6899
E-mail: phunt@ksu.edu
www.ksu.edu/music

Kansas State performing groups include five
band/wind ensembles, three jazz bands, one
orchestra, chamber music groups, one musical
theater group, four choruses, and one opera.

KANSAS WESLEYAN UNIVERSITY
DEPARTMENT OF MUSIC

100 E. Clafin
Salina, KS 67401
Phillip Miller
913-827-5541
Fax: 913-827-0927
www.kwu.edu

LABETTE COMMUNITY COLLEGE
DEPARTMENT OF MUSIC

Parsons, KS 67357
Robert Walker
516-421-3897
E-mail: robertw@labette.cc.ks.us
www.labette.cc.ks.us

MANHATTAN CHRISTIAN COLLEGE
MUSIC MINISTRY PROGRAM

1415 Anderson Ave.
Manhattan, KS 66502
Laurie Forsberg
913-539-3571
Fax: 913-539-0832
E-mail: lforsberg@mccks.edu
www.mccks.edu

MCPHERSON COLLEGE
DEPARTMENT OF MUSIC

P.O. Box 1402
McPherson, KS 67460
Stephanie Brunelli
620-241-0731
Fax: 620-241-8443
www.mcpherson.edu

NEOSHO COUNTY COMMUNITY COLLEGE
DEPARTMENT OF MUSIC

800 W. 14th St.
Chanute, KS 66720
Al Guinn
316-431-2820
Fax: 316-431-0082
E-mail: afguinn@neosho.cc.ks.us
www.neosho.cc.ks.us

NEWMAN UNIVERSITY
DEPARTMENT OF FINE ARTS

3100 McCormick St.
Wichita, KS 67213
Mark Clark
316-942-4291
www.newmanu.edu

OTTAWA UNIVERSITY
DEPARTMENT OF MUSIC

1001 S. Ceder St. #8
Ottawa, KS 66067
Byron Jenson
913-242-5200
Fax: 913-242-7429
E-mail: jensen@ottawa.edu
www.ottawa.edu

PITTSBURGH STATE UNIVERSITY
DEPARTMENT OF MUSIC
Pittsburgh, KS 66762
Dr. Anne Patterson
316-235-4466
Fax: 316-235-4468
www.pittstate.edu

SEWARD COUNTY COMMUNITY COLLEGE
DEPARTMENT OF MUSIC
P.O. Box 1137
Liberal, KS 67905
Darin Workman
316-629-2683
Fax: 316-626-3005
E-mail: dworkman@sccc.cc.ks.us
www.sccc.cc.ks.us

SOUTHWESTERN COLLEGE
DEPARTMENT OF MUSIC
100 College St.
Winfield, KS 67156
Micheal Wilder
316-229-6272
Fax: 316-229-6335
E-mail: mwilder@sckans.edu
www.sckans.edu

STERLING COLLEGE
DEPARTMENT OF MUSIC
P.O. Box 98
Sterling, KS 67579
Diane Lewis
620-278-2173
Fax: 620-278-2775
E-mail: dlewis@sterling.edu
www.stercolks.edu

TABOR COLLEGE
DEPARTMENT OF MUSIC
400 S. Jefferson St.
Hillsboro, KS 67063
Richard Cantwell
620-947-3121
Fax: 620-947-2607
E-mail: richardc@Tabor.edu
www.tabor.edu

UNIVERSITY OF KANSAS
DEPARTMENT OF MUSIC AND DANCE
452 Murphy Hall
Lawrence, KS 66045
785-864-3436
Fax: 316-229-6335
www.music.ukans.edu

WASHBURN UNIVERSITY
DEPARTMENT OF MUSIC
1700 S.W. College Ave.
Topeka, KS 66621
Kirt Saville
785-231-1010
Fax: 785-357-4168
E-mail: Kirt.saville@washburn.edu
www.washburn.edu/cas/music

Degrees: B.A. in Music, B.M. in performance, B.M. in Music Education

At Washburn University, "Learning for a Lifetime," is more than a motto... it is a call to action. Since 1865, the university has lived up to that call through educational excellence. Washburn's success is based on the highest standards for faculty, a commitment to individual student achievement. Interactivity between campus and community and an emphasis on technology and the future. Current enrollment stands at 6,600 students.

The department of music offers two degree programs. One program leads to the B.M. degree, with a major in music performance, or a major in music education. The second program leads to a B.A. degree, with a major in music. Students planning a professional career in music performance or in music education pursue the B.M. degree. The B.A. degree with a major in music is pursued by students who seek emphasis in music within the context of a Liberal Arts Education.

WICHITA STATE UNIVERSITY
SCHOOL OF MUSIC

1845 North Fairmount
Wichita, KS 67260
Dr. John W. Thomson
316-978-3500
Fax: 316-978-3625
E-mail: j.thomson@wichita.edu
www.wichita.edu

KENTUCKY

Population: 4,153,202 (2003 Estimate)

Capital City: Frankfort

Music Colleges and Universities: Alice Lloyd College, Asbury College, Asbury Theological Seminary, Ashland Community College, Bellarmine University, Berea College, Boyce College, Brescia University, Campbellsville University, Centre College, Cumberland College, Eastern Kentucky University, Elizabeth Community College, Georgetown College, Kentucky Christian College, Kentucky Mountain Bible College, Kentucky State University, Kentucky Wesleyan College, Lees College, Lindsey Wilson College, Morehead State University, Murray State University, Northern Kentucky University, Paducah Community College, Pikeville College, St. Catharine College, Thomas More College, Transylvania University, Union College, University of Kentucky, University of Kentucky at Louisville, University of Louisville, Western Kentucky University

Bird: Cardinal

Motto: United We Stand, Divided We Fall

Flower: Goldenrod

Tree: Tulip Tree

Residents Called: Kentuckians

Origin of Name: Based on the Iroquois Indian word "Ken-tah-ten," meaning "land of tomorrow"

Area: 40,411 square miles (37th largest state)

Statehood: June 1, 1792 (15th state)

Largest Cities: Lexington, Fayette, Louisville, Owensboro, Bowling Green, Covington, Hopkinsville, Frankfort, Henderson, Richmond, Jeffersontown

College Band Programs: Campbellsville University, Eastern Kentucky University, Kentucky State University, Northwestern State University of Louisiana, University of Kentucky, University of Louisville

KENTUCKY

ALICE LLOYD COLLEGE
DEPARTMENT OF MUSIC
100 Purpose Rd.
Pippa Passes, KY 41844
Richard Kennedy
606-368-6036
Fax: 606-368-6215
E-mail: richardkennedy@alc.edu
www.alc.edu

ASBURY COLLEGE
MUSIC DEPARTMENT
1 Macklem Dr.
Wilmore, KY 40390
Dr. Paul A. Rader
859-858-3511
Fax: 859-858-3921
E-mail: paularader@asbury.edu
www.asbury.edu

ASBURY THEOLOGICAL SEMINARY
DEPARTMENT OF MUSIC
204 North Lexington Ave.
Wilmore, KY 40390
William Goold
606-858-3581
Fax: 606-858-4509
www.ats.wilmore.ky.us

ASHLAND COMMUNITY COLLEGE
DEPARTMENT OF MUSIC
1400 College Dr.
Louisville, KY 41101
Barbara Nichols
606-329-2999
Fax: 606-325-8124
www.ashlandcc.org

BELLARMINE UNIVERSITY
DEPARTMENT OF MUSIC
2001 Newburg Rd.
Louisville, KY 40205-0671
Richard Burchard
502-452-8224
Fax: 502-452-8451
E-mail: rburchard@bellarmine.edu
www.bellamine.edu

BEREA COLLEGE
MUSIC DEPARTMENT
CPO 2194
Berea, KY 40403
Dr. Anne Rhodes
859-985-3466
Fax: 859-985-3912
E-mail: anne_solberg@berea.edu
www.berea.edu/mus/mus.home.html

Degrees: A.B. in Music, with various concentrations; A.B. Music Education, Instrumental and Vocal emphases

The music department offers private instruction in several instruments, and a variety of large and small instrumental and vocal ensembles. In addition it offers a succession of courses leading to a Bachelor of Arts degree in Music with several concentrations available (African-American Music, Appalachian Music, Keyboard Performance, Vocal Performance, and Wind Performance). The A.B. Music education degree is offered, with instrumental or vocal emphasis and K-12 certification. A music minor is also available. There are four choral ensembles (Black Music Ensemble, Chamber Singers, Concert Choir, and Women's Chorus) and seven instrumental ensembles (African-Latin Percussion Ensemble, Bluegrass Music Ensemble, Chamber Wind Ensemble, Contemporary Percussion Ensemble, Jazz Ensemble, Recorder Ensemble, and Wind Ensemble). The highly trained diverse music faculty consists of artist-teachers who are active performers as well as educators. More than 20 percent of the student body at Berea participates in ensembles and/or lessons.

BOYCE COLLEGE
2825 LEXINGTON RD.

Louisville, KY 40280-1812
Thomas Bolton
800-626-5525
Fax: 502-897-4066
E-mail: tbolton@sbts.edu
www.sbts.edu

Degrees: Bachelor of Science in Biblical Studies with a Major in Music

Boyce College, on the historic campus of the Southern Baptist Theological Seminary, is centrally located in beautiful Louisville, KY. Louisville is situated just hours from Chicago, St. Louis, Nashville, and Atlanta. In fact, Louisville is just a day's drive from more than half of the United States' population. Boyce College offers an outstanding program of theological education for ministry. It represents confessional fidelity, academic excellence, practical application, and a world vision of the gospel. We have brought together a world-class faculty and the Boyce College offers an unprecedented level of theological training and ministry experience.

Boyce College's music major offers the best of both worlds: a first rate theological education and a world class music program. Taught by the music faculty of Southern Seminary, the music major is second to none. Building upon Southern Seminary's renewed focus on the importance of worship in the life of the believer and the church, every element of Boyce's music program was designed to capitalize on your talents and interests, vocal or instrumental. In this way you will be prepared for the ministry of music leadership or the pursuit of a higher level of education.

BRESCIA UNIVERSITY
DEPARTMENT OF MUSIC

Owensboro, KY 42301
James White
502-685-3131
Fax: 502-686-4266
E-mail: jamesw@brescia.edu
www.brescia.edu

CAMPBELLSVILLE UNIVERSITY
SCHOOL OF MUSIC

1 University Dr.
Campbellsville, KY 42718
Trent Argo
270-789-5269
Fax: 270-789-5534
E-mail: gaddisjr@campbellsvile.edu
www.campbellsville.edu/music

Campbellsville's School of Music is one of the university's strongest assets and is an accredited institutional member of the National Association of Schools of Music (NASM). Its dedicated and highly qualified faculty is committed to excellence in musical performance and academics. Each music curriculum includes the study of music foundations, such as music theory, music history and literature and conducting. Each music student not only participates in a variety of ensembles, but also receives individual instruction in an applied music area leading up to the presentation of a senior recital. The Gosser Fine Arts Center houses large instrumental and choral/hand bell rehearsal rooms, practice rooms, classrooms, faculty teaching studios, music library, music technology lab and the 212-seat Gheens Recital Hall, which is one of the most up-to-date facilities in Kentucky. One hundred-plus majors enjoy performance opportunities in large and small ensembles in all areas of instrumental and choral music including opera workshop, auditioned touring choir, wind ensemble, marching band, jazz ensemble and orchestra.

CENTRE COLLEGE
DEPARTMENT OF MUSIC

600 W. Walnut St.
Danville, KY 40422-1309
Barbara Hall
606-238-5200
Fax: 606-238-5448
www.centre.edu

CUMBERLAND COLLEGE
DEPARTMENT OF MUSIC

7525 College Station Dr.
Williamsburg, KY 40769
Jeff Smoak
606-539-4332
Fax: 606-539-4332
E-mail: jsmoak@cc.cumber.edu
wwww.cumber.edu

EASTERN KENTUCKY UNIVERSITY
DEPARTMENT OF MUSIC

521 Lancaster Ave.
Richmond, KY 40475
Rob James
859-622-3266
Fax: 859-622-1333
E-mail: rob.james@eku.edu
www.music.eku.edu

ELIZABETH COMMUNITY COLLEGE
DIVISION OF HUMANITIES

Elizabethtown, KY 42701
Camille Hill
502-769-2371
Fax: 502-769-0736

GEORGETOWN COLLEGE
DEPARTMENT OF MUSIC

400 E. College St.
Georgetown, KY 40324-1696
Sonny Burnette
502-863-8100
Fax: 502-868-8888
www.georgetowncollege.edu

KENTUCKY CHRISTIAN COLLEGE
DEPARTMENT OF MUSIC

100 Academic Pkwy
Grayson, KY 41143
Dr. Mark Deakins
606-474-3290
Fax: 606-474-3157
E-mail: mdeakins@email.kcc.edu
www.kcc.edu

Degrees: BS in Church Music; B.S. in Music Education; B.S. Specialized Ministries; B.S. in Music Performance; B.S. in Music Business; B.S. in Contemporary Worship

Kentucky Christian College is a private college offering residence degrees in music ministry, music performance, music business and music education. The college is widely recognized for its excellence in choral music. The choirs have performed five times in Carnegie Hall and record for major Christian labels in Nashville, TN, at least once a year. Kentucky Christian College is known as the Great Commission College. Every student carries a 30-Bible major along with his/her chosen major. This prepares students to take the gospel into the work place where it is desperately needed. Students may choose from three degrees in church music – B.S. in Church Music, B.S. in Specialized Ministries, and B.S. in Contemporary Worship. Students may also choose Bachelor of Science degrees in Music Education, Music Business, and Music Performance.

KENTUCKY MOUNTAIN BIBLE COLLEGE
DEPARTMENT OF MUSIC
P.O. Box 10
Vancleve, KY 41385
John Finney
606-666-5000
Fax: 606-666-7744
www.kmbc.edu

KENTUCKY STATE UNIVERSITY
DIVISION OF FINE ARTS
400 E. Main St.
Frankfort, KY 40601
Timothy Chambers
502-597-5815
Fax: 502-597-5999
E-mail: tchambers@gwmail.kysu.edu
www.kysu.edu

KENTUCKY WESLEYAN COLLEGE
DEPARTMENT OF MUSIC
3000 Frederica St.
Owensboro, KY 42302
Diane Earle
270-926-3111
Fax: 270-926-3196
E-mail: dearle@kwc.edu
www.kwc.edu

LEES COLLEGE
DEPARTMENT OF MUSIC
Jackson, KY 41339
Kathy Smoot
606-666-8142
Fax: 606-666-8910
www.lees.hazcc.kctcs.net

LINDSEY WILSON COLLEGE
DEPARTMENT OF MUSIC
210 Lindsey Wilson St.
Columbia, KY 42778
Robert Reynolds
502-384-2126
Fax: 502-384-8050
E-mail: reynolds@lindsey.edu
www.lindsey.edu

MOREHEAD STATE UNIVERSITY
DEPARTMENT OF MUSIC
160 Baird Music Hall
University Blvd.
Morehead, KY 40351
Dr. Christopher S. Gallaher
606-783-2473
Fax: 606-783-5447
E-mail: c.gallaher@moreheadstate.edu
www.moreheadstate.edu

Degrees: B.M.E., B.M., B.A., M.M.

The Morehead State University department of music is widely respected throughout the United States as having one of the country's finest music education programs. By providing the academic programs of a great University within the atmosphere of a small community, the department offers programs with the "personal touch" unmatched by large universities.

Central to this program is a faculty of some 26 teachers and scholars and an excellent student body. During the regular school year, there are more than 200 majors in the department of music from more than 18 states, 6 foreign countries in addition to the Commonwealth of Kentucky.

The department of music is an institutional member of the NASM. The requirements for entrance and graduation are in accordance with the published regulations of NASM.

The department also offers a "Minor in Traditional Music" in conjunction with the Kentucky Center for Traditional Music.

MURRAY STATE UNIVERSITY
DEPARTMENT OF MUSIC
504 Fine Arts Building
Murrey, KY 42071
Dennis Johnson
270-762-6339
Fax: 270-762-3965
www.murraystate.edu

NORTHERN KENTUCKY UNIVERSITY
DEPARTMENT OF MUSIC
Nunn DR
Highland Heights, KY 41099
Dr. J. Randall Wheaton
859-572-6399
Fax: 859-572-6076
E-mail: wheatonr@nku.edu
www.music.nku.edu

PADUCAH COMMUNITY COLLEGE
DEPARTMENT OF MUSIC
P.O. Box 7380
Paducah, KY 42002
Norman Wurgler
502-554-9200
Fax: 502-554-6310
E-mail: norman.wurglar@pccky.com
www.pccky.com

PIKEVILLE COLLEGE
DEPARTMENT OF MUSIC
Sycamore St.
Pikeville, KY 41501
William Daniels
606-432-9200
Fax: 606-432-9328
www.pc.edu

ST. CATHARINE COLLEGE
DEPARTMENT OF MUSIC
2735 Bardstown Rd.
St. Catharine, KY 40061
Valarie Alexandra Valois
606-336-5082
Fax: 606-336-5031
www.sccky.edu

THOMAS MORE COLLEGE
MUSIC DEPARTMENT
333 Thomas More Pkwy.
Crestview Hills, KY 41017
606-344-3603
Fax: 606-344-3342
www.thomasmore.edu

TRANSYLVANIA UNIVERSITY
MUSIC PROGRAM
300 N. Broadway
Lexington, KY 40508
Ben Hawkins
859-233-8141
Fax: 859-233-8785
E-mail: bhawkins@transy.edu
www.transy.edu

UNION COLLEGE
DEPARTMENT OF MUSIC
310 College St.
Barbourville, KY 40906
Thomas McFarland
859-257-4900
Fax: 859-257-9576
www.unionky.edu

UNIVERSITY OF KENTUCKY
SCHOOL OF MUSIC

105 Fine Arts Bldg.
Lexington, KY 40506
859-257-4900
Fax: 859-257-9576
E-mail: hclarke@uky.edu
www.uky.edu/finearts/music

UNIVERSITY OF KENTUCKY AT LOUISVILLE
JEFFERSON COMMUNITY COLLEGE

109 E. Broadway
Louisville, KY 40292
Wesley Lites
502-584-0181
Fax: 502-584-0181

UNIVERSITY OF LOUISVILLE
SCHOOL OF MUSIC

Louisville, KY 40292
Academic Coordinator
502-852-6907
Fax: 502-852-0520
E-mail: koerselman@louisville.edu
www.louisville.edu

WESTERN KENTUCKY UNIVERSITY
DEPARTMENT OF MUSIC

1 Big Red Way
Bowling Green, KY 42101
David Lee
270-745-3751
Fax: 270-745-6855
E-mail: music@wku.edu
www.wku.edu/music

LOUISIANA

Population: 4,536,437 (2003 Estimate)

Capital City: Baton Rouge

Music Colleges and Universities: Centenary College of Louisiana, Delgado Community College, Grambling State University, Louisiana College, Louisiana State University, Louisiana Tech University, Loyola University at New Orleans, McNeese State University, New Orleans Baptist Theology Seminary, Nicholls State University, Northwestern State University, Northwestern State University at Louisiana, Our Lady of Holy Cross College, Southeastern Louisiana University, Southern University at Baton Rouge, Southern University at New Orleans, St. Joseph Seminary College, Tulane University, University of Louisiana at Lafayette, University of Louisiana at Monroe, University of New Orleans, Xavier University of Louisiana

Bird: Eastern Brown Pelican

Motto: Union, justice, and confidence

Flower: Magnolia

Tree: Bald Cypress

Residents Called: Louisianians

Origin of Name: Named in honor of France's King Louis XIV.

Area: 51,843 square mile (31st largest state)

Statehood: April 30, 1812 (18th state)

Largest Cities: New Orleans, Baton Rouge, Shreveport, LaFayette, Lake Charles, Kenner, Bossier City, Monroe, Alexandria, New Iberia

College Band Programs: Grambling State University, Louisiana State University, Northwestern State University, Southern University

LOUISIANA

CENTENARY COLLEGE OF LOUISIANA
HURLEY SCHOOL OF MUSIC
2911 Centenary Blvd.
Shreveport, LA 71104
Gale Odom
318-869-5235
Fax: 318-869-5248
E-mail: godom@centenary.edu
www.centenary.edu

The Hurley School of Music is a professional music school within a liberal arts college. It has been a member of the National Association of Schools of Music since 1936. Among its graduates are musicians with major symphonies and opera companies, church musicians, music scholars, and school and private music teachers. Ensembles include two major choral groups, wind ensemble, chamber orchestra, jazz band, percussion ensemble and chamber groups. The Hurley School of Music is housed in its own building, with a recital hall, a new choral wing and new instrumental rehearsal hall.

DELGADO COMMUNITY COLLEGE
DEPARTMENT OF MUSIC
615 City Park Ave.
New Orleans, LA 70119
Peter Cho
504-483-4959
Fax: 503-483-4954
www.dcc.edu

GRAMBLING STATE UNIVERSITY
DEPARTMENT OF MUSIC
Grambling, LA 71245
Larry Pannell
318-274-2682
Fax: 318-274-3723
www.gram.edu
Degrees: B.A. in Music

LOUISIANA COLLEGE
DEPARTMENT OF MUSIC
P.O. Box 604
Pineville, LA 71359
Dr. Cleamon R. Downs
318-487-7336
Fax: 318-487-7337
E-mail: burr@lacollege.edu
www.lacollege.edu

LOUISIANA STATE UNIVERSITY
SCHOOL OF MUSIC
Baton Rouge, LA 70803
Ronald D. Ross
225-578-3261
Fax: 225-578-2562
E-mail: rross@lsu.edu
www.music.lsu.edu

LOUISIANA TECHNICAL UNIVERSITY
DEPARTMENT OF MUSIC
SCHOOL OF THE PERFORMING ARTS
P.O. Box 8608
Ruston, LA 71272
Dr. Jon A. Barker
318-257-4200
Fax: 318-257-4571
E-mail: jbarker@latech.edu
http://performingarts.latech.edu
Degrees: B.A., B.M. in Music Performance, B.A. in Music Education, M.E in Music Education

The department of Music in the School of the Performing Arts is accredited by NASM and boasts a fine faculty, curriculum, facilities, and performance schedule. The vocal, strings, guitar, piano, and theory programs are housed in the Howard Center for the Performing Arts. The instrumental area of the department of music is housed in the band building, and includes two rehearsal halls, instrumental faculty studios, and offices for the Director of

Bands. Louisiana Tech is a fully accredited comprehensive institution within the University of Louisiana system, with graduate and undergraduate curricula. The school of the performing arts is recognized by the regents as an area of excellence and is a vital part of the College of Liberal Arts working closely with other units within the college. A new Steinway grand piano graces the recital hall. Other venues include the 1,300-seat Howard Center and the 120-seat Stone Theatre.

LOYOLA UNIVERSITY AT NEW ORLEANS
COLLEGE OF MUSIC

6363 St. Charles Ave.
New Orleans, LA 70118
Dr. Edward Kvet
504-865-3240
Fax: 504-865-3383
E-mail: admit@loyno.edu
www.loyno.edu

Degrees: Composition, Jazz Studies, Music Education, Music Business (Performance Track), Music Business (Non-performance track)

Music with Elective Studies, Music Theory, Music Therapy, Performance (Instrumental /Voice) and Piano Pedagogy

The College of Music, founded in 1932, gives students the opportunity to combine liberal arts studies with professional music courses in the only college of music conducted by the Jesuit fathers in the United States. The college fosters a spirit of closeness and communication. With a maximum enrollment of 300 students, small class sizes and a student faculty ratio of 6:1, students receive the individual attention inherent in quality education.

Performance is an integral part of each student's music education. Vocalists may perform with the University Chorus, the Chamber Singers, Opera Theatre, or the highly selective University Chorale. Instrumental performance opportunities include several large, distinguished ensembles such as the university sym-

phony orchestra, Loyola chamber orchestra, university concert band, wind ensemble, or one of the jazz bands. Specialized chamber ensemble experiences are available to all students.

As one of 28 Jesuit universities in the United States, Loyola shares the reputation for academic excellence that has come to be recognized internationally. This, combined with the College of Music's record for preparing students for professional music careers, has established Loyola University, New Orleans, as an educational leader in music.

MCNEESE STATE UNIVERSITY
DEPARTMENT OF MUSIC

4205 Ryan St.
Lake Charles, LA 70609
Michele K. Martin
318-475-5028
Fax: 318-475-5922
E-mail: mmartin@mail.mcneese.edu
www.mcneese.edu

NEW ORLEANS BAPTIST THEOLOGY SEMINARY
DIVISION OF CHURCH MUSIC MINISTRIES

3939 Gentilly Blvd.
New Orleans, LA 70126
Ken Gabrielse
504-282-4455
Fax: 504-816-8033
E-mail: kgabrielse@nobts.edu
www.nobts.edu

NICHOLLS STATE UNIVERSITY
DEPARTMENT OF PERFORMING ARTS

P.O. Box 2017
Thibodaux, LA 70310
Dr. Carol D. Britt
985-448-4600
Fax: 985-448-4674
E-mail: mus-cdb@nicholls.edu
www.nicholls.edu/perform

Degrees: Instrumental Music Education, Vocal Music Education, B.A. in music

Nicholls State University serves about 8,000 students. Situated in South Louisiana, the university draws students from around the country and abroad. The division of music is part of the school of Fine Arts. It is accredited by NASM. There are about 60 music majors, with majors in voice piano, and all band instruments. Nicholls is about 60 miles from New Orleans and Baton Rouge — close enough to take advantage of the culture of both cities. Jubilee — a festival of the arts and humanities, an annual spring even, offers many opportunities for student performances and internationally known performers and speakers. Nicholls' motto is "Come here. Go far." The division of music is large enough to offer the curricula needed by the students, and it is small enough for the faculty, staff, and students to develop caring relationships. Visit our Web site to read about activities and the faculty.

NORTHWESTERN STATE UNIVERSITY
DEPARTMENT OF MUSIC

Creative and Performing Arts
School of Music
Natchitoches, LA 71497
William Brent
318-342-4522
www.nsula.edu/capa/music

NORTHWESTERN STATE UNIVERSITY OF LOUISIANA
DEPARTMENT OF CREATIVE AND PERFORMING ARTS

College Ave.
Natchitoches, LA 71497
William Brent
318-357-4522
Fax: 318-357-5906
www.nsula.edu

Degrees: B.M. in Music education, B.M.E.

Instrumental, B.M.E. Vocal, B.M. in Performance, B.M. in Sacred Music, Master of Music

OUR LADY OF HOLY CROSS COLLEGE
DEPARTMENT OF MUSIC

4123 Woodland Dr.
New Orleans, LA 70131
Raymond Gitz
504-394-7744
Fax: 504-391-2421
E-mail: ritz@aol.com
www.olhcc.edu

SOUTHEASTERN LOUISIANA UNIVERSITY
MUSIC DEPARTMENT

Department of Music and Dramatic Arts
SLU P.O. Box 10815-0815
Hammond, LA 70402
David Evenson
985-549-2184
Fax: 985-549-2892
E-mail: devenson@selu.edu
www.selu.edu/music

Degrees: B.M. in performance; B.M.E.; M.M. in performance, M.M. in theory

The Music Department and Dramatic Arts boasts a lengthy heritage of excellence in the training of educators and professional musicians. Central to its mission are a faculty of sixteen full-time and nineteen part-time teachers and scholars, and a diverse student body from throughout the United States, and several foreign countries including Honduras, Bulgaria, Russia, Romania, and the Republic of Moldova. Southeastern's faculty is respected performers, composers, and educators, who take a deep and lasting interest in their students. Faculty are leaders in their fields, holding offices in state and national professional organizations and receiving national and university awards in teaching, research, and creative activity. They can be heard performing nationally and internationally in live concerts and on compact discs. Graduates have distinguished themselves as performers and educators in public school, colleges, and universities. The Music Department and Dramatic Arts is faculty accredited by the NASM.

SOUTHERN UNIVERSITY AT NEW ORLEANS
DIVISION OF MUSIC
6400 Press Dr.
New Orleans, LA 70126
Roger Dickerson
504-286-5346
Fax: 504-286-5131
E-mail: vgking@worldnet.att.net
www.suno.edu

SOUTHERN UNIVERSITY AT BATON ROUGE
OFFICE OF ADMISSIONS
Baton Rouge, LA 70813
225-771-3440
Fax: 225-771-2495
E-mail: admit@subr.edu
www.subr.edu

ST. JOSEPH SEMINARY COLLEGE
MUSIC PROGRAM
St. Benedict, LA 70457
Laura Wakeland
504-892-1800
E-mail: lwakela@wpo.it.luc.edu
www.stjoseph.luc.edu

TULANE UNIVERSITY
DEPARTMENT OF MUSIC
101 Dixon Hall
New Orleans, LA 70118
Anthony M. Cummings

504-865-5267
Fax: 504-865-5270
E-mail: music@tulane.edu
www.tulane.edu/~music

UNIVERSITY OF LOUISIANA AT LAFAYETTE
SCHOOL OF MUSIC
P.O. Box 41207
Lafayette, LA 70504
A. C. Himmes
337-282-6016
Fax: 337-482-5017
E-mail: ach5291@louisiana.edu
www.arts.louisiana.edu
Degrees: B.M., B.M.E., M.M.

The school of music's programs have been accredited by the NASM since 1952. The enrollment is approximately 200 undergraduate and graduate students. The faculty consists of twenty full-time faculty, twelve adjunct faculty, two laboratory assistants and twelve graduate assistants.

Recognized as a center for musical performance, composition, and research, the school of music is housed in 56,000 square foot Angelle Hall and hosts approximately 100 concerts, recitals, competitions, or other performances each year. All classrooms are equipped with modern audio, video and Ethernet capability. Facilities include 40 practice rooms and 3 large ensemble rehearsal rooms. Concert facilities include Angelle Hall Auditorium, a 900-seat hall, and the Choral-Recital Hall, a 125 seat hall used for lectures as well as recitals., Special facilities include the MIDI Lab, the Griffin Recording Studio and the Griffin Music Resource Center. These facilities are equipped with state of the art electronic and computer technology.

UNIVERSITY OF LOUISIANA AT MONROE

SCHOOL OF MUSIC

700 University Ave.
Monroe, LA 71209
Larry Edwards
318-342-1570
Fax: 318-342-1369
www.ulm.edu

UNIVERSITY OF NEW ORLEANS

DEPARTMENT OF MUSIC

Lakefront
New Orleans, LA 70148
Dr. Jeff Cox
504-280-6381
Fax: 504-280-6098
E-mail: unomusic@uno.edu
www.uno.edu/~music
Degrees: B.A., and M.M.

The Music Department at the University of New Orleans is a reflection of its community, one of the most musically significant, historically important, and culturally diverse cities of the world. By promoting the highest levels of musicianship, scholarship and creativity, the mission of the department is to train the musicians capable of furthering the music legacy of the city and of assuming significant positions in society through offering a B.A. with the emphasis in performance, jazz performance, theory/composition, and history and an M.M. in performance, jazz studies, composition and conducting. The creative activity of the department serves the cultural needs of the community through numerous performances by faculty and students. The Music Department's service activity includes the support of community music making it a commitment to the development of regional, national, and international partnerships. In addition, the Music Department serves the needs of non-majors through instruction and performance opportunities designed to nurture lifelong appreciation and support of music.

XAVIER UNIVERSITY OF LOUISIANA

DEPARTMENT OF MUSIC

Palmetto Pine St.
New Orleans, LA 70125
John Ware
504-483-7621
Fax: 504-482-2801
www.xula.edu

MAINE

Population: 1,285,159 (2003 Estimate)

Capital City: Augusta

Music Colleges and Universities: Bates College, Bowdoin College, Colby College, College of the Atlantic, Delta College, University of Maine, University of Maine at Augusta, University of Maine at Farmington, University of Maine at Fort Kent, University of Maine at Machias, University of Maine at Orono, University of Southern Maine

Bird: Chickadee

Motto: Dirigo – I direct

Flower: White pine cone and tassel

Tree: White pine

Residents Called: Mainers

Origin of Name: Assumed to be a reference to the state region being a mainland, different from its many surrounding islands.

Area: 35,387 square miles (39th largest state)

Statehood: March 15, 1820 (23rd state)

Largest Cities: Portland, Lewiston, Bangor, South Portland, Auburn, Brunswick, Biddeford, Sanford, Augusta, Scarborough

College Band Programs: University of Maine

MAINE

BATES COLLEGE
DEPARTMENT OF MUSIC
75 Russell St.
Lewiston, ME 04240
William Matthews
207-786-6139
Fax: 207-786-8335
E-mail: wmatthew@abacus.bates.edu
www.bates.edu

BOWDOIN COLLEGE
DEPARTMENT OF MUSIC
Gibson Hall
Brunswick, ME 04011
Linda Marquis
207-725-3321
Fax: 207-725-3748
E-mail: mhunter@bowdoin.edu
www.bowdoin.edu

COLBY COLLEGE
MUSIC DEPARTMENT
5670 Mayflower Hill
Waterville, ME 04901
Steven Saunders
207-872-3236
Fax: 207-872-3141
E-mail: dlkadyk@colby.edu
www.colby.edu/music
Degrees: B.A.

Colby's Music Department combines outstanding academic instruction in a liberal arts setting with many of the performance opportunities more typical of a conservatory or school of music. Students work closely with the eight faculty and sixteen instructors in instruments and voice, in course offerings ranging from music history and theory to musicianship, performance, conducting, composition, world music, jazz history, American popular music and African drumming.

Colby's instrumental and vocal instructors include some of the most represented teacher-performers in New England. Our artists-in-residence, the Portland String Quartet, regularly coach students and perform on campus, and the Music at Colby series brings artists of national stature to campus for concerts and master classes.

COLLEGE OF THE ATLANTIC
DEPARTMENT OF MUSIC
Bar Harbour, ME 04609
John Cooper
207-288-5015
Fax: 207-288-2328
E-mail: cooper@ecology.coa.edu
www.coa.edu

DELTA COLLEGE
DEPARTMENT OF MUSIC
1961 Delta Rd.
University Center, ME 48710
Paul Hill
517-686-9000
Fax: 517-686-8736
www.delta.edu

UNIVERSITY OF MAINE AT AUGUSTA
DEPARTMENT OF MUSIC
46 University Dr.
Augusta, ME 04330
Richard Nelson
207-621-3214
Fax: 307-621-3293
www.uma.maine.edu

Degrees: bachelor of arts in music, bachelor of music education and bachelor of music performance.

As a fully accredited member of the National Association of Schools of Music, the department also offers a complete range of music courses and performing experiences to all of the over 9,400 students on campus. The major vocal ensembles balance the major instrumental performing groups. A large number of chamber music ensembles is maintained as well. The school offers students a state-of-the-art facility for study and performance. There are teaching, rehearsal and performing studios for music, a "high tech" classroom, and a fully digital recording studio. Performances take place in a newly built 280-seat Minsky Recital Hall as well as in the Maine Center for the Arts, located on the University of Maine campus.

UNIVERSITY OF MAINE AT FARMINGTON
DEPARTMENT OF VISUAL AND PERFORMANCE ARTS
98 Main St.
Farmington, ME 04938
Phillip Carlsen
207-778-7072
Fax: 207-778-7247
E-mail: carlsen@maine.edu
www.umf.maine.edu

UNIVERSITY OF MAINE AT FORT KENT
DEPARTMENT OF PERFORMING ARTS
25 Pleasant St.
Fort Kent, ME 04743
Scott Brickman
207-834-7506
Fax: 207-834-7503
E-mail: brickman@maine.maine.edu
www.umfk.maine.edu

UNIVERSITY OF MAINE AT MACHIAS
DEPARTMENT OF MUSIC
9 O'Brien Ave.
201 Powers Hall
Machias, ME 04654
Eugene Nichols
207-255-1229
Fax: 207-255-4864
E-mail: gnichols@maine.edu
www.umm.maine.edu

UNIVERSITY OF MAINE ORONO
THE SCHOOL OF PERFORMING ARTS
5788 Class of 1944 Hall
Orono, ME 04459
Diane Roscetti
207-581-4700
Fax: 207-581-4701
E-mail: diane.roscetti@umit.maine.edu
www.ume.maine.edu/spa

UNIVERSITY OF SOUTHERN MAINE
DEPARTMENT OF MUSIC
Corthell Hall
37 College Ave.
Gorham, ME 04038
Peter Martin
207-780-5265
Fax: 207-780-5527
E-mail: pmartin@usm.maine.edu
www.usm.maine.edu/~mus

MARYLAND

Population: 5,459,305 (2003 Estimate)

Capital City: Annapolis

Music Colleges and Universities: Allegany College, Anne Arundel Community College, Baltimore School for the Arts, Chesapeake College, College of Notre Dame of Maryland, Columbia Union College, Community College of Baltimore City, Coppin State College, Frederick Community College, Frostburg State University, Garrett Community College, Goucher College, Hagerstown Community College, Hartford Community College, Hood College, Montgomery College, Morgan State University, Mount St. Mary's College, Peabody Conservatory of Music, Prince Georges Community College, Salisbury University, St. Mary's College of Maryland, The Peabody Institute of Johns Hopkins U., Towson University, United States Naval Academy, University of Maryland, University of Maryland at Baltimore County, University of Maryland at Eastern Shore, Washington Bible College, Washington College, Washington Conservatory of Music, Western Maryland College

Bird: Baltimore Oriole

Motto: Fatti Maschii Parole Femine – Strong deeds, gentle words

Flower: Black-eyed Susan

Tree: White Oak

Residents Called: Marylanders

Origin of Name: Named to honor Henrietta Maria, wife of England's King Charles I.

Area: 12,407 square miles (42nd largest state)

Statehood: April 28, 1788 (7th state)

Largest Cities: Baltimore, Frederick, Gaithersburg, Bowie, Rockville, Hagerstown, Annapolis, College Park, Salisbury, Cumberland

College Band Programs: John Hopkins University, Morgan State University, Towson University, University of Maryland

MARYLAND

ALLEGANY COLLEGE
DEPARTMENT OF HUMANITIES AND MUSIC
12401 Willowbrook Rd. S.E.
Cumberland, MD 21502
Melody Grew
301-784-5697
Fax: 301-784-1349
E-mail: mgrew@ac.cc.md.us
www.ac.cc.md.us

ANNE ARUNDEL COMMUNITY COLLEGE
DEPARTMENT OF PERFORMING ARTS
101 College Pkwy.
Arnold, MD 21012
Dr. Jean Turner Schreier
401-351-7000
Fax: 401-541-2489
E-mail: jtschreier@aacc.cc.md.us
www.aacc.cc.md.us

BALTIMORE SCHOOL FOR THE ARTS
712 Cathedral St.
Baltimore, MD 21201
Chris Ford
410-396-8392
Fax: 410-539-1430
www.bsfa.edu

CHESAPEAKE COLLEGE
DEPARTMENT OF MUSIC
P.O. Box 8
Wye Mills, MD 21679-0008
Music Department
301-822-5400
Fax: 410-827-5875
www.chesapeake.edu

COLLEGE OF NOTRE DAME OF MARYLAND
DEPARTMENT OF MUSIC
4701 N. Charles St.
Baltimore, MD 21210-2402
Ernest Ragogini
410-532-5386
Fax: 410-435-5937
E-mail: eragogini@ndm.edu
www.ndm.edu

COLUMBIA UNION COLLEGE
DEPARTMENT OF MUSIC
7600 Flower Ave.
Takoma Park, MD 20812-7796
James Bingham
301-270-9200
Fax: 301-270-1618
www.cuc.edu

COMMUNITY COLLEGE OF BALTIMORE CITY
DEPARTMENT OF MUSIC-ESSEX CAMPUS
7201 Rossville Blvd.
Baltimore, MD 21237-3899
William Watston
410-780-6521
Fax: 410-682-6871
E-mail: wwatson@ccbc.cc.md.us
www.ccbc.cc.md.us

COPPIN STATE COLLEGE
DEPARTMENT OF MUSIC
Baltimore, MD 21216
Charles Alston
800-635-3674
www.coppin.edu

FREDERICK COMMUNITY COLLEGE
DEPARTMENT OF MUSIC
7932 Opossumtown
Frederick, MD 21702
Jan Holly
301-846-2512
Fax: 301-846-2498
E-mail: jholly@fcc.cc.md.us
www.co.frederick.md.us

FROSTBURG STATE UNIVERSITY
MUSIC DEPARTMENT
101 Braddock Rd.
Frostburg, MD 21532
Dr. Ellen Grolman Schlegel
301-687-4109
Fax: 301-687-4784
E-mail: eschlegel@frostburg.edu
www.frostburg.edu

The structure of the program offers the following: concentration in vocal performance; concentration in music management; tracks in piano and instrumental performance; and a teaching certification option. The music department is housed in a new, $20 million performing arts facility with three recital halls, a state-of-the-art MIDI lab, a piano lab and a listening lab.

GARRETT COMMUNITY COLLEGE
DEPARTMENT OF MUSIC
Mosser Rd.
Mc Henry, MD 21541
Lillian Mitchell
301-387-3054
Fax: 301-387-3054
www.gcc.cc.md.us

GOUCHER COLLEGE
DEPARTMENT OF MUSIC
Baltimore, MD 21204
Lisa Weiss
410-337-6276
Fax: 410-769-5063
www.goucher.edu

HAGERSTOWN COMMUNITY COLLEGE
DEPARTMENT OF MUSIC
11400 Robinwood
Hagerstown, MD 21742
Dave Warner
301-790-2800
Fax: 301-393-3680
E-mail: warnerd@hcc.cc.md.us
www.hcc.cc.md.us

HARTFORD COMMUNITY COLLEGE
DEPARTMENT OF MUSIC
401 Thomas Run Rd.
Bel Air, MD 21015
Paul Lee
410-836-4291
Fax: 410-836-4363
E-mail: plabe@harford.cc.md.us
www.harford.cc.md.us

HOOD COLLEGE
COMMUNICATIONS
401 Rosemont Ave.
Frederick, MD 21701
Eileen Lishka
301-696-3429
Fax: 301-696-7653
E-mail: nlester@hood.edu
www.hood.edu

MONTGOMERY COLLEGE
DEPARTMENT OF MUSIC
51 Mannakee St.
Rockville, MD 20850
Molly Donnelly
301-279-5209
Fax: 301-251-7553
E-mail: mdonnell@mc.cc.md.us
www.montgomerycollege.edu

MORGAN STATE UNIVERSITY
MURPHY FINE ARTS CENTER
Room 151
Baltimore, MD 21251
Dr. Nathan M. Carter
401-319-3286
Fax: 401-319-3835
E-mail: ncarter@moac.morgan.edu
www.morgan.edu

MOUNT ST. MARY'S COLLEGE
DEPARTMENT OF VISUAL PERFORMING ARTS
16300 Emmetsburg Rd.
Emmetsburg, MD 21727
Kurt Blaugher
301-447-5308
Fax: 301-447-5755
www.msmary.edu

PEABODY CONSERVATORY OF MUSIC
JOHN HOPKINS UNIVERSITY
1 E. Mount Vernon Pl.
Baltimore, MD 21202
Barbara Lambert
410-659-8100
Fax: 410-659-8129
E-mail: lambert@peabody.jhu.edu
www.peabody.jhu.edu

Degrees: Minors in Music only

PRINCE GEORGES COMMUNITY COLLEGE
DEPARTMENT OF MUSIC
301 Largo Rd.
Upper Marlboro, MD 20774
Gary Kirkeby
301-322-0955
Fax: 301-808-0960
www.pg.cc.md.us

SALISBURY UNIVERSITY
DEPARTMENT OF MUSIC
Fulton Hall
Room 200
Salisbury, MD 21801
Richard Johnson
410-543-6385
Fax: 410-548-3002
E-mail: rjohnson@salisbury.edu
www.salisbury.edu

ST. MARY'S COLLEGE OF MARYLAND
DEPARTMENT OF MUSIC
St. Mary's City, MD 20686
David Froom
301-862-0225
Fax: 301-862-0958
www.smcm.edu

THE PEABODY INSTITUTE OF JOHNS HOPKINS UNIVERSITY
PEABODY PUBLIC INFORMATION OFFICE
1 E. Mount Vernon Place
Baltimore, MD 21202
Anne Garside
410-659-8180
www.peabody.jhu.edu

TOWSON UNIVERSITY
MUSIC DEPARTMENT
8000 York Rd.
Towson, MD 21252
Mary Ann Criss
410-830-2839
Fax: 410-830-2841
E-mail: mcriss@towson.edu
www.towson.edu/music

NAVAL ACADEMY
DEPARTMENT OF MUSIC
Alumni Hall
675 Decatur Rd.
Annapolis, MD 21402-1309
John Talley
410-293-2439
Fax: 410-293-3218
www.usna.edu

UNIVERSITY OF MARYLAND
SCHOOL OF MUSIC
2110 Clarice Smith Performing Arts
Center
College Park, MD 20742
Lois Ash
301-405-1313
Fax: 301-314-7966
E-mail: music-
admissions@umail.umd.edu
www.music.umd.edu

Degrees: B.A., B.M., B.M.E., M.A., M.M.,
D.M.A, and D.P

Located in the culturally vibrant corridor
between Washington D.C. and Baltimore, the
University of Maryland School of Music offers
all the opportunities of a conservatory with the
advantages of a world-class research university

UNIVERSITY OF MARYLAND BALTIMORE COUNTY
DEPARTMENT OF MUSIC
1000 Hilltop Cir.
Baltimore, MD 21250
Pat Benton
410-455-2942
Fax: 410-455-1181
E-mail: benton@umbc.edu
www.umbc.edu

UNIVERSITY OF MARYLAND EASTERN SHORE
DEPARTMENT OF FINE ARTS
Backbone Rd.
Princess Anne, MD 21853
Gerald Johnson
410-651-6571
Fax: 410-651-6105
www.umes.edu

WASHINGTON BIBLE COLLEGE
DEPARTMENT OF MUSIC
6511 Princess Garden Pkwy.
Lanham, MD 20706
Janice Kilgore Wood
301-521-1400
Fax: 301-552-2775
www.bible.edu

WASHINGTON COLLEGE
GIBSON DEPARTMENT OF MUSIC
Chesterton, MD 21620
Dr. Amzie Parcell
410-778-2800
Fax: 410-778-7850
E-mail: amzie.parcell@washcoll.edu
www.washcoll.edu

WASHINGTON CONSERVATORY OF MUSIC

5144 Mass. Ave.
Bethesda, MD 20816
Fax: 307-766-5326
www.washingtonconservatory.com

WESTERN MARYLAND COLLEGE
DEPARTMENT OF MUSIC

2 College Hill
Westminster, MD 21157
410-857-2595
Fax: 410-857-2729
E-mail: mboudrea@wmdc.edu
www.wmdc.edu

MASSACHUSETTS

Population: 6,424,140 (2003 Estimate)

Capital City: Boston

Music Colleges and Universities: American International College, Amherst College, Anna Maria College, Assumption College, Atlantic Union College, Berklee College of Music, Berkshire Community College, Boston College, Boston Conservatory, Boston University, Brandeis University, Bridgewater State College, Cape Cod Community College, Clark University, College of the Holy Cross, Dean College, Eastern Nazarene College, Emerson College, Emmanuel College, Endicott College, Fitchburg State College, Gordon College, Hampshire College, Harvard University, Holyoke Community College, Longy School of Music, Massachusetts College of Liberal Arts, Massachusetts Communications College, Massachusetts Institute of Technology, Mount Holyoke College, New England Conservatory, North Bennet Street School, Northeastern University, Northern Essex Community College, Our Lady of the Elms College, Pine Manor College, Regis College, Salem State College, Simmons College, Smith College, Springfield College, Tufts University, University of Massachusetts at Amherst, University of Massachusetts at Boston, University of Massachusetts at Dartmouth, University of Massachusetts at Lowell, Wellesley College, Westfield State College, Wheaton College, Wheelock College, Williams College, Worcester State College

Bird: Chickadee

Motto: Ense petit placidam sub libertate quietem – By the sword we seek peace, but peace only under liberty.

Flower: Mayflower

Tree: American Elm

Residents Called: Bay Staters

Origin of Name: Named after local Indian tribe whose name means "a large hill place."

Area: 10,555 square miles (44th largest state)

Statehood: February 6, 1788 (6th state)

Largest Cities: Boston, Worcester, Springfield, Lowell, Cambridge, Brockton, New Bedford, Fall River, Lynn, Quincy

College Band Programs: Boston College, Boston University, Harvard University, Massachusetts Institute of Technology (MIT) Marching Band, Worcester Polytechnic Institute's Pep Band, University of Massachusetts-Amherst, Williams College

MASSACHUSETTS

AMERICAN INTERNATIONAL COLLEGE
DEPARTMENT OF MUSIC
100 State St.
Springfield, MA 01109
Admissions
800-242-3142
E-mail: inquiry@www.aic.edu
www.aic.com

AMHERST COLLEGE
DEPARTMENT OF MUSIC
224 Arms Music Center
Amherst, MA 01002
David Reck
413-542-5812
Fax: 413-542-2678
E-mail: dbreck@amherst.edu
www.amherst.edu

ANNA MARIA COLLEGE
MUSIC PROGRAM
50 Sunset Lane
Worcester, MA 01612-1198
Irene Robinson
508-849-3450
Fax: 508-849-3334
E-mail: aransom@annamaria.edu
www.annamaria.edu

ASSUMPTION COLLEGE
DEPARTMENT OF ART AND MUSIC
500 Salisbury St.
Worcester, MA 01615-0005
Michelle Graveline
508-767-7386
Fax: 508-799-4502
E-mail: mgraveli@assumption.edu
www.assumption.edu

ATLANTIC UNION COLLEGE
DEPARTMENT OF MUSIC
P.O. Box 1000
South Lancaster, MA 01561
Erick Parris
978-368-2100
Fax: 978-368-2011
E-mail: info@atlanticuc.edu
www.atlanticuc.edu

BERKLEE COLLEGE OF MUSIC
1140 Boylston St.
Boston, MA 02215
Lee Eliot Berk
800-BERKLEE
Fax: 617-247-6978
E-mail: admissions@berklee.edu
www.berklee.edu

For over 55 years, Berklee College of Music has become the world's largest independent school of music. Today, it is widely recognized as the leading college for the study of contemporary music. Berklee's environment is designed to give its 3,500 students and 450 faculty members real-world learning experiences and the proper tools to help further their craft. It all adds up to the most complete music learning experience anywhere. With Boston as a backdrop, Berklee's state-of-the-art facilities provide students with opportunities to develop their skills and talent in every area from composition to performance to production. As so many successful graduates before him or her, each student will also learn how to make informed business and career decisions. Berklee's faculty reads like a "Who's Who" of the contemporary music world, including saxophonist Joe Lovano, and Walter Beasley; vocalist of Manhattan Transfer, Cheryl Bentyne; pianist JoAnne Brackeen; drummer Kenwood Dennard; guitarist Mick Goodrick; saxophonist Bill Pierce; and vibist Dave Samuels.

BERKSHIRE COMMUNITY COLLEGE
DEPARTMENT OF MUSIC

1350 West St.
Pittsfield, MA 01201
Ellen Shanahan
413-499-4660
Fax: 413-447-7840
E-mail: eshanaha@berkshirecc.edu
www.berkshirecc.edu

BOSTON COLLEGE
MUSIC DEPARTMENT

Lyons 407
Chestnut Hill, MA 02467-3805
T. Frank Kennedy
617-552-3018
E-mail: frkenned@bc.edu
www.bc.edu

BOSTON CONSERVATORY
MUSIC CONSERVATORY

Boston, MA 02215
Jennifer L. Benjamin
617-536-6340
Fax: 617-536-3176
E-mail:
jbenjamin@bostonconservatory.edu
www.bostonconservatory.edu

BOSTON UNIVERSITY
SCHOOL FOR THE ARTS, MUSIC DIVISION

855 Commonwzealth Ave.
Boston, MA 02215
Richard Cornell
617-353-3341
Fax: 617-353-7455
www.bu.edu/cfa

The Boston University School of Music offers a conservatory-style education with the advantages of being in a large university setting.

Undergraduate degrees can be obtained in performance, music education, history and literature, theory and composition.

BRANDEIS UNIVERSITY
DEPARTMENT OF MUSIC

P.O. Box 549110
MS 051
Waltham, MA 02254-9110
Eric Chasalow
781-736-3312
Fax: 781-736-3320
E-mail: chasalow@brandeis.edu
www.brandeis.edu

BRIDGEWATER STATE COLLEGE
DEPARTMENT OF MUSIC

Park Ave.
Bridgewater, MA 02325
Steven Young
508-531-1377
Fax: 508-531-1772
E-mail: s1young@bridgew.edu
www.bridgew.edu

CAPE COD COMMUNITY COLLEGE
DEPARTMENT OF MUSIC

2240 Lyanough Rd.
West Barnstable, MA 02668
Robert Kidd
508-362-2131
Fax: 508-375-4020
www.capecod.mass.edu

CLARK UNIVERSITY
DEPARTMENT OF VISUAL AND PERFORMING ARTS

950 Main St.
Worcester, MA 01610-1400
Gerald Castonguay
508-793-7340
Fax: 508-793-8844
E-mail: gcastonguay@clarku.edu
www.clarku.edu/clarkarts

COLLEGE OF THE HOLY CROSS

1 College St.
P.O. Box 151A
Worcester, MA 01510
Ann McDermott
508-793-2296
Fax: 508-793-3030
E-mail: skorde@holycross.edu
www.holycross.edu

The music department offers all Holy Cross students the opportunity to develop an understanding and appreciation of music through a wide range of courses in the history and theory of music, both on an introductory and an advanced level. It also provides an opportunity for further study to those who, by virtue of previous training and continuing serious interest, wish to focus in music. The major in music consists of a minimum of 10 courses. Required courses are four theory of music courses, two history of western music courses and senior seminar. Electives can include additional courses in history, theory, composition, ethnomusicology and performance in addition to required courses. Students who do not wish to enroll in the performance program of the college may meet the performance requirement for the major by participating in any one of the performing organizations of the college with the permission of the department chair. Facilities in the music department include a music library with state-of-the-art listening equipment and a sizable collection of scores, books, recordings and videotapes; practice rooms with pianos; classrooms; a studio for electronic and computer music; music notation workstations; and a variety of traditional instruments.

DEAN COLLEGE
DEPARTMENT OF MUSIC

Franklin, MA 02038
Nancy Kerr
508-541-1823
Fax: 508-541-1922
www.dean.edu

EASTERN NAZARENE COLLEGE
DEPARTMENT OF MUSIC

Quincy, MA 02170
Charles Seifert
617-773-6350
Fax: 617-773-6324
E-mail: seifertc@enc.edu
www.enc.edu

EMERSON COLLEGE
DEPARTMENT OF MUSIC

100 Beacon St.
Boston, MA 02170
Scott Wheeler
617-578-8780
Fax: 617-578-1501
E-mail: scott_wheeler@emerson.edu
www.emerson.edu

EMMANUEL COLLEGE
DEPARTMENT OF MUSIC

400 The Fenway
Boston, MA 02115-5725
Louise Cash
617-277-9340
Fax: 617-735-9801
E-mail: cash@emmanuel.edu
www.emmanuel.edu

ENDICOTT COLLEGE
NORTH SHORE CONSERVATORY OF MUSIC
376 Hale St.
Beverly, MA 01915
Music Department
800-325-1114
www.endicott.edu

FITCHBURG STATE COLLEGE
DEPARTMENT OF HUMANITIES AND MUSIC
160 Pearl St.
Fitchburg, MA 01420
Jane Fiske
978-665-3276
Fax: 978-665-3274
E-mail: jfiske@fsc.edu
www.fsc.edu

GORDON COLLEGE
DIVISION OF FINE ARTS
255 Grapevine Rd.
Wenham, MA 01984
Joanne Collins
508-927-2300
Fax: 508-921-1398
www.gordon.edu

The Music Department, a part of the Division of Fine Arts, offers degree programs (B.M., B.A.) in which students may specialize in performance, music education, theory, church music or liberal arts. The department, which has over 30 full-time and part-time instructors and 95 music majors, is fully accredited by the National Association of Schools of Music. The Interstate Certification Compact also certifies the music education program. Performance groups include the college choir, symphony orchestra, wind ensemble, chamber singers, women's choir, hand bell choir, jazz ensemble and many other small chamber organizations. Membership in these ensembles is open by audition to all students regardless of major.

HAMPSHIRE COLLEGE
DEPARTMENT OF MUSIC
West St.
Amherst, MA 01002
Daniel Warner
413-559-5586
Fax: 413-559-5481
E-mail: dcwmb@hampshire.edu
www.hampshire.edu

HARVARD UNIVERSITY
DEPARTMENT OF MUSIC
Music Building
105S/203S
Cambridge, MA 02138
Thomas Forrest Kelly
617-495-2791
Fax: 617-496-8081
E-mail: musicdpt@fas.harvard.edu
www.fas.harvard.edu/~musicdpt

HOLYOKE COMMUNITY COLLEGE
DEPARTMENT OF MUSIC
303 Homestead Ave.
Holyoke, MA 01040
Elissa Brill
413-552-2291
Fax: 413-534-8975
E-mail: ebrill@hcc.mass.edu
www.hcc.mass.edu

LONGY SCHOOL OF MUSIC
1 Follen St.
Cambridge, MA 02138
Robert Shay
617-876-0956
Fax: 617-354-8841
E-mail: music@longy.edu
www.longy.edu/main.htm

MASSACHUSETTS COLLEGE OF LIBERAL ARTS
DEPARTMENT OF FINE AND PERFORMANCE ARTS

375 Church St
North Adams, MA 01247
Christine Condaris
413-662-5101
Fax: 413-662-5010
E-mail: ccondaris@mcla.mass.edu
www.mcla.mass.edu

MASSACHUSETTS COMMUNICATIONS COLLEGE
RECORDING ARTS DEPARTMENT

10 Brookline Place
Brookline, MA 03445
617-267-7910
Fax: 617-236-7883

MASSACHUSETTS INSTITUTE OF TECHNOLOGY
DEPARTMENT OF MUSIC

Cambridge, MA 02139
Fred Harris
617-253-1000
E-mail: jhlyons@mit.edu
www.mit.edu

MOUNT HOLYOKE COLLEGE
DEPARTMENT OF MUSIC

Room 5, Pratt
South Hadley, MA 01075
Gary Steigerwalt
413-538-2306
Fax: 413-538-2547
E-mail: gsteiger@mtholyoke.edu
www.mtholyoke.edu/acad/music

NEW ENGLAND CONSERVATORY
OFFICE OF ADMISSIONS

290 Huntington Ave.
Boston, MA 02115
Allison Ball
617-585-1100
Fax: 617-262-0500
www.newenglandconservatory.edu.

NORTH BENNET STREET SCHOOL
ADMISSIONS

39 North Bennet St.
Boston, MA 02113
Robert G. Delaney
617-227-0155
Fax: 617-227-0155
E-mail: admissions@nbss.org
www.nbss.org

Piano Technology is a two-year program. The first year is devoted to tuning, regulation and some repair. The second year is devoted to the major repair, rebuilding and finishing of pianos. There is also a three-year violin-making program.

NORTHEASTERN UNIVERSITY
DEPARTMENT OF MUSIC

351 Ryder Hall
Boston, MA 02115
Bruce Ronkin
617-373-2440
Fax: 617-373-4129
E-mail: bronkin@lynx.neu.edu
www.music.neu.edu

NORTHERN ESSEX COMMUNITY COLLEGE
DEPARTMENT OF MUSIC

100 Elliott St.
Haverhill, MA 01830
Michael Finegold

978-738-7000
E-mail: mfinegold@necc.mass.edu
www.necc.mass.edu

OUR LADY OF THE ELMS COLLEGE
DIVISION OF HUMANITIES AND FINE ARTS
291 Springfield St.
Chicopee, MA 01013
Cristina Canales
413-594-2761
Fax: 413-594-2761
www.elms.edu

PINE MANOR COLLEGE
MUSIC PROGRAM
400 Heath St.
Chestnut Hill, MA 02467
Nia Chester
617-731-7000
Fax: 617-731-7199
E-mail: beamsmah@pmc.edu
www.pmc.edu

REGIS COLLEGE
DEPARTMENT OF MUSIC
235 Wellesley St.
Weston, MA 02193
Sheila Prichard
617-893-1820
Fax: 617-893-1820
E-mail: sheila.prichard@regiscollege
www.regiscollege.edu

SALEM STATE COLLEGE
DEPARTMENT OF MUSIC
352 Lafayette St.
Salem, MA 01970
Gregg Thaller
978-542-6456
Fax: 978-542-6296
E-mail: gthaller@salemstate.edu
www.salemstate.edu/music

SIMMONS COLLEGE
MARKETING
300 The Fenway
Boston, MA 02215
Lynette Benton
617-521-2000
E-mail: lynette.benton@simmons.edu
www.simmons.edu

SMITH COLLEGE
DEPARTMENT OF MUSIC
Northampton, MA 01063
Monica Jakuc
413-585-3150
Fax: 413-585-3180
E-mail: mjakuc@smith.edu
www.smith.edu/music

SPRINGFIELD COLLEGE
DEPARTMENT OF MUSIC
Springfield, MA 01109
Christopher Haynes
413-788-3277
E-mail:
christopher_haynes@spfldcol.edu
www.spfldcol.edu

TUFTS UNIVERSITY
DEPARTMENT OF MUSIC
20 Professors Row
Medford, MA 02155
John McDonald
617-627-3564
Fax: 617-627-3967
E-mail: ljones01@emerald.tufts.edu
www.tufts.edu/as/music

UNIVERSITY OF MASSACHUSETTS AT AMHERST
DEPARTMENT OF MUSIC
FAC/151 Presidents Dr.
Amherst, MA 01003
Marilyn Kushick
413-545-2227
Fax: 413-545-2092
E-mail: mkushick@music.umass.edu
www.umass.edu/music-dance

UNIVERSITY OF MASSACHUSETTS AT DARTMOUTH
COLLEGE OF VISUAL AND PERFORMANCE ARTS AND MUSIC
285 Old Westport Rd.
North Dartmouth, MA 02747
Eleanor Carlson
508-999-8568
Fax: 508-910-6587
E-mail: ecarlson@umassd.edu
www.umassd.edu

UNIVERSITY OF MASSACHUSETTS AT BOSTON
ENROLLMENT INFORMATION SERVICES
Wheatley Department of Music
100 Morrissey Blvd.
Boston, MA 02125
Jean Macgowan
617-287-6980
Fax: 617-287-6511
www.umb.edu

UNIVERSITY OF MASSACHUSETTS AT LOWELL
DEPARTMENT OF MUSIC
Lowell, MA 01854
Dr. William Moylan
978-934-3850
Fax: 978-934-3034
www.uml.edu/dept/music/home.htm

WELLESLEY COLLEGE
MUSIC DEPARTMENT
106 Central St.
Wellesley, MA 02481
Martin Brody
781-283-2077
Fax: 781-283-3687
www.wellesley.edu/Music/home.html

WESTFIELD STATE COLLEGE
DEPARTMENT OF MUSIC
577 Western Ave.
Westfield, MA 01086
Dr. Peter J. Demos
413-572-5300
Fax: 413-562-3613
E-mail: pdemos@wisdom.wsc.ma.edu
www.wsc.ma.edu

WHEATON COLLEGE
WATSON FINE AND PERFORMING ARTS
Department of Music
26 E. Main St.
Norton, MA 02766
Annette Blood
508-285-7722
Fax: 508-286-3565
E-mail: ablood@wheatonma.edu
www.wheatoncollege.edu

WHEELOCK COLLEGE
DEPARTMENT OF MUSIC
200 Riverway
Boston, MA 02215
Leo Collins
617-734-5200
Fax: 617-566-7369
E-mail: whe_lcollins@flo.org
www.wheelock.edu

WILLIAMS COLLEGE
DEPARTMENT OF MUSIC
Williamstown, MA 01267
David S. Kechley
413-597-2127
Fax: 413-597-3100
E-mail: david.s.kechley@williams.edu
www.williams.edu/depts.html

Symphonic Winds: The Symphonic Winds
consists of 40-45 musicians and is open to all
college brass, woodwind and percussion players. Rehearsals begin in mid-November in
preparation for several public concerts held in
Chapin Hall. The ensemble's goal is to perform a wide variety of traditional band repertoire as well as transcriptions and contemporary works. Student soloists, guest soloists, and
conductors (such as saxophonist Lynn Klock
and conductor Elliott Del Borgo) are featured.
Steven Dennis Bodner is director. The
Berkshire Symphony: The Berkshire
Symphony is conducted by Ronald Feldman
and includes nearly 70 members, half of whom
are students and half of whom are professional
musicians. The ensemble presents four major
concerts each season; the programs balance
orchestral standard with contemporary works.
The symphony received an ASCAP award for
innovative programming during the 1990-
1991 season, in which works for soloist and
orchestra by living American women composers (Joan Tower, Marilyn Bliss, Elizabeth
Vercoe and Ellen Taaffe Zwilich) were performed, one on each concert.

WORCESTER STATE COLLEGE
DEPARTMENT OF VISUAL AND PERFORMANCE ARTS
486 Chandler St.
Worcester, MA 01602
Charlie Nigro
508-793-8000
Fax: 508-929-8166
http://wwwfac.worcester.edu/athletic

MICHIGAN

Population: 10,115,680 (2003 Estimate)

Capital City: Lansing

Music Colleges and Universities: Adrian College, Albion College, Alma College, Andrews University, Aquinas College, Art Center Music School, Bethany Lutheran College, Calvin College, Central Michigan University, Concordia College, Cornerstone University, Eastern Michigan University, Ferris State University, Gogebic Community College, Grace Bible College, Grand Rapids Community College, Grand Valley State University, Great Lakes Christian College, Henry Ford Community College, Hillsdale College, Hope College, Interlochen Center for the Arts, Jackson Community College, Kalamazoo College, Kellogg Community College, Lake Michigan College, Lansing Community College, Macomb Community College Center Campus, Madonna University, Michigan State University, Michigan Technological University, Monroe Community College, Mott Community College, Muskegon Community College, Northern Michigan University, Northwestern Michigan College, Oakland Community College, Oakland University, Olivet College, Rochester College, Saginaw Valley State University, Schoolcraft College, Siena Heights University, Southwestern Michigan, Spring Arbor University, University of Michigan at Ann Arbor, University of Michigan at Dearborn, University of Michigan at Flint, Wayne State University, Western Michigan University, William Tyndale College

Bird: Robin

Motto: Si Quaeris Peninsulam Amoenam, Circumspice – If you seek a pleasant peninsula, look about you.

Flower: Apple Blossom

Tree: White pine

Residents Called: Michiganians

Origin of Name: Based on Chippewa Indian word "meicigama" meaning "great water" and refers to the Great Lakes.

Area: 96,810 square miles (11th largest state)

Statehood: January 26, 1837 (26th state)

Largest Cities: Detroit, Grand Rapids, Warren, Flint, Sterling Heights, Lansing, Ann Arbor, Livonia, Dearborn, Westland

College Band Programs: Central Michigan University, Eastern Michigan University, Michigan State University, Northern Michigan University, Michigan State University, University of Michigan, Western Michigan University

MICHIGAN

ADRIAN COLLEGE
DEPARTMENT OF MUSIC
110 South Madison St.
Adrian, MI 49221
Tom Hodgman
517-264-3331 x3925
Fax: 517-264-5161
E-mail: thodgman@adrian.edu
www.adrian.edu

ALBION COLLEGE
DEPARTMENT OF MUSIC
611 East Porter St.
Goodrich Chapel
Albion, MI 49224
Dr. Maureen Balke
517-629-0471
Fax: 517-629-0784
E-mail: mbalke@albion.edu
www.albion.edu/music

ALMA COLLEGE
DEPARTMENT OF MUSIC
614 West Superior St.
Alma, MI 48801-1599
David Zerbe
989-463-7213
Fax: 989-463-7979
E-mail: zerbe@alma.edu
www.alma.edu

ANDREWS UNIVERSITY
DEPARTMENT OF MUSIC
207 Hamel Hall
US 31/33 N.
Berrien Springs, MI 49014
Dr. Peter J. Cooper
269-471-3128
Fax: 269-471-6339
E-mail: pcooper@andrews.edu
www.andrews.edu/MUSIC

AQUINAS COLLEGE
DEPARTMENT OF MUSIC
1607 Robinson Rd. S.E.
Grand Rapids, MI 49506
Barbara W. McCargar
616-459-8281
Fax: 616-732-4487
E-mail: mccarbar@aquinas.edu
www.aquinas.edu

ART CENTER MUSIC SCHOOL
3975 Cass Ave.
Detroit, MI 48201
Denise Harvey
313-832-1711
http://comnet.org/acms

BETHANY LUTHERAN COLLEGE
DEPARTMENT OF MUSIC
700 Luther Dr.
Mankato, MI 56001-4436
Dennis Marzolf
507-344-5300
Fax: 507-344-7376
E-mail: dmarzolf@blc.edu
www.blc.edu

CALVIN COLLEGE
DEPARTMENT OF MUSIC
3201 Burton St. S.E.
Grand Rapids, MI 49546
Judith Czanko
616-957-6253
Fax: 616-957-6266
E-mail: jcza@calvin.edu
www.calvin.edu

CENTRAL MICHIGAN UNIVERSITY
SCHOOL OF MUSIC

Mt. Pleasant, MI 48859
Randi L'Hommedieu
517-774-3281
Fax: 517-774-3766
E-mail: randi.l'hommedieu@cmich.edu
www.mus.cmich.edu

Degrees: B.M.E., B.S., B.F.A., B.A., M.M., M.M.E

The CMU School of Music's faculty's reputation as outstanding performers, conductors, composers, and most importantly educators is known throughout the nation. Students in the school immediately sense an unyielding commitment to quality music education on the part of each faculty member.

One unique feature of this commitment is that university faculty members teach most undergraduate students, freshman through seniors. This means that the incoming freshman are offered the same educational and performing opportunities as upper class and graduate students. Students in the school of music, therefore, receive a personalized approach to their education.

The school places primary emphasis on the excellence of its faculty, staff and students. It is a place where students can achieve excellence through close interaction with dedicated and caring faculty. The school's programs encourage intellectual and music growth and prepare majors and minors for meaningful careers in music.

CONCORDIA COLLEGE
DEPARTMENT OF MUSIC

4090 Geddes Rd.
Ann Arbor, MI 48105-2705
Jeffrey Blersch
734-995-7300
Fax: 734-995-4610

CORNERSTONE UNIVERSITY
DEPARTMENT OF MUSIC

1001 E. Beltline Ave. N.E.
Grand Rapids, MI 49505-5803
Richard Stewart
616-222-1514
Fax: 616-222-1540
E-mail: rstewart@cornerstone.edu
www.cornerstone.edu

EASTERN MICHIGAN UNIVERSITY
DEPARTMENT OF MUSIC

Alexander Music Building
Room N101
Ypsilanti, MI 48197
David Woike
734-487-0244
Fax: 734-487-6939
E-mail: dave.woike@emich.edu
www.emich.edu

Why choose EMU? Full-time professors, rather than graduate assistants, teach most major classes at EMU. Course offerings provide a wide variety of class choices. Students find the educational environment at Eastern "stimulating." EMU faculty members are recognized for their dedicated teaching and outstanding performance skills. Students find faculty at EMU to be approachable, fair, caring, and fun to be around. EMU also has fine ensembles.

The orchestra, winds symphony, symphonic band and Barnhill Concert Band perform regularly, often visiting area schools and participating (by invitation) in the Midwestern Music Conference. They are known for the difficulty of their repertoire and their exemplary performing skills. The bands often break up into performing chamber groups, work in clinic situations with area high school groups, and through the band fraternity and sorority, participate in meaningful charity events. The nearly 200-member marching band stirs up excitement on EMU football Saturdays, and on several occasions, has performed at televised professional football games. And, the band is the featured attraction at our annual Bandorama in historic Pease Auditorium. EMU's Pep Band generates excitement during the basketball season. EMU's jazz ensemble and percussion ensemble play to standing-room-only crowds. In early 2001, the EMU Symphony Orchestra spent a weekend "on retreat" in Detroit, working with DSO musicians, and attending their Saturday night orchestra concert. They have collaborated in opera, ballet and other dance productions, and performed with professional entertainers like Marvin Hamlisch. Every fall, the orchestra and band team up to present a children's concert that is so popular with local school children that EMU's 1,400-seat Pease Auditorium is filled to capacity in two consecutive performances. EMU also has excellent performing ensembles, including University Choir (which plans to return for a third time next year to sing in New York's Carnegie Hall), Chamber Choir (which has toured the southeast and western United States, Mexico, and Europe), Women's Chorus and Collegium Musicum (a vocal-instrumental ensemble specializing in 18th- and 20th-century music).

FERRIS STATE UNIVERSITY
DEPARTMENT OF HUMANITIES
Big Rapids, MI 49307
Department Head
231-591-9971
Fax: 231-591-2188
www.ferris.edu

GOGEBIC COMMUNITY COLLEGE
DEPARTMENT OF MUSIC
Ironwood, MI 49938
Alex Mariniak
906-932-4962
E-mail:
alex.marciniak@faculty.gogebic.cc.mi.us
www.gogebic.cc.mi.us

GRACE BIBLE COLLEGE
DEPARTMENT OF MUSIC
1011 Aldon St. S.W.
Wyoming, MI 49509-1921
Jasonm Werkema
616-538-2330
Fax: 616-538-0599
www.gbcol.edu

GRAND RAPIDS COMMUNITY COLLEGE
DEPARTMENT OF MUSIC
Music Department
143 Bostwick Ave. N.E.
Grand Rapids, MI 49503
Lynn K. Asper
616-234-3940
Fax: 616-234-3973
E-mail: lasper@post.grcc.cc.mi.us
www.grcc.cc.mi.us

GRAND VALLEY STATE UNIVERSITY
DEPARTMENT OF MUSIC
1 Campus Dr.
Allendale, MI 49401
John Schuster-Craig
616-895-3484
www.gvsu.edu

GREAT LAKES CHRISTIAN COLLEGE
DEPARTMENT OF MUSIC
6211 W. Willow Hwy.
Lansing, MI 48917-1231
Esther Hetrick
517-321-0242
Fax: 517-321-5902
E-mail: ehetrick@glcc.edu
www.glcc.edu

HENRY FORD COMMUNITY COLLEGE
DEPARTMENT OF PERFORMANCE ARTS AND MUSIC
Dearborn, MI 48128
Jay Korinek
313-845-9634
Fax: 313-845-9658
www.henryford.cc.mi.us

HILLSDALE COLLEGE
DEPARTMENT OF MUSIC
Hillsdale, MI 49242
James Hollerman
517-437-7341
Fax: 517-607-2665
E-mail: cheryl.thomas@hillsdale.edu
www.hillsdale.edu

HOPE COLLEGE
MUSIC DEPARTMENT
127 E. 12th St.
Holland, MI 49423
Dr. Stuart Sharp
616-395-7642
Fax: 616-395-7182
E-mail: sharp@hope.edu
www.hope.edu

Degrees: B.A./B.M. in Performance,
Instrumental Music Education and Vocal
Music Education

INTERLOCHEN CENTER FOR THE ARTS
ADMISSIONS
P.O. Box 199
Traverse City, MI 49643
Tom Bewley
231-276-7472
Fax: 231-276-7464
www.interlochen.org

JACKSON COMMUNITY COLLEGE
DEPARTMENT OF MUSIC
Jackson, MI 49204
Ronald Douglas
517-787-0800
Fax: 517-789-1623
www.jackson.cc.mi.us

KALAMAZOO COLLEGE
DEPARTMENT OF MUSIC
1200 Academy St.
Kalamazoo, MI 49006
Dr. Leslie Tung
269-337-7070
Fax: 269-337-7067
E-mail: tung@kzoo.edu
www.kzoo.edu/music
Degrees: B.A.

The college offers an undergraduate experience of rigorous liberal arts scholarship and opportunities for experiential education in both domestic and international settings. Through the nationally recognized "K-Plan," students are provided an array of opportunities to develop increasing independence as they engage in intellectual and aesthetic inquiry, discriminate among moral and ethical values, and develop a humane knowledge of self in the context of history and society. The music department seeks to cultivate an understanding of the language and history of music and to nurture artistic skill and musicianship. Applied music and an ensemble program are at the center of the curriculum. Frequent performance opportunities are available through music ensembles and individual instruction. Performance facilities in the recently renovated music building (2001) include a concert hall and a recital hall. In addition, our students perform in Stetson Chapel and in several venues off campus. The college has an outstanding collection of early keyboard instruments (Dowd harpsichord, Schreiner positive organ, and McCobb fortepiano), a reconstructed 1907 Steinway concert grand piano and a newly purchased Hamburg Steinway concert grad.

Courses in music theory, music history, conducting, composition, and electives in combination with applied music provide an integrated approach to the discipline. Computer software, practice rooms, several rehearsal halls, and music instruments are available.

KELLOGG COMMUNITY COLLEGE
DEPARTMENT OF MUSIC
450 North Ave.
Battle Creek, MI 49017
Deric Craig
616-965-3931
Fax: 616-965-0280
E-mail: craigd@kellogg.cc.mi.us
www.kellogg.cc.mi.us

LAKE MICHIGAN COLLEGE
DEPARTMENT OF MUSIC
2755 E. Napier Ave.
Benton Harbor, MI 49017
Elife Schults-Berndt
616-927-8100
Fax: 616-927-6587
E-mail: bernt@lmc.cc.mi.us
www.lmc.cc.mi.us

LANSING COMMUNITY COLLEGE
MUSIC PROGRAM
P.O. Box 40010
Lansing, MI 48901
Michael Nealon
517-483-1018
Fax: 517-483-1473
E-mail: michael_nealon@lcc.edu
www.lcc.edu

MACOMB COMMUNITY COLLEGE CENTER CAMPUS
DEPARTMENT OF MUSIC
44575 Garfield Rd.
Clinton Township, MI 48038
John Krnacick
810-286-2045
Fax: 810-286-2272
www.macomb.cc.mi.us

MADONNA UNIVERSITY
DEPARTMENT OF MUSIC
36600 Schoolcraft Rd.
Livonia, MI 48150
Linette Popoff-Parks
734-432-5709
Fax: 734-432-5393
www.munet.edu

MARYGROVE COLLEGE
DEPARTMENT OF MUSIC
8425 W. McNichols Rd.
Detroit, MI 48221
Ellen Duncan
313-927-1252
Fax: 313-927-1345
E-mail: eduncan@marygrove.edu
www.marygrove.edu

MICHIGAN STATE UNIVERSITY
SCHOOL OF MUSIC
Music Building
East Lansing, MI 48824
James Forger
517-353-5340
Fax: 517-432-2880
E-mail: forger@msu.edu
www.music.msu.edu

The Michigan State University School of Music is known throughout the world and

U.S. as a leading professional training ground for composers, music educators, music therapists, and performers. It boasts one of the leading music education areas and African Studies programs in the nation, and presents more than 275 concerts on campus and throughout the United States annually. The school of music is made up of more than 600 students from across the nation, and has significant international representation. An outstanding, diverse faculty of more than 70 resident artists and scholars, along with more than 65 graduate assistants, provide instruction and guidance. The faculty is noted for devotion to teaching, excellence in performance, creating innovative and imaginative curricula, producing creative works and conducting significant research in many areas of music. The school of music consists of two neighboring buildings that include numerous classrooms, a complex of four computer music studios, a 20-seat computer-assisted instruction classroom, a music education resource room, a music therapy clinic, a psychology of music laboratory, recording facilities, rehearsal and practice rooms and teaching studios. The school is located adjacent to the main library, which houses music collections within the 15,000-square-foot Fine Arts Library.

MICHIGAN TECHNOLOGICAL UNIVERSITY
DEPARTMENT OF FINE ARTS AND MUSIC
1400 Townsend Dr.
Houghton, MI 49921
Milton Olsson
906-487-1841
Fax: 906-487-1841
www.fa.mtu.edu

MONROE COMMUNITY COLLEGE
DEPARTMENT OF MUSIC
15555 S. Rainsville Rd.
Monroe, MI 49931
William McCloskey
734-384-4152
Fax: 734-384-4160
E-mail:
wmccloskey@mail.monroe.cc.mi.us
www.monroe.cc.mi.us

MOTT COMMUNITY COLLEGE
DEPARTMENT OF MUSIC
1401 East Court St.
Flint, MI 48503
Charles Iwanusa Jr.
313-762-0943
www.mcc.edu

MUSKEGON COMMUNITY COLLEGE
DEPARTMENT OF MUSIC
Muskegon, MI 49440
Scott Cutting
616-773-9131
www.muskegon.cc.mi.us

NORTHERN MICHIGAN UNIVERSITY
DEPARTMENT OF MUSIC
1401 Presque Isle Ave.
Marquette, MI 49855
Dr. Donald R. Grant
906-227-2568
Fax: 906-227-2165
E-mail: dgrant@nmu.edu
www.nmu.edu/music

NORTHWESTERN MICHIGAN COLLEGE
DEPARTMENT OF MUSIC
1701 East Front
Traverse City, MI 49684
Mark Puchala
231-995-1338
Fax: 231-995-1696
www.nmc.edu

OAKLAND COMMUNITY COLLEGE
DEPARTMENT OF MUSIC
Orchard Ridge
Farmington, MI 48334
Nick Valenti
810-471-7795
Fax: 810-471-7544

OAKLAND UNIVERSITY
DEPARTMENT OF MUSIC, THEATRE, AND DANCE
Rochester, MI 48309
Karl Boelter
248-370-2030
Fax: 248-370-2041
E-mail: boelter@oakland.edu
www.otus.oakland.edu

From an excellent location accessible to all area cultural events, OU offers music in a dynamic growing environment rich with performance opportunities and a world-class faculty.

OLIVET COLLEGE
DEPARTMENT OF ARTS AND COMMUNICATION
MUSIC PROGRAM
320 S. Main St.
Olivet, MI 49076
Gary Wertheimer
616-749-7616
Fax: 616-749-7695
www.olivetcollege.edu

ROCHESTER COLLEGE
DEPARTMENT OF MUSIC
800 W. Avon Rd.
Rochester Hills, MI 48307
Joe Bentley
248-218-2000
Fax: 248-218-2005
E-mail: jbentley@rc.edu
www.rc.edu

SAGINAW VALLEY STATE UNIVERSITY
DEPARTMENT OF MUSIC
7400 Bay Rd.
May City, MI 48710
Marc Peretz
517-790-4159
E-mail: mhp@tardis.svsu.edu
www.svsu.edu

SCHOOLCRAFT COLLEGE
DEPARTMENT OF MUSIC
18600 Haggerty Rd.
Livonia, MI 48152
Bradley Bloom
313-462-4400
Fax: 313-462-4495
www.schoolcraft.cc.mi.us

SIENA HEIGHTS UNIVERSITY
DEPARTMENT OF MUSIC
1247 E. Siena Heights Dr.
Adrian, MI 49221
Susan Matych-Hager
517-264-7899
Fax: 517-265-3380
E-mail: smatyc@sienahts.edu
www.sienahts.edu

SOUTHWESTERN MICHIGAN
DEPARTMENT OF FINE AND PERFORMANCE ARTS
58900 Cheery Grove Rd.
Dowagiac, MI 49047
Jonathan Korzun
616-782-1225
Fax: 616-782-8414
E-mail: jkorzun@smc.cc.mi.us
www.smc.cc.mi.us

SPRING ARBOR UNIVERSITY
DEPARTMENT OF MUSIC
P.O. Box 219
Spring Arbor, MI 49283
Bruce Brown
517-750-1200
Fax: 517-750-2108
E-mail: bbrown@admin.arbor.edu
www.arbor.edu

UNIVERSITY OF MICHIGAN AT ANN ARBOR
SCHOOL OF MUSIC
1100 Baits Dr.
2290 Moore Bldg.
Ann Arbor, MI 48109
Sam Robinson
734-764-0584
Fax: 734-763-6616
www.music.umich.edu

Founded in 1880 when the University of Michigan engaged Calvin B. Cady as its first faculty member in music, the school of music is one of the oldest and largest music schools in the United States. It has consistently ranked among the top half-dozen music schools and conservatories for as long as such polls have been conducted. Earl V. Moore, one of music's greatest educators, headed the school from 1923-1960, developing programs that are still widely emulated throughout the U.S. In 1964, the school of music moved to its new building on north campus; the building was subsequently named for Dean Emeritus Moore. With over 1,000 students from all 50 states and almost two dozen countries, the school is located in a park-like setting on the university's north campus, in the city of Ann Arbor, a classic college town in the tradition of Cambridge and Berkeley, where intellectual, artistic and recreational activities abound. The school of music provides performance training comparable to Julliard or Curtis and academic training in music comparable to Princeton and Yale. The school contains rehearsal facilities, two concert halls, 45 performance-teaching studios, 18 classrooms, 135 practice rooms and other special facilities.

UNIVERSITY OF MICHIGAN AT DEARBORN
DEPARTMENT OF HUMANITIES
4901 Evergreen Rd.
Dearborn, MI 48128
Dr. John Constant
313-593-5433
Fax: 313-593-5551
E-mail: jgconsta@umich.edu
www.umd.umich.edu

UNIVERSITY OF MICHIGAN AT FLINT

DEPARTMENT OF MUSIC

French Hall 126
Flint, MI 48502
Lois Alexander
810-762-3377
Fax: 810-762-3326
E-mail: chumov@umflint.edu
www.flint.umich.edu/departments/mus

WAYNE STATE UNIVERSITY

DEPARTMENT OF MUSIC

1321 Old Main
Detroit, MI 48202
Dennis J. Tini
313-577-1795
Fax: 313-577-5420
E-mail: music@wayne.edu
www.music.wayne.edu
Degrees: B.M., M.M., B.A., and
Graduate Certificate in Orchestral
Studies

Part of the college of fine, performing and
communication arts, the Wayne State
University Department of Music has 16 full-
time and over 60 adjunct faculty. Located in
the heart of Detroit's University Cultural
Center, it enrolls over 325 music majors. Since
1918, the department has been recognized for
its artistic and academic excellence. The
department is fully accredited by the NASM,
and 22 members of the part-time faculty are
members of the Detroit Symphony Orchestra.
Aspiring musicians have the opportunity to
study with professional musicians of regional,
national and international acclaim at one of
the largest urban research universities in the
United States. Our renovated facilities in Old
Main feature a new recording studio and a
digital synth-lab; expanded rehearsal and
office space; updated library/computer labs;
and the new 160-seat Music Recital Hall.

WESTERN MICHIGAN UNIVERSITY

SCHOOL OF MUSIC

1903 W. Michigan Ave.
Kalamazoo, MI 49008
616-387-4667
Fax: 616-387-1113
E-mail: richardohearn@wmich.edu
www.wmich.edu/music

WILLIAM TYNDALE COLLEGE

DEPARTMENT OF MUSIC

35700 E. 12th Mile Rd.
Farmington Hills, MI 48331
Kimberly Swan
248-553-7200
Fax: 248-553-5963
E-mail: kswan@williamtyndale.edu
www.williamtyndale.com

MINNESOTA

Population: 5,102,518 (2003 Estimate)

Capital City: Saint Paul

Music Colleges and Universities: Anoka Ramsey Community College at Coon Rapids, Augsburg College, Bemidji State University, Bethel College, Carleton College, College of St. Benedict, College of St. Catherine, College of St. Scholastica, Concordia College at Morehead, Crown College, Fergus Falls Community College, Gustavus Adolphus College, Hamline University, Hibbing Community College, Itasca Community College, Macalester College, Martin Luther College, Minneapolis Community and Technology College, Minnesota Bible College, Minnesota State College Southeast Technical, Minnesota State University at Mankato, Minnesota State University at Moorhead, Moorhead State University, Musictech College, Normandale Community College, North Central Bible College, North Hennepin Community College, Northland Community and Technology College, Northwestern College, Red Wing Technical College, Ridgewater College, Riverland Community College, Southwest State University, St. Cloud State Univer, St. John's University, St. Mary's University of Minnesota, St. Olaf College, University of Minnesota at Crookston, University of Minnesota at Duluth, University of Minnesota at Morris, University of Minnesota at Twin Cities, University of St. Thomas, Vermillion Community College, Winona State University, Worthington Community College

Bird: Common Loon

Motto: L'Etoile du nord – The star of the north

Flower: Pink and white lady's-slipper

Tree: Red Pine

Residents Called: Minnesotans

Origin of Name: It is based on the Dakota Sioux Indian word for "sky-tinted water," referring to the Minnesota River or the state's many lakes.

Area: 86,943 square miles (12th largest state)

Statehood: May 11, 1858 (32nd state)

Largest Cities: Minneapolis, Saint Paul, Duluth, Rochester, Bloomington, Brooklyn Park, Plymouth, Eagan, Coon Rapids, Burnsville

College Band Programs: University of Minnesota

MINNESOTA

ANOKA RAMSEY COMMUNITY COLLEGE AT COON RAPIDS
DEPARTMENT OF MUSIC
11200 Mississippi Blvd. N.W.
Coon Rapids, MN 55433-3470
Carlyle Davidson
763-427-2600
www.an.cc.mn.us

AUGSBURG COLLEGE
DEPARTMENT OF MUSIC
2211 Riverside Ave.
Minneapolis, MN 55454
Dr. Robert Stacke
612-330-1028
Fax: 612-330-1264
E-mail: stacke@augsburg.edu
www.augsburg.edu/music

BEMIDJI STATE UNIVERSITY
DEPARTMENT OF MUSIC
1500 Birchmont Dr. N.E.
Bemidji, MN 56601
Del Lyren
218-755-2915
Fax: 218-755-4369
E-mail: dlyren@bemidjistate.edu
www.bemidjistate.edu

BSU is a beautiful campus located in the north woods country of Northern Minnesota. The music building is located next to Lake Bemidji. We offer excellent training for anyone interested in a music performance or music education degree. With approximately 100 majors and minors, our department is large enough to offer many performance opportunities and small enough to offer individual attention.

BETHEL COLLEGE
DEPARTMENT OF MUSIC
3900 Bethel Dr.
St. Paul, MN 55112
Music Department Chair
651-638-6400
Fax: 651-638-6001
E-mail: c-reents@bethel.edu
www.bethel.edu

CARLETON COLLEGE
MUSIC DEPARTMENT
1 North College St.
Northfield, MN 55057
Music Department Chair
507-646-4347
Fax: 507-646-5561
E-mail: music@carleton.edu
www.carleton.edu

Music performance and study in the context of a small, highly selective liberal arts college.

COLLEGE OF ST. CATHERINE
DEPARTMENT OF MUSIC
2004 Randolph
Saint Paul, MN 55105-1794
Arlene Goter
651-690-6690
Fax: 651-690-8819
E-mail: agoter@stkate.edu
www.stkate.edu

COLLEGE OF ST. BENEDICT
BENEDICTA ARTS CENTER
37 S. College Ave., BAC 116A
St. Joseph, MN 56374
Deb Guertin
612-363-5796
Fax: 612-363-6097
E-mail: gwalker@csbsju.edu
www.csbsju.edu

COLLEGE OF ST. SCHOLASTICA
DEPARTMENT OF MUSIC
1200 Kenwood Ave.
Duluth, MN 55811-4199
Marianne Sandstrom
218-723-6038
Fax: 218-723-5991
E-mail: msandstr@css.edu
www.css.edu/depts/music

CONCORDIA COLLEGE AT MOORHEAD
MUSIC DEPARTMENT
901 8th St. S.
Moorhead, MN 56562
Dr. Robert J. Chabora
218-299-4414
Fax: 218-299-3058
E-mail: chabora@cord.edu
www.cord.edu/music

Degrees: B.A. (Music and Music Education)

The department of music at Concordia College at Moorhead is widely recognized for excellence in music making. Its fully accredited, rigorous B.A. and B.M. programs (in Music, Music Education, Performance and Theory) contribute broadly to a student-centered, liberal arts academic environment, and generate an exceptional quality of music performance rare at the undergraduate level. The department's premier touring ensembles (The Concordia Choir, Band and Orchestra) enjoy national and international acclaim, and perpetuate their respective legacies through a growing list of Concordia Recordings. Artist faculties, who are much in demand on the stage, are first and foremost gifted teachers and dedicated mentors. The department's 200-plus music majors and 45 faculty are housed in the beautiful, expanded and newly renovated Hivdsten Hall of Music. Like all departments at Concordia the Department of Music seeks to nurture the development of the whole person and to imbue in each student the benefits of comprehensive learning and of a global vision, and to provide opportunities not only for professional preparation, but also for personal, social and spiritual development through faith-based education and lives of service.

CROWN COLLEGE
DEPARTMENT OF MUSIC
6425 County Rd. 30
Saint Bonifacius, MN 55375
David Donelson
952-446-4231
Fax: 952-446-4149
E-mail: hyndmann@crown.edu
www.crown.edu

FERGUS FALLS COMMUNITY COLLEGE
DEPARTMENT OF MUSIC
1414 College Way
Fergus Falls, MN 5637-1009
Teresa Ashworth
218-739-7500
Fax: 218-739-7475
E-mail: tashworth@ff.cc.mn.us
www.ff.cc.mn.us

GUSTAVUS ADOLPHUS COLLEGE
MUSIC DEPARTMENT
800 W. College Ave.
St. Peter, MN 56082
Dr. Ann Pesavento
507-933-7364
Fax: 507-933-7641
E-mail: apesaven@gustavus.edu
www.gustavus.edu

HAMLINE UNIVERSITY
DEPARTMENT OF MUSIC

1536 Hewitt Ave.
Mail #16
Saint Paul, MN 55104
Rees Allison
612-523-2231
Fax: 612-523-3066
E-mail: rallison@gw.hamline.edu
www.hamline.edu/cla/academics/music

HIBBING COMMUNITY COLLEGE
DEPARTMENT OF MUSIC

Hibbing, MN 55746
Thomas Palmsheim
218-262-6729
www.hcc.mnscu.edu

ITASCA COMMUNITY COLLEGE
DEPARTMENT OF MUSIC

Grand Rapids, MN 55744
Robert Perterson
218-327-4477
Fax: 218-327-4350
www.itasca.mnscu.edu

MACALESTER COLLEGE
DEPARTMENT OF MUSIC

1600 Grand Ave.
St. Paul, MN 55105
Robert Peterson
651-696-6382
Fax: 651-696-6785
E-mail: petersonr@macalester.edu
www.macalester.edu

MARTIN LUTHER COLLEGE
DEPARTMENT OF MUSIC

1995 Luther Ct
New Ulm, MN 56073
Kermit Moldenhaur
507-354-8221
Fax: 507-354-8225
www.mlc-wels.edu

MINNEAPOLIS COMMUNITY AND TECHNOLOGY COLLEGE
DEPARTMENT OF MUSIC

1501 Hennepin Ave.
Minneapolis, MN 55403
Stephen Solum
612-341-7233
Fax: 612-341-7075
www.mctc.mnscu.edu

MINNESOTA BIBLE COLLEGE
DEPARTMENT OF MUSIC

920 Mayowood Rd. S.W.
Rochester, MN 55902
Gary Sprague
507-288-4563
Fax: 507-288-9046

MINNESOTA STATE COLLEGE SOUTHEAST TECHNICAL
INSTRUMENT REPAIR
BAND INSTRUMENT REPAIR PROGRAM

308 Pioneer Rd.
Red Wind, MN 55066
John Huth
800-657-4849
Fax: 651-385-6378
E-mail: jhuth@southeasttech.mnscu.edu
www.southeasttech.mnscu.edu

The music instrument repair programs at
MSC-ST are designed to offer both educators

and performers viable career alternatives within the field of music.

MINNESOTA STATE UNIVERSITY AT MANKATO
Music Department
Department of Music
PAC 202
Mankato, MN 56001
John Lindberg
507-389-2118
E-mail: john.lindberg@mnsu.edu
www.intech.mnsu.edu/music

MINNESOTA STATE UNIVERSITY AT MOORHEAD
Department of Music
1104 7th Ave. S
Moorhead, MN 56563
David Ferriera
218-236-2101
Fax: 218-236-4097
E-mail: music@mnstate.edu
www.mnstate.edu

MUSICTECH COLLEGE
Admissions
19 Exchange St. E.
St. Paul, MN 55101
Debbie Sandridge
612-291-0177
Fax: 612-291-0366
www.musictech.com

NORMANDALE COMMUNITY COLLEGE
Department of Music
9700 France Ave. S.
Bloomington, MN 55431
Ona Pinsoneult
952-487-8200
Fax: 952-287-8439
www.nr.cc.mn.cc

NORTH CENTRAL BIBLE COLLEGE
Department of Music
910 Elliot Ave. South
Minneapolis, MN 55404
Larry Bach
612-343-4700
Fax: 612-343-4778

NORTH HENNEPIN COMMUNITY COLLEGE
Department of Music
7411 85th Ave. N
Brooklyn Park, MN 55445
Jerry Sandvik
612-424-0792
Fax: 612-424-0929
www.ndsu.nodak.edu

NORTHLAND COMMUNITY AND TECHNOLOGY COLLEGE
Department of Music
1101 Hwy. 1 E.
Thief River Falls, MN 56701
Linda Sameulson
218-681-0733
Fax: 218-681-0724
E-mail: lsameulson@northland.cc.mn.us
www.northland.cc.mn.us

NORTHWESTERN COLLEGE
DEPARTMENT OF MUSIC
3003 Snelling Ave. N.
St. Paul, MN 55113
Dr. Gerry Bouma
651-631-5255
Fax: 651-631-5124
E-mail: gdb@nwc.edu
www.nwc.edu

RED WING TECHNICAL COLLEGE
MINNESOTA SOUTHEAST TECHNICAL
1250 Homer Rd.
Winona, MN 55987
Music Department
800-372-8164
www.southeasttech.mnscu.edu

RIDGEWATER COLLEGE
DEPARTMENT OF MUSIC
2010 15th Ave. N.W.
Willmar, MN 56201
Darc Lease Gubrud
320-235-5114
Fax: 320-231-6602
E-mail: dlease@ridgewater.mnscu.edu
www.ridgewater.mnscu.edu

RIVERLAND COMMUNITY COLLEGE
DEPARTMENT OF MUSIC
1900 8th Ave. N.W.
Austin, MN 55912
Scott Blankenbaker
507-433-0547
Fax: 507-433-0515
E-mail: sblanken@river.cc.mn.us
www.riverland.cc.mn.us
Degrees: A.A.

Riverland community College is a two-year
comprehensive community college offering
3,000 students outstanding opportunities in
transfer and career education. Students may
choose to work toward an A.A. degree while
studying music. An A.F.A. degree has been
developed specifically for music majors with a
target date of Fall 2004 for implementation.
Riverland offers a friendly, collegial atmosphere with a department small enough to feel
personal, but large enough to provide many
exciting educational opportunities. Private and
class instruction, performing ensembles, theory, and survey courses are offered in a rapidly
growing, active department. Riverland's choirs
have appeared at Lincoln Center, Carnegie
Hall, and in other venues throughout North
America.

SOUTHWEST STATE UNIVERSITY
DEPARTMENT OF MUSIC
1501 State St.
Marshall, MN 56258
Charles Kauffman
507-537-7234
Fax: 507-537-7014
E-mail:
kauffman@ssu.southwest.msus.edu
www.southwest.msus.edu

ST. CLOUD STATE UNIVERSITY
DEPARTMENT OF MUSIC - PAC 238
720 4th Ave. S
Saint Cloud, MN 56301
Bruce Wood
320-255-3223
Fax: 320-255-2902
www.stcloudstate.edu

ST. JOHN'S UNIVERSITY
DEPARTMENT OF MUSIC
P.O. Box 2000
Collegeville, MN 56321
Deb Guertin
320-363-3371
E-mail: dguertin@csbsju.edu
www.csbsju.edu/music

ST. MARY'S UNIVERSITY OF MINNESOTA
SCHOOL OF THE ARTS AND MUSIC
700 Terrace Heights #58
Winona, MN 55987
Janet Heukeshoven
507-452-4430
Fax: 507-457-1611
E-mail: jheukesh@smumn.edu
www.smumn.edu/music

Degrees: B.A. Music Performance, Music Education, Music Industry (two tracks: music business and sound recording and technology), and B.A. in music (general studies degree)

The St. Mary's Music Department offers a challenging and enriching curriculum for music majors and minors, as well as many musical opportunities for non-majors. Music majors prepare themselves for careers in music education (both instrumental and vocal with classroom music), music industry (music technology on/or music business) or graduate school. Most SMU music education students complete the Master's of Instruction degree in their fifth year, thus obtaining both a B.A. in music and M of I degree for their professional teaching licensure. The music faculties are both active professionals and nurturing mentors for students. Students and faculty present an ambitious calendar of recitals and concerts throughout the year. Major ensembles at SMU include: concert band, wind ensemble, concert choir, chamber singers, jazz ensemble, jazz combos, academy chamber orchestra, batuaca-ta percussion ensemble, and many instrumen-tal chamber ensembles. Studies in music allow students to enhance their spiritual and person-al lives, and develop the basis for life-long appreciation of music and the arts in a Catholic, liberal arts university setting.

ST. OLAF COLLEGE
DEPARTMENT OF MUSIC
1520 St. Olaf Ave.
Northfield, MN 55057
Mary Hakes
507-646-3297
Fax: 507-646-3527
E-mail: music@stolaf.edu
www.stolaf.edu/depts/music
Degrees: B.M.

Integrating the artistic standards of a professional program with the intellectual rigors and academic breadth of the liberal arts, the St. Olaf College Music Department and its 60-plus faculty members offer extensive opportunities to explore, practice and celebrate the musician's art with an ongoing commitment to a distinctive ensemble program, and excellent individualized instruction, and a comprehensive undergraduate music curriculum. The St. Olaf Music program is well known nationally and internationally through its annual tours, recordings, and television broadcasts of its famous Christmas Festival. These well-known components of the program are only the most obvious examples of a rich and high quality music program specifically fashioned to serve the undergraduate musician. St. Olaf offers both the Bachelor of music degree with majors in performance, music education, theory-composition and church music; and a music major in the Bachelor of arts degree, including opportunities for emphasis in music history and literature and theory-composition.

UNIVERSITY OF MINNESOTA AT CROOKSTON
DEPARTMENT OF MUSIC AND THEATRE

2900 University Ave.
Crookston, MN 56716
George French
218-281-8266
Fax: 218-281-8080
E-mail: gfrench@mail.crk.umn.edu
www.crk.umn.edu

UNIVERSITY OF MINNESOTA AT DULUTH
DEPARTMENT OF MUSIC

231 Humanities Bldg.
10 University Dr.
Duluth, MN 55812
Judith Kritzmire
218-726-8206
Fax: 218-726-8210
www.d.umn.edu/music

UNIVERSITY OF MINNESOTA AT MORRIS
DEPARTMENT OF MUSIC

Morris, MN 56267
James Carlson
320-589-2111
Fax: 320-589-6253
E-mail: carlsoja@mrs.umn.edu
www.mrs.umn.edu/academic/music

UNIVERSITY OF MINNESOTA AT TWIN CITIES
FERGUSON HALL

2016 Fourth St. S.
Minneapolis, MN 55445
Wayne Lu
612-624-5093

Fax: 612-624-8001
www.music.umn.edu

Degrees: Sixteen different bachelor's, master's and doctoral degrees

The University of Minnesota School of music is a comprehensive music school located in a national land grant and research university of 44,000 students. Fifty fulltime and forty adjunct faculty, many drawn from the Minnesota Orchestra, St. Paul Chamber Orchestra and other professional organizations, provide instructional leadership to more than 600 music majors, 340 undergraduates, and 260 graduates. State of the art classroom, rehearsal and performance facilities are part of the West Bank Arts Quarter, a unique physical, curricular and performance environment for the university's arts disciplines. Sixteen different comprehensive degree programs are offered from bachelors to doctorate with multiple tracks designed to fit the needs of individual students. Located in Minneapolis-St. Paul, one of America's most vibrant music learning laboratories, the School of Music offers outstanding academic and musical opportunities with much collaboration and partnerships with metropolitan music organizations. For more information, visit the school of music Web site.

UNIVERSITY OF ST. THOMAS
DEPARTMENT OF MUSIC

2115 Summit Ave.
BEC 9
Saint Paul, MN 55105
Matthew George
652-962-5850
Fax: 652-962-5976
E-mail: mjgeorge@stthomas.edu
www.stthomas.edu

VERMILLION COMMUNITY COLLEGE

DEPARTMENT OF MUSIC

1900 E. Camp St.
Ely, MN 55731
Susan Germek
218-365-3256
Fax: 218-365-7207
http://kardassia.vcc.mnscu.edu

WINONA STATE UNIVERSITY

DEPARTMENT OF MUSIC

P.O. Box 5838
Winona, MN 55987
Dr. Harry A. Mechell
507-457-5250
Fax: 507-457-5620
www.winona.msus.edu/music

WINONA STATE UNIVERSITY

DEPARTMENT OF MUSIC

P.O. Box 5838
Winona, MN 55987
Catherine Schmidt
507-457-5250
Fax: 507-457-5624
E-mail: cschmidt@winona.edu
www.winona.msus.edu

WORTHINGTON COMMUNITY COLLEGE

DEPARTMENT OF MUSIC

P.O. Box 107
Worthington, MN 56187
Galen Benton
507-372-2107
Fax: 507-372-5801
www.mnwest.mnscu.edu

MISSISSIPPI

Population: 2,934,996 (2003 Estimate)

Capital City: Jackson

Music Colleges and Universities: Alcorn State University, Belhaven College, Blue Mountain College, Copiah-Linoln Community College, Delta State University, Hinds Community College, Itawamba Community College, Jackson State University, Jones County Junior College, Meridian Community College, Millsaps College, Mississippi College, Mississippi Gulf Coast College, Mississippi State University, Mississippi University for Women, Mississippi Valley State University, Northeast Mississippi Community College, Pearl River Community College, Rust College, Tougaloo College, University of Mississippi, University ofSouthern Mississippi, Wesley College, William Carey College

Bird: Mockingbird

Motto: Virtute Et Armis – By valor and arms

Flower: Magnolia

Tree: Magnolia

Residents Called: Mississippians

Origin of Name: Possibly based on Chippewa Indian words "mici zibi," loosely meaning great river.

Area: 48,434 square miles (32nd largest state)

Statehood: December 10, 1817 (20th state)

Largest Cities: Jackson, Gulfport, Biloxi, Hattiesburg, Greenville, Meridian, Tupelo, Southaven, Vicksburg, Pascagoula

College Band Programs: Mississippi College, Mississippi State University, University of Mississippi, University of Southern Mississippi

MISSISSIPPI

ALCORN STATE UNIVERSITY
DEPARTMENT OF FINE ARTS

1000 ASU Dr. #29
Lorman, MS 39096
Donzell Lee
601-877-6261
Fax: 601-877-6262
E-mail: dlee@lorman.alcorn.edu
www.alcorn.edu

BELHAVEN COLLEGE
DEPARTMENT OF MUSIC

1500 Peachtree St
Jackson, MS 49201
Christopher Shelt
601-974-6471
Fax: 601-968-9998
E-mail: cshelt@belhaven.edu
www.belhaven.edu

BLUE MOUNTAIN COLLEGE
DEPARTMENT OF MUSIC

201 W. Main
P.O. Box 160
Blue Mountain, MS 38610
Charles Meyer
601-685-4771
Fax: 601-685-4776
E-mail: cmeyer@bmc.edu
www.bmc.edu

COPIAH-LINCOLN COMMUNITY COLLEGE
DEPARTMENT OF MUSIC

P.O. Box 649
Wesson, MS 39191-0649
Brad Johnson
601-643-8431
Fax: 601-643-8212
E-mail: brad.johnson@colin.cc.ms.us
www.colin.cc.ms.us

DELTA STATE UNIVERSITY
DEPARTMENT OF MUSIC

P.O. Box 3256
Cleveland, MS 38733
Douglas Wheeler
662-846-4615
Fax: 662-846-4605
E-mail: dwheeler@deltastate.edu
www.deltastate.edu

HINDS COMMUNITY COLLEGE
DEPARTMENT OF MUSIC

P.O. Box 1100
Raymond, MS 39154
Berry Rhines
601-857-3271
Fax: 601-857-3458
E-mail: bsrhines@hinds.cc.ms.us
www.hinds.cc.ms.us

ITAWAMBA COMMUNITY COLLEGE
DEPARTMENT OF MUSIC

602 W. Hill St.
Fulton, MS 38843-1099
Jerry Cogdell
662-862-8000
Fax: 662-862-8410
E-mail: jwcogdell@icc.cc.ms.us
www.iccms.edu

Degrees: A.A.

Itawamba Community College is a fully accredited member of the Southern Association of Colleges and Schools. The music curriculum offers freshman and sophomore level music courses that transfer to four-year institutions.

Performing organizations and opportunities include marching band; concert bands; choir; woodwind; brass, percussion, vocal, jazz, and pop-rock ensembles; student recital; music theater; and music technology.

JACKSON STATE UNIVERSITY
DEPARTMENT OF MUSIC

Jackson, MS 39217
Dr. Jimmy James Jr.
601-979-2141
Fax: 610-968-2568
E-mail: jjames@ccaix.jsums.edu
www.jsums.edu

JONES COUNTY JUNIOR COLLEGE
DEPARTMENT OF MUSIC

900 S. Court St.
Ellisville, MS 39437-3901
Jeff Brown
601-477-4094
Fax: 601-477-4017
E-mail: jeff.brown@jcjc.cc.ms.us
www.jcjc.cc.ms.us

Degrees: A.A. (major in music education or music)

The Jones County Junior college music department features courses designed to meet the requirements of university degree programs for major in music performance or music education. The Jones Band and Choir are among the best known in the southeastern United States. The band has performed at the Macy's Thanksgiving Day Parade, the Orange Bowl Parade, the Tournament of Roses Parade and the Marshall Field's Jungle Elf Parade in Chicago. The Choir has performed in Dallas, Atlanta, Minneapolis, New York and London, England.

MERIDIAN COMMUNITY COLLEGE
DEPARTMENT OF MUSIC

910 Hwy. 19 N
Meridian, MS 39307
Robert Hermetz
601-483-8241
Fax: 601-482-3936
www.mcc.cc.ms.us

MILLSAPS COLLEGE
DEPARTMENT OF MUSIC

Department of Performing Arts
1701 North State St.
Jackson, MS 39210
Tim Cooker
601-974-1000
Fax: 601-974-1059
E-mail: cokertc@okra.millsaps.edu
www.millsaps.edu

MISSISSIPPI COLLEGE
DEPARTMENT OF MUSIC

P.O. Box 4201
Clinton, MS 39058
Dr. Richard Joiner
601-925-3440
Fax: 601-925-3945
E-mail: joiner@mc.edu
www.mc.edu

The MC music faculty possesses performance experience, career involvement, advanced degrees and a commitment to its mission of providing the finest and most complete professional education in music.

MISSISSIPPI GULF COAST COLLEGE

DEPARTMENT OF MUSIC

Perkinston, MS 39573
Becky Guevara
601-928-6211
Fax: 601-928-6386
www.mgccc.cc.ms.us

MISSISSIPPI STATE UNIVERSITY

DEPARTMENT OF MUSIC

P.O. Box 9734
Mississippi State, MS 39762
Michael Brown
662-325-3070
Fax: 662-325-0250
E-mail: mbrown@colled.msstate.edu
www.msstate.edu

Degrees: Music Education Major:
Instrumental Music Education Emphasis, Vocal
Music Education Emphasis

MISSISSIPPI UNIVERSITY FOR WOMEN

DIVISION OF FINE AND PERFORMING ARTS

P.O. Box W-70
Columbus, MS 39701
Dr. Michael D. Garrett
662-329-7342
E-mail: mgarrett@muw.edu
www.muw.edu/fine_arts

MISSISSIPPI VALLEY STATE UNIVERSITY

MUSIC DEPARTMENT

Itta Bena, MS 38941
Lawrence Horn
601-254-3482
Fax: 601-254-3485
E-mail: lhorn@msvu.edu
www.mvsu.edu

NORTHEAST MISSISSIPPI COMMUNITY COLLEGE

DEPARTMENT OF MUSIC

100 Cumminham Blvd.
Booneville, MS 38829
Jerry Rains
662-728-7751
Fax: 662-728-1165
E-mail: jrains@necc.cc.ms.us
www.necc.cc.ms.us

PEARL RIVER COMMUNITY COLLEGE

DEPARTMENT OF MUSIC

101 Hwy. 11 N.
Poplaville, MS 39470
Archie Rawls
601-403-1180
Fax: 601-403-1138
E-mail: arawls@prcc.cc.ms.us
www.prcc.cc.ms.us

RUST COLLEGE

DEPARTMENT OF MUSIC

Holly Springs, MS 38635
Norman Chapman
601-252-4661
www.rustcollege.edu

TOUGALOO COLLEGE
DEPARTMENT OF MUSIC

500 W. County Line Rd.
Tougaloo, MS 39174
Ben Bailey
601-977-7758
Fax: 601-977-7824
www.tougaloo.edu

UNIVERSITY OF MISSISSIPPI
DEPARTMENT OF MUSIC

132 Meek Hall, P.O. Box 1848
University, MS 38677
Dr. Steven F. Brown
662-915-7268
Fax: 662-915-1230
E-mail: music@olemiss.edu
www.olemiss.edu/depts/music
Degrees: B.A., B.M., M.M., and D.A.

The department of music at the University of
Mississippi prepares professional musicians
and educators, and has graduates teaching and
performing throughout the nation.

Over 160 students are enrolled as majors in
the department of music. The size is ideal in
affording a pleasant atmosphere and ensuring
proper instrumentation for the larger ensembles as well as individual attention for students
in private applied music study, in classes and in
the many small ensembles. Performance facilities for music include: the Gertrude Ford
Center, a 1,300-seat theatre/concert hall, the
240-seat Meek Auditorium, commonly used as
a recital hall, the Fulton Chapel, a 650-seat
concert hall used jointly by the department of
theatre arts, Paris-Yates Chapel, seating 250,
and the home of the university's 32 rank,
1642-pipe organ.

UNIVERSITY OF SOUTHERN MISSISSIPPI

P.O. Box 5031
Hattiesburg, MS 39406
Charles Elliot
601-266-5363
Fax: 601-266-5081
E-mail: charles.elliott@usm.edu
www.arts.usm.edu

WESLEY COLLEGE
DEPARTMENT OF MUSIC

P.O. Box 1070
Florence, MS 39073
Beverly Porter
601-845-2265
Fax: 601-845-2266
www.wesleycollege.com

WILLIAM CAREY COLLEGE
DEPARTMENT OF MUSIC

P.O. Box 14
498 Tuscan Ave.
Hattiesburg, MS 39401
Milfred Valentine
601-582-6175
Fax: 601-582-6454
www.wmcarey.edu

MISSOURI

Population: 5,751,680 (2003 Estimate)

Capital City: Jefferson City

Music Colleges and Universities: Avila College, Calvary Bible College and Theological Seminary, Central Methodist College, Central Missouri State University, College of the Ozarks, Cottey College, Crowder College, Drury College, Evangel University, FFontbonne College,Hannibal La Grange College, Jefferson College, Lincoln University, Lindenwood University, Maryville University, Mineral Area College, Missouri Southern State College, Missouri Western State College, Northwest Missouri State University, Park University, Rockhurst College, Saint Louis University, Southeast Missouri State University, Southwest Baptist University, Southwest Missouri State University, St. Louis Community College at Forest Park, St. Louis Community College at Meramec, St. Paul School of Theology, Stephens College, Tarkio College, Three Rivers Community College, Truman State University, University of Missouri, University of Missouri at Columbia, University of Missouri at Rolla, University of Missouri at St. Louis, Washington University, Webster University, William Jewell College, William Woods University

Bird: Bluebird

Motto: Salus Populi Suprema Lex Esto – The welfare of the people shall be the supreme law.

Flower: Hawthorn

Tree: Flowering Dogwood

Residents Called: Missourians

Origin of Name: Named after Missouri Indian tribe whose name means "town of the large canoes."

Area: 69,709 square miles (21st largest state)

Statehood: August 10, 1821 (24th state)

Largest Cities: Kansas City, Saint Louis, Springfield, Independence, Columbia, Saint Joseph, Lee's Summit, Saint Charles, Saint Peters

College Band Programs: Central Missouri University, , University of Missouri-Columbia, University of Missouri-Rolla

MISSOURI

AVILA COLLEGE

Department of Music
11901 Wornall Rd.
Kansas City, MO 64145-1007
Amity Bryson
816-501-3651
Fax: 816-501-2442
E-mail: brysonah@mail.avila.edu
www.avila.edu

CALVARY BIBLE COLLEGE AND THEOLOGICAL SEMINARY
DEPARTMENT OF MUSIC

15800 Calvary Rd.
Kansas City, MO 64147-1303
Mr. Paul Vander Mey
816-322-0110
Fax: 816-331-4474
E-mail: musicdir@calvary.edu
www.calvary.edu

Degrees: B.A. or B.S. in Church Music;
B.M.E.; B.A. or B.S. in Music and Youth
Ministry; B.A. or B.S. in a combination major
that includes music

The Calvary Bible College Music Department
provides excellence and ministry for students
in the music programs it offers. Young musicians come to Calvary to study music in preparation to serve God, the church and the community. Calvary is the ideal place for music
students looking for high quality music education, small class sizes, caring teachers, personal
attention and plenty of opportunities to participate and perform. Music majors graduate
with a double major in music and Bible. The
music department offers four-degree programs
in music.

CENTRAL METHODIST COLLEGE
SWINNEY CONSERVATORY OF MUSIC

411 CMC Square
Fayette, MO 65248
Dr. Ron Shroyer
660-248-6317
Fax: 660-248-6357
E-mail: rshroyer@cmc.edu
www.cmc.edu

CENTRAL MISSOURI STATE UNIVERSITY
DEPARTMENT OF MUSIC

Utt 111A
Warrensburg, MO 64093
Dr. Charles A. McAdams
660-543-4530
Fax: 660-543-8271
E-mail: mcadams@cmsu1.cmsu.edu
www.cmsu.edu/music

Degrees: B.A., B.M., Bachelor of Music
Education, M.A.

Central has a long tradition of excellence with
its first graduates in the 1920s. We now offer
four degrees and have over 200 music majors
and 22 full-time faculty. Our largest program
is the Bachelor of Music Education degree
preparing elementary and secondary school
music teachers. In fact, more Missouri certified
teachers graduated from Central than from
any single instruction. We offer majors in
voice, piano, organ, and all major orchestral
instruments, including guitar. Our B.M. degree
has five performance, piano pedagogy,
Jazz/commercial, and music technology. Music
technology is our newest emphasis and is primarily an audio recording/audio engineering
degree. Central is large enough to offer two
large choirs, three bands, a marching band,
two jazz bands, and a full orchestra, yet small
enough to still provide a nurturing and supportive environment.

COLLEGE OF THE OZARKS
DEPARTMENT OF MUSIC
Point Lookout, MO 65726
Bruce Gerlach
417-334-6411
Fax: 417-335-2618
E-mail: gerlach@cofo.edu
www.cofo.edu

COTTEY COLLEGE
DEPARTMENT OF MUSIC
601 Laclede Ave.
Neosho, MO 64850-9165
Theresa Forrester Spencer
417-667-8181
Fax: 417-667-8103
www.cottey.edu

CROWDER COLLEGE
DEPARTMENT OF MUSIC
601 Laclede Ave.
Neosho, MO 64850-9165
Marsha Wilson Thomson
417-451-3223
Fax: 417-451-4280
E-mail: mthomson@crowdercollege.net
www.crowdercollege.net

DRURY COLLEGE
DEPARTMENT OF MUSIC
900 N. Benton Ave.
Springfield, MO 65802-3712
Tijuna Julian
417-873-7296
Fax: 417-873-7898
E-mail: tjulian@lib.drury.edu
www.drury.edu

EVANGEL UNIVERSITY
DEPARTMENT OF MUSIC
1111 N. Glenstone Ave.
Springfield, MO 65802
John Shows
417-865-2815
E-mail: showsj@evangel.edu
www.evangel.edu

FONTBONNE COLLEGE
DEPARTMENT OF FINE ARTS
6800 Wyndown Blvd.
St. Louis, MO 63105-3098
Catherine Connor-Talasek
314-889-1431
Fax: 314-889-1451
www.fontbonne.edu

HANNIBAL LA GRANGE COLLEGE
DEPARTMENT OF MUSIC
2800 Palmyra Rd.
Hannibal, MO 63401
John Booth
314-221-3675
Fax: 314-221-6594
E-mail: jbooth@hlg.edu
www.hlg.edu

JEFFERSON COLLEGE
DEPARTMENT OF MUSIC
1000 Viking Dr.
Hillsboro, MO 63050-2440
Mindy Selsor
636-797-3000
Fax: 636-789-4012
E-mail: mselsor@jeffco.edu
www.jeffco.edu

LINCOLN UNIVERSITY
DEPARTMENT OF FINE ARTS
201 Elliaf Hall
Jefferson City, MO 65101
Steven Houser
573-681-5280
Fax: 573-681-5438
E-mail: housers@lincolnu.edu
www.lincolnu.edu

LINDENWOOD UNIVERSITY
DEPARTMENT OF MUSIC
209 S. KingsHwy. St
Saint Charles, MO 63391
Marsha Parker
314-916-1912
Fax: 314-949-1693
E-mail: mparker@lindenwood.edu
www.lindenwood.edu

MARYVILLE UNIVERSITY
DEPARTMENT OF MUSIC
13550 Conway Rd.
St. Louis, MO 63141
Katia Georgieff
314-529-9300
www.maryville.edu

MINERAL AREA COLLEGE
DEPARTMENT OF MUSIC
Park Hills, MO 63601
Jerry Walters
573-431-4593
Fax: 573-518-2164
www.mac.cc.mo.us

MISSOURI SOUTHERN STATE COLLEGE
MUSIC DEPARTMENT
3950 E. Newman Rd.
Joplin, MO 64801
Dr. Phillip C. Wise
417-625-9318
Fax: 417-625-3030
E-mail: wise-p@mail.mssc.edu
www.mssc.edu/music

MISSOURI WESTERN STATE COLLEGE
DEPARTMENT OF MUSIC
4525 Downs Dr.
Joseph, MO 64507
Dr. F.M. Gilmour
816-271-4420
Fax: 816-271-5974
E-mail: gilmour@griffon.mwsc.edu
www.mwsc.edu/music

Missouri Western State College has nearly 5,600 students. The department of music, led by chairperson Dr. F.M. Gilmour, has 125 majors in the diverse music offerings. Students can gain a degree and certification in music education with an instrumental or vocal certification (or both). They can also choose a bachelor of arts degree aimed at following different areas of music business: commercial music/jazz studies emphasis, commercial music/business emphasis, or commercial music/recording/studio emphasis. Missouri Western also offers a strong Bachelor of Arts degree in performance. Missouri Western has an excellent faculty and fine facilities. Outstanding band scholarships and talent awards are available.

NORTHWEST MISSOURI STATE UNIVERSITY
DEPARTMENT OF MUSIC
800 University Dr.
Maryville, MO 64468
Dr. Ernest Woodruff
660-562-1315
Fax: 660-562-1326
E-mail: ewoodru@mail.nwmissouri.edu
www.nwmissouri.edu/~music

PARK UNIVERSITY
DEPARTMENT OF MUSIC
8700 N.W. River Park Dr.
Parkville, MO 64152
Timothy Corrao
816-584-6484
E-mail: tcorrao@mail.park.edu
www.park.edu

ROCKHURST COLLEGE
DEPARTMENT OF MUSIC
1100 Rockhurst Rd.
Kansas City, MO 64110
Timothy McDonald
816-501-4000
Fax: 816-501-4169
E-mail:
timothy.mcdonald@rockhurst.edu
www.rockhurst.edu

ST. LOUIS UNIVERSITY
DEPARTMENT OF FINE AND PERFORMANCE ART AND MUSIC
221 N. Grand Blvd.
St. Louis, MO 63101
Suzanne Lee
314-977-2410
Fax: 314-977-2999
E-mail: leesr@slu.edu
www.slu.edu

SOUTHEAST MISSOURI STATE UNIVERSITY
MUSIC DEPARTMENT
108 A Brandt Music Hall
M/S 7800
Cape Girardeau, MO 63701
Barry W. Bernhardt
573-651-2334
Fax: 573-651-2431
E-mail: bbernhardt@semo.edu
www.semo.edu

SOUTHEAST MISSOURI STATE UNIVERSITY
DEPARTMENT OF MUSIC
1 University Plaza MS7800
Brandt Music Hall, Room 108
Cape Girardeau, MO 63701
Dr. Gary Miller
573-651-2141
Fax: 573-651-2431
http://www5.semo.edu/music

The department of music at Southeast offers both the variety of performing and learning experiences found at a large university, and the individual attention and relaxed atmosphere expected of a small college. Southeast is fully accredited by the National Association of Schools of Music. The department of music has over 120 music majors and has full and adjunct instructors in each area. Our full and adjunct faculty represents all areas of musical study, including performance, composition, electronic music and world music. This outstanding group of educators has performed both nationally and abroad with recognition in Canada, China, England, Ireland, Japan, Scotland and the Ukraine. The overall student to faculty ratio is 18:1, which provides students with the attention and instruction that they deserve and expect. Southeast Missouri State University is a public university founded in 1873, that has evolved into a comprehensive state university with more than 150 academic programs. Located in Cape Girardeau, "on the banks" of the Mississippi River, Southeast has nearly 400 full-time faculty. Music faculty with degrees from universities such as Cornell, Julliard and the London College of Music work with students in size-controlled classes. The department of music has over 15 ensembles, encompassing every performance area. Scholarship assistance is available through competitive auditions held each spring semester, by appointment.

SOUTHWEST BAPTIST UNIVERSITY
DEPARTMENT OF MUSIC
1600 University Ave.
Bolivar, MO 65613
Jeffery Waters
417-326-1630
Fax: 417-326-1637
E-mail: jwaters@sbuniv.edu
www.sbuniv.edu

SOUTHWEST MISSOURI STATE UNIVERSITY
DEPARTMENT OF MUSIC
901 S. National
Springfield, MO 65804
Dr. John Prescott
417-836-5749
Fax: 417-836-7665
www.smsu.edu/contrib/music

ST. LOUIS COMMUNITY COLLEGE AT FOREST PARK
DEPARTMENT OF MUSIC
5600 Oakland Ave.
St. Louis, MO 63110
James Hegerty
314-644-9769
Fax: 314-951-9406
E-mail: jhegerty@st1cc.cc.mo.us
www.stlcc.cc.mo.us/fp

ST. LOUIS COMMUNITY COLLEGE AT MERAMEC
DEPARTMENT OF MUSIC
11333 Big Bend Rd.
St. Louis, MO 63122
Ron Stillwell
314-984-7639
Fax: 314-984-7254
www.stlcc.cc.mo.us

ST. PAUL SCHOOL OF THEOLOGY
DEPARTMENT OF MUSIC
5123 E. Truman Rd.
Kansas City, MO 64127
Marian Thomas
816-483-9600
Fax: 816-483-9605
E-mail: spst@spst.edu
www.spst.edu

STEPHENS COLLEGE
DEPARTMENT OF PERF ARTS-MUSIC
P.O. Box 2077
Columbia, MO 65201
Pam Ellsworth
573-876-7117
www.stephens.edu

TARKIO COLLEGE
DEPARTMENT OF MUSIC
Tarkio, MO 64491
Gary Declue
816-736-4131
Fax: 816-736-5268
www.tarkioalumni.org

THREE RIVERS COMMUNITY COLLEGE

DEPARTMENT OF MUSIC

2080 Three Rivers Blvd.
Poplar Bluff, MO 63901
Cindy White
573-840-9639
Fax: 573-840-9603
E-mail: cwhite@trcc.cc.mo.us
www.trcc.cc.mo.us

TRUMAN STATE UNIVERSITY

DIVISION OF FINE ARTS

100 E. Normal St.
Kirksville, MO 63501-4221
Robert Jones
660-785-4417
Fax: 660-785-7463
E-mail: finearts@truman.edu
www.truman.edu

UNIVERSITY OF MISSOURI AT COLUMBIA

DEPARTMENT OF MUSIC

140 Fine Arts Building
Columbia, MO 65211.
Dr. Alex Pickard
573-882-7361
Fax: 573-884-7444
E-mail: plattm@missouri.edu
www.missouri.edu/~musicwww

Degrees: B.A., B.M., B.S. (Education) M.M., M.A., Ph.D. (Education)

Founded in 1907, the school of music is comprised of 34 full-time faculty members and has 220 music majors. It is small enough to permit close, personal interaction between students and faculty, but large enough to provide many wonderful opportunities for talented students to excel. Fully accredited by the NASM, the school offers a B.A. in music or a B.M. degree with majors in Performance (piano, voice,

strings, woodwinds, percussion or brass), music history, music theory and composition. Master of Music programs include performance, music theory, composition, conducting, accompanying, and piano pedagogy. The M.A. can be earned in music history. The B.S. in Music education, M.Ed., M.A.Ed. and Ph.D. programs are offered in conjunction with the college of curriculum and instruction. Performing ensembles include three concert bands, orchestra, four choirs, jazz bands, Marching Mizzou, and various chamber groups.

UNIVERSITY OF MISSOURI AT KANSAS CITY

CONSERVATORY OF MUSIC

Kansas City Conservatory of Music
4949 Cherry St.
Kansas City, MO 64110
Dr. James Elswick
816-235-2900
Fax: 816-235-5264
E-mail: pembrookr@umkc.edu
www.umkc.edu/conservatory

The UMKC Conservatory of Music has been the Midwest's most comprehensive training center for music and dance since 1906. With nearly 500 students and 65 faculty at two facilities on UMKC's midtown Volker campus, the conservatory plays a major role in the culturally thriving Kansas City area. Performance opportunities are available in orchestra, wind ensemble, jazz, choral ensembles, opera, winds, brass, percussion, strings and dance. Admission is by audition and fulfillment of academic standards. Audition requests are required 30 days prior to the audition date.

UNIVERSITY OF MISSOURI AT ROLLA
DEPARTMENT OF PERFORMING ARTS
127 Castleman Hall
1870 Mine Cr
Rolla, MO 65409
Shelly Plank
573-341-4185
Fax: 573-341-6992
E-mail: splank@umr.edu
www.umr.edu/~music

UNIVERSITY OF MISSOURI AT ST. LOUIS
DEPARTMENT OF MUSIC
8001 Natural Bridge Rd.
St. Louis, MO 63121
Lonard Ott
314-516-5981
Fax: 314-516-6593
E-mail: leonard_ott@umsl.edu
www.umsl.edu/~music

WASHINGTON UNIVERSITY
DEPARTMENT OF MUSIC
1 Brookins Dr.
CB 1032
St. Louis, MO 63130
Dolores Pesce
314-935-5581
Fax: 314-935-4034
E-mail: wlharry@artsci.wustl.edu
www.artsci.wustl.edu/~music

WEBSTER UNIVERSITY
DEPARTMENT OF MUSIC
470 E. Lockwood Ave.
St. Louis, MO 63119
Micheal Parkinson
314-968-7032
Fax: 314-963-5048
E-mail: parkinmi@webster.edu
www.webster.edu/depts/finearts/music

WILLIAM JEWELL COLLEGE
DEPARTMENT OF MUSIC
500 College Hill
Liberty, MO 64068
Donald Brown
816-781-7700
Fax: 816-415-5027
E-mail: brownd@william.jewell.edu
www.jewell.edu

WILLIAM WOODS UNIVERSITY
VISUAL AND PERFORMING ARTS
1 University Ave.
Fulton, MO 65251
Paul Clervi
573-592-4367
Fax: 573-592-1623
E-mail: pclervi@williamwoods.edu
www.wmwoods.edu

MONTANA

Population: 937,462 (2003 Estimate)

Capital City: Helena

Music Colleges and Universities: Dawson Community College, Miles Community College, Montana State University at Billings, Montana State University at Bozeman, Northern Montana College, Rocky Mountain College, University of Great Falls, University of Montana, Western Montana College

Bird: Western Meadowlark

Motto: Oro y plata – Gold and Silver

Flower: Bitterroot

Tree: Ponderosa pine

Residents Called: Montanans

Origin of Name: Based on Spanish word for "mountainous"

Area: 147,046 square miles (4th largest state)

Statehood: November 8,1889 (41st state)

Largest Cities: Billings, Missoula, Great Falls, Butte, Bozeman, Helena, Kalispell, Havre, Anaconda, Miles City

College Band Programs: Montana State University

MONTANA

DAWSON COMMUNITY COLLEGE
DEPARTMENT OF MUSIC
2715 Dickinson St
Miles City, MT 59301-4774
Jim Schultz
406-377-9463
Fax: 406-377-8132
E-mail: Jim_S@dawson.edu
www.dawson.cc.mt.us

MILES COMMUNITY COLLEGE
DEPARTMENT OF MUSIC
2715 Dickinson St
Miles City, MT 59301
Glenna James
406-232-3031
www.mcc.cc.mt.us

MONTANA STATE UNIVERSITY AT BILLINGS
DEPARTMENT OF MUSIC
1500 North 30th St.
Billings, MT 59101
Dr. Gary Behm
406-657-2350
Fax: 406-657-2051
E-mail: gbehm@msubillings.edu
www.msubillings.edu

MONTANA STATE UNIVERSITY AT BOZEMAN
DEPARTMENT OF MUSIC
186 Howard Hall
P.O. Box 173420
Bozeman, MT 59717
Johan Jonsson
406-994-3562
Fax: 406-994-6656

E-mail: music@montana.edu
www.montana.edu/music

Degrees: B.A. in music, B.M.E., and M.M.

The Montana State University Department of Music annually enrolls approximately 100 music majors and an additional 2,000 non-majors in a variety of academic, performance, and pedagogical activities. While its primary role is to develop and maintain programs, which prepare students for careers in music teaching, the department of music provides a musical environment in which students pursue the music arts. A faculty comprised of outstanding musician/teachers provides instruction in music.

The department of music is an asset to the cultural and intellectual life of Montana State University and the community of Bozeman. Students, faculty, ensembles, and guest artists present more than 100 recitals and concerts annually. Many performing ensembles, ranging from the Chamber Orchestra, Wind Ensemble, and Chorale, to the Studio Jazz Lab and the "Spirit of the West" Marching Band, provide opportunities for all university students to actively continue their music endeavors. Many of these ensembles have represented the department of music at national conferences and through the international tours.

The department of music is a Wonderful Environment in which to study and perform. Come to Montana State University – Bozeman and continue to make music with us.

NORTHERN MONTANA COLLEGE
DEPARTMENT OF MUSIC
Havre, MT 59501
Janice Wiberg
406-265-7821
www.nmclites.edu

ROCKY MOUNTAIN COLLEGE
DEPARTMENT OF MUSIC

1511 Poly Dr.
Billings, MT 59101
Dr. David Reynolds
800-877-6259
Fax: 406-259-9751
E-mail: reynoldd@rocky.edu
www.rocky.edu
Degrees: B.A. in Music Performance,
B.A. in Education

Rocky Mountain College is the oldest college in Montana, celebrating its 125th anniversary in 2003. The campus occupies approximately 60 park-like acres in the northwest residential section of Billings, the largest community in Montana. The college is affiliated with the United Church of Christ, United Methodist Church, and the Presbyterian Church (U.S.A.). Rocky Mountain College has a student population of approximately 850 and is known for distinctive programs in aviation, equestrian studies, physician assistant training, teacher education, and the fine and performing arts. For decades the college has enjoyed a distinguished reputation for offering quality musical study to both music majors and non-music majors. All ensemble participation, including the college band, choir, and jazz ensemble, is open to qualified students. Our music education graduates have taken positions in many of the most significant public school music programs in the region, and our performance graduates have attained success in several of the most prestigious graduate schools in the country. There are core faculty of five in the music department, supplemented by a cadre of nine adjunct artists, many of which perform in the Billings Symphony. Special programs in the music department include a course in creativity, a biennial study abroad trip to Bavaria and Austria, and an endowed recital series, which brings professional performers to campus annually. A music technology lab, with fifteen state-of-the-art computers, synthesizers, and music writing software has recently been added to Losekamp Hall, the home of the music program.

UNIVERSITY OF GREAT FALLS
DEPARTMENT OF MUSIC

1301 20th St. S.
Great Falls, MT 59405
William Furdell
406-791-5370
Fax: 406-791-5395
E-mail: wfurdell@ugf.edu
www.ugf.edu

UNIVERSITY OF MONTANA
DEPARTMENT OF MUSIC

Missoula, MT 59812
Thomas Cook
406-243-6880
Fax: 406-243-2441
www.sfa.umt.edu/music

WESTERN MONTANA COLLEGE
FINE ARTS DEPARTMENT

710 S. Atlantic
Dillon, MT 59725
Dale Misenhelter
406-683-7242
Fax: 406-683-7493
www.wmc.edu

NEBRASKA

Population: 1,749,069 (2003 Estimate)

Capital City: Lincoln

Music Colleges and Universities: Central Community College Platte, Chadron State College, College of St. Mary, Concordia College, Creighton University, Dana College, Doane College, Grace University, Hastings College, Midland Lutheran College, Nebraska Wesleyan University, Northeast Community College, Peru State College, Southeast Community College at Beatrice, Union College, University of Nebraska, University of Nebraska at Kearney, University of Nebraska at Omaha, Wayne State College, Western Nebraska Community College, York College

Bird: Western Meadowlark

Motto: Equality before the law

Flower: Goldenrod

Tree: Eastern Cottonwood

Residents Called: Nebraskans

Origin of Name: Name based on an Oto Indian word that means "flat water," referring to the Platte River.

Area: 77,358 square miles (16th largest state)

Statehood: March 1, 1867 (37th state)

Largest Cities: Omaha, Lincoln, Bellevue, Grand Island, Kearney, Fremont, Hastings, North Platte, Norfolk, Columbus

College Band Programs: University of Nebraska-Lincoln

NEBRASKA

CENTRAL COMMUNITY COLLEGE PLATTE
DEPARTMENT OF MUSIC
P.O. Box 1027
Columbus, NE 68602-1027
Rex Hash
402-563-1270
Fax: 402-562-1201
www.cccneb.edu

CHADRON STATE COLLEGE
MEMORIAL HALL
1000 Main St.
Chadron, NE 69337
William Winki
308-432-6375
Fax: 308-432-6464
E-mail: wwinkle@csc.edu
www.csc.edu

COLLEGE OF ST. MARY
DEPARTMENT OF MUSIC
1901 S. 72nd ST
Omaha, NE 68124-2301
Patricia Will
402-399-2622
Fax: 402-399-2341
www.csm.edu

CONCORDIA COLLEGE
DEPARTMENT OF MUSIC
800 N. Columbia Ave.
Seward, NE 68434-1556
Charles Ore
402-643-3651
Fax: 402-643-4073

CREIGHTON UNIVERSITY
MUSIC PROGRAM
2500 California Plane
Omaha, NE 68178
Marilyn Keilmiarz
402-280-2509
Fax: 402-280-2320
E-mail: mkieln@creighton.edu
www.creighton.edu

DANA COLLEGE
ADMISSIONS
2848 College Dr.
Blair, NE 68008
800-444-7310
Fax: 402-426-7332
E-mail: kberg@acad2.dana.edu
www.dana.edu

DOANE COLLEGE
DEPARTMENT OF MUSIC
1014 Boswell
Crete, NE 68333
Jay Gilbert
402-826-2161
Fax: 402-826-8278
E-mail: jgilbert@doane.edu
www.doane.edu

GRACE UNIVERSITY
DEPARTMENT OF MUSIC
1311 South 9th St.
Omaha, NE 68108-3629
Greg Zielke
402-449-2800
Fax: 402-341-9587
E-mail: gdzielke@graceu.edu
www.graceuniversity.edu

HASTINGS COLLEGE
DEPARTMENT OF MUSIC

P.O. Box 269
Hastings, NE 68902
402-461-7448
Fax: 402-461-7428
www.hastings.edu

MIDLAND LUTHERAN COLLEGE
DEPARTMENT OF MUSIC

900 N. Clarkson
Fremont, NE 68025
Charles Wilhite
402-721-5480
Fax: 402-727-6223
E-mail: wilhite@mlc.edu
www.mlc.edu

NEBRASKA WESLEYAN UNIVERSITY
MUSIC DEPARTMENT

5000 St. Paul Ave.
Lincoln, NE 68504
Dr. Patrick M. Fortney
402-465-7501
E-mail: pmf@nebrwesleyan.edu
http://music.nebrwesleyan.edu

Nebraska Wesleyan University is a private liberal arts college, accredited by NCA and NASM. It features a small student/teacher ratio, 13 performing ensembles and 21 full- and part-time artist faculty.

NORTHEAST COMMUNITY COLLEGE
DEPARTMENT OF MUSIC

801 E. Benjamin Ave.
Norfolk, NE 68702
Linda Boullion
402-844-7354
Fax: 402-844-7402

E-mail: lindab@northeastcollege.com
www.alpha.necc.cc.ne.us

PERU STATE COLLEGE
DEPARTMENT OF MUSIC

P.O. Box 10
Peru, NE 68421
David Edris
402-872-2368
Fax: 402-872-2412
E-mail: edrisd@bobcat.peru.edu
www.peru.edu

SOUTHEAST COMMUNITY COLLEGE AT BEATRICE
DEPARTMENT OF MUSIC

4771 W. Scott Rd.
Beatrice, NE 68501
Robert Mitchell
402-228-8266
Fax: 402-228-2218
E-mail: rmitchel@scc.ne.us
www.southeast.edu

UNION COLLEGE
DEPARTMENT OF MUSIC

3800 S. 48th St.
Lincoln, NE 68501
Daniel Lynn
402-486-2553
Fax: 402-486-2528
E-mail: dalynn@ucollege.edu
www.ucollege.edu

UNIVERSITY OF NEBRASKA
SCHOOL OF MUSIC

P.O. Box 880100
Lincoln, NE 68588
Colleen Nyhoff
402-472-2503

Fax: 402-472-8962
E-mail: cnyhoff@unl.edu
www.music.unl.edu

UNIVERSITY OF NEBRASKA AT KEARNEY
DEPARTMENT OF MUSIC AND PERFORMING ARTS
2506 12th Ave.
Kearney, NE 68849
John Kundel
308-865-8526
Fax: 308-865-8806
www.unk.edu

UNIVERSITY OF NEBRASKA AT OMAHA
DEPARTMENT OF MUSIC
6001 Dodge St.
Omaha, NE 68182
James R. Saker
402-554-3446
Fax: 402-554-2252
E-mail: jsaker@mail.unomaha.edu
http://music.unomaha.edu
Degrees: B.M. and M.M.

A vibrant, metropolitan university in the state's largest city, the University of Nebraska at Omaha has an enrollment of 16,000 students, and is a residential campus with several new and beautifully appointed residence halls. The campus is located in the heart of Omaha, a sophisticated city with a diverse population of more than 500,000. Music making in Omaha is represented by an active Symphony and Opera Company, and many community and semi-professional performing groups. UNOmaha is in a unique position to take advantage of these resources.

The department is located in the beautifully landscaped Strauss Performing Arts Center, which is nestled near the focal point of the campus, a campanile that houses a carillon of forty-seven bells. The complex itself boasts a tunable recital hall and well-equipped class-

rooms and rehearsal spaces. The center serves as a nexus of musical activity not only for the university, but for the city of Omaha as well.

With a faculty of 35 full- and part-time members, UNOmaha is a fully accredited member of the NASM. The department enrolls 200 undergraduate and graduate students programs leading to the B.M. degree with concentrations in composition, music education, music technology, and performance. Also, M.M. degrees can be with concentrations in conducting, music education and performance as well.

WAYNE STATE COLLEGE
FINE ARTS DIVISION
1111 Main St.
Wayne, NE 68787
Linda Christensen
402-375-7359
Fax: 402-375-7204
E-mail: lichris1@wsc.edu
www.wsc.edu

WESTERN NEBRASKA COMMUNITY COLLEGE
DEPARTMENT OF MUSIC
1601 E. 27th St.
Scottsbluff, NE 69361
Dale Skornia
308-635-6046
Fax: 308-635-6100
E-mail:
dskornia@hannibal.wncc.cc.ne.us
www.wncc.cc.ne.us

YORK COLLEGE
DEPARTMENT OF MUSIC
York, NE 68467
Clark Roush
402-363-5610
Fax: 402-363-5712
E-mail: croush@york.edu
www.york.edu

NEVADA

Population: 2,442,375 (2003 Estimate)

Capital City: Carson City

Music Colleges and Universities: University of Nevada at Las Vegas, University of Nevada at Reno, Western Nevada Community College

Bird: Mountain Bluebird

Motto: All for our country

Flower: Sagebrush

Tree: Single leaf pinon and Bristlecone pine

Residents Called: Nevadans

Nickname: The Silver State

Area: 110,567 square miles (7th largest state)

Statehood: October 31, 1864 (36th state)

Largest Cities: Las Vegas, Reno, Henderson, North Las Vegas, Sparks, Carson City, Elko, Boulder City, Mesquite, Fallon

College Band Programs: University of Nevada-Las Vegas

NEVADA

UNIVERSITY OF NEVADA AT LAS VEGAS
COLLEGE OF FINE AND PERFORMING ARTS
4505 S. Maryland Pkwy.
Las Vegas, NV 89154
Jeff Koep
702-895-3332
Fax: 702-895-4239
www.unlv.edu

UNIVERSITY OF NEVADA AT RENO
DEPARTMENT OF MUSIC
Reno, NV 89557
Michael Cleveland
775-784-6145
Fax: 775-784-6896
www.unr.edu/artsci/music

WESTERN NEVADA COMMUNITY COLLEGE
DEPARTMENT OF MUSIC
2201 W. College Pkwy.
Carson City, NV 89703
Joseph De Flyer
775-445-4249
Fax: 775-887-3154
www.wncc.cc.ne.us

NEW HAMPSHIRE

Population: 1,272,601 (2003 Estimate)

Capital City: Concord

Music Colleges and Universities: Colby-Sawyer College, Dartmouth College, Franklin Pierce College, Keene State College, Notre Dame College, Plymouth State College, Rivier College, St. Anselm College, University of New Hampshire

Bird: Purple Finch

Motto: Live free or die

Flower: Purple lilac

Tree: White birch

Residents Called: New Hampshirites

Nickname: The Granite State

Area: 9,351 square miles (46th largest state)

Statehood: June 21, 1788 (9th state)

Largest Cities: Manchester, Nashua, Concord, Derry, Rochester, Salem, Dover, Merrimack, Londonderry, Hudson

College Band Programs: Dartmouth College, University of New Hampshire

NEW HAMPSHIRE

COLBY-SAWYER COLLEGE
DEPARTMENT OF FINE AND PERFORMING ARTS
100 Main St.
New London, NH 03257
Donna Sparks
603-526-3787
E-mail: welcome@colby-sawyer.edu
www.colby-sawyer.edu

DARTMOUTH COLLEGE
DEPARTMENT OF MUSIC
Hinman P.O. Box 6187
Hanover, NH 03755
Larry Polansky
603-646-2139
Fax: 603-646-2551
E-mail: Larry.polansky@Dartmouth.edu
www.dartmouth.edu

FRANKLIN PIERCE COLLEGE
MUSIC DEPARTMENT
Rindge, NH 03461
David Brandes
603-899-4006
Fax: 603-899-4324
E-mail: scharfpe@fpc.edu
www.fpc.edu

KEENE STATE COLLEGE
DEPARTMENT OF MUSIC
229 Main St.
Keene, NH 03435
Music Administrative Assistant
603-358-2177
Fax: 603-358-2973
E-mail: phitchne@keene.edu
www.keene.edu

Degrees: B.M., B.A.

Keene State College has approximately 100 music majors, 9 full-time music faculty and 15 adjunct music faculty on a liberal arts college campus of 5,000 students. The music programs are accredited by the NASM.

The music major program at Keene State College provides preparation for a wide range of career opportunities. In the Bachelor of Music degree program, students may choose teaching in the public school, teaching in privately owned studios, or professional performance. In the Bachelor of Arts degree programs, students may pursue interests in four specializations: Music Theory, Music Composition, Music history and literature, or (for elementary education majors) Music for Classroom Teachers. Entrance to any of these programs is contingent upon passing an audition on a traditional instrument or voice.

NOTRE DAME COLLEGE
DEPARTMENT OF MUSIC
2321 Elm St.
Manchester, NH 03104
Anita Marchesseault
603-669-4298
Fax: 603-644-8316
www.notredamecollege.edu

PLYMOUTH STATE COLLEGE
MUSIC AND THEATER DEPARTMENT
Department of Music
17 High St.
MSC 37
Plymouth, NH 03264-1595
Dr. Jonathan C. Santore
603-535-2334
Fax: 603-535-2645
E-mail: jsantore@mail.plymouth.edu
www.plymouth.edu/psc/music

Degrees: B.S. Music Education; B.A., Music with options in Vocal Performance and

Pedagogy, Piano performance and Pedagogy, Music Technology and Contract (student self-design); B.A., theatre arts with option in music theatre performance.

The Plymouth State College Department of Music, Theatre, and Dance offers the music and music-related degrees described above in the context of an interdisciplinary department housing all the performing arts. This gives our students unique opportunities for academic and artistic growth, and for participation in a variety of performing, creative, and educational experiences. Students who choose our department also receive a great deal of individual attention and mentoring from a dedicated faculty. Our department is housed in the Silver Cultural Arts Center, one of the most beautiful facilities of its type in Northern New England, and home to a strong annual concert/ performance series by visiting artists.

RIVIER COLLEGE
DEPARTMENT OF ART AND MUSIC

420 Main St.
Nashua, NH 03060
Clifford Davis
603-888-1311
Fax: 603-897-8817
E-mail: cldavis@rivier.edu
www.rivier.edu

ST. ANSELM COLLEGE
DEPARTMENT OF FINE ARTS AND MUSIC

100 St. Anslem Dr.
Manchester, NH 03102
Katherine Hoffman
603-641-7000
Fax: 603-641-7116
www.anselm.edu

UNIVERSITY OF NEW HAMPSHIRE
PAUL CREATIVE ARTS CENTER

PCAC 30 College Rd.
Durham, NH 03824
Isabel Gray
603-862-2404
Fax: 603-862-3155
www.unh.edu/music

NEW JERSEY

Population: 8,600,685 (2003 Estimate)

Capital City: Trenton

Music Colleges and Universities: Bergen Community College, Brookdale Community College, Caldwell College, Camden County College, College of New Jersey, College of St. Elizabeth, County College of Morris, Drew University, Fairleigh Dickinson University Madison, Felician College, Georgian Court College, Kean University, Mercer County Community College, Monmouth University, Montclair State University, New Jersey City University, Princeton University, Ramapo College of New Jersey, Raritan Valley Community College, Richard Stockton College, Rowan University, Rutgers University, Rutgers University at New Brunswick, Rutgers University at Newark, Seton Hall University, Trenton State College, William Paterson University

Bird: Eastern Goldfinch

Motto: Liberty and Prosperity

Flower: Violet

Tree: Red Oak

Residents Called: New Jerseyites

Nickname: The Garden State

Area: 8,722 square miles (47th largest state)

Statehood: December 18, 1787 (3rd state)

Largest Cities: Newark, Jersey City, Paterson, Elizabeth, Edison Township, Woodbridge, Township, Dover Township, Hamilton, Trenton, Camden

College Band Programs: Princeton University, Rutgers University

NEW JERSEY

BERGEN COMMUNITY COLLEGE
DIVISION OF ARTS AND HUMANITIES
400 Paramus Rd.
Paramus, NJ 07652-1508
Dr. Linda Marcel
201-447-9279
Fax: 201-612-5240
E-mail: lmarcel@bergen.cc.nj.us
www.bergen.edu

BROOKDALE COMMUNITY COLLEGE
DEPARTMENT OF MUSIC
765 Newman Springs Rd.
Lincroft, NJ 07738
Joseph Accurso
732-224-2345
E-mail: jaccurso@brookdale.cc.nj.us
www.brookdale.cc.nj.us

CALDWELL COLLEGE
DEPARTMENT OF MUSIC
9 Ryerson Ave.
Caldwell, NJ 07006
Laura Greenwald
973-618-3520
Fax: 973-618-3467
E-mail: lgreen@caldwell.edu
www.caldwell.edu

CAMDEN COUNTY COLLEGE
DEPARTMENT OF MUSIC
P.O. Box 200
Blackwood, NJ 08012
Judith Rowlands
856-227-7200
Fax: 856-374-4969
www.camdencc.edu

COLLEGE OF NEW JERSEY
DEPARTMENT OF MUSIC
P.O. Box 7718
Ewing, NJ 08628
Dr. Robert E. Parrish
609-771-2551
Fax: 609-637-5182
E-mail: music@tcnj.edu
www.tcnj.edu/~music

COLLEGE OF ST. ELIZABETH
DEPARTMENT OF MUSIC
Morristown, NJ 07960
Teresa Walters
201-539-1600
www.cse.edu

COUNTY COLLEGE OF MORRIS
DEPARTMENT OF MUSIC
214 Center Grove Rd.
Randolph, NJ 07869
Susuan Cook
973-325-4300
Fax: 978-328-5445
E-mail: scook@ccm.edu
www.ccm.edu

DREW UNIVERSITY
DEPARTMENT OF MUSIC
36 Madison Ave.
Madison, NJ 07940
Lydia Ledeen
201-408-3422
Fax: 201-408-3768
E-mail: lledeen@drew.edu
www.depts.drew.edu

FAIRLEIGH DICKINSON UNIVERSITY MADISON
DEPARTMENT OF FINE ARTS
Madison, NJ 07940
Louis Gordon
201-593-8638
www.fdu.edu

FELICIAN COLLEGE
DEPARTMENT OF S. MAIN ST.
Lodi, NJ 07644
James Boyce
201-778-1190
www.felician.edu

GEORGIAN COURT COLLEGE
DEPARTMENT OF MUSIC, HUMANITIES, AND MUSIC
900 Lakewood Ave.
Lakewood, NJ 08701
Myra Malamut
732-364-2200
Fax: 732-905-8571
E-mail: malamutm@georgian.edu
www.georgian.edu
Degrees: B.A. in Music

The Music Program at Georgian Court College provides a rigorous and thorough education within the framework of a small department, which cares for each and every student. Three tracks within the major allow students to major in Applied Music, Teacher of Music Certification, or Music as a double major with Education. Georgian Court College is a small college with outstanding ensembles: Concert Band, Jazz Band, String Orchestra, Flute Ensemble, Chorale, and Court Singers provide performance experiences for students, as well as numerous recitals and opportunities to solo within campus special events.

Georgian Court College's program in Music is within the Undergraduate day Division for Women. The campus, a national historic landmark, is known for its beauty in its architecture, arboretum, and beautiful gardens. Located near the New Jersey shore and with access to cultural events in Manhattan and Philadelphia, Georgian Court College is an ideal place to major in Music in an atmosphere conducive to learning yet with a variety of nearby cultural and recreational opportunities.

KEAN UNIVERSITY
DEPARTMENT OF MUSIC
1000 Morris Ave.
Union, NJ 07083
Mark Terenzi
908-527-2107
Fax: 908-527-2635
www.kean.edu

MERCER COUNTY COMMUNITY COLLEGE
DEPARTMENT OF MUSIC
P.O. Box B
Trenton, NJ 08690
James Kelly
609-586-4800
Fax: 609-586-2318
E-mail: kellyj@mccc.edu
www.mccc.edu

MONMOUTH UNIVERSITY
DEPARTMENT OF MUSIC AND THEATRE ARTS
West Long Branch, NJ 07764
John Burke
732-571-3442
Fax: 732-263-5330
www.monmouth.edu

MONTCLAIR STATE UNIVERSITY
DEPARTMENT OF MUSIC
Upper Montclair, NJ 07043
Dr. Ting Ho
973-655-7212
Fax: 973-655-5279
E-mail: ho_ting@hotmail.com
www.montclair.edu/music

The department of music at Montclair State University has been training professional musicians for more than 45 years. Just 14 miles from Manhattan, our program attracts a distinguished faculty and guest artists to teach and perform every semester, while enabling students to take advantage of New York City's concerts, open rehearsals and extensive resources. The department offers undergraduate and graduate degrees in performance, theory/composition, music education and music therapy. Instruction is based on a rigorous traditional approach, combined with methodologies from the most up-to-date research available. Our philosophy is that students should be exposed to all facets of music, including performance, theory and music history, regardless of their particular concentration. Professional development is key to the music program. While activities such as ensemble and performance preparation are part of the required curriculum, additional experiences are offered through special programs and affiliations of the faculty. The department sponsors a full roster of 12 performing ensembles and more than 100 concerts each year. Facilities include three concert halls, faculty teaching studios, practice rooms, an electronic music studio and a computer/MIDI-keyboard lab. The department is fully accredited by the National Association of Schools of Music (NASM). The music therapy program is approved by the National Association for Music Therapy.

NEW JERSEY CITY UNIVERSITY
DEPARTMENT OF MUSIC, DANCE, AND THEATRE
2039 Kennedy Blvd.
Jersey City, NJ 07305
Dr. Edward Raditz
201-200-2017
Fax: 201-200-3130
E-mail: eraditz@njcu.edu
www.njcu.edu

PRINCETON UNIVERSITY
DEPARTMENT OF MUSIC
Woolworth Center of Musical Studies
Princeton, NJ 08544
Scott Burnham
609-258-4241
Fax: 609-258-6793
E-mail: sburnham@princeton.edu
www.music.princeton.edu

RAMAPO COLLEGE OF NEW JERSEY
SCHOOL OF CONTEMPORARY ARTS
505 Ramapo Valley Rd.
Mahwah, NJ 07430
Mack Brandon
201-529-7368
Fax: 201-529-7481
www.ramapo.edu

RARITAN VALLEY COMMUNITY COLLEGE
DEPARTMENT OF PERFORMANCE ARTS AND MUSIC
P.O. Box 3300
Somerville, NJ 08876
Roger Briscoe
908-231-8813
Fax: 908-595-0213

E-mail: rbriscoe@raritanval.edu
www.raritanaval.edu

RICHARD STOCKTON COLLEGE
Music Sub-Track Area
P.O. Box 195
Pomona, NJ 08240
Kenneth Dollarhide
609-652-4505
Fax: 609-652-4550
www.stockton.edu

ROWAN UNIVERSITY
Wilson Hall
201 Mullica Hill Rd.
Glassboro, NJ 08028
Larry De Pasquale
609-256-4555
Fax: 609-256-4644
E-mail: depasquale@rowan.edu
www.rowan.edu/mars

RUTGERS UNIVERSITY
Camden Department of Fine Arts and Music Program
Music Program
Camden, NJ 08102
Dr. Wibert Davis Jerome
856-225-6239
Fax: 856-225-6176
E-mail: wdj@crab.rutgers.edu
http://rutgers.edu

RUTGERS UNIVERSITY AT NEWARK
Department of Visual and Performing Arts
Newark, NJ 07102
Annette Juliano
973-353-5119
Fax: 973-353-1392
www.andromeda.rutgers.edu

RUTGERS UNIVERSITY AT NEW BRUNSWICK
Mason Gross School of the Arts
33 Livingston Ave.
New Brunswick, NJ 08901
Nancy Darling
732-932-3848
Fax: 732-932-1517
E-mail: ndarling@rci.rutgers.edu
http://musicweb.rutgers.edu

SETON HALL UNIVERSITY
Department of Art and Music
400 South Orange Ave.
South Orange, NJ 07079
Jeanette Hile
201-761-9459
Fax: 201-275-2386
http://artsci.shu.edu/artmusic

TRENTON STATE COLLEGE
Department of Music
Ewing, NJ 08628
609-771-2551
Fax: 609-771-3422

WILLIAM PATERSON UNIVERSITY
Department of Music
Wayne, NJ 07470
Diane Falk Romaine
973-720-2315
Fax: 973-720-2217
E-mail: falkd@wpunj.edu
www.wpunj.edu

NEW MEXICO

Population: 1,928,443 (2003 Estimate)

Capital City: Santa Fe

Music Colleges and Universities: College of Sante Fe, Eastern New Mexico University, New Mexico Highlands University, New Mexico Junior College, New Mexico State University, New Mexico Tech, San Juan College, University of New Mexico, Western New Mexico University

Bird: Roadrunner

Motto: Crescit eundo – It grows as it goes

Flower: Yucca flower

Tree: Pinon

Residents Called: New Mexicans

Origin of Name: Named by the Spanish for lands north of the Rio Grande River.

Area: 121,593 square miles (5th largest state)

Statehood: January 6, 1912 (47th state)

Largest Cities: Albuquerque, Las Cruces, Santa Fe, Rio Rancho, Roswell, Farmington, Alamogordo, Clovis, Hobbs, Carlsbad

College Band Programs: New Mexico State University

NEW MEXICO

COLLEGE OF SANTA FE
Department of Performing Arts
17600 St. Michaels Dr.
Sante Fe, NM 87505-7615
Steven Miller
505-473-6196
Fax: 505-473-6021
E-mail: cmp@csf.edu
www.cfs.edu

Degrees: Contemporary Music, B.A., B.F.A.

EASTERN NEW MEXICO UNIVERSITY
School of Music
Portales, NM 88130
John Olsen
505-562-2671
Fax: 505-562-2381
E-mail: john.olsen@enmu.edu
www.enmu.edu

The Eastern New Mexico University School of Music is located on a beautiful and scenic campus in Portales. Professional programs in music prepare students for careers in performance, public school or private studio teaching, music theatre, music business and graduate school. Degrees offered include: bachelor of music education (choral/instrumental) with K-12 certification; bachelor of music performance (piano, instrumental or vocal); bachelor of music with music theatre emphasis; bachelor of science in music; bachelor of science in music with elective studies in business. One hundred percent placement rate for music education graduates.

NEW MEXICO HIGHLANDS UNIVERSITY
Student Recruitment
P.O. Box 9000
Las Vegas, NM 87701
Tim Cossaart
505-454-3593
Fax: 505-454-3068
E-mail: timcossaart@nmhu.edu
www.nmhu.edu

NEW MEXICO JUNIOR COLLEGE
Department of Music
Lovington Hwy.
Hobbs, NM 88240
Sue Bennett
505-392-4510
Fax: 505-392-2527
www.nmjc.cc.nm.us

NEW MEXICO STATE UNIVERSITY
Music Department
P.O. Box 3001
3F
Las Cruces, NM 88003
Dr. Greg Fant
505-646-2421
Fax: 505-646-8199
E-mail: music@nmsu.edu
www.nmsu.edu/~music

NEW MEXICO TECH
Music Program
801 Leroy
Socorro, NM 87801
Douglas Dunston
505-835-5445
Fax: 505-385-5544
www.nmt.edu

SAN JUAN COLLEGE
DEPARTMENT OF MUSIC
4601 College Blvd.
Farmington, NM 87402
Keith Cochrane
505-566-3386
Fax: 505-566-3385
E-mail: cochrane@sjc.cc.nm.us
www.sjc.cc.nm.us
Degrees: Music Associate of Arts Degree

UNIVERSITY OF NEW MEXICO
DEPARTMENT OF MUSIC
Center for the Arts
Albuquerque, NM 87131
505-277-2126
Fax: 505-277-0708
www.unm.edu

WESTERN NEW MEXICO UNIVERSITY
EXPRESSIVE ARTS DEPT - MUSIC
1000 W. College Ave.
P.O. Box 680
Silver City, NM 88062
Dr. Ben Tucker
505-538-6614
Fax: 505-538-6619
E-mail: tuckerb@silver.wnmu.edu
www.wnmu.edu

Degrees: B.S., B.A. in Music, with
Performance or Music Education with
Concentrations

Boasting one of the finest performance auditoriums in the Southwest, this friendly university overlooks picturesque Silver City on the edge of the Gila Wilderness in Southwestern New Mexico. Music opportunities abound at WNMU for music majors and non-majors alike in both university ensembles and a wide array of community music organizations and events. With a total university enrollment of under 3,000 and a dedicated professional music faculty, personal attention is one of the important advantages of studying at WNMU, an ideal place for college study. WNMU offers baccalaureate degrees in music with a particular emphasis on music education. Graduates of WNMU are currently teaching music in schools throughout the southwest and as far away as Alaska.

NEW YORK

Population: 19,206,184 (2003 Estimate)

Capital City: Albany

Music Colleges and Universities: Adelphi University, Alfred University, Bard College, Barnard College, Baruch College, Binghamton University, Borough of Manhattan Community College, Bronx Community College, Brooklyn College, Brooklyn Conservatory of Music, Broome Community College, Canisius College, Cayuga County Community College, Chautauqua School of Music, City College of New York, City University of New York, City University of New York at Brooklyn, City University of New York at City College, City University of New York at Grad Center, City University of New York at Hunter College, City University of New York at Jay College, City University of New York at Lehman College, City University of New York at Medgar Evers, City University of New York at York University, Colgate University, College of St. Rose, Columbia University, Concordia College, Cornell University, Corning Community College, Crane Institute for Music Business, Daemen College, Dalcroze School of Music, Dutchess Community College, Eastern U.S. Music Camp at Colgate University, Eastman School of Music of the University of Rochester, Elmira College, Erie Community College, Erie Community College at North, Erie Community College at South, Finger Lakes Community College, Five Towns College, Fordham University, Hamilton College, Hartwick College, Hebrew Union College, Hobart and William Smith College, Hofstra University, Houghton College, Institute of Audio Research, Ithaca College, Jamestown Community College, Jewish Theological Seminary of America, Julliard School of Music, Keuka College, Kingsborough Community College, LaGuardia Community College, Long Island University at Brooklyn, Long Island University at CW Post, Malloy College, Manhattan School of Music, Manhattanville College, Mannes College of Music, Mercy College, Monroe Community College, Nassau Community College, Nazareth College, New School University, New York Technical College, New York University, Niagara County Community College, Nyack College, Onondaga Community College, Orange County Community College, Packer Collegiate Institute, Queen's College, Queensborough Community College, Rensselaer Polytechnic Institute, Robert Wesleyan College, Rockland Community College, Rockland Summer Institute, Russell Sage College, Sarah Lawrence College, Schenectady County Community College, Skidmore College, St. Bonaventure University, St. John's University, St. Lawrence University, Stony Brook University, Suffolk County Community College, SUNY at Binghamton, SUNY at Buffalo, SUNY at Cortland, SUNY at Fredonia, SUNY at Geneseo, SUNY at New Paltz, SUNY at Oneonta, SUNY at Oswego, SUNY at Plattsburgh, SUNY at Potsdam, SUNY at Purchase College, SUNY at Stony Brook, Syracuse University, Teachers College, Tompkins Cortland Community College, Ulster County Community College, Union College, University at Albany, University of Rochester, Utica College of Syracuse, Vassar College, Villa Maria College of Buffalo, Wagner College, Wells College, Westchester Conservatory of Music

Bird: Bluebird

Motto: Excelsior

Flower: Rose

Tree: Sugar maple

Largest Cities: New York, Buffalo, Rochester, Yonkers, Syracuse, Albany, New Rochelle, Mount Vernon, Schenectady, Utica

College Band Programs: Columbia University, Cornell University, Syracuse University, SUNY-Buffalo

NEW YORK

ADELPHI UNIVERSITY
MUSIC ADMISSIONS
DEPARTMENT OF MUSIC
1 South Ave.
Garden City, NY 11530
Paul Moravec
516-877-4295
Fax: 516-877-4296
www.adelphi.edu

ALFRED UNIVERSITY
DEPARTMENT OF MUSIC
26 N. Main St
Alfred, NY 14802
Luanne Crosby
607-871-2251
Fax: 607-871-2339
E-mail: performs@alfred.edu
www.alfred.edu

BARD COLLEGE
MUSIC PROGRAM
Annedale-on-the-Hudson, NY 12504
Joan Tower
845-758-7251
E-mail: tower@bard.edu
www.bard.edu

BARNARD COLLEGE
DEPARTMENT OF MUSIC
3009 Broadway
P.O. Box 37
New York, NY 10027
Gail Archer
212-854-5096
Fax: 212-854-7491
E-mail: garcher@Barnard.edu
www.barnard.edu

BARUCH COLLEGE
DEPARTMENT OF FINE AND PERFORMING ARTS
17 Lexington Ave.
P.O. Box A-1209
New York, NY 10010
Mimi D'aponte
212-802-5660
Fax: 212-346-8166
E-mail: mgdbb@cunyvm.cuny.edu
www.baruch.cuny.edu

BINGHAMTON UNIVERSITY
DEPARTMENT OF MUSIC
P.O. Box 6000
Binghamton, NY 13903
Jane Zuckerman
607-777-2592
Fax: 607-777-4425
E-mail: jzucker@binghamton.edu
http://music.binghamton.edu
Degrees: B.A. in music; B.M. and M.M.

Binghamton University's Music Department offers an exciting curriculum of academic and performance opportunities in ensembles, studio, and in the classroom. The offerings are designed to serve the students who are interested in majoring in music and students for whom music studies represent an enriching complement to other areas of endeavor. Accredited by the NASM, the department offers undergraduate and graduate major studies in most instruments and voice, choral and instrumental conducting, composition, music history, and music theory. In addition, the University offers an M.M. in Opera degree in cooperation with the Tri Cities Opera, the region's prestigious professional training company. The Music Department is housed in the Fine Arts building which offers excellent classrooms, studios, large rehearsal rooms, concert halls, and practice rooms. The university's Anderson Center for the Arts, one of America's premier arts centers, is the home of 450-seat Chamber Hall and a 1,200-seat Concert Theater.

BOROUGH OF MANHATTAN COMMUNITY COLLEGE
DEPARTMENT OF MUSIC
199 Chambers St.
New York, NY 10007
Douglas Anderson
212-220-1464
Fax: 212-220-1285
www.bmcc.cuny.edu

BRONX COMMUNITY COLLEGE
ART AND MUSIC
Department of Music
University Ave. W. 181 St.
Bronx, NY 10453
Ruth Bass
718-289-5100
Fax: 718-289-6433
www.bcc.cuny.edu

BROOKLYN COLLEGE
CONSERVATORY OF MUSIC
2900 Bedford Ave.
Brooklyn, NY 11210-2889
Bruce Macintyre
718-951-5286
www.brooklyn.cuny.edu

BROOKLYN CONSERVATORY OF MUSIC
58 Seventh Ave.
Brooklyn, NY 11217
Leomaris Sanchez
718-461-8910
Fax: 718-866-2450
www.brooklynconservatory.com

The Brooklyn Conservatory is a community music school offering low-cost tuition for music lessons and classes for students aged 18 months to senior citizens. Jazz and classical are available.

BROOME COMMUNITY COLLEGE
DEPARTMENT OF MUSIC
P.O. Box 1017
Binghamton, NY 13902-1017
Micheal Kinney
607-778-5000
Fax: 607-778-5394
E-mail: kinney_m@sunybroome.edu
www.sunybroome.edu

CANISIUS COLLEGE
DEPARTMENT OF MUSIC
2001 Main St.
Buffalo, NY 14208
Penelope Lips
716-888-2201
Fax: 716-888-3230
E-mail: lips@canisius.edu
www.canisius.edu

CAYUGA COUNTY COMMUNITY COLLEGE
DEPARTMENT OF MUSIC
Franklin St
Auburn, NY 13021
David Richards
315-255-1743
Fax: 315-255-1743
www.cayuga-cc.edu

CHAUTAUQUA SCHOOL OF MUSIC
P.O. Box 1098
Chautauqua, NY 14722
Peter J. Schoenbach
716-357-6233
Fax: 716-357-9014
E-mail: amarshaus@chautauqua-inst.com
http://music.ciweb.org

Degrees: credits available through SUNY Fredonia, NY 14063

A summer studying music at Chautauqua Institution is like no other educational experience. Going far beyond excellent instruction, students of music may also attend concerts, plays, films, operas, art exhibits, and relax in the beauty of Chautauqua's famous lakeside grounds.

Students of orchestral instruments (ages 17-25) participate in all three components of the instrumental program: orchestra, chamber music, and private instruction.

Our voice department offers lessons, role preparation, diction classes and vocal coaching by a full-time staff of teachers, coaches and resident state director along with numerous guest artists for students 18 and older.

Chautauqua piano strives to understand and encourage a unique and exciting mixture of traditional and innovative classes and concerts for pianists 16 and older in a one-on-one course study designed for each participant. Summer school facilities are equipped with new Kawai pianos.

CITY UNIVERSITY OF NEW YORK
DEPARTMENT OF PERFORMANCE AND CREATIVE ARTS

2800 Victory Blvd., IP 203
Staten Island, NY 10314-6609
Syliva Kahan
718-982-2520
Fax: 718-982-2537
E-mail: kahan@postbox.csi.cuny.edu
www.csi.cuny.edu

Degrees: B.A. and B.S.

The College of Staten Island is situated on a beautiful wooded campus in one of New York City's outer boroughs, one half-hour from Manhattan. CSI's outstanding Music Program offers two degrees in the Bachelor of Arts and the Bachelor of Science, within the context of a liberal arts education. The program integrates the four traditional music disciplines – theory, musicianship, history and literature, and performance/composition – in an innova-

tive and cross-disciplinary curriculum. The course offerings, including Jazz Studies, Electronic Music, and (beginning in 2004-05) Music Education, prepare students for careers in teaching, scholarship, performance, and the music industry. Students receive both rigorous training and supportive individual attention from professors and arts-faculty who are active in New York City's thriving music and intellectual life. Classes are taught in the College's magnificent Center for the Arts, which boasts an acoustically excellent Recital Hall, a Concert Hall, a Theater and a Black Box Theater.

CITY UNIVERSITY OF NEW YORK AT BROOKLYN
CONSERVATORY OF MUSIC

2900 Bedford Ave.
Brooklyn, NY 11210-2889
Bruce Macintyre
718-951-5286
Fax: 718-951-4502
www.brooklyn.cuny.edu

CITY UNIVERSITY OF NEW YORK AT CITY COLLEGE
DEPARTMENT OF MUSIC

Convent Ave. and W. 138 St
New York, NY 10031
James Watts
212-650-5411
Fax: 212-650-5428
www.cuny.edu

Degrees: Ph.D./D.M.A. Programs in Music; the Graduate Center only offers doctoral level degrees)

CITY UNIVERSITY OF NEW YORK AT GRAD CENTER
DEPARTMENT OF MUSIC
365 Fifth Ave.
New York, NY 10016
Peg Rivers
212-817-8602
Fax: 212-817-1529
E-mail: privers@gc.cuny.edu
www.web.gc.cuny.edu/dept/music/index.htm

CITY UNIVERSITY OF NEW YORK AT HUNTER COLLEGE
DEPARTMENT OF MUSIC
695 Park Ave.
New York, NY 10021
Paul F. Mueller
212-772-5020
Fax: 212-772-5022
E-mail:
paul.mueller@hunter.cuny.edu
www.hunter.cuny.edu

CITY UNIVERSITY OF NEW YORK AT JAY COLLEGE
DEPARTMENT OF ART MUSIC AND PHIL
445 W. 59th St
New York, NY 10019-1029
John Pittman
212-237-8335
www.york.cuny.edu

CITY UNIVERSITY OF NEW YORK AT LEHMAN COLLEGE
DEPARTMENT OF MUSIC
Bronx, NY 10468
Bernard Shockett
212-960-8247
www.cuny.edu

CITY UNIVERSITY OF NEW YORK AT MEDGAR EVERS
DEPARTMENT OF MUSIC
1150 Carroll St
Brooklyn, NY 11225-2201
Edna Edet
www.cuny.edu

CITY UNIVERSITY OF NEW YORK AT YORK UNIVERSITY
DEPARTMENT OF MUSIC
94 20 Guy Brewer Blvd.
Jamaica, NY 11451
David Erst
718-262-2400
www.cuny.edu

COLGATE UNIVERSITY
MUSIC DEPARTMENT
13 Oak Dr.
Hamilton, NY 13346
Roberta Healey
315-228-7642
Fax: 315-228-7557
E-mail: rhealey@colgate.edu
www.colgate.edu

COLLEGE OF ST. ROSE
DEPARTMENT OF MUSIC
432 Western Ave.
Albany, NY 12203
Paul Evoskevich
518-454-5178
Fax: 518-454-2146
E-mail: reelsole@yahoo.com
www.strose.edu

Degrees: B.S. in music education, B.S. in music industry, M.M. in performance, jazz studies, music industry, and piano pedagogy

When you walk into the Saint Rose Music

Building, you will hear the voices of our distinguished faculty members mentoring the talented young musicians. Since it is rare to have more than a dozen students in a music class, within a very short period of time our professors know all our students by name, enabling them to genuinely give each student the individual attention that he or she desires and deserves. Our music students all seem to know each other and the small size of our programs creates a spirit of positive competitiveness in which students help each other be the best musicians possible.

COLUMBIA UNIVERSITY
MUSIC PERFORMANCE OFFICE
DEPARTMENT OF MUSIC
2960 Broadway
New York, NY 10027
Deborah Bradley
212-854-3825
Fax: 212-854-8191
E-mail: db511@columbia.edu
www.music.columbia.edu/music-department.html

CONCORDIA COLLEGE
CONCORDIA CONSERVATORY OF MUSIC
171 White Plains
Bronxville, NY 10708
Timothy Schultz
914-337-9300
Fax: 914-337-4500
E-mail: tps@concordia-ny.edu
www.concordia-ny.edu

Located just 30 minutes north of New York City in a beautiful suburb, Concordia College draws its applied music faculty from some of the finest performing organizations in the world. Arts management majors gain experience through internships with corporations such as Sony, Colbert Artists Management, Steinway and Sons and Lincoln Center.

CORNELL UNIVERSITY
MUSIC DEPARTMENT
101 Lincoln Hall
Ithaca, NY 14853
Mark Davis Scatterday
607-255-4097
Fax: 607-254-2877
E-mail: cjb2@cornell.edu
www.cornell.edu

CORNING COMMUNITY COLLEGE
DEPARTMENT OF MUSIC
1 Academic Dr.
Corning, NY 14830
James Hudson
607-962-9298
Fax: 607-962-9456
E-mail: hudson@corning-cc.edu
www.corning-cc.edu

DAEMEN COLLEGE
MUSIC DEPARTMENT
4380 Main St.
Amherst, NY 14226
Chester L. Mais
716-839 3600
Fax: 716-839-8516
E-mail: cmais@daemen.edu
www.daemen.edu

DALCROZE SCHOOL OF MUSIC
129 WEST 67TH ST.
New York, NY 10023
Yana Joseph
212-501-3380
Fax: 212-874-7865
E-mail: dalcroze2@aol.com
www.dalcroze.com

The Dalcroze School of Music offers the Dalcroze Certificate – three teacher-training programs in Dalcroze eurhythmics, instrumental instruction and dance. Classes for personal and/or professional enrichment are available. No audition is necessary for those classes.

DUTCHESS COMMUNITY COLLEGE
PERFORMING ARTS AND COMMUNICATIONS
53 Pendell Rd.
Poughkeepsie, NY 12601-1512
Kelly Conner
914-431-8625
Fax: 914-431-8985
E-mail: conner@sunydutchess.edu
www.sunyditchess.edu

ELMIRA COLLEGE
DEPARTMENT OF MUSIC
Park Place
Elmira, NY 14901
Mark Spicer
607-735-1949
Fax: 607-351-7580
E-mail: mspicer@elmira.edu
www.elmira.edu

ERIE COMMUNITY COLLEGE
DEPARTMENT OF LIBERAL ARTS AND HUMANITIES
121 Ellicott St.
Buffalo, NY 14203
Kathleen McGuigan-Sadoff
716-842-2770
Fax: 716-842-1972
www.ecc.edu

ERIE COMMUNITY COLLEGE- NORTH
LIBERAL ARTS AND HUMANITIES
Williamsville, NY 14221
Paul Stencel
716-851-1319
Fax: 716-851-1429
www.ecc.edu

ERIE COMMUNITY COLLEGE - SOUTH
LIBERAL ARTS AND HUMANITIES
4041 Southwestern Blvd.
Orchard Park, NY 14127
Alan Schmdt
www.ecc.edu

FINGER LAKES COMMUNITY COLLEGE
DEPARTMENT OF MUSIC
4355 Lakeshore Dr.
Canandaigua, NY 14424-8347
Eleanor Rideout
716-394-3500
Fax: 716-395-5005
www.fingerlakes.edu

FIVE TOWNS COLLEGE
DEPARTMENT OF MUSIC
305 N. Service Rd.
Dix Hills, NY 11746
Music Department
516-424-7000
Fax: 806-747-2294
www.fivetowns.edu

FORDHAM UNIVERSITY
DEPARTMENT OF ART AND MUSIC
Faculty Memorial Hall 447
Bronx, NY 10458
Jack Spalding
718-817-4890
Fax: 718-817-4929
www.fordham.edu

HAMILTON COLLEGE
DEPARTMENT OF MUSIC
198 College Hill Rd.
Clinton, NY 13323
Dr. Lydia Hamessley
315-859-4261
E-mail: lhamessl@hamilton.edu
www.hamilton.edu

HARTWICK COLLEGE
DEPARTMENT OF MUSIC
Anderson Center
Oneonta, NY 13820
Sandra McKane
607-431-4800
Fax: 607-431-4813
E-mail: mckanes@hartwick.edu
www.hartwick.edu/music

HEBREW UNION COLLEGE
SCHOOL OF SACRED MUSIC
1 W. 4th St
New York, NY 10012
Isreal Goldstein
212-674-5300
Fax: 212-388-1720
E-mail: igoldstein@huc.edu
www.huc.edu

HOBART AND WILLIAM SMITH COLLEGE
DEPARTMENT OF MUSIC
Geneva, NY 14456
Dr. Patricia Ann Myers
315-781-3401
Fax: 315-781-3560
E-mail: myers_p@hws.edu
www.hws.edu

HOFSTRA UNIVERSITY
MUSIC DEPARTMENT
Emily Lowb Hall
Room 101B
112 Hofstra University
Hempstead, NY 11570
Mark Anson Cartwright
516-463-5490
Fax: 516-463-6393
E-mail: mushzc@hofstra.edu
www.hofsrta.edu

HOUGHTON COLLEGE
DEPARTMENT OF MUSIC
School of Music
1 Willard Ave.
Houghton, NY 14744
Ben King
585-567-9516
Fax: 585-567-9517
E-mail: ben.king@houghton.edu
www.houghton.edu

The school of music has 10 full-time faculty, 120 music majors, new $8 million facility, a full range of performance and teaching facilities.

INSTITUTE OF AUDIO RESEARCH
ADMISSIONS
64 University Place
New York, NY 10003-4595
Mark L. Kahn
212-777-8550
Fax: 212-677-6549
E-mail: iarny@aol.com
www.audioschool.com

ITHACA COLLEGE
3322 WHALEN CENTER FOR MUSIC
Ithaca, NY 14850
Townsend A. Plant
607-274-3366
Fax: 607-274-1727
E-mail: tplant@ithaca.edu
www.ithaca.edu/music

Degrees: B.M., and B.A.

The Ithaca College School of Music is one of the largest private undergraduate schools of music in the United States. 56 full-time resident faculties create a student-to-teacher ratio of 8:1. Small classes and the one-on-one weekly interaction between student and private teacher have developed professional performance and outstanding music educators noted for their musicianship and pedagogical skills. In 1999, the James J. Whalen Center for Music had its grand opening. The center doubled the size of the existing Ford Hall Facility to form a stunning complex which adds a beautiful new recital hall, two large rehearsal halls, 30 new faculty studios, two recording studios, an electro acoustic suite of three studios, a computer classroom and lab, and a music education suite, and it is situated in Ithaca College's breath-taking residential campus overlooking Cayuga Lake in the Finger Lakes region of New York State. Students in the school of music become part of a rich musical heritage, eventually taking their place in the long line of alumni who work and perform in virtually every area of music. Ithaca graduates are educators and administrators in public schools and at colleges and universities throughout the country, as well as performers in such prestigious organizations as the Metropolitan Opera, the Chicago Symphony, the New York Philharmonic, and the Boston Symphony. Others work in important positions throughout the music industry, including music publishing, artist management, and recording.

JAMESTOWN COMMUNITY COLLEGE
DEPARTMENT OF MUSIC
525 Falconer St.
Jamestown, NY 14791
Wade Davenport
716-665-5220
Fax: 716-665-9110
www.sunyjcc.edu

JEWISH THEOLOGICAL SEMINARY OF AMERICA
3080 Broadway
College of Jewish Music
New York, NY 10027
Boaz Tarsi
212-678-8037
Fax: 212-678-8947
www.jtsa.edu

JULLIARD SCHOOL OF MUSIC
COMMUNICATIONS OFFICE
60 Lincoln Plaza
New York, NY 10023
Paul Mlyn
212-799-5000
Fax: 212-769-0263
www.julliard.edu

KEUKA COLLEGE
DEPARTMENT OF MUSIC
Keuka Park, NY 14478
Joanne Desotelle
315-536-4411
Fax: 315-536-5216
E-mail: jdesotel@mail.keuka.edu
www.keuk.edu

KINGSBOROUGH COMMUNITY COLLEGE
DEPARTMENT OF COMMUNICATIONS AND PERFORMANCE ARTS
2001 Oriental Blvd.
Brooklyn, NY 11235
John Williams
718-368-5591
Fax: 718-368-4879
E-mail: chesse@kbcc.cuny.edu
www.kbcc.cuny.edu

LAGUARDIA COMMUNITY COLLEGE
DEPARTMENT OF HUMANITIES AND PERFORMING ARTS
3110 Thomson Ave.
Long Island City, NY 11101
John Williams
718-482-5694
Fax: 718-482-5599
www.lagcc.cuny.edu

LONG ISLAND UNIVERSITY AT BROOKLYN
DEPARTMENT OF MUSIC
1 University Plaza
Brooklyn, NY 11201
Robert Aquino
718-488-1668
Fax: 718-488-1372

E-mail: raquino@liu.edu
www.liu.edu

Degrees: B.F.A. (Jazz Studies); B.A. (traditional Music); B.S. (Music Education)

L.I.U is one of the few jazz studies programs in the New York Metropolitan area. A student's music program can be tailored to include other concentrations such as minor or double major in Media Arts, Business, etc. Students are allowed to study privately off campus for credit with top professionals in the music field. L.U.U. is a multi-campus, highly-diverse, independent university. It is the seventh largest in the U.S. The Brooklyn Campus is constructing its new state-of-the-art Kumble Theatre with new rehearsal and practice rooms. Students have the opportunity to perform in various instrumental and vocal ensembles. With small classes, students receive personalized attention to guidance. Scholarships are available.

LONG ISLAND UNIVERSITY AT CW POST
DEPARTMENT OF MUSIC
720 Northern Blvd.
Brookville, NY 11548
Alexander Dashnaw
516-299-2474
Fax: 516-299-2884
E-mail: music@cwpost.liu.edu
www.liu.edu/~svpa/music

MALLOY COLLEGE
DEPARTMENT OF MUSIC
1000 Hempstead Ave.
Rockville Center, NY 11570
Daniel McGann
516-678-5000

MANHATTAN SCHOOL OF MUSIC
120 CLAREMONT AVE.
New York, NY 10027
Richard Adams
212-749-2802
Fax: 212-749-5471
E-mail: radams@msmnyc.edu
www.msmnyc.edu

MANHATTANVILLE COLLEGE
DEPARTMENT OF MUSIC
2900 Purchace St
Purchase, NY 10577
Anthony Lamagra
914-323-5260
Fax: 914-323-5383
E-mail: lamagraa@mville.edu
www.mville.edu

MANNES COLLEGE OF MUSIC
NEW SCHOOL UNIVERSITY
150 West 85th St.
New York, NY 10024
Joel Lester
212-580-0210
Fax: 212-580-1738
E-mail:
mannesadmissions@newschool.edu
www.mannes.edu

Mannes College of Music, a division of New School University, holds a proud place in the forefront of American music education. Throughout its 75 years of existence, it has led the way with programs considered among the best in the world for broad musical training and the encouragement of artistic growth. Its distinguished faculty includes some of New York City's most prominent musicians, as well as internationally known ensembles. Students at Mannes College of Music receive rigorous professional training as members of a friendly and supportive school community dedicated to artistic attainment. In an age of mass educa-tion, Mannes maintains small classes and an intimate atmosphere that permit a close and sustained contact among students, faculty, and administration. In the larger context, students have the benefit of full access to the richness of New York City's musical and cultural life. The college itself is an important contributor to music in New York. Members of the Mannes community of faculty, students and alumni are active in every kind of musical endeavor. In addition, external programs of the college bring into the school some of the most creative and exciting personalities of the current scene for courses, master classes and special lectures.

MERCY COLLEGE
MUSIC PROGRAM
555 Broadway
Dobbs Ferry, NY 10522
Joshua Berrett
914-674-7420
Fax: 914-674-7488
www.mercynet.edu

MONROE COMMUNITY COLLEGE
DEPARTMENT OF VISUAL AND PERFORMANCE ARTS
Rochester, NY 14692
Randall Johnson
716-292-2000
Fax: 716-427-2749
www.monroecc.edu

NASSAU COMMUNITY COLLEGE
DEPARTMENT OF MUSIC
1 Education Dr.
Garden City, NY 11530
Richard Brooks
516-572-7447
Fax: 516-572-9791
E-mail: musoff@sunynassau.edu
www.sunynassau.edu

NAZARETH COLLEGE
DEPARTMENT OF MUSIC
4245 East Ave.
Rochester, NY 14618
Barbara Staropoli
716-389-2700
Fax: 716-586-2452
E-mail: brstarop@naz.edu
www.naz.edu

NEW SCHOOL UNIVERSITY
JAZZ AND CONTEMPORARY MUSIC PROGRAM
55 W. 13th St., 5th Floor
New York, NY 10011
212-229-5896
Fax: 212-229-8936
E-mail: jazzadm@newschool.edu
www.newschool.edu/jazz

NEW YORK TECHNICAL COLLEGE
PROGRAM OF MUSIC
300 Jay St. #A630
Brooklyn, NY 11201
Charles Porter
718-260-5018
Fax: 718-260-5198
www.cuny.edu

NEW YORK UNIVERSITY
DEPARTMENT OF MUSIC
24 Waverly Place
Room 268
New York, NY 10003
Stanley Boorman
212-998-8300
Fax: 212-995-4147
E-mail: sb11@nyu.edu
www.nyu.edu

NIAGARA COUNTY COMMUNITY COLLEGE
DEPARTMENT OF MUSIC
Sanborn, NY 14132
Paul Ferington
716-614-5999
Fax: 716-614-6826
www.niagaracc.suny.edu

NYACK COLLEGE
DEPARTMENT OF MUSIC
1 South Blvd.
Nyack, NY 10960
Glenn Koponen
845-358-1710
Fax: 845-348-8838
E-mail: koponen@nyackcollege.edu
www.nyackcollege.edu

ONONDAGA COMMUNITY COLLEGE
DEPARTMENT OF MUSIC
Syracuse, NY 13220
Selma Moore
740-588-1482
Fax: 315-469-2240
www.sunyocc.edu

ORANGE COUNTY COMMUNITY COLLEGE
DEPARTMENT OF ARTS AND COMMUNICATIONS
115 South St.
Middletown, NY 10940
Mark Strunksy
845-341-4787
Fax: 845-341-4789
www.sunyorange.edu

PACKER COLLEGIATE INSTITUTE
DEPARTMENT OF MUSIC
Brooklyn, NY 11201
Robert Crendell

QUEENS COLLEGE
AARON COPLAND SCHOOL OF MUSIC
65-30 Kassena Blvd.
Flushing, NY 11364
Hubert S. Howe, Jr.
718-997-3800
Fax: 718-997-3849
E-mail: Hubert_Howe@qc.edu
www.qc.edu/music

QUEENSBOROUGH COMMUNITY COLLEGE
DEPARTMENT OF MUSIC
Flushing, NY 11364
Dorothea Austin
718-631-6393
Fax: 718-423-9620
www.qcc.cuny.edu

RENSSELAER POLYTECHNIC INSTITUTE
DEPARTMENT OF ARTS
110 8th St.
IEAR Studios
Troy, NY 12180
Laura Garrison
518-276-8362
Fax: 518-276-4780
E-mail: garril@rpi.edu
www.arts-rpi.edu

ROBERT WESLEYAN COLLEGE
DIVISION OF FINE ARTS
2301 Westside Dr.
Rochester, NY 14624
Dr. Noel Magee
716-594-6411
Fax: 716-594-6371
www.roberts.edu

ROCKLAND COMMUNITY COLLEGE
DEPARTMENT OF MUSIC
145 College Rd.
Suffern, NY 10901
James Naismith
914-574-4000
www.sunyrockland.edu

ROCKLAND SUMMER INSTITUTE
P.O. Box 161
Tallman, NY 10982
Dr. Edward Gold
www.rsimusic.org

RUSSELL SAGE COLLEGE
DEPARTMENT OF MUSIC
Troy, NY 12180
Micheal Musial
518-244-2248
E-mail: musiam@sage.edu
www.sage.edu

SARAH LAWRENCE COLLEGE
ADMISSIONS OFFICE
1 Mead Way
Bronxville, NY 10708
Barbara Michael
914-337-0700
E-mail: protzman@mail.slc.edu
www.slc.edu

SCHENECTADY COUNTY COMMUNITY COLLEGE
DEPARTMENT OF MUSIC
78 Washington Ave.
Schenectady, NY 12305
William Meckley
518-381-1230
Fax: 518-346-7511
E-mail: mecklewa@gw.sunysccc.edu
www.sunyscc.edu

SKIDMORE COLLEGE
DEPARTMENT OF MUSIC
815 North Broadway
Saratoga Springs, NY 12866
Charles M. Joseph
518-580-5705
Fax: 518-580-5694
E-mail: cjoseph@skidmore.edu
www.skidmore.edu

ST. BONAVENTURE UNIVERSITY
MUSIC PROGRAM
St. Bonaventure, NY 14778
Dr. Les Sabina
716-375-2000
Fax: 716-375-2690
E-mail: lsabina@sbu.edu
www.sbu.edu/academics_arts.html

ST. JOHNS UNIVERSITY
DEPARTMENT OF FINE ARTS-MUSIC
8000 Utopia Pkwy
Jamaica, NY 11439
Anthony Lowell
718-990-6250
Fax: 718-990-2075
E-mail: lowella@stjohns.edu
www.stjohns.edu

ST. LAWRENCE UNIVERSITY
DEPARTMENT OF MUSIC
20 Ramoda Dr.
Canton, NY 13617
Norman Hessert
315-379-5192
Fax: 315-379-7425
E-mail: nhessert@stlawu.edu
http://web.stlawu.edu

STONY BROOK UNIVERSITY
DEPARTMENT OF MUSIC
Stony Brook, NY 10010
Daniel Weymouth
631-632-7330
Fax: 631-632-7404
E-mail:
Daniel.Weymouth@StonyBrook.edu
www.sunysb.edu/music

Degrees: B.A. with a major in music; Master of Arts, Master of Music, Ph.D., M.A. and Ph.D.: Program in the History and Theory of Music; Composition M.M. and D.M.A. Performance

Stony Brook's programs have grown out of an unusual partnership between the academy and the conservatory. The music department has distinguished and well-balanced faculty in the areas of music history, theory, composition, and performance. The degree programs are designed to favor interaction among music disciplines that have traditionally been kept separate. For example, the performance programs at Stony Brook all have an academic component. Graduate courses typically have a healthy mix of students from all areas. A number of courses are team taught by two or more faculty members, examining topics from several disciplinary viewpoints. Several examine music in a broader social context, drawing on such disciplines as ethnomusicology, cultural studies, and feminist theory. Interdisciplinary studies are central to the educational philosophy of the department.

The music of the 20th and 21st centuries is a particular emphasis of both the performance and academic programs. But other areas are also amply represented. Students can choose seminars from a broad spectrum of topics, ranging from medieval music theory to popular music.

SUFFOLK COUNTY COMMUNITY COLLEGE
DEPARTMENT OF MUSIC
533 College
Seldon, NY 11784
Craig Boyd
516-451-4346
Fax: 516-451-4697
E-mail: boydc@sunysuffolk.edu
www.sunysoffolk.edu

SUNY AT FREDONIA
SCHOOL OF MUSIC
Mason Hall Room 1004
Fredonia, NY 14063
Peter J. Schoenbach
716-673-3151
Fax: 716-673-3154
E-mail: peter.schoenbach@fredonia.edu
www.fredonia.edu/som

The current college enrollment represents diverse majors in the arts, humanities and the natural and social sciences, as well as professional programs in many areas. It is primarily an undergraduate teaching institution consistently rated as one of the best small four-year comprehensive colleges in the United States. The school of music dates from 1867 and is today a nationally recognized school of 500 undergraduates and 75 graduate majors with full accreditation by the National Association of Schools of Music. It offers both bachelor and master of music degree programs in performance, composition and music education and other baccalaureate degrees in applied music, music therapy, sound recording and musical theatre. The school of music currently

has 36 full-time and 35 part-time faculty members; facilities for instruction and performance are superior. The village of Fredonia is situated between the south shore of Lake Erie and the Allegany foothills in scenic western New York, midway between Buffalo, N.Y. and, Erie, Penn.

SUNY AT BINGHAMTON
DEPARTMENT OF MUSIC
P.O. Box 6000
Binghamton, NY 13902
Jane Zuckerman
607-777-2589
Fax: 607-777-4425
E-mail: jzucker@binghamton.edu
http://music.binghamton.edu

SUNY AT BUFFALO
STUDENT PROGRAMS OFFICE
DEPARTMENT OF MUSIC
Baird Hall, Room 226
Buffalo, NY 14260
Michael P. Burke
716-645-2758
Fax: 716-645-3824
E-mail: mpburke@acsu.buffalo.edu
www.music.buffalo.edu

SUNY AT CORTLAND
DEPARTMENT OF PERFORMING ARTS
P.O. Box 2000
Cortland, NY 13045
Karen Bals Simmerman
607-753-2811
Fax: 607-753-5728
E-mail: balsk@cortland.edu
www.cortland.edu

SUNY AT GENESEO
School of Performing Arts
Music Program/One College Circle
Geneseo, NY 14454
Jack Johnston
716-245-5824
Fax: 716-245-5826
E-mail: johnston@geneseo.edu
www.geneseo.edu

SUNY AT NEW PALTZ
Department of Music
75 S. Manheim Blvd. Suite 8
New Paltz, NY 12561
Lee Pritchard
845-257-2700
Fax: 845-257-3121
E-mail: pritchal@lan.newpaltz.edu
www.newpaltz.edu/music

SUNY AT ONEONTA
Department of Music
School of Music
Oneonta, NY 13820
Dr. Robert Barstow
607-436-3415
Fax: 607-436-2718
E-mail: BARSTORS@ONEONTA.EDU
www.oneonta.edu/academics/music

SUNY AT OSWEGO
Music Department
Tyler Hall
Oswego, NY 13126
Stanley Gosek
315-341-2980
Fax: 315-312-5642
www.oswego.edu

SUNY AT PLATTSBURGH
State University College
101 Broad St
Plattsburgh, NY 12901
Jo Ellen Miano
518-564-2180
Fax: 518-564-2197
E-mail: joellen.miano@plattsburgh.edu
www.plattsburgh.edu

SUNY AT POTSDAM
The Crane School of Music
P.O. Box IN
44 Pierrepont A
Potsdam, NY 13676
Alan Soloman
315-267-2415
Fax: 315-267-2413
E-mail: solomon@potsdam.edu
www.potsdam.edu/crane

SUNY AT PURCHASE COLLEGE
Conservatory of Music
735 Anderson Hill Rd.
Purchase, NY 10577
Music Department
914-251-6700
Fax: 914-251-6702
E-mail: music@purchase.edu
www.purchase.edu

SUNY AT STONY BROOK
Music Department
Department of Music
Room 3304 Staller Center
Stony Brook, NY 11794
Judy Lochhead
631-632-7330
Fax: 631-632-7404
E-mail: jlochhead@notes.cc.sunysb.edu
www.sunysb.edu/music

SYRACUSE UNIVERSITY
SETNOR SCHOOL OF MUSIC
Syracuse, NY 13244-1010
Joseph Downing
315-443-5892
Fax: 315-443-1935
E-mail: jdowning@syr.edu
http://vpa.syr.edu
Degrees: B.M., B.A., and M.M.

TEACHERS COLLEGE
PROGRAM IN MUSIC EDUCATION
525 W. 120th St.
P.O. Box 139
New York, NY 10027
Harold Abelels
212-678-3283
Fax: 212-678-4048
E-mail: hfa2@columbia.edu
www.tc.columbia.edu

TOMPKINS CORTLAND COMMUNITY COLLEGE
DEPARTMENT OF MUSIC
170 N. Rd.
P.O. Box 39
Dryden, NY 13053
Diane Casey
607-844-8211
Fax: 607-844-9665
www.sunytccc.edu

ULSTER COUNTY COMMUNITY COLLEGE
DEPARTMENT OF MUSIC
Stone Ridge, NY 12484
Richard Olsen
914-687-5060
www.sunyulster.edu

UNION COLLEGE
DEPARTMENT OF MUSIC
Schenectady, NY 12308
Hilary Tan
518-388-6785
E-mail: tannh@union.edu
www.union.edu

UNIVERSITY AT ALBANY
MUSIC DEPARTMENT
PAC 310
Albany, NY 12222
Dr. Reed Hoyt
518-442-4187
E-mail: rhoyt@csc.albany.edu
www.albany.edu/music

The department of music offers B.A. degrees as a general program (36 credits) and as a departmental program (54 credits) in composition, theory, music history, performance, music technology and conducting. Ensembles consist of chorale, chamber singers, band, orchestra, jazz ensemble, percussion ensemble, electronic music ensemble and chamber ensemble. The Performing Arts Center houses a recital hall, a concert hall, several theatres, instrumental and choral rehearsal rooms and extensive practice facilities as well as classrooms and faculty offices.

UNIVERSITY OF ROCHESTER
DEPARTMENT OF MUSIC
Todd 207
P.O. Box 270052
Rochester, NY 14627
Jean Caruso
716-275-2828
Fax: 716-273-5337
E-mail: opal@mail.rochester.edu
www.rochester.edu/eastman

UTICA COLLEGE OF SYRACUSE
DEPARTMENT OF MUSIC
Burrstone Rd.
Utica, NY 13502
Louis Angelini
315-792-3172
Fax: 315-792-3292
www.utica.edu

VASSAR COLLEGE
MUSIC DEPARTMENT
Poughkeepsie, NY 12604
914-437-7319
Fax: 914-437-7114
E-mail: mijacobs@vassar.edu
http://vassar.edu/~music

VILLA MARIA COLLEGE OF BUFFALO
DEPARTMENT OF MUSIC
240 Pini Ridge Rd.
Buffalo, NY 14225
James Kurzdorfer
716-896-0700
Fax: 716-891-9020
E-mail: kurzdorferj@villa.edu
www.villa.edu

WAGNER COLLEGE
DEPARTMENT OF MUSIC
One Campus Rd.
Staten Island, NY 10301
David Schulenburg
718-390-3313
Fax: 718-390-3392
E-mail: dschulen@wagner.edu
www.wagner.edu

WELLS COLLEGE
DEPARTMENT OF MUSIC
Aurora, NY 13026
Crawford Thorburn
315-364-3347
Fax: 315-364-3227
www.wells.edu

WESTCHESTER CONSERVATORY OF MUSIC
20 Soundview Ave.
White Plains, NY 10606
Robert Arthurs
914-761-3900
Fax: 914-761-3984
www.musicconservatory.org

NORTH CAROLINA

Population: 8,571,004 (2003 Estimate)

Capital City: Raleigh

Music Colleges and Universities: Appalachian State University, Barton College, Bennett College, Blue Ridge Community College at Flat Rock, Brevard College, Campbell University, Catawba College, Chowan College, Coastal Carolina Community College, College of the Albemarle, Davidson College, Duke University, East Carolina University, Eastern Music Festival, Elizabeth City State University, Elon University, Fayetteville State University, Fayetteville Tech Community College, Gardner Webb University, Gaston College, Greensboro College, Guilford College, Guilford Tech Community College, Jamestown College, John Wesley College, Johnson C. Smith University, Lees-McRae College, Lenoir Community College, Lenoir-Rhyne College, Livingstone College, Louisburg College, Mars Hill College, Meredith College, Methodist College, Mitchell Community College, Montreat College, MMount Olive College,North Carolina AandT State University, North Carolina Central University, North Carolina School of the Arts, North Carolina State University, North Carolina Wesleyan College, Peace College, Pheiffer University, Piedmont Baptist College, Queens College, Rockingham Community College, Salem College, Sandhills Community College, Shaw University, Southeast Baptist Theology Seminary, St. Augustine's College, Surry Community College, University of North Carolina at Asheville, University of North Carolina at Chapel Hill, University of North Carolina at Charlotte, University of North Carolina at Greensboro, University of North Carolina at Pembroke, University of North Carolina at Wilmington, Wake Forest University, Warren Wilson College, Western Carolina University, Wilkes Community College, Wilmington Academy of Music, Wingate University, Winston-Salem State University

Bird: Cardinal

Flower: Dogwood

Tree: Pine

Motto: Esse Quam Videri – To be, rather than to seem

Residents Called: North Carolinians

Area: 53,821 square miles (28th state)

Statehood: November 21, 1789 (12th state)

Origin of Name: Taken from "Carolus," the Latin word for Charles and named after England's King Charles I.

Largest Cities: Charlotte, Raleigh, Greensboro, Durham, Winston-Salem, Fayetteville, Cary, High Point, Wilmington, Asheville

College Band Programs: Appalachian State University, Duke University, East Carolina University, Elizabeth City State University, Fayetteville State University, North Carolina Central University, North Carolina State University, University of North Carolina-Chapel Hill

NORTH CAROLINA

APPALACHIAN STATE UNIVERSITY
MUSIC DEPARTMENT

Mariam Cannon Hayes School of Music
813 Rivers St.
Boone, NC 28608
William G. Harbinson
828-262-6459
Fax: 828-262-6446
E-mail: music@appstate.edu
www.music.appstate.edu
Degrees: B.S., and M.M.

The Mariam Cannon School of Music is the prime purveyor of music for the University, presenting an exciting and stimulating array of cultural events throughout the year. The faculty of the Hayes School of music, composed of thirty-seven nationally recognized teachers, performers and composers, is a major element in sustaining the creative atmosphere that surrounds Appalachian. The community is treated to a broad spectrum of faculty and student programs including solo recitals, instrumental and vocal ensemble concerts, chamber music and opera. The Hayes School of Music is among the leading music education institutions in the region and maintains a reputation of excellence in undergraduate and graduate instruction. Young musicians pursue studies in music education, music therapy, music performance, sacred music, composition/theory and music industry. Performances of the faculty and students of the Hayes School of Music are presented in the beautiful Rosen Concert Hall and the Recital Hall of the Broyhill Music Center.

BARTON COLLEGE
DEPARTMENT OF COMMUNITY AND PERFORMANCE ARTS

P.O. Box 5618
Wilson, NC 27893-7000
Jane Bostick
800-345-4973
Fax: 919-399-7000
E-mail: dbostick@barton.edu
www.barton.edu

BENNETT COLLEGE
DEPARTMENT OF MUSIC

900 E. Washington Ave.
Greensboro, NC 27410
Dr. David Pinnix
336-517-2316
Fax: 336-373-0569
www.bennett.edu

BLUE RIDGE COMMUNITY COLLEGE AT FLAT ROCK
DEPARTMENT OF MUSIC

College Dr.
Flat Rock, NC 28721
Earl Medlin
828-694-1821
Fax: 826-694-1690
E-mail: earlm@blueridge.edu
www.blueridge.cc.nc.us

BREVARD COLLEGE
DEPARTMENT OF MUSIC

400 N. Broad St.
Breward, NC 28712
Kay Hoke
828-884-8211
Fax: 828-884-3790
E-mail: skhoke@brevard.edu
www.brevard.edu

CAMPBELL UNIVERSITY
DEPARTMENT OF MUSIC
Buies Creek, NC 27506
Moran Whitley
910-893-1495
Fax: 910-893-1515
E-mail:
whitley@mailcenter.campbell.edu
www.campbell.edu

CATAWBA COLLEGE
DEPARTMENT OF MUSIC
2300 W. Innes St
Salisbury, NC 28144
Renee McCachren
704-637-4345
Fax: 704-637-4736
www.catawba.edu

CHOWAN COLLEGE
MUSIC DEPARTMENT
220 Jones Dr.
Murfreesboro, NC 27855
Dr. Dennis McIntire
252-398-6236
Fax: 252-398-1301
E-mail: mcintd@chowan.edu
www.chowan.edu

In a small, nurturing environment, the department of music offers qualified students the opportunity to become well-trained musicians capable of pursuing graduate studies in music or professional careers in a variety of music-related fields. The degree programs stress training in basic musical disciplines, proficiency in applied and theoretical areas as well as the completion of a liberal arts core curriculum. The department also provides all college students and community members the opportunity to enrich their musical experiences through participation in choral and instrumental ensembles, to increase their knowledge in music appreciation classes and to attend musical performances. The department of music aggressively supports the cultural life of the college and community.

COASTAL CAROLINA COMMUNITY COLLEGE
DEPARTMENT OF MUSIC
444 Western Blvd.
Jacksonville, NC 28546-6816
Michael Daugherty
910-455-1221
Fax: 910-455-7027
E-mail: daugmuse@hotmail.com
www.coastalcarolina.org

COLLEGE OF THE ALBEMARLE
DEPARTMENT OF MUSIC
Elizabeth City, NC 27909
Hank Rion
252-335-0821
Fax: 252-335-2011
E-mail: hrion@albemarle.edu
www.albemarle.cc.nc.us

DAVIDSON COLLEGE
MUSIC DEPARTMENT
P.O. Box 358
Davidson, NC 28036
William Lawing
704-894-2357
Fax: 704-892-2593
E-mail: lybrickels@davidson.edu
www.davidson.edu

DUKE UNIVERSITY
MUSIC DEPARTMENT

P.O. Box 90665
Durham, NC 27708-0665
Department Head
919-660-3300
Fax: 919-660-3301
E-mail: ksilb@duke.edu
www.duke.edu

For students seeking a professional career in music or pursuing music as an avocation, Duke offers: a curriculum that combines theory, history, and performance; a low student-faculty ratio; a distinguished faculty of scholars, composers, and performers with expertise in a broad range of subjects; 13 different vocal and instrumental performing groups, open to major and non-majors alike; opportunities to work with renowned visiting artists and composers; annual concert series focusing on a wide variety of periods and styles; a music library with more than 85,000 books, scores, journals, and microfilms, housed in the Mary Duke Biddle Music Building; superb practice facilities and a wide-ranging collection of historical instruments.

At the graduate level, the department of music offers programs leading to the A.M. and Ph.D. in composition and musicology, and the A.M. in performance practice. The programs include courses, seminars, and independent study in composition, ethnomusicology, music history, music theory and analysis, performance practice and interpretation, and interdisciplinary studies.

EAST CAROLINA UNIVERSITY

School of Music
AJ Fletcher Music Cent
Greenville, NC 27858
Michael A. Dorsey
252-328-6851
Fax: 252-328-6258
E-mail: dorseym@mail.ecu.edu

www.music.ecu.edu

The East Carolina University School of Music is one of the largest, most noted and comprehensive music programs in the southeast. The successful record of our graduates in a broad range of careers is our highest achievement and a continuing source of pride. The school is housed in the A.J. Fletcher Music Center, a facility designed exclusively for music. All music classes are held in the center, which features two large rehearsal halls and a 300-seat recital hall. Within the center are two electronic piano labs, five organs, more than 50 practice rooms, faculty studios, the music library and the center for music technology. The music library's collection contains more than 61,000 books, scores, periodicals and media materials representative of all types and periods of music. The state-of-the-art Center for Music Technology is an outstanding resource and teaching facility. Our artists-teachers provide students with valuable musical experience and a solid foundation for success in the music profession.

EASTERN MUSIC FESTIVAL
PIEDMONT JAZZ FESTIVAL

P.O. Box 22026
Greensboro, NC 2742
Jazz Festival Hotline
336-271-2600
www.easternmusicfestival.com

ELIZABETH CITY STATE UNIVERSITY
MUSIC DEPARTMENT

Elizabeth City, NC 27909
Music Department
252-335-3359
Fax: 252-335-3779
www.ecsu.edu

ELON UNIVERSITY
DEPARTMENT OF MUSIC

Campus Dr.
P.O. Box 2800
Elon, NC 27244
Kimberly Rippy
336-278-5600
Fax: 336-278-5609
E-mail: krippy@elon.edu
www.elon.edu/music

Degrees: B.S. in Music Education, B.A. in Music Performance, B.A. Music, music minor, Jazz Studies

The Elon University Music Department's mission is to provide a dynamic, challenging and intellectually rich environment where students are actively engaged and encouraged to develop creativity and excellence in the study and performance of diverse musical styles. By offering career-oriented/professional programs in music education, and music performance, the Music Department prepares students for graduate school or careers in performance and/or teaching. Elon's Fine Arts Center boasts numerous Steinway concert grand pianos; McCrary Theatre, a fully equipped theatre and concert hall; Yeager Recital Hall, with digital recording capabilities; modular practice rooms; and a music technology lab. Newly renovated Whitley Auditorium houses a new, custom-built Cassavant pip organ. Performance and experiential learning opportunities include a variety of instrumental and/or choral ensembles; recording projects in Elon's digital recording facility featuring ProTools recording;/editing software; and Elon's nationally recognized Study Abroad program. At Elon, students gain real-world skills and experiences in a liberal arts setting.

FAYETTEVILLE STATE UNIVERSITY
DEPARTMENT OF FINE ARTS

R105 Rosenthal Bldg.
Fayetteville, NC 28301
Robert Owens
910-486-1457
Fax: 910-486-1572
www.uncfsu.edu

Degrees: Music Education Major

FAYETTEVILLE TECH COMMUNITY COLLEGE
DEPARTMENT OF MUSIC

P.O. Box 35236
Fayetteville, NC 28303-0236
Stanley Holgate
919-678-8295
Fax: 919-678-8477
www.faytech.cc.nc.us

GARDNER WEBB UNIVERSITY
DEPARTMENT OF FINE ARTS

P.O. Box 298
Boiling Springs, NC 28017
Stephen Plate
704-406-4480
Fax: 704-403-920
E-mail: splate@gardner-webb.edu
www.gardner-webb.edu

GASTON COLLEGE
DEPARTMENT OF MUSIC

201 Hwy. 321 S.
P.O. Box 45
Dallas, NC 28034-1402
Alex Hegenbart
704-922-6346
Fax: 704-922-6440
www.gaston.cc.nc.us

GREENSBORO COLLEGE
DEPARTMENT OF MUSIC

815 W. Market St.
Greensboro, NC 27403
Jane McKinney
336-272-7102
Fax: 336-271-6634
E-mail: mckinneyj@gborocollege.edu
www.gborocollege.edu

Degrees: Bachelor of Music Education, Bachelor of Arts in Music, Bachelor of Science in music, a Certificate in Church Music and a Minor in Music

Greensboro College has been known for over one-hundred-and-fifty years for the quality of its music programs and graduates. Located in the heart of a city that boasts of its cultural offerings, students enjoy not only concerts and recitals on campus but those offered throughout the city as well as in neighboring Piedmont Triad communities. With a student population a little over 1,200, class size is small and allows for individual attention to student needs. Private lessons are taught in all classical orchestral instruments, piano, organ, and voice. Within the context of the valuable liberal arts undergraduate education, the curricula for the Bachelor of Arts in Music, the Bachelor of Science in Music, and the Bachelor of Music Education allows for focused study in music along with a disciplined pursuit of knowledge. Students are also given a wide range of music experiences and ensembles also including marching band, opera workshop and clinics with internationally renowned musicians.

GUILFORD COLLEGE
MUSIC DEPARTMENT

5800 W. Friendly Ave.
Greensboro, NC 27410
Timothy H. Lindeman
336-316-2430
Fax: 336-316-2959
E-mail: tlindema@guilford.edu
www.guilford.edu

GUILFORD TECHNICAL COMMUNITY COLLEGE
DEPARTMENT OF COMMUNICATIONS AND FINE ARTS

P.O. Box 309
Jamestown, NC 58401
Mark Wheller
910-334-4822
www.technet.gtcc.cc.nc.us

JAMESTOWN COLLEGE
DEPARTMENT OF MUSIC

6000 College Lane
Jamestown, NC 58401
William Wojnar
701-252-3467
Fax: 701-253-4318
E-mail: wojnar@acc.jc.edu
www.jc.edu

JOHN WESLEY COLLEGE
MUSIC PROGRAM

2314 N. Centennial St.
High Point, NC 27265-3136
Deniis Renfroe
336-889-2262
Fax: 336-889-2261
E-mail: drenfroe@johnwesley.edu
www.johnwesly.edu

JOHNSON C. SMITH UNIVERSITY
SCHOOL OF MUSIC AND FINE ARTS
100 Beatties Ford Rd.
Charlotte, NC 28216
Dr. Gregory Thompson
704-378-1000
Fax: 704-371-6752
E-mail: gthompson@jcsu.edu
www.jcsu.edu/music.html

LEES-MCRAE COLLEGE
DEPARTMENT OF PERFORMING ARTS
P.O. Box 128
Banner Elk, NC 28604
Janet Speer
828-898-8721
Fax: 828-898-8814
E-mail: speerj@lmc.edu
www.lmc.edu

LENOIR COMMUNITY COLLEGE
DEPARTMENT OF ARTS AND SCIENCES
P.O. Box 188
Kinston, NC 28502-0188
Carolyn Howett
252-527-6223
Fax: 252-527-2704
E-mail: cmh367@email.lenoir.cc.nc.us
www.lenoir.cc.nc.us

LENOIR-RHYNE COLLEGE
DEPARTMENT OF MUSIC
P.O. Box 7355
Hickory, NC 28603
Daniel Kiser
828-328-1747
Fax: 828-327-7073
www.lrc.edu

LIVINGSTONE COLLEGE
DEPARTMENT OF MUSIC
701 W. Monroe St.
Salisbury, NC 28144
William Crowder
704-216-6145
Fax: 704-216-6143
E-mail: wcrowde@livingstone.edu
www.livingstone.edu

LOUISBURG COLLEGE
DIVISION OF HUMANITIES
Louisburg, NC 27549
Gayle Green
919-496-2521
Fax: 919-496-1788
www.louisburg.edu

MARS HILL COLLEGE
DEPARTMENT OF MUSIC
205 Moore St.
Mars Hill, NC 28754
Dr. Joel Reed
828-689-1131
Fax: 828-689-1211
E-mail: jreed@mhc.edu
www.mhc.edu/music

MEREDITH COLLEGE
Music Department
3800 Hillsborough St.
Raleigh, NC 27607
Dr. David Lynch
919-760-8536
Fax: 919-760-2359
E-mail: lynchd@meredith.edu
www.meredith.edu

Meredith College, an accredited institutional member of NASM, offers about 95 majors, 40 faculty; a comprehensive private college for women; strong programs in choral music, voice, piano, strings, woodwinds, orchestra. Several competitive scholarships are available to entering freshmen music majors.

METHODIST COLLEGE
DEPARTMENT OF MUSIC
5400 Ramsey St.
Fayetteville, NC 28311
Jane Gardner
919-630-7158
Fax: 919-630-7513
E-mail: gardiner@methodist.edu
www.methodist.edu/music

The Methodist College Music Department offers five music programs with concentrations in either vocal or keyboard music.

MITCHELL COMMUNITY COLLEGE
Department of Music
Statesville, NC 28677
Jane Heymann
704-878-3200
www.mitchell.cc.nc.us

MONTREAT COLLEGE
DEPARTMENT OF MUSIC
310 Gaither Cir.
Montreat, NC 28757
Eunice Stackhouse
828-669-8011
Fax: 828-669-9554
E-mail: estackhouse@montreat.edu
www.montreat.edu

MOUNT OLIVE COLLEGE
MUSIC PROGRAM
634 Henderson St.
Mount Olive, NC 28365
Alan Armstrong
Fax: 704-658-8934
E-mail: mocmus@juno.com
www.mountolive.edu

NORTH CAROLINA AANDT STATE UNIVERSITY
DEPARTMENT OF MUSIC
1601 E. Market St.
Greensboro, NC 27420
Micheal Day
336-334-7926
Fax: 336-334-7484
www.ncat.edu

NORTH CAROLINA CENTRAL UNIVERSITY
DEPARTMENT OF MUSIC
801 Fayetteville St.
Durham, NC 27707
Brennetta Simpson
919-530-7211
Fax: 919-530-7979
E-mail: rcoleman@wpo.edu
www.nccu.edu

NORTH CAROLINA SCHOOL OF THE ARTS
SCHOOL OF MUSIC
1533 S. Main St.
Winston-Salem, NC 27117
Sue Miller
336-770-3255
Fax: 336-770-3248
E-mail: suemiller@ncarts.edu
www.ncarts.edu

North Carolina School of the Arts offers professional performance training with world renowned artist faculty – limited enrollment.

NORTH CAROLINA STATE UNIVERSITY

DEPARTMENT OF MUSIC

Cates Ave.
P.O. Box 7311
Raleigh, NC 27695
Robert Petters
919-515-2981
Fax: 919-515-4204
E-mail: susan_mazzochi@ncsu.edu
www.fis.ncsu.edu/music

Degrees: Minors only in music: emphasis in Music Performance, Music Theory and Composition and Music History and Literature.

NORTH CAROLINA WESLEYAN COLLEGE

DEPARTMENT OF MUSIC

3400 N. Wesleyan Blvd.
Rocky Mount, NC 27804
Micheal McAllister
919-985-5100
Fax: 919-977-3701
www.ncwc.edu

PEACE COLLEGE

DEPARTMENT OF MUSIC

15 E. Peace St
Raleigh, NC 27604
Virginia Vance
919-508-2000
Fax: 919-508-2326
E-mail: vvance@peace.edu
www.peace.edu

PHEIFFER UNIVERSITY

DEPARTMENT OF MUSIC

P.O. Box 960
Hwy. 52 N.
Misenheimer, NC 28109
Jean Raines
704-463-1360
Fax: 704-463-1363
E-mail: jraines@pfeiffer.edu
www.pfeiffer.edu

PIEDMONT BAPTIST COLLEGE

716 Franklin St.
Division of Music
Winston-Salem, NC 27101
Troy Crain
800-937-5097
Fax: 336-725-5522
E-mail: admissions@pbc.edu
www.pbc.edu

Degrees: B.A. Music Major, B.S. music Education (K-12), B.A. Music/Youth, and Music minor

As an independent fundamental Baptist Bible College, Piedmont is preparing students for church-related music vocations, including church music ministry, and public or private school teaching. Students in all programs receive a major in Bible as well as in their professional area. They may select piano, voice, or an orchestral instrument as their proficiency area. The B.A. music major is a performance and church music ministry degree. The B.S. Music Education degree prepares students to teach grades K-12, including general music, band and choir. The B.A. music/youth degree offers dual preparation for students who will be both music and youth ministers in churches. A music minor ranging from 24-28 hours may be added to any non-music degree. Faculty are highly qualified and experienced and PBC is situated in a richly cultural area. Piedmont is accredited by TRACS.

QUEENS UNIVERSITY OF CHARLOTTE
DEPARTMENT OF MUSIC
1900 Selwyn Ave.
Charlotte, NC 28274
Julie Dean
704-337-2213
Fax: 704-337-2356
E-mail: deanjm@queens.edu
www.queens.edu

ROCKINGHAM COMMUNITY COLLEGE
DEPARTMENT OF MUSIC
Wentworth, NC 27375
Patricia Harden
919-342-4261
www.rcc.cc.nc.us

SALEM COLLEGE
SCHOOL OF MUSIC
610 S. Church St
Winston-Salem, NC 27108
David Schildkret
336-721-2636
Fax: 336-721-2683
www.salem.edu

SANDHILLS COMMUNITY COLLEGE
MUSIC PROGRAM
3395 Airport Rd.
Pinehurst, NC 28374
Tim Haley
910-692-6185
Fax: 910-692-2756
E-mail: haleyt@email.sandhills.cc.nc.us
www.sandhills.cc.nc.us

SHAW UNIVERSITY
DEPARTMENT OF VISUAL AND PERFORMING ARTS
118 E. South St.
Raleigh, NC 27601
Dr. James Abbington
919-546-8200
Fax: 919-546-8367
E-mail: jabbing@shawu.edu
www.shawuniversity.edu

SOUTHEAST BAPTIST THEOLOGY SEMINARY
DEPARTMENT OF MUSIC
P.O. Box 1889
Wake Forest, NC 27587
John Boozer
919-863-8316
Fax: 919-863-8315
E-mail: jboozer@sebts.edu
www.sebts.edu

ST. AUGUSTINE'S COLLEGE
DEPARTMENT OF MUSIC
Raleigh, NC 27611
William Dargen
919-824-4451
Fax: 919-834-6473
www.st-aug.edu

SURRY COMMUNITY COLLEGE
MUSIC PROGRAM
P.O. Box 304
Dobson, NC 27017
Benny Younger
336-386-8121
Fax: 336-386-8951
www.surry.cc.nc.us

UNIVERSITY OF NORTH CAROLINA AT ASHEVILLE

DEPARTMENT OF MUSIC

1 University Heights
CPO 2290 UNCA
Asheville, NC 28804
Dr. Wayne J. Kirby
828-251-6432
Fax: 828-251-6814
E-mail: music@unca.edu
www.unca.edu/music

Degrees: B.S. in Music Technology; B.A. in Music (Jazz Studies or General Music Studies)

UNCA offers two-degree programs: the Bachelor of Science in Music Technology and the Bachelor of Arts in Music. The B.A. program allows the student to pursue either a Jazz Studies track or a General Music track. Both degree programs are grounded in a nationally acclaimed liberal arts curriculum. This special feature of the UNCA experience helps students prepare not only for entry-level jobs but also, and more importantly, for leadership roles in the music professions of the twenty-first century.

The UNCA recording facilities include a hybrid on-campus digital/analog multi-track studio which houses a variety of microphones, limiters/compressors, noise gates, noise reduction systems, DAT recorders, ProTools LE, Sound Forge, CD Architect, etc. Analog and digital remote recording systems are available for student use. Audio and video tie-lines connect our 614-seat auditorium to the control from for use as an auxiliary studio for recording large ensembles.

UNIVERSITY OF NORTH CAROLINA AT CHAPEL HILL

DEPARTMENT OF MUSIC

CB #3320 Hill Hall
Chapel Hill, NC 27599
Jeffrey Fuchs

919-962-1039
Fax: 919-962-3376
E-mail: jfuchs@email.unc.edu
www.unc.edu/depts/music

UNIVERSITY OF NORTH CAROLINA AT CHARLOTTE

DEPARTMENT OF MUSIC

9201 University Circle
Charlotte, NC 28223
Dr. Royce Lumpkin
704-547-2472
Fax: 704-687-6806
www.uncc.edu

UNIVERSITY OF NORTH CAROLINA AT GREENSBORO

DEPARTMENT OF MUSIC

P.O. Box 26167
Greensboro, NC 27402
John R. Locke
336-334-5789
Fax: 336-334-5497
E-mail: lockej@uncg.edu
www.uncg.edu/~lockej

UNIVERSITY OF NORTH CAROLINA AT PEMBROKE

DEPARTMENT OF MUSIC

P.O. Box 1510
Pembroke, NC 28372
George Walter
910-521-6230
Fax: 910-521-6390
E-mail: george.walter@uncp.edu
www.uncp.edu/music

UNIVERSITY OF NORTH CAROLINA AT WILMINGTON
DEPARTMENT OF MUSIC
601 S. College Rd.
Wilmington, NC 28403
Frank Bongiorno
910-962-3390
Fax: 910-962-7106
E-mail: uncwmus@uncwil.edu
www.uncwil.edu/music

WAKE FOREST UNIVERSITY
DEPARTMENT OF MUSIC
P.O. Box 7345
Winston-Salem, NC 27109
Dr. David B. Levy
336-758-5364
Fax: 336-758-4935
E-mail: brehmcj@wfu.edu
www.wfu.edu

WARREN WILSON COLLEGE
DEPARTMENT OF MUSIC
P.O. Box 9000
Asheville, NC 28815
Steven Williams
828-298-3325
Fax: 828-299-4841
E-mail: swilliams@warren-wilson.edu
www.warren-wilson.edu

WESTERN CAROLINA UNIVERSITY
DEPARTMENT OF MUSIC
Cullowhee, NC 28723
Robert Kehrberg
828-227-7242
Fax: 828-227-7266
E-mail: rkehrberg@email.wcu.edu
www.wcu.edu

WILKES COMMUNITY COLLEGE
DEPARTMENT OF MUSIC
P.O. Box 120
Wilkesboro, NC 28697
Anita Crunk
910-651-8600
Fax: 910-651-8749
www.wilkes.edu

WILMINGTON ACADEMY OF MUSIC
1635 Ellington Ave.
Wilmington, NC 28401
910-392-1590
www.academyofmusic.com

WINGATE UNIVERSITY
DEPARTMENT OF MUSIC
P.O. Box 3088
Wingate, NC 28174
Judy Hutton
704-233-8313
Fax: 704-233-8309
E-mail: jhutt@wingate.edu
www.wingate.edu/home.asp

WINSTON-SALEM STATE UNIVERSITY
DEPARTMENT OF FINE ARTS AND MUSIC
P.O. Box 19432
Winston-Salem, NC 27110
Lee David Legette
336-750-2520
Fax: 336-750-2522
www.wssu.edu

NORTH DAKOTA

Population: 642,848 (2003 Estimate)

Capital City: Bismarck

Music Colleges and Universities: Bismarck State College, Dickinson State University, Minot State University, North Dakota State University, University of Mary, University of North Dakota Grand Forks, Valley City State University

Bird: Western Meadowlark

Motto: Liberty and union, now and forever, one and inseparable.

Flower: Wild Prairie Rose

Tree: American Elm

Residents Called: North Dakotans

Origin of Name: Dakota is the Sioux Indian word for "friend."

Area: 70,704 square miles (19th largest state)

Statehood: November 2, 1889 (39th state)

Largest Cities: Fargo, Bismarck, Grand Forks, Minot, Mandan, Dickinson, Jamestown, West Fargo, Williston, Wahpeton

College Band Programs: North Dakota State University, University of Mary

NORTH DAKOTA

BISMARCK STATE COLLEGE
DEPARTMENT OF MUSIC
Bismarck, ND 58501
Deirdre Fay
800-445-5073
E-mail: fay@media.mit.edu
www.bismarckstate.edu

DICKINSON STATE UNIVERSITY
DEPARTMENT OF FINE ARTS AND MUSIC
Dickinson, ND 58601
Ken Haught
701-227-2308
Fax: 701-227-2006
E-mail: ken.haught@dsu.nodak.edu
www.dickinsonstate.org

MINOT STATE UNIVERSITY
DIVISION OF MUSIC
500 University Ave. W.
Minot, ND 58707
Aurora Dokken
701-858-3185
Fax: 701-858-3823
E-mail: dokkena@minotstateu.edu
www.minotstateu.edu

NORTH DAKOTA STATE UNIVERSITY
DIVISION FINE ARTS
P.O. Box 5691
Fargo, ND 58105
John Miller
701-231-7932
Fax: 701-231-2085
www.ndsu.nodak.edu/finearts

Degrees: Vocal or instrumental music education (B.S. in music education), vocal or instrumental music performance (B.A. in music), music theory/composition (BA in music), music history/literature (BA in music), or general music (BA in music). A master's degree in education with a music emphasis is also offered.

UNIVERSITY OF MARY
DEPARTMENT OF MUSIC
7500 University Dr.
Bismarck, ND 58501
Scott Prebys
701-255-7500
Fax: 701-255-7685
E-mail: sprebys@umary.edu
www.umary.edu

Degrees: Music, and Music Teaching

UNIVERSITY OF NORTH DAKOTA AT GRAND FORKS
DEPARTMENT OF MUSIC
P.O. Box 7125/UND
Grand Forks, ND 58202
Gary Towne
701-777-2644
Fax: 701-777-3320
E-mail: gary_Towne@und.nodak.edu
www.und.edu/dept/undmusic
Degrees: Music, Music Education, Music Education - Instrumental, Music Education; Choral, Music Performance, Music Therapy

VALLEY CITY STATE UNIVERSITY
DEPARTMENT OF MUSIC

101 S.W. College St.
Valley City, ND 58072
Diana Skroch
701-845-7272
Fax: 701-845-7275
E-mail:
diana_skroch@mail.vcsu.nodak.edu
www.vcsu.nodak.edu

Degrees: K-12 Certification/ Music in B.S. Ed.

Major Music/ (B.A., B.S.); Minor Music/ (B.A., B.S., B.S. in Ed.); Composite Major Music/(B.S. in Ed.)

OHIO

Population: 11,480,268 (2003 Estimate)

Capital City: Columbus

Music Colleges and Universities: Antioch College, Ashland University, Athenaeum of Ohio, Baldwin-Wallace College, Bluffton College, Bowling Green State University, Capital University, Case Western Reserve University, Cedarville University, Central State University, Cincinnati Bible College and Seminary, Cleveland Institute of Music, Cleveland State University, College of Mount St. Joseph, College of Wooster, Cuyahoga Community College at Metropolitan, Cuyahoga Community College at West, Dana School of Music, Denison University, Heidelberg College, Hiram College, John Carroll University, Kent State University at Kent, Kent State University at Salem, Kent State University at Tuscarawas,

Kenyon College, Lake Erie College, Lorain County Community College, Lourdes College, Malone College, Marietta College, Miami University, Mount Union College, Mount Vernon Nazarene College, Muskingum College, Oberlin Conservatory of Music, Ohio Dominican College, Ohio Northern University, Ohio State University, Ohio State University at Lima, Ohio University, Ohio University at Lancaster, Ohio University at Zanesville, Ohio Wesleyan University, Otterbein College, Recording Workshop, Shawnee State Community College, Shawnee State University, Sinclair Community College, University of Akron, University of Cincinnati, University of Dayton, University of Findlay, University of Toledo, Walsh University, Wilberforce University, Wittenberg University, Wright State University, Xavier University, Youngstown State University

Bird: Cardinal

Motto: With God all things are possible

Origin of Name: From the Iroquois Indian word for "good river."

Statehood: March 1, 1803 (17th state)

Flower: Scarlet Carnation

Tree: Buckeye

Residents Called: Ohioans

Area: 44,828 square miles (34th largest state)

Largest Cities: Columbus, Cleveland, Cincinnati, Toledo, Akron, Dayton, Parma, Youngstown, Canton, Lorain

College Band Programs: Bowling Green State University, Miami University, Kent State University, Ohio Northern University, Ohio State University, Ohio University, University of Cincinnati, University of Toledo

OHIO

ANTIOCH COLLEGE
MUSIC DEPARTMENT
795 Livermore St.
Yellow Springs, OH 45387
Department
937-769-1000
Fax: 937-767-6450
www.antioch-college.edu

ASHLAND UNIVERSITY
DEPARTMENT OF MUSIC
Arts and Humanities Bldg.
331 College Ave.
Ashland, OH 44805
Rowland F. Backley Jr.
419-289-5100
Fax: 419-289-5638
E-mail: rblackle@ashland.edu
www.ashland.edu

ATHENAEUM OF OHIO
DEPARTMENT OF MUSIC
6616 Beechmont Ave.
Cincinnati, OH 45230-5900
Anthony DiCello
513-231-2223
Fax: 513-231-3254
E-mail: tdicello@mtsm.org
www.mtsm.org

BALDWIN-WALLACE COLLEGE
CONSERVATORY OF MUSIC
275 Eastland Rd.
Berea, OH 44017
Anita S. Evans
440-826-2362
Fax: 440-826-3239
E-mail: aevans@bw.edu
www.bw.edu/academics/conservatory

The Conservatory of Music is within a liberal arts college near Cleveland. Bachelor of Music degrees are conferred in performance, musical theatre, music therapy, composition, theory, history and literature. Also offered is the bachelor of music education degree and music management program. The conservatory provides personal attention from esteemed faculty and numerous performance opportunities.

BLUFFTON COLLEGE
DEPARTMENT OF MUSIC
280 W. College Ave.
Bluffton, OH 45817-1196
Eric Fulcomer
800-488-3251
Fax: 419-358-3323
E-mail: admissions@bluffton.edu
www.bluffton.edu

Degrees: Bachelor of Arts in Music; Music with concentrations in music business, music ministry, performance studies, and piano pedagogy; and Music Education

The Bluffton College music department has a long history of offering quality music education from performance ensembles to preparation for music teachers. Performance opportunities include three choirs: Camerata Singers, Bluffton College Chorale, and Choral Society; two bands: Bluffton College-Community Concert Band and Jazz Ensemble; the Lima Symphony Orchestra; annual staged production and numerous smaller ensembles. Bluffton College is an accredited institutional member of the NASM. The music department is housed in Mosiman Hall that houses classrooms, studios, practice rooms, a music library and an electronic music lab. Connected to the music building is Yoder Recital Hall, built in 1996, that offers a beautiful performance facility to both students and prominent artists in a yearly artist series. The Bluffton College music department offers majors in music education, music (liberal arts), and music with concentrations in performance studies, music ministry, piano pedagogy, and music business. A music minor is also available to students majoring in another discipline.

BOWLING GREEN STATE UNIVERSITY
COLLEGE OF MUSICAL ARTS
Moore Musical Arts Center
Bowling Green State, OH 43403-0290
Dr. Kathleen Moss
419-372-8577
Fax: 419-372-2938
E-mail: kmoss@bgnetbgsu.edu
www.bgsu.edu/colleges

The College of Musical Arts has achieved national recognition for its outstanding faculty and student performers, and for its academic programs in preparing students to be music scholars, educators and performers. The College of Musical Arts is located in the Moore Musical Arts Center, a $9 million state-of-the-art teaching and performance facility, including over 70 practice rooms, a 250-seat Bryan Recital Hall, a 850-seat Kobacker Concert Hall, two rehearsal halls with observatories and state-of-the-art music technology and recording studios. There are approximately 400 undergraduate and 100 graduate music students with 56 full-time and distinguished faculty, including specialists on every instrument. Fourteen large ensembles and over 20 instrumental and vocal chamber music ensembles perform frequently on and off campus. Auditions for entrance and scholarships may be scheduled by visiting the Web site or by calling the coordinator of music admissions.

CAPITAL UNIVERSITY
ADMISSIONS OFFICE
Columbus, OH 43029
Celia Alspach
614-236-6101
Fax: 614-236-6935
E-mail: calspach@capital.edu
www.capital.edu

CASE WESTERN RESERVE UNIVERSITY
DEPARTMENT OF MUSIC
10900 Euclid Ave.
Cleveland, OH 44106
Ross W. Duffin
216-368-2400
Fax: 216-368-6557
E-mail: pdm3@po.cwru.edu
www.cwru.edu

CEDARVILLE UNIVERSITY
DEPARTMENT OF MUSIC
251 N. Main St.
Cedarville, OH 45314-0601
Roscoe Smith
937-766-7728
Fax: 937-766-7661
E-mail: roscoes@cedarville.edu
www.cedarville.edu

Degrees: B.M. degrees in church music, ministry, keyboard pedagogy, music composition, performance, music education (B.M.E.) – choral or instrumental and a B.A. in music

The purpose of the Music Department at Cedarville University is to help develop an appreciation and understanding of the music arts consistent with a biblical worldview. The department seeks to help students gain an understanding of the reusability of stewardship, service, and worship that is placed upon those to whom God has given musical talents.

Performance opportunities open to all Cedarville University students include Concert Choral, Men's Glee Club, Women's Choir, University Jazz Singers, Jubilaté, Piano Ensemble, Symphonic Band, Brass Choir, Jazz Band, Orchestra, and Pep Band.

CENTRAL STATE UNIVERSITY
DEPARTMENT OF FINE AND PERFORMING ARTS
Wilberforce, OH 45384
Donna Henderson
937-376-6403
www.centralstate.edu

CINCINNATI BIBLE COLLEGE AND SEMINARY
DEPARTMENT OF MUSIC AND WORSHIP
2700 Glenway Ave.
Cincinnati, OH 45204
Gary Gregory
513-244-8165
Fax: 513-244-8140
E-mail: musicworship@cincybible.edu
www.cincybible.edu

CLEVELAND INSTITUTE OF MUSIC
INSTITUTE OF MUSIC
11021 E. Blvd.
Cleveland, OH 44121
Jeffery Sharkey
216-791-5000
Fax: 216-791-1530
E-mail: jxs206@po.cwru.edu
www.cim.edu

Cleveland Institute of Music is a leading international conservatory that provides a professional, world-class education in the art of music.

CLEVELAND STATE UNIVERSITY
Music Department
2001 Euclid Ave.
Cleveland, OH 44115-2212
Dr. Christine Smith-Dorey
216-687-5039
Fax: 216-687-9279

E-mail: chang75@csuohio.edu
www.csuohio.edu/music

Located in the heart of one of America's most vibrant cultural centers, Cleveland State University makes use of the city's rich musical resources to provide students with a complete spectrum of educational opportunities. Faculty is drawn from the internationally renowned Cleveland Orchestra and other noted professional instrumental and vocal organizations. The award-winning Cleveland Chamber Symphony, a professional ensemble nationally recognized for the commission and performance of contemporary music, is in residence in the CSU department of music. Completed in 1990, the CSU Music and Communication Building provides students with a state-of-the-art facility for the study and performance of music. Music scholarships are available to qualified undergraduate students, regardless of academic major. Graduate tuition grants and teaching assistantships are available to qualified students pursuing the master of music degree.

COLLEGE OF MOUNT ST. JOSEPH
5701 Delhi Rd.
Cincinnati, OH 45233
Ulli Brinksmeier
513-244-4435
Fax: 513-244-4222
E-mail: ulli_brinksmeier@mail.msj.edu
www.msj.edu

COLLEGE OF WOOSTER
SCHEIDE MUSIC CENTER
535 E. University
Wooster, OH 44691
Thomas Wood
330-263-2033
Fax: 330-263-2051
E-mail: twood@acs.wooster.edu
www.wooster.edu/music

Wooster has long enjoyed a distinguished reputation for the quality of its music program and the professional preparation it affords its graduates. Young musicians in increasing numbers are realizing the advantages of earning a music degree from a liberal arts college. With its tradition of academic achievement, wide variety of music degree offerings, and a music department that offers unusual quality and breadth of experience for an institution of its size, Wooster is the ideal choice for the student who seeks rigorous professional music training within the context of an excellent liberal arts curriculum. The primary music facility, the Scheide Music Center, is a fully-equipped, $5 million facility which contains five classrooms, 11 teaching studios, 23 practice rooms, rehearsal rooms for large ensembles, an audio library, and an electronic music studio. The building's centerpiece is the elegant Gault Recital Hall (designed by Maurice Allen of TMP Associates with acoustical design and engineering by Lawrence Kirkegaard and Associates, Chicago). The College of Wooster offers four degree programs in music (bachelor of music, bachelor of music education in public school teaching, bachelor of music education in music therapy and a bachelor of arts) as well as the option of designing a special major, pursuing a double major, or following a minor in music.

CUYAHOGA COMMUNITY COLLEGE - METROPOLITAN
DEPARTMENT OF MUSIC

2900 Community College Ave.
Cleveland, OH 441153196
Thomas Horning
216-987-4525
Fax: 216-987-4370
E-mail: thomas.horning@tri-c.cc.oh.us
www.tri-c.cc.oh.us

CUYAHOGA COMMUNITY COLLEGE - WEST
DEPARTMENT OF MUSIC

11000 W. Pleasant Valley Rd.
Parma, OH 44130-5114
Gary Scott
216-987-5532
E-mail: gary.scott@tri-c.cc.oh.us
www.infonet.tri-c.cc.oh.us

DANA SCHOOL OF MUSIC
YOUNGSTOWN STATE UNIVERSITY

One University Plaza
Youngstown, OH 44555
Dr. Ted Perkins
330-742-3636
Fax: 330/742-2341
E-mail: tlperkins@cc.ysu.edu
www.fpa.ysu.edu/music
Denison University
Department of Music
P.O. Box M
Granville, OH 43023
Andrew Glendening
740-587-6220
Fax: 740-587-6417
E-mail: glendening@denison.edu
www.denison.edu

HEIDELBERG COLLEGE
DEPARTMENT OF MUSIC

310 E. Market St.
Tiffin, OH 44883
Douglas McConnell
419-338-2073
Fax: 419-448-2124
E-mail: dmcconne@heidelberg.edu
www.heidelberg.edu

HIRAM COLLEGE
DEPARTMENT OF MUSIC

Music Department
201 Frohring Music Bldg.
Hiram, OH 44234
Dr. Justin Kelly
330-569-5294
Fax: 330-569-6093
E-mail: kellyjm@hiram.edu
www.hiram.edu

Hiram College is an accredited institutional member of the National Association of Schools of Music. The department of music offers a major in music, with specific tracks in music education, music history and theory, and music performance. The department also offers a minor in music. Frohring Music Hall contains classrooms, studios and practice rooms, stereo systems, video tape equipment, a room equipped with computer and synthesizer work stations for classroom instruction and an electronic music studio. A large collection of music scores, tapes, compact discs and records is housed in the Hiram College Library.

JOHN CARROLL UNIVERSITY
MUSIC PERFORMANCE AREA AND FINE ARTS

Cleveland, OH 44101
E. James Kotora
216-397-1609
E-mail: jkotora@jcu.edu
www.jcu.edu

KENT STATE UNIVERSITY
HUGH A. GLAUSER SCHOOL OF MUSIC

P.O. Box 5190
Kent, OH 44242
John Lee
330-672-2172
Fax: 330-672-7837
E-mail: leejohnm@kent.edu

www.kent.edu
Degrees: B.M., B.A.

KENT STATE UNIVERSITY AT SALEM
DEPARTMENT OF MUSIC

2491 State Rte. 45 S.
Salem, OH 44460
Jeffrey Nolte
330-332-0361
Fax: 330-332-9256
E-mail: nolte@salem.kent.edu
www.salem.kent.edu

KENT STATE UNIVERSITY AT TUSCARAWAS
DEPARTMENT OF MUSIC

University N.E.
New Philadelphia, OH 44663
Gregg Andrews
216-339-3391
Fax: 216-339-3321
www.tusc.kent.edu

KENYON COLLEGE
DEPARTMENT OF MUSIC

Storer Hall 30
Gambier, OH 43022
Benjamin R. Locke
740-427-5197
Fax: 740-427-5512
E-mail: lockeb@kenyon.edu
www.kenyon.edu

LAKE ERIE COLLEGE
DEPARTMENT OF FINE ARTS

P.O. Box 354
391 W. Washington St.
Painesville, OH 44077
Paul Gothard
440-352-3361
www.lec.edu

LORAIN COUNTY COMMUNITY COLLEGE
DEPARTMENT OF MUSIC
Elyria, OH 44035
Robert Beckstrom
216-365-4191
Fax: 216-365-6519
www.lorainccc.edu

LOURDES COLLEGE
DEPARTMENT OF MUSIC
6832 Convent Blvd.
Sylvania, OH 43560
Ann Carmen Barone
419-885-3211
Fax: 419-824-3513
E-mail: acarmen@lourdes.edu
www.lourdes.edu

MALONE COLLEGE
DEPARTMENT OF MUSIC
515 25th St. N.W.
Canton, OH 44709
Leslie Covell
330-471-8231
Fax: 330-471-8474
E-mail: lcovell@malone.edu
www.malone.edu

MARIETTA COLLEGE
DEPARTMENT OF MUSIC
Marietta, OH 45750
Daniel Monek
740-376-4696
Fax: 740-376-4529
E-mail: monekd@marietta.edu
www.marietta.edu

MIAMI UNIVERSITY
DEPARTMENT OF MUSIC
Oxford, OH 45056
Judith Delzell
513-529-3014
Fax: 513-529-3027
E-mail: delzeljk@muohio.edu
www.muohio.edu/music

Degrees: B.M. in Music Education; B.M. in Performance; B.A. in Music; M.M. in Music Education; M.M. in Performance

Miami University has been recognized as one of the country's top schools that are academically challenging, offer the best value and offer the best freshman housing according Kaplan Publishing's The Unofficial, Unbiased, Insider's Guide to the 320 most interesting colleges (2002). Miami was also ranked among the top 21 public universities "Best Buys" in the Fiske Guide to Colleges 2003. No other Ohio university was so recognized. In the publication, the Department of Music was singled out as one of the university's strongest programs. There is a wonderful sense of community between faculty and students in this department of approximately 200 undergraduate music majors and 25 graduate students. Faculty members rather than graduate students teach all music classes, except for class piano. Our program is large enough to offer a rich and substantial array of musical and educational opportunities, yet small enough to foster a strong sense of community.

MOUNT UNION COLLEGE
DEPARTMENT OF MUSIC
1972 Clark Ave.
Alliance, OH 44601
Dr. Scott W. Dorsey
330-823-2180
Fax: 330-823-2144
E-mail: dorseysw@muc.edu
www.muc.edu/mu

MOUNT VERNON NAZARENE COLLEGE
DEPARTMENT OF MUSIC
800 Martinsburg Rd.
Mount Vernon, OH 43050
David Liles
740-397-2769
Fax: 740-397-2769
E-mail: dliles@mvnc.edu
www.mvnc.edu

MUSKINGUM COLLEGE
DEPARTMENT OF MUSIC
57 N. Layton Dr.
New Concord, OH 43762
William Schlacks
740-826-9095
Fax: 740-826-9090
E-mail: wschlacks@muskingum.edu
www.muskingum.edu

OBERLIN CONSERVATORY OF MUSIC
OBERLIN COLLEGE
Public Relations
77 W. College St.
Oberlin, OH 44074
Marci Janas
440-775-8413
Fax: 440-776-8942
E-mail: marci.janas@oberlin.edu
www.oberlin.edu/con

The Oberlin Conservatory provides thorough and professional music training. Its faculty consists of highly regarded musicians who maintain active careers as performers, composers, theoreticians and historians. Founded in 1865, the conservatory is internationally recognized as one of the finest music schools in the United States. A conservatory student's program includes private study and solo and ensemble performance, plus courses in music history and music theory. Individual instruction is highly valued, and there is one faculty member for every eight students. Most faculty members live in Oberlin, so teachers and students get to know one another in the studio and outside academic contexts —

over coffee at the De Café, at post-concert receptions, at parties at professors' homes, at various campus events. The Oberlin Conservatory is a division of Oberlin College, making it a major music school linked with a preeminent liberal arts college. Degree candidates in the conservatory take at least 20 percent of their courses in non-music subjects in the College of Arts and Sciences, and most may elect up to 40 percent. This approach provides balance between intense professional training and broad general education.

OHIO DOMINICAN COLLEGE
DEPARTMENT OF MUSIC
1216 Sunbury Rd.
Columbus, OH 43219
Micheal Pavone
www.ohiodominican.edu

OHIO NORTHERN UNIVERSITY
MUSIC DEPARTMENT
525 S. Main St.
Ada, OH 45810
Dr. Edwin L Williams
419-772-2151
Fax: 419-772-2488
E-mail: e-williams@onu.edu
www.onu.edu

Degrees: B.M., and B.A.

The music department offers five major degree programs and collaborates in providing a sixth. Students may choose the Bachelor of Music Degree with a major in music education, performance, composition or elective studies in business. Some students choose the Bachelor of Arts curriculum who have a definite interest in music as a major but may also have interests in other academic areas. The Bachelor of Arts degree has become popular for students who wish to add a second major. The music department also collaborates with the Department of Communication Arts in offering the Bachelor of Fine Arts in Musical Theater.

Nineteen performing groups are currently active on campus to offer music students an opportunity to gain experience in a wide variety of music and musical styles. Membership in our ensembles also provides them an opportunity to rehearse and perform with outstanding artists of national or international stature.

OHIO STATE UNIVERSITY
School of Music
110 Weigel Hall
1866 College Rd.
Columbus, OH 43210
Dr. David Frego
614-292-2870
Fax: 614-292-1102
E-mail: frego.1@osu.edu
www.arts.ohio-state.edu/Music

Degrees: B.M., B.M.E., B.A., M.M., M.A., D.M.A., Ph.D.

The OSU School of Music, an accredited institutional member of the NASM, offers outstanding professional training and academic degrees. With a full-time faculty of about 60, the school has approximately 330 undergraduate students and 170 graduate students majoring in performance, music education, musicology, jazz studies, music theory, and composition. Metropolitan Opera sopranos Barbara Daniels and Diane Kesling; composers Clare Grundman, Stephen Montague, Carman Moore, and Vince Mendoza; TELARC founder and CEO Jack Renner; and internationally renowned clarinetist Richard Stoltzman are a few of the school's alumni. The School of Music is ranked 24th nationally (11th nationally among public institutions) by US News and World Report.

OHIO STATE UNIVERSITY, LIMA CAMPUS
Department of Music
4240 Campus Dr.
Lima, OH 45804
Richard Mallonee
419-995-8349
Fax: 419-995-8884
E-mail: mallonee.1@osu.edu
www.lima.ohio-state.edu

OHIO UNIVERSITY
Department of Music
440 Music Bldg.
Athens, OH 45701
Dr. Sylvia Henry
740-593-4244
Fax: 740-593-1429
E-mail: henrys@ohio.edu
www.ohiou.edu/music

OHIO UNIVERSITY AT LANCASTER
Department of Music
1570 Granville Pike
Lancaster, OH 43130
John Furlow
614-654-6711
Fax: 614-687-9497
E-mail: furlow@ohio.edu
www.ohiou.edu/lancaster

OHIO UNIVERSITY AT ZANESVILLE
Department of Music
1425 Newark Rd.
Zanesville, OH 43701
William Christy
740-588-1482
Fax: 740-453-6161
E-mail: christyw@ohio.edu
www.zanesville.ohiou.edu

OHIO WESLEYAN UNIVERSITY
DEPARTMENT OF MUSIC
Sanborn Hall
Delaware, OH 43015
Dr. Cameron D. Bennett
740-368-3700
Fax: 740-368-3723
E-mail: cdbennet@owu.edu
www.owu.edu

OTTERBEIN COLLEGE
DEPARTMENT OF MUSIC
One Otterbein College
Westerville, OH 43081
Dr. Craig Johnson
614-823-1508
Fax: 614-823-1118
www.otterbein.edu

RECORDING WORKSHOP
455 Massieville Rd.
Chillicothe, OH 45601
Jim Rosebrook
740-663-2544
Fax: 740-663-2427
E-mail: info@recordingworkshop.com
www.recordingworkshop.com

SHAWNEE STATE COMMUNITY COLLEGE
DEPARTMENT OF MUSIC
940 2nd St.
Portsmouth, OH 45662
Leslie Williams
614-354-3205
Fax: 614-335-2416

SHAWNEE STATE UNIVERSITY
DEPARTMENT OF MUSIC
Portsmouth, OH 45662
Jerry Holt
614-354-3205
Fax: 614-355-2416
www.shawnee.edu

SINCLAIR COMMUNITY COLLEGE
DEPARTMENT OF MUSIC
444 W. 3rd St
Dayton, OH 45402
Robert Rickman
937-512-2541
E-mail: bruckman@sinclair.edu
www.sinclair.edu

THE UNIVERSITY OF AKRON
SCHOOL OF MUSIC
Akron, OH 44325
Dr. William K. Guegold
330-972-7590
Fax: 330-972-6409
E-mail: WGuegold@AOL.com
www3.uakron.edu/faa/schools/music.html

UNIVERSITY OF CINCINNATI
COLLEGE CONSERVATORY OF MUSIC
P.O. Box 210003
Cincinnati, OH 45221
Douglas Lowry
513-556-3737
Fax: 513-556-3320
E-mail: lowryda@uc.edu
www.ccm.uc.edu

The College Conservatory of Music (CCM) has been called "One of this country's leading conservatories" by the New York Times. A $93.2 million village for the performing and electronic media was completed in 1999. CCM offers programs in music performance, music education, conducting, acting, musical theater, voice, stage production, television and audio. More than 1,000 performances take place each year, with opportunities for all student instrumentalists to perform with orchestras, wind symphonies, and large and small chamber ensembles. The prestigious faculty attract students from all over the world. CCM offers quality education at an affordable price with over $4 million available in scholarship awards. Visit the Web site for further information and listen to students perform.

UNIVERSITY OF DAYTON
DEPARTMENT OF MUSIC

300 College Park
Dayton, OH 45469
Donna Cox
937-229-3936
Fax: 937-229-3916
E-mail: donna.cox@notes.udayton.edu
www.udayton.edu/~music

The University of Dayton Department of Music is fully accredited by the National Association of Schools of Music. Students have a distinctive opportunity to enrich their backgrounds in music, as well as enjoy the wide variety of liberal arts offerings by the university. Performance opportunities include Pride of Dayton Marching Band, symphonic wind ensemble, university concert band, Dayton Jazz Ensemble, jazz lab band, jazz combos, Flyer Pep Band, indoor drum line, University Chorale, choral union, Ebony Heritage Singers, musical theatre, opera workshop, Hands in Harmony (sign-sing), and a wide variety of chamber ensembles. The Dayton area provides rich, cultural opportunities for the university student, including the Dayton Philharmonic Orchestra, Dayton Opera, and the Dayton Bach Society (chorus). Opening in 2002, the brand new Shuster Performing Arts Center, downtown Dayton, will be a state-of-the-art performance facility. Music education and music therapy majors will find a variety of field experience opportunities in the immediate area. A large number of area schools have high-quality music programs, providing the music education major with quality experiences. For the therapy major, there are plenty of area hospitals, assisted-care facilities, schools, and other programs for practicum experiences.

UNIVERSITY OF FINDLAY
DEPARTMENT OF MUSIC

1000 N. Main St
Findlay, OH 45840-3695
Michael Anders
419-434-4531
Fax: 419-434-4822
E-mail: anders@findlay.edu
www.findlay.edu

Degrees: Minor in Musical Arts

Although the University of Findlay does not offer a professional degree in music, it has a long tradition of training excellent musicians from other academic areas, as well as fostering extensive performance opportunities for students pursuing degrees in all academic disciplines. The mission of the UF Music Department is "to effectively train the avocational musician to the highest level possible and foster an appreciation for the musical arts in all persons through live performances, applied music study, and traditional and non-traditional classroom experiences." Performance opportunities at UF include, among others, the Concert-Chorale, University Singers, Marching Band, Wind Ensemble, Jazz Ensemble, annual spring musical production, and applied music study in 20 different fields of study (including all areas of voice, piano, strings, woodwinds, brass, percussion, and composition). UF is the ideal choice for the student who is seeking nurturing, yet rigorous, musical training while pursuing a professional degree within another academic area.

UNIVERSITY OF TOLEDO
DEPARTMENT OF MUSIC AND DANCE
2801 W. Bancroft
Toledo, OH 43606
Dr. Raymond Marchionni
419-530-2448
Fax: 419-530-8483
E-mail: utmusic@utoledo.edu
www.utoledo.edu

WALSH UNIVERSITY
DEPARTMENT OF FINE ARTS
2020 Easton St. N.W.
Canton, OH 44720
Dorothy Ling
216-497-0900
Fax: 216-499-8518
E-mail: dling@walsh.edu
www.walsh.edu

WILBERFORCE UNIVERSITY
DEPARTMENT OF MUSIC
P.O. Box 1001
Wilberforce, OH 45384
James Williams
937-376-2911
www.wilberforce.edu

WITTENBERG UNIVERSITY
DEPARTMENT OF MUSIC
Krieg Hall
P.O. Box 720
Springfield, OH 45501
Trudy Faber
937-327-7341
Fax: 937-327-7347
E-mail: tfaber@wittenberg.edu
www.wittenberg.edu/academics/music

Degrees: B.A. in Music, Bachelor of Music
Education, B.M. in church music, performance
or composition

Wittenberg is a small liberal arts college with
an outstanding reputation for the quality of its
programs. The combination of a broad academic education with specialization in a chosen area of music makes our graduates very
marketable. Our B.A. in music includes
enough self-selection for a student to also con-
centrate in other areas such as management or
English, resulting in an education that can
meet specific goals. In addition, we offer the
Bachelor of Music Education degree and a
B.M. in the areas of performance, church
music, and composition. The National
Association of Music Schools approves all our
programs; Wittenberg has been accredited by
NASM since 1931. Highly qualified faculties,
both full-time and adjunct, offer excellent
instruction in all areas. Of special interest is
our computer composition lab. We have a top-
quality lab with cutting edge facilities, thanks
to the very generous gifts of donors. The professor in charge of the lab is himself an internationally recognized composer who has won
numerous ASCAP awards and commissions to
write major works. If a student loves music but
decides not to major, we have a very strong
minor. Scholarships are available to all students on the basis of talent.

WRIGHT STATE UNIVERSITY
DEPARTMENT OF MUSIC
3640 Colonel Glenn Hwy.
Dayton, OH 45435
Beth Millard
937-775-2347
Fax: 937-775-3786
E-mail: beth.millard@wright.edu
www.wright.edu

WSU offers a comprehensive education in all
degree programs. WSU ensembles regularly
perform at state and national festivals and conventions, and several tours nationally and
internationally. The department is housed in
the Creative Arts Center, which has two performance halls and a state-of-the-art computer
laboratory for the study of music. The campus
is entirely accessible to the handicapped.

XAVIER UNIVERSITY
DEPARTMENT OF MUSIC

3800 Victory Pkwy.
Cincinnati, OH 45207
Dona Buel
513-745-3801
Fax: 513-745-3343
E-mail: buel@xu.edu
www.xu.edu

OKLAHOMA

Population: 3,538,843 (2003 Estimate)

Capital City: Oklahoma City

Music Colleges and Universities: Bartlesville Wesleyan College, Cameron University, Carl Albert State College, East Central University, Eastern Oklahoma State College, Langston University, Margaret E. Petree School of Music, Northeastern Oklahoma A&M College, Northeastern State University, Northwestern Oklahoma State University, Oakland City University, Oklahoma Baptist University, Oklahoma Christian University, Oklahoma State University, Southwestern Oklahoma State University, University of Oklahoma, University of Science and Arts of Oklahoma, University of Tulsa

Bird: Scissor-tailed Flycatcher

Motto: Labor omnia vincit – Labor conquers all things

Flower: Mistletoe

Tree: Redbud

Residents Called: Oklahomans

Origin of Name: Based on Choctaw Indian words for "red man."

Area: 69,903 square miles (20th largest state)

Statehood: November 16, 1907 (46th state)

Largest Cities: Oklahoma City, Tulsa, Norman, Lawton, Broken Arrow, Edmond, Midwest City, Enid, Moore, Stillwater

College Band Programs: University of Oklahoma

OKLAHOMA

BARTLESVILLE WESLEYAN COLLEGE
MUSIC PROGRAM
2201 Silverlake Rd.
Bartlesville, OK 74006-6233
Steve Hughs
918-333-6295
Fax: 918-335-6210
www.bwc.edu

CAMERON UNIVERSITY
DEPARTMENT OF MUSIC
2800 W. Gore Blvd.
Lawton, OK 73505
Scott Richard Klein
580-581-2440
Fax: 580-581-5764
E-mail: scottk@cameron.edu
www.cameron.edu

CARL ALBERT STATE COLLEGE
DEPARTMENT OF MUSIC
1507 S. McKenna St
Poteau, OK 74953-5207
Chuck Cole
918-647-8660
Fax: 918-647-2980
www.casc.cc.ok.us

EAST CENTRAL UNIVERSITY
MUSIC DEPARTMENT
Ada, OK 74820
Dennis Silkebakken
580-310-5390
Fax: 580-310-0752
www.ecok.edu

EASTERN OKLAHOMA STATE COLLEGE
DEPARTMENT OF MUSIC
3701 S. 35 Service Rd.
Oklahoma City, OK 73129
Paul Enis
918-465-2361
www.eosc.edu

LANGSTON UNIVERSITY
DEPARTMENT OF MUSIC
P.O. Box 1500
Langston, OK 73050
Mark Davis
405-466-2936
Fax: 405-466-2990
E-mail: mhdavis@lunet.edu
www.lunet.edu

MARGARET E. PETREE SCHOOL OF MUSIC
DEAN'S OFFICE
2501 North Blackwelder
Oklahoma City, OK 73106
405-521-5474
www.okcu.edu/music

NORTHEASTERN OKLAHOMA A&M COLLEGE
DEPARTMENT OF FINE ARTS AND MUSIC
200 I St. N.E.
Miami, OK 74354
Andrea Leonard
918-540-6138
Fax: 918-540-6490
www.neoam.cc.ok.us

NORTHEASTERN STATE UNIVERSITY
DEPARTMENT OF MUSIC
Tahlequah, OK 74464
Robert Daniel
918-456-5511
Fax: 918-458-2348
E-mail: danielrm@cherokee.nsuok.edu

NORTHWESTERN OKLAHOMA STATE UNIVERSITY
DEPARTMENT OF MUSIC
709 Oklahoma Blvd.
Alva, OK 73717
Mike Knedler
405-327-8590
Fax: 405-327-8524
E-mail: jmknedler@nwosu.edu
www.nwosu.edu

OAKLAND CITY UNIVERSITY
PETREE COLLEGE OF MUSIC
2501 N. Blackwelder Ave.
Oklahoma City, OK 73106
Mark Edward Parker
405-521-5315
Fax: 405-521-5971
E-mail: mamowry@okcu.edu
www.okcu.edu/music

OKLAHOMA BAPTIST UNIVERSITY
DIVISION OF MUSIC
500 W. University St.
P.O. Box 61276
Shawnee, OK 74801
Paul Hammond
405-878-2305
Fax: 405-878-2328
E-mail: pul_hammond@mail.okbu.edu
www.okbu.edu

OKLAHOMA CHRISTIAN UNIVERSITY
DEPARTMENT OF MUSIC
P.O. Box 11000
Oklahoma City, OK 73136
John Fletcher
405-425-5530
Fax: 405-425-5480
E-mail: john.fletcher@oc.edu
www.oc.edu

OKLAHOMA STATE UNIVERSITY
MUSIC DEPARTMENT
Stillwater, OK 74078
William Ballenger
405-744-8997
Fax: 405-744-9324
E-mail: musica@okstate.edu
http://music.okstate.edu

SOUTHWESTERN OKLAHOMA STATE UNIVERSITY
100 CAMPUS DR.
Weatherford, OK 73096
Dr. Terry Segress
580-774-3708
Fax: 580-774-3714
E-mail: segrest@swosu.edu
www.swosu.edu/deps/music

Degrees: B.M. in Performance (Vocal, Instrumental, Keyboard), Music Business and Music Therapy, Bachelor of Music Education in Instrumental and Vocal, M.M. in Performance and Music Education.

Southwestern Oklahoma State University is a fully accredited, state supported co-educational school located in Weatherford, Oklahoma, a town of approximately 10,000 people. Weatherford is located 70 miles west of Oklahoma City on Interstate 40. The University has an enrollment of approximately 4,700 students. Students may choose from a wide variety of academic programs offered by the five different schools comprising the university. They include the school of the arts and sciences, the school of business, school of education, school of health sciences, and the graduate school. The SWOSU department of music, which is part of the school of arts and sciences is accredited by the National Association of Schools of Music, the National Council for the Accreditation of Teacher Education, the North Central Association of Colleges and Secondary Schools, and the National Association of Music Therapy.

UNIVERSITY OF OKLAHOMA
SCHOOL OF MUSIC

500 W. Boyd St.
Room 138
Norman, OK 73019
Carl Rath
405-325-2081
Fax: 405-325-7574
E-mail: oumusic@ou.edu
www.ou.edu

The school of music is located in a brand new building, Catlett Music Center. There is one concert hall, which is named Paul F. Sharp Concert Hall. This hall seats about 1,000 people. Our recital hall, Pitman Recital Hall, holds about 200 people. We currently have about 350 undergraduate students and 200 graduate students.

UNIVERSITY OF SCIENCE AND ARTS OF OKLAHOMA
MUSIC DEPARTMENT

P.O. Box 82345
Chickasha, OK 73018
Dr. Dan Hanson
405-574-1297
Fax: 405-574-1220
E-mail: dhanson@usao.edu
www.usao.edu

UNIVERSITY OF TULSA
DEPARTMENT OF MUSIC

600 S. College Ave.
Tulsa, OK 74112
Frank Ryan
918-631-2262
Fax: 918-631-3589
E-mail: frank-ryan@utulsa.edu
www.cas.utulsa.edu/music

The School of Music is dedicated to providing professional, comprehensive musical education for students preparing for careers in the field of music and, as part of a comprehensive university, to enriching the curriculum with special course offerings and a variety of ensemble experiences available to all students. The School of Music offers both liberal arts and professional degree programs. The B.A. degree (bachelor of arts) is offered in both general music studies and also with a special emphasis on jazz studies. In cooperation with the School of Art, the Department of Theatre and the College of Business Administration, the B.A. degree is also offered with a major in arts administration. The B.M. degree (bachelor of music) is offered with majors in performance, music composition and music theory. The B.M.E. degree (bachelor of music education) is offered in instrumental and vocal music, and in vocal music with piano as the principal instrument. Additionally, the bachelor of music education is offered in all three of these areas with an emphasis on jazz techniques. Students may also receive a minor in music by completing 12 to 15 hours of selected music courses.

OREGON

Population: 3,629,528 (2003 Estimate)

Capital City: Salem

Music Colleges and Universities: Britt Institute, Lewis and Clark College, Oregon State University, Portland State University, University of Oregon School of Music, University of Portland, Western Oregon University, Willamette University

Bird: Western Meadowlark

Motto: Alis Volat Propiis – She Flies With Her Own Wings

Flower: Oregon Grape

Tree: Douglas Fir

Residents Called: Oregonians

Origin of Name: Origin and meaning of name unknown. May have been derived from that of the Wisconsin River shown on a 1715 French map as "Ouaricon-sint."

Area: 98,386 square miles (9th largest state)

Statehood: February 14, 1859 (33rd state)

Largest Cities: Portland, Eugene, Salem, Gresham, Hillsboro, Beaverton, Medford, Springfield, Bend, Corvallis

College Band Programs: Oregon State University, University of Oregon

OREGON

BRITT INSTITUTE
517 W. 10TH
Medford, OR 97504
Angela Warren
541-779-0847
www.brittfest.org

LEWIS AND CLARK COLLEGE
DEPARTMENT OF MUSIC
125 Evans Center
Portland, OR 97219
Gil Seeley
503-768-7460
Fax: 503-768-7475
E-mail: seeley@lclark.edu
www.lclark.edu/dept/music

OREGON STATE UNIVERSITY
DEPARTMENT OF MUSIC
101 Benton Hall
Corvallis, OR 97331
Marlan Carlson
541-737-4061
Fax: 541-737-4268
E-mail: mcarlson@orst.edu
www.orst.edu

PORTLAND STATE UNIVERSITY
DEPARTMENT OF MUSIC
P.O. Box 751
Portland, OR 97207
Harold K. Gray Jr.
503-725-3011
Fax: 503-725-8215
E-mail: grayh@pdx.edu
www.fpa.pdx.edu/music.html

UNIVERSITY OF OREGON SCHOOL OF MUSIC
1225 University of Oregon
Eugene, OR 97403
Laurie Goren
541-346-3761
Fax: 541-346-0723
E-mail: amclucas@oregon.uoregon.edu
www.music.uoregon.edu

The University of Oregon is a fully-accredited institution for degrees in music through the doctoral level, offering major programs in music performance, music education, composition, theory, jazz studies and music technology. Facilities include 540-seat Beall Concert Hall, acclaimed for its superb acoustics; microcomputer laboratory; Clavinova digital keyboard lab; and three studios for creating electroacoustic music.

UNIVERSITY OF PORTLAND
DEPARTMENT OF MUSIC
5000 Willamette Blvd.
Portland, OR 97203
Kenneth Kleszynski
503-943-7294
Fax: 503-283-7399
E-mail: kkleszyn@up.edu
www.up.edu

WESTERN OREGON UNIVERSITY
DEPARTMENT OF MUSIC
Smith Hall 102
Monmouth, OR 97361
Diane R. Baxter
503-838-8275
Fax: 503-838-8880
E-mail: baxterd@wou.edu
www.wou.edu

WILLAMETTE UNIVERSITY
MUSIC DEPARTMENT

900 State St.
Salem, OR 97301
Martin Behnke
503-370-6255
Fax: 503-370-6260
E-mail: wumusic@willamette.edu
www.willamette.edu

PENNSYLVANIA

Population: 12,366,455 (2003 Estimate)

Capital City: Harrisburg

Music Colleges and Universities: Albright College, Allegheny College, Bloomsburg University, Bryn Mawr College, California University of Pennsylvania, Carnegie-Mellon University, Clarion University of Pennsylvania, Curtis Institute of Music, Dickinson College, Drexel University, Duquesne University, Edinboro University of Pennsylvania, Franklin and Marshall College, Geneva College, Gettysburg College, Haverford College, Indiana University of Pennsylvania, Lafayette College, LaSalle University, Lebanon Valley College, Lehigh University, Lock Haven University of Pennsylvania, Lycoming College, Mansfield University, Marywood University, Millersville University, Moravian College, Pennsylvania State University, Susquehanna University, Swarthmore College, Technology Institute for Music, Temple University, The Music Academy, University of Pennsylvania, University of Pittsburgh, University of the Arts, Villanova University, West Chester University, Wide World Music, York College

Bird: Ruffed Grouse

Motto: Virtue, Liberty, and Independence

Flower: Mountain Laurel

Tree: Eastern Hemlock

Residents Called: Pennsylvanians

Origin of Name: Named in honor of Admiral William Penn, father of the state's founder, William Penn.

Area: 46,058 square miles (33rd largest state)

Statehood: December 12, 1787 (2nd state)

Largest Cities: Philadelphia, Pittsburgh, Allentown, Erie, Upper Darby Township, Reading, Scranton, Bethlehem, Lower Merion Twp, Lancaster

College Band Programs: Carnegie-Mellon University, Indiana University of Pennsylvania, Lehigh University, Millersville University, Pennsylvania State University, University of Pennsylvania, University of Pittsburgh, West Chester University

PENNSYLVANIA

ALBRIGHT COLLEGE
DEPARTMENT OF MUSIC
13th and Bern St.
P.O. Box 15234
Reading, PA 19612
Andrew Kaye
610-921-7870
Fax: 610-921-2381
E-mail: beckyb@alb.edu
www.alb.edu

ALLEGHENY COLLEGE
DEPARTMENT OF MUSIC
Arnold Hall
520 North Main
Meadville, PA 16335
Dr. Lowell Hepler
814-332-3304
Fax: 814-337-3352
E-mail: lhepler@alleg.edu
www.alleg.edu

BLOOMSBURG UNIVERSITY
DEPARTMENT OF MUSIC
400 E. Second St.
Bloomsburg, PA 17815
Mark Jelinek
570-389-4284
Fax: 570-389-4289
E-mail: mjelinek@bliimu.edu
www.bloomu.edu

BRYN MAWR COLLEGE
ARTS PROGRAM
101 North Merion Ave.
Bryn Mawr, PA 19010
Michael Isador
610-526-5210
www.brynmawr.edu

CALIFORNIA UNIVERSITY OF PENNSYLVANIA
DEPARTMENT OF MUSIC
Music Department
250 University Ave.
California, PA 15419
Max Gonano
724-938-4242
Fax: 724-938-4256
E-mail: gonano@cup.edu
www.cup.edu

CARNEGIE-MELLON UNIVERSITY
SCHOOL OF MUSIC
5000 Forbes Ave.
Pittsburgh, PA 15131
Alexis Cribbs
412-268-4118
Fax: 412-268-1431
E-mail: music-admissions@andrew.cmu.edu
www.cmu.edu

CLARION UNIVERSITY OF PENNSYLVANIA
DEPARTMENT OF MUSIC
840 Wood St.
Clarion, PA 16214
Dr. Lawrence J. Wells
814-393-2287
Fax: 814-393-2723
E-mail: wells@clarion.edu
www.clarion.edu

CURTIS INSTITUTE OF MUSIC
ADMISSIONS OFFICE
1726 Locust St.
Philadelphia, PA 19103-6187
Music Department
215-893-5262

Fax: 215-893-7900
E-mail: admissions@curtis.edu
www.curtis.edu

DICKINSON COLLEGE
WAIDNER ADMISSIONS HOUSE
P.O. Box 1773
Carlisle, PA 17013-2896
Blake Wilson
717-245-1231
Fax: 717-245-1937
E-mail: wilson@dickinson.edu
www.dickinson.edu

DREXEL UNIVERSITY
ARTS AND SCIENCES
3141 Chestnut St.
Philadelphia, PA 19104
Alfread Blatter
215/895-2620
Fax: 215-895-2452
E-mail: perfarts@drexel.edu
www.coas.drexel.edu

DUQUESNE UNIVERSITY
MARY PAPPERT SCHOOL OF MUSIC
600 Forbes Ave.
Pittsburgh, PA 15282
Nicholas Jordanoff
412-396-6080
Fax: 412-396-5479
E-mail: jordanof@duq.edu
www.duq.edu

The Mary Pappert School of Music, which is accredited by NASM, has an enrollment of approximately 400 students in its undergraduate and graduate programs. The faculty consists of 26 full-time and over 75 adjunct professionals – many of whom are members of the Pittsburgh Symphony, Pittsburgh Opera, and Pittsburgh Ballet Theatre orchestras. The school, having recently added 68 new

Steinway pianos, is now counted among a select group of prestigious schools of music that are officially designated "All Steinway Schools." The undergraduate degree majors are in music education, music therapy, music performance with classical, jazz, and sacred music tracks, and music technology with performance, composition, and sound recording tracks. The master's degree programs are in music performance, theory and composition, sacred music and music education. In music education, the student has the option of the regular semester program, the summers-only program, or the online program. The artist diploma program is offered in performance. The School of Music offers $1.5 million in undergraduate music talent scholarships and graduate assistantships.

EDINBORO UNIVERSITY OF PENNSYLVANIA
HEATHER HALL
Edinboro, PA 16444
Peter Van Den Honert
814-732-2555
Fax: 814-732-2629
E-mail: vandenhonert@edinboro.edu
www.edinboro.edu

The music department at Edinboro University provides music students with a wealth of opportunities in musical performance and study. Many of our graduates teach in elementary and secondary schools, while others go on to graduate study, or pursue careers in the music industry or performance.

FRANKLIN AND MARSHALL COLLEGE
MUSIC DEPARTMENT
P.O. Box 3003
Lancaster, PA 17604-3003
Bruce Gustafson
717-291-4346
Fax: 717-399-7168

E-mail: deb.miller@fandm.edu
www.fandm.edu

Degrees: B.A., music major, music minor-general; music minor performance

At Franklin and Marshall, we believe that music has a central place in liberal arts education. Our purpose is to provide students the means of opportunity to interact on intellectual and aesthetic levels with the art of music.

Those taking music courses work closely with faculty members, and all students have access to professionally directed instrumental and choral ensembles.

The newly renovated Barshinger Center provides a worl-class concert hall to serve as the centerpiece of the College's thriving music program. The setting is elegant and acoustically vibrant and serves as a venue for visiting musicians of higher caliber.

GENEVA COLLEGE
DEPARTMENT OF MUSIC

3200 College Ave.
Beaver Falls, PA 15010
Donald B. Kephart
724-846-5100
Fax: 724-847-6687
E-mail: dbk@geneva.edu
www.geneva.edu

GETTYSBURG COLLEGE
DEPARTMENT OF MUSIC

P.O. Box 403
300 N. Washington St.
Gettysburg, PA 17325
Dr. John William Jones
717-337-6131
Fax: 717-337-6099
E-mail: jjones@gettysburg.edu
www.gettysburg.edu

HAVERFORD COLLEGE
DEPARTMENT OF MUSIC

370 Lancaster Ave.
Haverford, PA 19041
Curt Cacioppo
610-896-1008
Fax: 610-896-4902
E-mail: tlloyd@haverford.edu
www.haverford.edu

INDIANA UNIVERSITY OF PENNSYLVANIA
DEPARTMENT OF MUSIC

101 Cogswell Hall
Indiana, PA 15705
Dr. Lorraine Wilson
724-357-4452
Fax: 724-357-1324
E-mail: lpw@grove.iup.edu
www.arts.iup.edu/music

LAFAYETTE COLLEGE
DEPARTMENT OF MUSIC

Easton, PA 18042
Dr. J. Larry Stockton
610-330-5356
Fax: 610-330-5058
E-mail: stocktoj@lafayette.edu
www.lafayette.edu

LASALLE UNIVERSITY
FINE ARTS DEPARTMENT

1900 West Olney Ave.
Philadelphia, PA 19141
Dr. Charles White
215-951-1098
Fax: 215-951-1892
E-mail: white@lasalle.edu
www.lasalle.edu

LEBANON VALLEY COLLEGE
DEPARTMENT OF MUSIC

101 N. College Ave.
Annville, PA 17003-1400
Dr. Mark Mecham
717-867-6275
Fax: 717-867-6390
E-mail: mecham@lvc.edu
www.lvc.edu

Housed in the Blair Music Center, the department of music at Lebanon Valley College has a long tradition of excellence in music. Accredited by the National Association of Schools of Music since 1941, the department serves 240 majors in four undergraduate programs, and launched a new, summers-only master of music in music education degree in the summer of 2001.

LEHIGH UNIVERSITY
DEPARTMENT OF MUSIC

420 E. Packer Ave.
Bethlehem, PA 18015
Nadine Sine
610-758-3839
Fax: 610-758-6470
E-mail: nadine.sine@lehigh.edu
www.lehigh.edu

Lehigh offers a liberal arts degree with concentrations in performance, history and literature, theory and composition. The program is designed to allow students to double major in other fields. The new arts center has a 1,000-seat concert hall. Outstanding student ensembles include philharmonic orchestra, university choir, jazz, opera and music theatre and marching band.

LOCK HAVEN UNIVERSITY OF PENNSYLVANIA
MUSIC DEPARTMENT

208 Price Performance Center
Lock Haven, PA 17745
John Schmidt
570-893-2263
Fax: 570-893-2819
E-mail: jschmidt@lhup.edu
www.lhup.edu

LYCOMING COLLEGE
DEPARTMENT OF MUSIC

700 College Place
Williamsport, PA 17701
Gary M. Boerckel
570-321-4000
Fax: 570-321-4090
E-mail: boerckel@lycoming.edu
www.lycoming.edu

MANSFIELD UNIVERSITY
ADMISSIONS OFFICE

Alumni Hall
Mansfield, PA 16933
Brian Barden
570-662-4243
Fax: 570-662-4121
E-mail: bbarden@mnsfld.edu
http://admissions.mnsfld.edu

MARYWOOD UNIVERSITY
MUSIC DEPARTMENT

2300 Adams Ave.
Scranton, PA 18509
Dr. James Moyer
717-348-6268
Fax: 717-961-4768
E-mail: music@ac.marywood.edu
www.marywood.edu

The programs in music provide a framework

for students to master the professional and leadership skills necessary for various careers in music, while at the same time enabling them to develop their highest potential. The strength of the programs lies in a solid core of music classes required of all music students along with comprehensive musical development, which permits a student to specialize in a chosen field. The music department has the following facilities in the performing arts center: 1,100-seat theater, performing arts studio seating 125, digital piano lab, two harpsichords, two harps, practice facilities – including a complement of band and orchestra instruments, multiple copies of orchestral scores, choral library, vocal solo library, small library of reference books, curriculum lab and learning center, two microcomputer labs, biofeedback lab and multiple organs.

MILLERSVILLE UNIVERSITY
DEPARTMENT OF MUSIC

P.O. Box 1002
Millersville, PA 17551
Dr. Micheal Houlahan
717-872-3357
Fax: 717-871-2304
E-mail:
Micheal.Houlahan@millersville.edu
http://muweb.millersville.edu/~music

MORAVIAN COLLEGE
DEPARTMENT OF MUSIC

1200 Main St.
Bethlehem, PA 18018
James Barnes
610-861-1300
Fax: 610-861-3956
E-mail: music@moravian.edu
www.moravian.edu

PENNSYLVANIA STATE UNIVERSITY
SCHOOL OF MUSIC

233 Music Building
University Park, PA 16802
Irene Kohute
814-865-0431
Fax: 814-865-6785
E-mail: rgreen@psu.edu
www.music.psu.edu

Degrees: B.M., B.A., B.M.A., B.S. in music education, twelve graduate degrees, and six integrated undergraduate-graduate degrees

The Penn State School of music has experienced significant growth in both quantity and quality over the past several years, and prides itself on providing a wide range of degree offerings, from the Bachelor's degrees in performance, music education, and music arts to the doctor of philosophy degree in music education. Over 300 students currently major in music at the University Park campus. The faculty consists of 50 full-time artist/teachers. In addition to providing professional instruction for music majors the School of Music Faculty is committed to enriching the arts experience for the entire University community, both through performance and instruction. Each semester, nearly 150 student and faculty performances are scheduled in Penn State facilities: the 500-seat Esber Recital Hall, the 900-seat Schwab Auditorium, and the 2,300-seat Eisenhower Auditorium in addition to other venues. In addition, dozens of performances are presented throughout the Commonwealth, the nation, and abroad.

SUSQUEHANNA UNIVERSITY
DEPARTMENT OF MUSIC

514 University Ave.
Selinsgrove, PA 17870
Heather Loomis
570-372-4309
Fax: 570-372-2789
E-mail: musicdept@susqu.edu
www.susqu.edu/music

Degrees: B.M. in Performance, Music Education, and Church Music; B.A. in Music

Located in central Pennsylvania, Susquehanna has an enrollment of approximately 1,900 students from 30 states and a dozen countries. Our music program has over 100 majors with a faculty of 10 full-time and 17 part-time members. We are pleased to offer our students several music majors and minors to choose from within the framework of a liberal arts institution. More than a dozen performing ensembles are available for students to participate in, regardless of major. Countless non-music majors take lessons and perform in ensembles throughout the department and are integral members of our program. Minors in music technology, theory/literature, and performance are also available. In February 2003, our new Center for Music and Art was dedicated. These facilities include the 320-seat Sretansky Concert Hall, 32 practice rooms and renovated classroom and teaching space. Susquehanna's Department of Music is fully accredited by the National Association of Schools of Music.

SWARTHMORE COLLEGE
DEPARTMENT OF MUSIC AND DANCE

500 College Ave.
Swarthmore, PA 19081
Michael Marissen
610-328-8237
Fax: 610-328-8551
E-mail: mmariss1@swarthmore.edu
www.swarthmore.edu

TECHNOLOGY INSTITUTE FOR MUSIC
OFFICE OF MUSIC ACTIVITIES

305 Maple Ave.
Wyncote, PA 19095
John Dunphy
610-519-7214
Fax: 610-519-7596
www.music.villanova.edu

TEMPLE UNIVERSITY
BOYER COLLEGE OF MUSIC

2001 N. 13th St.
Philadelphia, PA 19122
Richard Brodhead
215-204-8301
Fax: 215-204-4957
E-mail: brodhead@astro.temple.edu
www.temple.edu/music

Temple University's Esther Boyer College of Music offers comprehensive, professional education in music — baccalaureate through doctorate — for performers, educators, therapists, and scholars. Students enjoy a 10:1 student to faculty ratio. Our world-renowned faculty includes many members of the Philadelphia Orchestra, as well as many other noted recording and performing artists. Students also enjoy the cultural advantages of the City of Philadelphia.

THE MUSIC ACADEMY
519 WEST COLLEGE AVE.

State College, PA 16801
Music Department
814-238-3451
www.musicacademy.org

UNIVERSITY OF PENNSYLVANIA
MUSIC DEPARTMENT

201 S. 34th St.
Philadelphia, PA 19104
215-898-9664
Fax: 215-573-2106
E-mail: music@sas.upenn.edu
www.sas.upenn.edu/music

UNIVERSITY OF PITTSBURGH
DEPARTMENT OF MUSIC
110 Music Bldg.
Pittsburgh, PA 15260
John Goldsmith
412-624-4508
Fax: 412-624-4186
www.pitt.edu/~musicdpt/index.html

UNIVERSITY OF THE ARTS
COLLEGE OF THE PERFORMING ARTS
Office of Admissions
320 South Broad St.
Philadelphia, PA 19102
Barbara Elliot
215-717-6342
Fax: 215-545-8056
E-mail: mdicciani@uarts.edu
www.uarts.edu

Degrees: B.M. in Jazz Studies (performance or concentration), Master of Music in Jazz Studies (performance), Master of Arts in Teaching in Music Education

The School of Music at the University of the Arts is distinguished by its emphasis on Jazz and American music idioms. The school offers Bachelor and Master degrees in Jazz studies, and a Master of Arts in Teaching in Music Education. There are three large ensembles, and more than 40 small jazz groups performing all styles of traditional, contemporary, and Latin jazz. Faculty include world-renowned artists Carl Allen, Jimmy Bruno, Charles Fambrough, John Fedchock, Tim Hagans, Jeff Jarvis, Pat Martino, John Swana, and Gerald Veasley. Alumni include Stanley Clarke, Kenny Barron, Robin Eubanks, Gerry Brown, Lew Tabackin, and TV/FIL composers Edd Kalehoff and John Davis. Recent guest artists include Patti Austin, Jack DeJohnette, Kurt Elling, John Faddis, Chris Potter, McCoy Tyner, Dave Weckl, and the Yellojackets. The school of music continues to grow its long-held tradition of excellence which Grammy-winning saxo-phonist Michael Brecker called "...one of the premier schools of jazz in the universe as we know it". Uarts, located in the heart of downtown Philadelphia on the Avenue of the Arts, is the nation's only university devoted exclusively to education and training in performing, visual and media arts.

VILLANOVA UNIVERSITY
INTERCOLLEGIATE JAZZ FESTIVAL
800 Lancaster Ave.
Villanova, PA 19085
George Pinchock
610-519-7214
Fax: 610-519-7596
www.villanova.edu

WEST CHESTER UNIVERSITY
SCHOOL OF MUSIC
Swope Hall
West Chester, PA 19383
Timothy Blair
610-436-2739
Fax: 610-436-2873
E-mail: tblair@wcupa.edu
www.wcupa.edu

WIDE WORLD MUSIC
49 Warring Dr.
Delaware Water, PA 18327
717-476-0550
www.worldwidemusic.com

YORK COLLEGE
DIVISION OF MUSIC
York, PA 17405
Frederick Schreiner
717-846-7788
Fax: 717-849-1602
www.ycp.edu

RHODE ISLAND

Population: 1,057,191 (2003 Estimate)

Capital City: Providence

Music Colleges and Universities: Brown University, Providence College, University of Rhode Island

Bird: Rhode Island Red

Motto: Hope

Flower: Violet

Tree: Red Maple

Residents Called: Rhode Islanders

Origin of Name: Possibly named in honor of the Greek Island of Rhodes or was named Roode Eylandt by Adriaen Block, Dutch explorer, because of its red clay.

Area: 1,545 square miles (the smallest state)

Statehood: May 29, 1790 (13th state)

Largest Cities: Providence, Warwick, Cranston, Pawtucket, East Providence, Woonsocket, Coventry, North Providence, Cumberland, West Warwick

College Band Programs: Brown University

RHODE ISLAND

BROWN UNIVERSITY
ORWIG MUSIC BUILDING

1 Young Orchard Ave. P.O. Box 1924
Providence, RI 02912
Gerald M. Shapiro
401-863-3234
Fax: 401-863-1256
E-mail: Gerald_Shapiro@brown.edu
www.brown.edu

PROVIDENCE COLLEGE
DEPARTMENT OF MUSIC

549 River Ave.
Providence, RI 02918
Gail Himrod
401-865-2183
Fax: 401-865-2761
E-mail: cbarry@providence.edu
http://websvr.providence.edu/Music

Degrees: The Department of Music offers a
Bachelor of Arts in Music, a Bachelor of Arts
in Music/Music Education and a minor in
music

The department of Music offers the study of
music in a balanced and creative atmosphere
that emphasizes the theoretical, historical, and
educational foundations of music in a Liberal
Arts context. Ample opportunity is provided
for vocal and instrumental study and performance on an individual basis as well as in a variety of choral and instrumental ensembles.

The music degree has five areas of specialization: History/Literature; Theory Composition;
Performance; Jazz and Church Music. It is
possible to double major, combining music
with another department. The music education
degree program balances the requirements of
both music and education departments with
the College's Liberal Arts program. This K-12
music education program prepares students for
certification. Requirements for the minor
include history, theory, private study, and participation in an ensemble. A new center for the
Arts will be completed for the 2004-2005 academic year and will include performance areas,
classrooms, offices and student practice rooms.

RHODE ISLAND COLLEGE
NAZARIAN CENTER FOR THE PERFORMING ARTS

600 Mount Pleasant Ave.
Providence, RI 02908-1991
401-456-9883
www.ric.edu

Degrees: Bachelor of Music, Bachelor of
Science in Music Education, Bachelor of Arts,
Minor in Music, Minor in Jazz Studies, Master
of Music Education, Master of Arts in
Teaching

UNIVERSITY OF RHODE ISLAND
DEPARTMENT OF MUSIC

105 Upper College Rd.
Suite 2
Kingston, RI 02881
Gerard Heroux
401-874-5584
Fax: 401-874-2772
E-mail: muslib@uri.edu
www.uri.edu/artsci/mus

SOUTH CAROLINA:

Population: 4,184,327 (2003 Estimate)

Capital City: Columbia

Music Colleges and Universities: Bob Jones University, Clemson University, College of Charleston, Converse College, Furman University, Newberry College, South Carolina State University, University of South Carolina at Aiken, University of South Carolina at Columbia, Winthrop University

Bird: Great Carolina Wren

Motto: Animis Opibusque Parati / Dum Spiro Spero – Prepared in mind and resources / While I breathe, I hope

Flower: Yellow Jessamine

Tree: Sabal Palmetto

Residents Called: South Carolinians

Origin of Name: Named in honor of England's King Charles I

Area: 32,007 square miles (40th largest state)

Statehood: May 23, 1788 (8th state)

Largest Cities: Columbia, Charleston, North Charleston, Greenville, Rock Hill, Mount Pleasant, Spartanburg, Sumter, Hilton Head Island, Florence

College Band Programs: Clemson University, Furman University, University of South Carolina-Columbia

SOUTH CAROLINA

BOB JONES UNIVERSITY

Division of Music
P.O. Box 34533
Greenville, SC 29614
David Christ
864-242-5100
Fax: 864-467-9302
www.bju.edu

Bob Jones University is a Christian liberal arts university (fundamental in doctrine and evangelistic in emphasis) offering more than 100 majors. A music faculty of over 60 includes specialists in all fields. The faculty's training represents leading graduate schools and conservatories from around the world. Students have excelled in contests on the local, state, regional, and national level. Our facilities are unsurpassed in Christian education and serve approximately 250 music majors, 150 music minors.

CLEMSON UNIVERSITY
DEPARTMENT OF PERFORMING ARTS

211 Brooks Center
Clemson, SC 29634-0525
Dr. Richard E. Goodstein
864-656-3043
Fax: 864-656-1013
E-mail: perf-arts-l@clemson.edu
www.clemson.edu/Perf-Arts
Degrees: B.A.

Clemson University features a distinctive B.A. degree, which combines the disciplines of music and theater. The curriculum includes hands-on experiences in performing arts production technologies with classes in performance and arts history and theory in order to prepare students for entry into a wide variety of traditional, commercial, and community-based barriers. Students can choose from among 75 minors in order to customize their degree to their individual interests. The degree emphasizes multidisciplinary and collaborative performing arts and service learning as partners to traditional performance studies.

The production studies in performing arts degree is designed to provide students with diverse and essential skills and experiences that are marketable in today's international, multicultural workplace. Housed in the beautiful Brooks Center for the Performing Arts, the Clemson University Department of Performing Arts features state-of-the-art technology, including the 1,000-seat Brooks Theatre, a new ProTools recording studio and a 12-station music technology lab.

COLLEGE OF CHARLESTON
SIMONS CENTER FOR THE ARTS

Room 315B
Charleston, SC 29424
Music Department
843-953-5927
Fax: 843-953-4914
E-mail: music@cofc.edu
www.cofc.edu

CONVERSE COLLEGE
MUSIC DEPARTMENT

Petrie School of Music
580 E. Main St.
Spartanburg, SC 29302
Ms. Suzanne Brown
864-579-7509
Fax: 864-596-9167
E-mail: suzanne.brown@converse.edu
www.converse.edu

Established in 1889, Converse College is a liberal arts college for women with a professional school of music. The Petrie School of Music is an accredited, charter member of the National Association of Schools of Music (NASM). Majors include performance (all instruments), music education, piano pedagogy, composition, theory and music history. The B.A. degree is offered with concentrations in general music or music business. Double major opportunities are also available. The low 7:1 student-faculty ratio allows students to learn in small classes and receive individualized instruction from a distinguished faculty of artists who are active in performance, composition and research. The faculty is complemented by a guest artist series featuring acclaimed musicians in master classes and concerts. The curriculum is enhanced by two nationally-recognized performance halls, one of the largest music libraries in the southeast, teaching studios and classrooms, 30 practice rooms, music technology labs, Steinway pianos, Casavant and Schantz pipe organs, and instrument collections for student use. Performing opportunities include Converse Sinfonietta, festival orchestra, wind ensemble, chamber winds, chorale, festival chorus, opera theatre, a student recital series and numerous chamber ensembles.

FURMAN UNIVERSITY
DEPARTMENT OF MUSIC

3300 Poinsett Hwy.
Greenville, SC 29613
Marcella Frese
864-294-2086
Fax: 864-294-3035
E-mail: furmanmusic@furman.edu
www.furman.edu

Degrees: B.M.: Music Education (all areas), Music Theory, Church Music Performance (vocal, orchestral, keyboard, wind percussion); B.A. in music offers double major options

Housed on one of the most beautiful campuses in the nation, Furman offers students a flexible, engaged curriculum housed in state-of-the-art facilities backed by a fully accredited program with five pre-professional degrees. More than twenty ensembles provide musical outlets for students, regardless of major, including an all-undergraduate symphony orchestra. Band programs include Marching Band, Symphonic Band, Wind Ensemble, and several chamber groups. For singers, offerings include Opera Theater, Furman Choral, Chamber Choir, and the widely recognized Furman singers. Pianists and organists study privately with outstanding artist faculty, gaining performing experience through weekly recitals, chamber music opportunities, concerto concerts, ensemble concerts, and much more. The first rate surroundings of the Daniel Music Building, Herring Music Pavilion, McAllister Auditorium and Daniel Memorial Chapel provide classrooms, practice rooms, music library and technology space, stunning performing venues as well as studios and offices for the University's largest departmental faculty. Music scholarships available for majors, non-majors.

NEWBERRY COLLEGE
MUSIC DEPARTMENT

2100 College St.
Newberry, SC 29108
Dr. Sally Cherrington
803-321-5174
Fax: 803-321-5627
E-mail: scherrington@newberry.edu
www.newberry.edu

SOUTH CAROLINA STATE UNIVERSITY
DEPARTMENT OF VISUAL AND PERFORMING ARTS

Orangeburg, SC 29117
Ronald J. Sajeant
803-536-7101
Fax: 803-536-7192
www.scsu.edu

UNIVERSITY OF SOUTH CAROLINA AT AIKEN
DEPARTMENT OF FINE ARTS

Aiken, SC 29801
William House
803-648-3306
Fax: 803-641-3691
www.usca.edu

UNIVERSITY OF SOUTH CAROLINA AT COLUMBIA

SCHOOL OF MUSIC

Columbia, SC 29208
Mr. Jablonski
803-777-4280
Fax: 803-777-6508
E-mail: jjablonski@mozart.sc.edu
www.music.sc.edu

Degrees: B.A., B.M. in performance, theory, composition, music education, jazz studies; M.M. in performance, opera, theory, composition, history, conducting, and jazz studies; Ph.D. in music Education, D.M.A. in performance, conducting, and composition

The school of music at the University of South Carolina is a comprehensive music program that is housed in a beautiful state of the art facility. Approximately 320 undergraduates and 120 graduate music majors study with more than 50 artist/teachers in a wide variety of degree programs. A fully equipped recording studio, high-tech class rooms, and an excellent library support both academic and performance programs. Total enrollment at the Columbia, SC, campus is 23,000 students. USC is located in a metropolitan area of 400,000.

WINTHROP UNIVERSITY

DEPARTMENT OF MUSIC

129 Conservatory of Music
Rock Hill, SC 29733
Donald M. Rogers
803-323-2255
Fax: 803-323-2343
E-mail: rogersd@winthrop.edu
www.winthrop.edu
Degrees: B.A., B.M.E., B.M., M.A., M.M.

More than 7,000 students pursue 80 undergraduate and 50 graduate degrees and options at Winthrop University, a state-assisted university located in Rock Hill, S.C., a city of 50,000 in the Charlotte, N.C. metropolitan area. Winthrop has received 100 percent national accreditation in all eligible programs, the first comprehensive teaching institution among the South Carolina's senior colleges to reach that level of national accreditation. Winthrop has been identified in the US News and World Report ranking as a top 10 Southern Regional University for the last 10 years. The University boasts a 15:1 student to faculty ratio, with the average class size from 10-33 students. The department of music enjoys a long and distinguished history as an outstanding music program. An accredited institutional member of the NASM since 1940, the department boasts a strong faculty of 34 dedicated and caring professors delivering a quality curriculum. Students have an opportunity to learn how to compose music using MIDI synthesizers and computer, to perform solo or in 17 renowned ensembles, and to teach music incorporating the latest methodologies. Nearly 170 undergraduate and graduate students pursue a quality and varied curriculum.

SOUTH DAKOTA

Population: 773,464 (2003 Estimate)

Capital City: Pierre

Music Colleges and Universities: Black Hills State University, Dakota State University, Northern State University, South Dakota State University, University of South Dakota

Bird: Ring-necked Pheasant

Motto: Under God the people rule

Flower: Pasque Flower

Tree: Black Hills Spruce

Residents Called: South Dakotans

Origin of Name: South Dakota is the land of the famous Sioux or Dacotah Indians. Dakota Territory and later South Dakotans were named for the tribe.

Area: 77,121 square miles (17th largest state)

Statehood: November 2, 1889 (40th state)

Largest Cities: Sioux Falls, Rapid City, Aberdeen, Watertown, Brookings, Mitchell, Pierre, Yankton, Huron, Vermillion

SOUTH DAKOTA

AUGUSTANA COLLEGE
MUSIC DEPARTMENT
2001 S. Summit Ave.
Sioux Falls, SD 57197
800-727-2844
www.augie.edu
Degrees: Music, B.A. Instrumental
Emphasis, Music education major,
Minor

BLACK HILLS STATE UNIVERSITY
MUSIC DEPARTMENT
Fine and Applied Arts Department
1200 University St.
Unit 9097
Spearfish, SD 57799-9097
Dr. Janeen Larsen
605-642-6241
Fax: 605-642-6762
E-mail: janeenlarsen@bhsu.edu
www.bhsu.edu

Degrees: B.S. in Education: Music; B.S. in
Liberal Arts: Music

Black Hills State University is a small liberal
arts university in a beautiful and scenic location with many skiing, biking and hiking trails
nearby. A new music facility has recently been
completed with a new recital hall, band room,
choir room, recording studio and practice
rooms. The program features individual faculty mentoring by experienced teachers and a
cooperative group spirit among the students.
BHSU has long been a center for teacher education, and is fully accredited by NCATE. The
music program is fully accredited by the
National Associated of Schools of Music as
well. Students who choose the non-teaching
music program often minor in Entrepreneurial
Studies of Business.

DAKOTA STATE UNIVERSITY
MUSIC DEPARTMENT
820 N. Washington
Madison, SD 57042
Dr. Eric Johnson
605-256-5646
Fax: 605-256-5021
E-mail: johnsone@columbia.dsu.edu
www.dsu.edu

NORTHERN STATE UNIVERSITY
SCHOOL OF FINE ARTS
NSU Music and Theatre Department
1200 S. Jay St.
Aberdeen, SD 57401
Dr. Alan Lafave
605-626-2497
Fax: 605-626-2263
E-mail: lafavea@northern.edu
www.northern.edu/music/index.htm

SOUTH DAKOTA STATE UNIVERSITY
LINCOLN MUSIC HALL
P.O. Box 2212
Brookings, SD 57007
Corliss Johnson
605-688-6691
Fax: 605-688-4307
www.sdstate.edu

UNIVERSITY OF SOUTH DAKOTA
MUSIC DEPARTMENT
414 E. Clark St.
Vermillion, SD 57069
Dr. Larry Schou
605-677-5274
Fax: 605-677-5988
E-mail: lschou@usd.edu
www.usd.edu/cfa/Music

Degrees: B.M. and M.M.

The mission of the department of music at the University of South Dakota is to provide students with the necessary knowledge and skills to become professional musicians — performers, educators, scholars and life-long learners. Through performance, classroom studies, and guided research, students are provided opportunities for musical development and personal enrichment. The department of music is housed in the Warren M. Lee Center for the Fine Arts — a 140,000 square foot state-of-the-art facility that includes studios, galleries, labs, concert halls and a 450-seat proscenium theatre. The department of music facility includes: 16 faculty studios, 8 graduate assistantship studios, 15 practice rooms, Colton Tal Hall (seats 200), 2 rehearsal halls, and 2 electronic music studios/piano labs.

On main campus, large ensemble music events are held in Slagle Auditorium (seats 2,000). Throughout its history, the University of South Dakota has produced 13 Rhodes Scholars. Recently, five U students were awarded four of the nation's most prestigious scholarships — the Fullbright, Truman, Goldwater and Udall scholarship. Rarely is one school home to recipients of these four scholarships in a single year. In fact, the 2002 wards put the U among a group of only 13 colleges and universities across the country to have earned such honors.

TENNESSEE

Population: 5,968,606 (2003 Estimate)

Capital City: Nashville

Music Colleges and Universities: Austin Peay State University, Belmont University, Carson-Newman College, Fisk University, Lee University, Lipscomb University, Middle Tennessee State University, Navy Music Program, Rhodes College, Tennessee State University, Tennessee Technological University, Union University, University of Memphis, University of Tennessee at Knoxville, University of Tennessee at Martin, University of the South, Vanderbilt University

Bird: Mockingbird

Motto: Agriculture and Commerce

Flower: Iris

Tree: Tulip Tree

Residents Called: Tennesseans

Origin of Name: Named after Cherokee Indian villages called "Tanasi"

Area: 42,146 square miles (36th largest state)

Statehood: June 1, 1796 (16th state)

Largest Cities: Memphis, Nashville, Knoxville, Chattanooga, Clarksville, Murfreesboro, Jackson, Johnson City, Kingsport, Franklin

College Band Programs: Middle Tennessee State University,

University of Tennessee

TENNESSEE

AUSTIN PEAY STATE UNIVERSITY
DEPARTMENT OF MUSIC
Music Department
601 College St.
Clarksville, TN 37044
Bob Lee
931-648-7011
Fax: 931-221-7529
E-mail: leeb@apsu.edu
www.apsu.edu

BELMONT UNIVERSITY
SCHOOL OF MUSIC
1900 Belmont Blvd.
Nashville, TN 37212
Dr. Sharon Gregg
615-460-6408
Fax: 615-386-0239
E-mail: greggs@mail.belmont.edu
www.belmont.edu/music

Degrees: B.M., B.A., and M.M.

Belmont's School of Music offers its students a winning combination of large university resources and personal, small college service. Our world-class instructors, wide variety of degrees and state-of-the-art studio resources and performance halls place us among the best music schools in the country — yet our students also benefit from a sense of community rare in large universities. Located at the end of history music row, near the heart of Nashville, TN, Belmont's quiet, neighborhood campus provides a peaceful, inspiring environment for musicians to participate and learn.

CARSON-NEWMAN COLLEGE
MUSIC DEPARTMENT
Jefferson City, TN 37760
Donald Measels
865-471-3328
Fax: 865-471-3502
E-mail: measels@cn.edu
www.cn.edu

EAST TENNESSEE STATE UNIVERSITY
DEPARTMENT OF MUSIC
Box 70267
Johnson City, TN 37614-0054
423-439-1000
www.etsu.edu

Degrees: Bachelor of Music in Instrumental, Music Education, Bachelor of Music in Vocal Music Education, Bachelor of Music in Keyboard/Vocal Music Education, Bachelor of Music in Performance, Music minor, Master of Music Education

FISK UNIVERSITY
FACULTY OF MUSIC
1000 17th Ave. North
Nashville, TN 37208
Paul Kwami
615-329-8666
Fax: 615-329-8850
E-mail: pkwami@fisk.edu
www.fisk.edu

LEE UNIVERSITY
SCHOOL OF MUSIC
1130 Parker St.
Cleveland, TN 37320-3450
P.O. Box 3450
Dr. Stephen W. Plate
423-614-8240
Fax: 423-614-8242
E-mail: music@leeuniversity.edu
www.leeuniversity.edu

Degrees: B.A., B.M., B.M.E., B.S., and
M.C.M.

The Lee University School of Music is an institutional member of the National Association of Schools of Music. The School of Music offers programs of study designed to prepare men and women for the performance or instruction of the music arts by developing skills needed to become music performers, educators, ministers, private instructors, or music business professionals. It serves its majors by providing intensive, personalized studio instruction and other specialized courses in vocal and instrumental music. The primary music facility, the Curtsinger Music Building, is a fully equipped educational facility which includes five classrooms, 19 teaching studios, 25 practice rooms, two rehearsal rooms for large ensembles, an audio library, a MIDI Lab, and an electronic piano lab.

LIPSCOMB UNIVERSITY
MUSIC DEPARTMENT
3901 Granny White Pike
Nashville, TN 37204
Marcia Hughes
615-279-5765
E-mail: marcia.hughes@lipscomb.edu
http://music.lipscomb.edu

Degrees: B.A. in Music and B.S. in Music Teaching, Instrumental Teaching, Vocal Performance, Instrumental Performance, Piano Performance, and Theory/Composition.

Minors are offered in General Music and Church Music. Music scholarships are available to majors, minors, and some other participants.

MIDDLE TENNESSEE STATE UNIVERSITY
SCHOOL OF MUSIC
P.O. Box 47
Murfreesboro, TN 37132
Dr. Roger Kugler
615-898-2469
E-mail: daliquo@mtsu.edu
www.mtsu.edu/~music

NAVY MUSIC PROGRAM
5722 INTEGRITY DR.
Millington, TN 38054
Mark Hammond
901-874-5784
www.bupers.navy.mil/navymusic

RHODES COLLEGE
DEPARTMENT OF MUSIC
2000 N. Pkwy.
Memphis, TN 38122
Dr. Timothy Sharp
901-843-3782
Fax: 901-843-3789
E-mail: sharp@rhodes.edu
www.rhodes.edu

The mission of the Rhodes Music Department is to foster creativity and to develop the skills of students, while instilling a passion for quality and an appreciation of the universal importance of the arts. Students are encouraged to become aware of the great variety of musical styles, both past and present, and to recognize the wide range of musical activity currently available. They are invited to explore their individual interests in music and to discover ways to apply their own musical capabilities within society. The Bachelor of Arts degree in music is a liberal arts degree designed to prepare students for graduate studies, to develop a satisfying avocation, and to serve as preparation for a wide range of careers. Students from various backgrounds are welcome to pursue this degree. Course offerings are in the areas of music theory, music history and literature, applied music and ensembles.

TENNESSEE STATE UNIVERSITY
DEPARTMENT OF MUSIC
3500 John A. Merritt Blvd.
Nashville, TN 37209
Dr. Ralph Simpson
615-963-5971
Fax: 615-963-5346
E-mail: rsimpson@tnstate.edu
www.tnstate.edu/arts_science

TENNESSEE TECHNOLOGICAL UNIVERSITY
DEPARTMENT OF MUSIC
P.O. Box 5045
Cookeville, TN 38505
Arthur Labar
931-372-3161
Fax: 931-372-6279
E-mail: alabar@tntech.edu
www.tntech.edu

UNION UNIVERSITY
DEPARTMENT OF MUSIC
1050 Union University Dr.
Jackson, TN 38305
Dr. Betty Bedsole
731-661-5226
Fax: 731-661-5017
E-mail: bbedsole@uu.edu
www.uu.edu/dept/music
Union is a four-year, Christian liberal arts college associated with Tennessee

Baptist Convention. The music department is housed in a new state-of-the-art fine arts building.

UNIVERSITY OF MEMPHIS
DEPARTMENT OF MUSIC
3775 Central Ave.
Memphis, TN 38152
Kay Yager
901-678-2541
Fax: 901-678-3096
E-mail: music@memphis.edu
www.memphis.edu

UNIVERSITY OF TENNESSEE AT KNOXVILLE
149 Music Bldg.
Knoxville, TN 37996
Dr. Gary D. Sousa
865-974-3241
Fax: 865-974-1941
E-mail: music@utk.edu
www.fmusic.utk.edu

UNIVERSITY OF TENNESSEE AT MARTIN
DEPARTMENT OF MUSIC
102 Fine Arts Bldg.
Martin, TN 38238
Kevin Lambert
731-587-7402
Fax: 731-587-7415
E-mail: klambert@utm.edu
www.utm.edu

UNIVERSITY OF THE SOUTH
MUSIC DEPARTMENT
735 University Ave.
Sewanee, TN 37383
Robert Delcamp
931-598-1000

Fax: 931-598-1145
E-mail: rdelcamp@sewanee.edu
www.sewanee.edu

VANDERBILT UNIVERSITY
BLAIR SCHOOL OF MUSIC

2400 Blakemore Ave.
Nashville, TN 37212
Dwayne P. Sagen
615-322-7651
Fax: 615-343-0324
E-mail: dwayne.p.sagan@vanderbilt.edu
www.vanderbilt.edu/blair

Degrees: B.M. in Performance, composition,
musical arts, and teacher education

Blair School of Music... if you are looking for
the perfect balance between a finely tuned
music school and a highly regarded university,
consider the Blair School of Music at
Vanderbilt University. Vanderbilt is one of only
three top twenty universities in the nation to
boast an acclaimed, accredited undergraduate
school of music, the only one whose school of
music is solely for undergraduates. The talented musicians we attract expect the best. They
want conservatory quality music training with
excellent teachers, frequent performance
opportunities, and great facilities. They want
to participate in their school's top ensembles,
so we deliberately limit our admission numbers, because we are selective, our students
study and perform with musicians who are
equally dedicated. The student-to-faculty ratio
of 4:1 provides opportunities to work closely
with the world-class musicians on our faculty.
And for musicians, Nashville is an ideal college
town, home to a sizeable segment of the global
music industry in a progressive city of New
South.

TEXAS

Population: 22,356,654 (2003 Estimate)

Capital City: Austin

Music Colleges and Universities: Abilene Christian University, Austin College, Baylor University, Del Mar College, East Texas Baptist University, Frank Phillips College, Howard Payne University, International Festival-Institute, Lamar University, Our Lady of the Lake University, Rice University, Sam Houston State University, Southern Methodist University, Southwest Texas State University, Southwestern University, St. Mary College, Stephen F. Austin State University, Texas A&M University, Texas A&M University at Commerce, Texas Christian University, Texas Technological University, Texas Woman's University, Trinity University, University of Houston, University of North Texas, University of Texas at Arlington, University of Texas at Austin, University of Texas at El Paso, University of Texas at Houston, University of Texas at San Antonio, West Texas A&M University

Bird: Mockingbird

Motto: Friendship

Flower: Bluebonnet

Tree: Pecan

Residents Called: Texans

Origin of Name: Based on a word used by Caddo Indians meaning "friends."

Area: 268,601 square miles (2nd largest state)

Statehood: December 29, 1845

Largest Cities: Houston, Dallas, San Antonio, Austin, El Paso, Fort Worth, Arlington, Corpus Christi, Plano, Garland, University of Texas-El Paso, University of Texas-Austin

College Band Programs: Baylor University, Rice University, Southern Methodist University, Stephen F. Austin State University, Texas A&M University, Texas A&M University-Kingsville, Texas Christian University, Texas Tech University, University of Houston

TEXAS

ABILENE CHRISTIAN UNIVERSITY
MUSIC DEPARTMENT
Abilene, TX 79699
Dr. Sheila Hilton
915-674-2199
Fax: 915-260-2608
http://music.acu.edu

AUSTIN COLLEGE
MUSIC DEPARTMENT
900 N. Grand Ave.
Sherman, TX 75090
Daniel Dominick
903-813-2461
Fax: 903-813-2273
www.austincollegemusic.com

Austin College is a private, liberal arts college of which the music department is an important part, with four full-time and nine adjunct faculty. We offer three choral organizations, a full jazz band, and smaller ensembles for strings, brass, and winds. The college and community also support a regional volunteer and professional symphony orchestra that plays a full season of concerts in a renovated 1930s concert hall. The degree program includes courses in music theory, history, applied, and supporting electives for a major that is well-suited to continued graduate study.

BAYLOR UNIVERSITY
SCHOOL OF MUSIC
P.O. Box 97408
Waco, TX 76798
William May
254-710-1221
Fax: 254-710-1191
E-mail: william_may@baylor.edu
www.baylor.edu

DEL MAR COLLEGE
DIVISION OF ARTS AND SCIENCES
101 Baldwin Blvd.
Corpus Christi, TX 78404-3897
Joy Kairies
800-652-3357
E-mail: jkairies@delmar.edu
www.delmar.edu

EAST TEXAS BAPTIST UNIVERSITY
MUSIC DEPARTMENT
1209 North Grove
Marshall, TX 75670
Robert Spencer
903-935-7963
Fax: 903-934-8114
www.etbu.edu

FRANK PHILLIPS COLLEGE
DEPARTMENT OF MUSIC
Borger, TX 79008
Judy Strecker
806-274-5311
Fax: 806-274-6835
E-mail: jstrecke@fpc.cc.tx.us
www.fpc.cc.tx.us

HOWARD PAYNE UNIVERSITY
SCHOOL OF MUSIC AND FINE ARTS
1000 Fisk
Brownwood, TX 76801
Dr. Allen Reed
915-646-2502
Fax: 915-649-8945
E-mail: areed@hputx.edu
www.hputx.edu

INTERNATIONAL FESTIVAL-INSTITUTE

Hwy 237 at Jaster Rd.
Round Top, TX 78954-0089
Alain G. Declert
979-249-3086
Fax: 979-249-3100
http://festivalhill.org

LAMAR UNIVERSITY
DEPARTMENT OF MUSIC THEATER AND DANCE

P.O. Box 10044
Beaumont, TX 77710
Dr. L. Randolph Babin
409-880-8144
Fax: 409-880-8143
E-mail: babinlr@hal.lamar.edu
www.lamar.edu

The department of music, theatre and dance at Lamar serves an average of 180 students, including about 125 music majors. Degrees offered include the bachelor of music degree with specializations in performance, composition and music education. Performing groups include a cappella choir, chamber orchestra, concert band, grand choir, jazz band, opera theatre and symphonic band, as well as numerous smaller ensembles (clarinet quartet, sax quartet, brass quintet, woodwind quintet, string quartet). Students may audition for competitive scholarships in varying amounts. Additional scholarship support is available from the university, based on academic achievement and student need.

OUR LADY OF THE LAKE UNIVERSITY
DEPARTMENT OF MUSIC

411 S.W. 24th St.
San Antonio, TX 78207
Sister Madalyn Pape

210-434-6711
Fax: 210-436-0824
E-mail: papem@lake.ollusa.edu
www.ollusa.edu

Our Lady of the Lake University is a small Catholic college (enrollment of about 3,500) in San Antonio. It is sponsored by the Congregation of Divine Providence. The department seeks to involve as many students as possible in music courses and ensembles, regardless of major. Ensembles include vocal, mariachi, flute, clarinet, wind, brass, recorder and guitar ensembles. Currently a proposal is in process to establish a B.A. in music. Instructors are highly competent and include members of the San Antonio Symphony. Opportunities in San Antonio provide many on- and off-campus opportunities for performing and attending concerts. Current chair of the music department is Sister Madlyn Pape.

RICE UNIVERSITY
SHEPHERD SCHOOL OF MUSIC

MS 532
P.O. Box 1892
Houston, TX 77251
Bradley Blunt
713-348-4854
Fax: 713-348-5317
E-mail: bblunt@rice.edu
www.rice.edu

SAM HOUSTON STATE UNIVERSITY
SCHOOL OF MUSIC

1801 Ave. I. Suite 225
Huntsville, TX 77341
Dr. Rod Cannon
936-294-1360
Fax: 936-294-3765
E-mail: mus_rmc@shsu.edu
www.shsu.edu/~music

SOUTHERN METHODIST UNIVERSITY
MEADOWS SCHOOL OF THE ARTS
Division of Music
P.O. Box 750356
Dallas, TX 75275
Anthony de Bruyn
214-768-1951
Fax: 214-768-4669
www.smu.edu

SOUTHWEST TEXAS STATE UNIVERSITY
SCHOOL OF MUSIC
601 University Dr.
San Marcos, TX 78666-4616
Doug Skinner
512-245-2651
Fax: 512-245-8181
E-mail: ds23@swt.edu
www.finearts.swt.edu/music

Degrees: B.M., B.A., and M.M.

375 undergraduate and 65 graduate students are enrolled in the school of music. NASM accredited the school, which offers a unique opportunity for aspiring musicians who receive a comprehensive education from a faculty upholding high music standards.

Jazz ensembles have performed at festivals in France, Switzerland, Italy and Holland. The orchestra toured in Austria, the Czech Republic, England, Germany, Poland and Scotland. The chorale performed at Carnegie Hall. The marching band appeared on television and marched at festivals in Ireland.

Sound Recording Technology students participate in commercial recording sessions in a studio housing computer labs, digital editing stations and electronic audio labs while completing their degree.

SOUTHWESTERN UNIVERSITY
DEPARTMENT OF MUSIC
P.O. Box 770
Georgetown, TX 78627
Dr. Kenneth Sheppard
512-863-1358
Fax: 512-863-1422
www.southwestern.edu

ST. MARY COLLEGE
DEPARTMENT OF FINE ARTS-MUSIC
4100 S. 4th St.
Leavenworth, TX 66048
William Krusemark
913-682-5151
Fax: 913-758-6140
www.smcks.edu

STEPHEN F. AUSTIN STATE UNIVERSITY
DEPARTMENT OF MUSIC
P.O. Box 13043, SFA Station
Nacogdoches, TX 75962
Dr. Ron Anderson
936-468-4602
Fax: 409-468-5810
E-mail: randerson@sfasu.edu
www.finearts.sfasu.edu/music/music.html

Known as one of the top music education training centers in Texas, the department of music at Stephen F. Austin State University has assembled an outstanding faculty dedicated to the professional training of talented students in all areas of music. More than 250 music majors receive instruction in the Tom and Peggy Wright Music Building, which features the 350-seat Cole Concert Hall, an intimate recital hall, rehearsal halls for the bands, choirs, orchestras, and a percussion suite, as well as faculty studios and 30 student practice rooms. The department also occupies teaching areas in the Griffith Fine Arts Building and gives many concerts in the 1,000-seat Turner

Auditorium. It offers many special activities, including summer band, choir, and orchestra camps, summer opera and chamber music festivals, and a regional symphony orchestra: the Orchestra of the Pines. The department is fully accredited by the National Association of Schools of Music and is a member of the Texas Music Educators Association, the Texas Association of Music Schools and the Texas Music Educators Conference.

TEXAS A&M UNIVERSITY
DEPARTMENT OF MUSIC
405 Academic Building
4240 TAMU
College Station, TX 77843
Dr. Peter Lieuwen
979-845-3355
Fax: 979-458-1266
E-mail: lieuwen@neo.tamu.edu
http://clla.tamu.edu/perf

TEXAS A&M UNIVERSITY, COMMERCE
DEPARTMENT OF MUSIC
Music Department
P.O. Box 3011
Commerce, TX 75429
Gene Lockhart
903-886-5303
Fax: 903-468-6010
E-mail: Gene_Lockhart@tamu-com-merce.edu
www7.tamu-commerce.edu/music

Members of the outstanding applied faculty are all active as professionals in the Dallas/Ft. Worth area. The university is located just 60 miles from downtown Dallas. Please contact the office for an audition date and scholarship information.

TEXAS CHRISTIAN UNIVERSITY
DEPARTMENT OF MUSIC
TCU P.O. Box 297500

Fort Worth, TX 76129
Blaise Ferrandino
817-257-7020
Fax: 817-257-7344
E-mail: b.ferrandino@tcu.edu
www.music.tcu.edu/music

TEXAS TECHNOLOGICAL UNIVERSITY
ADMISSIONS DEPARTMENT
Lubbock, TX 79409
806-742-2225
Fax: 806-742-2294
E-mail: m.smith@ttu.edu
www.ttu.edu/~music

TEXAS WOMAN'S UNIVERSITY
PERFORMING ARTS DEPARTMENT
304 Administration Dr.
P.O. Box 425768
Denton, TX 76204
Dr. Janice Killian
940-898-2505
Fax: 940-898-2494
www.twu.edu/as/pa

TRINITY UNIVERSITY
DEPARTMENT OF MUSIC
715 Stadium Dr.
San Antonio, TX 78212
Dr. James Worman
210-999-8212
Fax: 210-999-8170
E-mail: jworman@trinity.edu
www.trinity.edu/departments/music

UNIVERSITY OF HOUSTON
MOORES SCHOOL OF MUSIC
16 Cullen Blvd.
Houston, TX 77251
David Tomatz
713-743-3009

Fax: 713-743-3166
E-mail: info@www.music.uh.edu
www.uh.edu/music

Degrees: B.A. in Music, Music Applied, and
Music Education

UNIVERSITY OF NORTH TEXAS
COLLEGE OF MUSIC
P.O. Box 311367
Denton, TX 76203
Dr. Joán Groom-Thornton
940-565-2791
Fax: 940-565-3700
E-mail: undergrad@unt.edu
www.music.unt.edu

UNIVERSITY OF TEXAS AT ARLINGTON
DEPARTMENT OF MUSIC
P.O. Box 19105
Arlington, TX 76019
817-272-3471
Fax: 817-272-4343
E-mail: music@uta.edu
www.uta.edu/music

UNIVERSITY OF TEXAS AT AUSTIN
SCHOOL OF MUSIC
Austin, TX 78712
512-471-7764
Fax: 512-471-2333
E-mail: utmusic@www.utexas.edu
http://utexas.edu
University of Texas at El Paso
Music Department
500 W. University Ave.
El Paso, TX 79968
Ron Hufstad
915-747-5606
Fax: 915-747-5023
E-mail: rhufstad@utep.edu

www.utep.edu/music

Programs of study include music education,
performance, theory and composition, conducting and music theater.

UNIVERSITY OF TEXAS AT HOUSTON
MOORES SCHOOL OF MUSIC
Suite 120
Houston, TX 77204
David Ashley White
713-743-3009
Fax: 713-743-3166
www.uth.tmc.edu

UNIVERSITY OF TEXAS AT SAN ANTONIO
DIVISION OF MUSIC
6900 North Loop
1604 West
San Antonio, TX 78249
Joe Stuessy
210-458-4355
Fax: 210-458-4381
http://utsa.edu

Outstanding artist faculty in beautiful facility,
including recital hall, theater, classrooms, and
soundproof practice rooms.

WEST TEXAS A&M UNIVERSITY
DEPARTMENT OF MUSIC AND DANCE
WT P.O. Box 60879
Canyon, TX 79015
Ted Dubois
806-651-2840
Fax: 806-651-2958
E-mail: tdubois@mail.wtamu.edu
www.wtamu.edu

UTAH

Population: 2,438,132 (2003 Estimate)

Capital City: Salt Lake City

Music Colleges and Universities: Brigham Young University, College of Eastern Utah, Dixie State College, University of Utah, Utah State University

Bird: California Seagull

Motto: Industry

Flower: Sego lily

Tree: Blue Spruce

Residents Called: Utahns

Origin of Name: Taken from the name of the Ute Indians, whose name means "people of the mountains."

Area: 84,904 square miles (13th largest state)

Statehood: January 4, 1896 (45th state)

Largest Cities: Salt Lake City, West Valley City, Provo, Sandy, Orem, Ogden, West Jordan, Layton, Taylorsville, St. George

College Band Programs: University of Utah

UTAH

BRIGHAM YOUNG UNIVERSITY
DEPARTMENT OF MUSIC

C-550 HFAC
Provo, UT 84602
Mike Ohman
801-422-3749
E-mail: michael_ohman@byu.edu
www.byu.edu

Brigham Young University — founded, supported, and guided by The Church of Jesus Christ of Latter-day Saints — is dedicated to educating the whole person through a synthesis of spiritual and professional education. The university seeks to enhance not only the intellectual lives but also the social, cultural and spiritual lives of its students. Through these students, as well as its faculty and facilities, BYU symbolizes one of the Church's fundamental articles of faith: "We believe in being honest, true, chaste, benevolent, virtuous, and in doing good to all men...If there is anything virtuous, lovely, or of good report or praiseworthy, we seek after these things." The art of music — as expressed through performance, composition, and teaching or communication media — is built on a foundation of knowledge and skills. Knowledge comes from study and research in music theory, literature, history and performance practices as well as from study in other arts and sciences. Skills come from applying knowledge to the instrument or voice and developing the tools of musicianship. The mission of the School of Music is to offer quality instruction that will enable students to think clearly about diverse kinds of music and to create, perform and teach music well. We strive to develop strong moral character, leading students to lifelong learning and service. The School of Music is housed in the Harris Fine Arts Center, a comprehensive complex that includes five theatres, a piano lab, organ lab, computer music lab, recording studio, several libraries and many practice rooms and classrooms. Additional large rehearsal spaces and teaching studios for music, dance, theatre and media music students are found in the Knight Mangum Building. BYU's School of Music is comprehensive, with 50 full-time and 49 part-time faculty teaching private instruction, ensembles, education, music theory and history and conducting, plus other exciting fields of study. Our focus is on cultivating individual talents and fostering some of the country's most respected music ensembles.

COLLEGE OF EASTERN UTAH
DEPARTMENT OF MUSIC

451 East 400 N.
Price, UT 84501
Gregory Benson
435-613-5378
Fax: 435-613-4102
E-mail: gbenson@ceu.edu
www.ceu.edu

DIXIE STATE COLLEGE
MUSIC DEPARTMENT

St. George, UT 84770
Gary Caldwell
435-652-7997
Fax: 435-656-4026
E-mail: caldwell@dixie.edu
www.dixie.edu

DSC Music Department fills the first two years for music majors or minors. Courses offered include first- and second-year music theory and ear-training; four choral ensembles, including college chorus, chamber singers, women's choir and southwest chorale; two orchestras, including chamber orchestra and southwest symphony; three bands, including symphonic band, jazz ensemble and jazz combo; woodwind choir; brass choir; private study for majors/minors.

UNIVERSITY OF UTAH
SCHOOL OF MUSIC

1375 E. Presidents Cir.
204 DGH
Salt Lake City, UT 84112-0030
Robert Walzel
801-581-6762
Fax: 801-581-5683
E-mail: robert.walzel@music.utah.edu
www.music.utah.edu

Degrees: B.M. – Performance, Music
Education, Composition, Music Theory, Music
History and Literature; B.A. in Music M.A. in
Musicology; M.M. – Performance, Music
Education, Conducting, Composition, Music
Theory, Music History; Ph.D. – Music
Education, Composition

A comprehensive music school located in the
beautiful Salt Lake Valley, the University of
Utah School of Music is a fully accredited
member of the NASM. A faculty of leading
scholars, composers and performers, including
several members of the Utah Symphony
Orchestra, support programs of the school of
music. Graduates have distinguished themselves through careers including those as members of major symphony orchestras, as performers with professional opera and music
theater companies, as university professors,
and as public school teachers. Serving primarily students from Utah, and the inter-Mountain
West, the School of Music enrolls students
from many of the United States as well as
countries in Europe, Asia and South America.

UTAH STATE UNIVERSITY
MUSIC DEPARTMENT

4015 Old Main Hill
Logan, UT 84322
435-797-3028
Fax: 435-797-1826
E-mail: musicdep@cc.usu.edu
www.music.usu.edu
Weber State University
Department of Music
1905 University Circle
Ogden, UT 84408-1905
Dr. Michael A. Palumbo
801-626-6437
www.weber.edu

Degrees: Bachelor of Music, Bachelor of
Music Education, Bachelor of Music in
Performance, Bachelor of Music in Keyboard
Pedagogy, Bachelor of Music in Vocal
Pedagogy , Music Minor, Music Honors

WESTMINSTER COLLEGE
DEPARTMENT OF MUSIC

1840 South 1300 East
Salt Lake City, UT 84105
801-832-2437 or 800-748-4753
E-mail: c-quinn@wcslc.edu
www.wcslc.edu
Degree: Minor only in Music

VERMONT

Population: 620,987 (2003 Estimate)

Capital City: Montpelier

Music Colleges and Universities: Bennington College, Middlebury College, University of Vermont

Bird: Hermit Thrush

Motto: Freedom and unity

Flower: Red Clover

Tree: Sugar Maple

Residents Called: Vermonters

Origin of Name: Based on "verts monts," French for green mountains.

Area: 9,615 square mile (45th largest state)

Statehood: March 4, 1791

Largest Cities: Burlington, Essex, Rutland, Colchester, South Burlington, Bennington, Brattleboro, Hartford, Milton, Barre

VERMONT

BENNINGTON COLLEGE

Route 67A
Dickinson Building
Bennington, VT 05201
Stephen Siegel
802-440-4610
Fax: 802-440-4511
www.bennington.edu

CASTLETON STATE COLLEGE
DEPARTMENT OF MUSIC

Castleton, VT 05735
802-468-5611
Fax: 802-468-5237
E-mail: information@castleton.edu
www.csc.vsc.edu

Degrees: Bachelor of Arts in Music Education
(BAMUSED), Bachelor of Arts in Music
(BAMUS). Music Education majors specialize
in Instrumental, Choral, or Elementary Music;
Minor in Music

GREEN MOUNTAIN COLLEGE
VISUAL AND PERFORMING ARTS DEPARTMENT

One College Cir.
Poultney, Vermont 05764-1199
800-776-6675
Fax: 802-287-8099
E-mail: www.GreenMtn.edu
www.greenmtn.edu

Degrees: B.A., and Visual and Performing Arts
with a music concentration

JOHNSON STATE COLLEGE
ARTS DEPARTMENT

337 College Hill
Johnson VT 05656
800-635-2356
Fax: 802-635-1230
E-mail: jscapply@badger.jsc.vsc.edu
www.jsc.vsc.edu
Degree: B.A. Music

MIDDLEBURY COLLEGE
MUSIC DEPARTMENT

Room 307, Center for the Arts
Middlebury, VT 05753
Deborah Young
802-443-5221
Fax: 802-443-2057
E-mail: young@middlebury.edu
www.middlebury.edu/~music

UNIVERSITY OF VERMONT
MUSIC DEPARTMENT

Redstone Campus
Burlington, VT 05405
David Neiweem
802-656-3040
Fax: 802-656-7895
E-mail: music@zoo.uvm.edu
www.uvm.edu/~music

VIRGINIA

Population: 7,385,529 (2003 Estimate)

Capital City: Richmond

Music Colleges and Universities: Armed Forces School of Music, Bridgewater College, College of William and Mary, Ferrum College, George Mason University, Hollins University, James Madison University, Mary Washington College, Norfolk State University, Old Dominion University, Radford University, Randolph-Macon Woman's College, Roanoke College, Shenandoah University, University of Richmond, University of Virginia, Virginia Commonwealth University, Virginia Tech, Virginia Union University, Virginia Wesleyan College, Washington and Lee University

Bird: Cardinal

Motto: Sic Semper Tyrannis – Thus Always to Tyrants

Flower: Dogwood

Tree: Dogwood

Residents Called: Virginians

Origin of Name: Named for England's "Virgin Queen," Elizabeth I.

Area: 42,769 square miles (35th largest state)

Statehood: June 25, 1788 (10th state)

Largest Cities: Virginia Beach, Norfolk, Chesapeake, Richmond, Newport News, Arlington, Hampton, Alexandria, Portsmouth, Roanoke

College Band Programs: James Madison University, Liberty University, University of Virginia, Virginia Tech

VIRGINIA

ARMED FORCES SCHOOL OF MUSIC

1420 Gator Blvd.
Norfolk, VA 23521-2617
George N. Thompson
757-462-7501
Fax: 757-462-7294
E-mail: SOM.00@cnet.navy.mil
www.cnet.navy.mil/som

Located aboard the Naval Amphibious Base in Norfolk, the Armed Forces School of Music provides specialized training for selected personnel of the Army, Navy, and Marine Corps, and is the first stop after basic training for instrumentalists and vocalists seeking to join the ranks of America's military bands. This unique facility, the largest of its kind in the world, provides basic to advanced levels of instruction geared toward preparing soldiers, sailors and marines for the challenges of performance within a wide variety of military ensembles. Graduates of the Armed Forces School of Music go on to become musical ambassadors throughout the United States and abroad as members of U.S. Army, Navy and Marine Corps bands.

BRIDGEWATER COLLEGE
DEPARTMENT OF MUSIC

402 E. College St.
Bridgewater, VA 22812
Dr. Jesse Hopkins
540-828-5303
Fax: 540-828-5637
E-mail: jhopkins@bridgewater.edu
www.bridgewater.edu

Degrees: B.A. in music or in music education; minors in church music and music business

The music department at Bridgewater College serves the various needs of the academic community with the Carter Center for worship and music as the site of most musical activity.

Students from all majors are invited to participate in one or more of the choral, instrumental or chamber ensembles, and private study is available to singers and players. Students who choose music as a career may focus on performance and/or elect to gain certification to teach vocal or instrumental music in the public schools. A special concentration in church music is offered and supported by the College's strong choral tradition and outstanding rehearsal and performance facilities for organists. Regular study and performance tours to international centers of music are a part of the music curriculum.

COLLEGE OF WILLIAM AND MARY
DEPARTMENT OF MUSIC

P.O. Box 8795
Williamsburg, VA 23187
Katherine Preston
757-221-1071
Fax: 757-221-3171
E-mail: eacova@wm.edu
www.wm.edu

FERRUM COLLEGE
PERFORMING AND VISUAL ARTS

Ferrum, VA 24088
Dr. Jody D. Brown
540-364-4354
Fax: 540-364-4203
E-mail: erose@ferrum.edu
www.ferrum.edu

GEORGE MASON UNIVERSITY
COLLEGE OF VISUAL AND PERFORMING ARTS

MSN 3E3
4400 University Dr.
Fairfax, VA 22030-4444
Ms. Wendy Basinger
703-993-1380

Fax: 703-993-1394
E-mail: music@gmu.edu
www.gmu.edu/departments/music

Degrees: B.M., B.A., M.M., D.A. and Ph.D.

Located 15 miles outside of the nation's capital, George Mason University is in the heart of one of the richest cultural centers in the US. The Music Department offers a B.M. in performance and music education; B.A. in music, minor in jazz studies, M.M. in performance, music education, conducting, and composition. Also offers a D.A. in community college education with a concentration in music, and a PhD. in education with a minor in music.

Part of the college of visual and performing arts, the Music Department boasts over 50 nationally and internationally recognized full-time and part-time artist-faculty instructors. Continual seminars workshops, master classes, and courses in music and wellness are prominent features of the curriculum. Over 100 student and faculty performances are given annually on campus throughout the capital region. Venues include a 2,000-seat concert hall and a 500-seat theatre. In addition to the rigorous academic curriculum, the department hosts exciting national events including the National Trump Competition, Saxophone Symposium, and one of the nation's largest Orff Schulwerk Certification programs for music educations. Auditions required. For more information and audition dates contact the Music Department.

HOLLINS UNIVERSITY
MUSIC DEPARTMENT

P.O. Box 9643
Roanoke, VA 24020
Judith Cline
540-362-6514
Fax: 540-362-6218
E-mail: jcline@hollins.edu
www.hollins.edu/undergrad/music/music.htm

JAMES MADISON UNIVERSITY
SCHOOL OF MUSIC

800 S. Main St.
Harrisonburg, VA 22807
Dr. Mellasenah Y. Morris
540-568-3851
Fax: 540-568-7819
E-mail: music_admit@jmu.edu
www.jmu.edu/music

MARY WASHINGTON COLLEGE
DEPARTMENT OF MUSIC

Pollard 110
1301 College Ave.
Fredericksburg, VA 22401
Patricia Norwwod
540-654-1012
Fax: 540-654-1966
E-mail: pnorwood@mwc.edu
www.mwc.edu/musc

Degrees: B. A. in Music

Mary Washington College allows students to earn a liberal arts degree in music in a challenging academic environment. The music department offers unusual breadth of opportunities for the major, double major, or non-major who wishes to remain an active performer at the collegiate level. The music training allows alumni to pursue graduate degrees in the field, teach in the public schools, join the music management environment or open their own studios. The music facility, Pollard Hall, contains a recital hall, classrooms, teaching studios, practice rooms, rehearsal space for large ensembles, and an audio library while contiguous Dupont Hall contains the electronic music studio.

NORFOLK STATE UNIVERSITY
MARKETING
700 Parks Ave.
Norfolk, VA 23504
Cecilia Ramirez
757-823-8373
Fax: 757-823-8544
E-mail: cramirez@nsu.edu
www.nsu.edu

OLD DOMINION UNIVERSITY
DEPARTMENT OF MUSIC
Hampton Blvd.
Norfolk, VA 23529
Dennis Zeisler
757-683-4061
Fax: 757-683-5000
E-mail: dzeisler@odu.edu
www.odu.edu/al/music

RADFORD UNIVERSITY
DEPARTMENT OF MUSIC
E. Main St.
Radford, VA 24142
Eugene C. Fellin
540-831-5177
Fax: 540-831-6133
E-mail: efellin@radford.edu
www.radford.edu/~musc-web
Degrees: B.M., B.A., B.S., M.A., M.S.

The undergraduate professional music program at Radford University offers opportunities for students to prepare for careers as teachers of music in elementary, middle, and secondary schools; for careers in music therapy for careers in music business; and for advanced professional graduate study. The undergraduate liberal arts program in the department of music offers opportunities for the study of music irrespective of specific career aspirations, for emphases, which may meet the needs of individual students, and for

preparation to study music at the graduate level. The department provides and promotes music activities for the university and community; and provides instruction and experiences in music for majors and non-majors, enhanced by multi-cultural perspectives and the benefits of new technology.

The Master of Arts program provides advanced study for musicians and music scholars in preparation for professional careers or doctoral study. The Master of Science program provides advanced study and opportunities for music therapists to refine existing competencies and to attain new ones.

RANDOLPH-MACON WOMAN'S COLLEGE
ADMISSIONS DEPARTMENT
2500 Rivermont Ave.
Lynchburg, VA 24503
Pat LeDonne
434-947-8100
Fax: 434-947-8138
E-mail: pledonne@rmwc.edu
www.rmwc.edu

ROANOKE COLLEGE
FINE ARTS DEPARTMENT
221 College Lane
Salem, VA 24153
Dr. Bruce L. Partin
540-375-2096
Fax: 540-375-2354
E-mail: partin@roanoke.edu
www.roanoke.edu

SHENANDOAH UNIVERSITY
1460 UNIVERSITY DR.
Winchester, VA 22601
Charlotte Collins
800-432-2266
Fax: 540-665-4627

E-mail: ccollins@su.edu
www.su.edu

Shenandoah Conservatory offers intense, specialized, professional training in instrumental and vocal music, theatre and dance. Students work with a faculty of active professionals as they develop artistically and intellectually for careers in the performing arts. Programs of study lead to over 30 degrees at the undergraduate and graduate levels. Shenandoah Conservatory offers dozens of ensemble experiences, from jazz to dance and opera. Students perform throughout the region, including regional concerts at the Kennedy Center in Washington, D.C., and at universities and public schools throughout the Mid-Atlantic region and New York. The Ohrstrom-Bryant Theatre/Ruebush Complex is a hub for vocal music programs and the theatre program. In addition to a 630-seat auditorium, the Ohrstrom-Bryant Theatre Complex houses the intimate Glaize Studio for children's theatre, as well as rehearsal space, make-up rooms, scene and costume shops. Ruebush Hall houses instructional space, faculty studios, practice rooms, choral and band rehearsal halls, a digital recording studio and a musical instrument digital interface (MIDI) laboratory. The newly renovated Armstrong Hall is home to the instrumental music programs with faculty and practice studios and a 550-seat auditorium. Singleton Hall houses the Dorothy Ewing Dance Studio, the dance program and a black box theatre.

UNIVERSITY OF RICHMOND
DEPARTMENT OF MUSIC

28 Westhampton Way
Richmond, VA 23173
Gene Anderson
804-289-8277
Fax: 804-287-6814
E-mail: ganderso@richmond.edu
www.music.richmond.edu

UNIVERSITY OF VIRGINIA
MCINTIRE DEPARTMENT OF MUSIC

Charlottesville, VA 22903
Walter Ross
804-924-3052
Fax: 804-924-6033
E-mail: music@virginia.edu
www.virginia.edu/~music/index.html

VIRGINIA COMMONWEALTH UNIVERSITY
DEPARTMENT OF MUSIC

922 Park Ave.
Richmond, VA 23285
JoAnne Welling
804-828-1166
Fax: 804-237-0230
E-mail: lsjohnst@saturn.vcu.edu
www.vcu.edu/artweb/Music

VIRGINIA TECH
DEPARTMENT OF MUSIC

241 Squires
Blacksburg, VA 24060
David Widder
540-231-5685
Fax: 540-231-5034
E-mail: dwidder@vt.edu
www.music.vt.edu

The Virginia Tech Music Department provides high-quality training to a select number of music majors, as well as ensembles and courses for large numbers of non-music majors. Instruction takes place in a handsome modern facility which has superb rehearsal rooms, well-designed practice rooms and music teaching studios, a beautiful, acoustically engineered recital salon, and laboratories with state-of-the-art electronic equipment for music study, recording and digital music. The curriculum offers an excellent liberal arts education with a low professor/student ratio combined with the library, computer facilities and cultural interaction which only a major, comprehensive university can provide. Learning is enhanced by the use of music technology across the curriculum and innovative programs in performance, music education and theory/composition. Students may design a degree plan combining music with virtually all other majors offered by the university. Virginia Tech faculty artists and scholars have performed and lectured at conventions, in music festivals and on concert series throughout the United States and in Canada, Europe, Asia and South America.

VIRGINIA UNION UNIVERSITY
Music Department

1500 North Lombardy St.
Richmond, VA 23220
Dr. Willis Barnett
804-347-5929
Fax: 804-354-5929
www.vuu.edu

The department of music at VUU is a small and intimate, one-on-one instruction, family-oriented department with an excellent faculty with loads of musical experience and expertise.

VIRGINIA WESLEYAN COLLEGE
Music Department

1584 Wesleyan Dr.
Norfolk, VA 23502
804-455-3200
Fax: 804-461-5025
E-mail: ljordananders@vwc.edu
www.vwc.edu

WASHINGTON AND LEE UNIVERSITY
Department of Music

Lexington, VA 24450
Timothy Gaylard
540-463-8855
Fax: 540-463-8104
http://music.wlu.edu

WASHINGTON

Population: 6,254,397 (2003 Estimate)

Capital City: Olympia

Music Colleges and Universities: Central Washington University, Eastern Washington University, Renton Technical College, Seattle Pacific University, University of Puget Sound, University of Washington School of Music, Washington State University, Western Washington University, Whitman College

Bird: Willow Goldfinch

Motto: Alki – Bye and Bye

Flower: Pink Rhododendron

Tree: Western Hemlock

Residents Called: Washingtonians

Origin of Name: Named after George Washington.

Area: 71,303 square miles (18th largest state)

Statehood: November 11, 1889 (42nd state)

Largest Cities: Seattle, Spokan, Tacoma, Vancouver, Bellevue, Everett, Federal Way, Kent, Yakima, Bellingham

College Band Programs: University of Washington, Washington State University

WASHINGTON

CENTRAL WASHINGTON UNIVERSITY
DEPARTMENT OF MUSIC

400 East 8th Ave.
Ellensburg, WA 98922-7450
Dr. Peter Gries
509-963-1216
Fax: 509-963-1239
E-mail: griesp@cwu.edu
www.cwu.edu/~music

Degrees: B.M., B.A., and M.M.

The Music Department provided opportunities for all students to develop into self-sufficient, secure and well-informed musicians and attempts to instill in them an aspiration for continual growth in knowledge and acquisition of skills. Academic coursework, ensemble experience and applied music study are directed to these goals. The department's ensembles are particularly strong, with its major groups being invited consistently to regional and national professional meetings. We have two wind ensembles, orchestras, chamber orchestra, chamber choir, choir, three jazz bands, three jazz choirs and many smaller groups all performing each quarter. Our composition program focuses on cutting edge technology, such as composing with Palm Pilots. The department has about 265 majors, with have being in music education, 75 in performance, 15 each in composition and music business and 12-14 graduate students. The music faculty is highly active in performance and professional service and takes ride in supporting the needs of each student.

EASTERN WASHINGTON UNIVERSITY
MUSIC DEPARTMENT, MS-100

526 5th St.
Cheney, WA 99004-2431
Colleen Hegney
509-359-2241
Fax: 509-359-7028
E-mail: chegney@ewu.edu
www.ewu.edu

RENTON TECHNICAL COLLEGE
MUSICAL INSTRUMENT REPAIR

3000 N.E. Fourth St.
Renton, WA 98056
Daryl L. Hickman
425-235-2453
Fax: 425-235-7832
E-mail: dhickman@rtc.ctc.edu
www.renton-tc.ctc.edu

SEATTLE PACIFIC UNIVERSITY
DEPARTMENT OF MUSIC

3307 Third Ave. West
Seattle, WA 98119
Romona Holmes
206-281-3415
Fax: 206-281-2771
E-mail: ramonaho@spu.edu
www.spu.edu

UNIVERSITY OF PUGET SOUND
SCHOOL OF MUSIC

1500 North Warner St.
Tacoma, WA 98416
Keith Ward
253-879-3730
Fax: 253-879-2906
E-mail: kward@ups.edu
www.ups.edu

UNIVERSITY OF WASHINGTON
SCHOOL OF MUSIC

P.O. Box 353450
Seattle, WA 98195
Robin Mccabe
206-543-1201

Fax: 206-685-9499
E-mail: mccabe@u.washington.edu
www.music.washington.edu

WASHINGTON STATE UNIVERSITY
MUSIC AND THEATRE ARTS
P.O. Box 645300
Pullman, WA 99164
Dr. James Schoepflin
509-335-7757
Fax: 509-335-4245
E-mail: music_and_theatre@wsu.edu
http://wsu.edu/MusicandTheatre
WSU music activities are located in
beautiful, newly enlarged and remodeled
Kimbrough Hall, with multiple perform-
ance spaces, state-of-the-art recording
studio and world-class music library.
Western Washington University

DEPARTMENT OF MUSIC
516 High St.
MS 9107
Bellingham, WA 98225-9107
Judy Korski
360-650-3130
Fax: 360-650-7538
E-mail: judy.korski@cc.wwu.edu
www.wwu.edu/music
Degrees: B.A., B.M., and M.M.

The department of music has a heritage, which
reaches back to the founding of Whatcom
Normal School in 1893. for years, its superb
faculty of artist-teachers has prepared students
with the comprehensive knowledge and skill to
meet the demands of artist, teacher, composer,
historian, arranger, and scholar. All music
majors receive applied study with a large faculty of artist-teachers. At WWU the relationship
between scholarly study and performance
blends emerging and established talent in a
unique environment.

The facilities include a 700-seat concert hall,
two large rehearsal halls, classrooms, computer
assisted instruction lab, electronic music studio, practice rooms, ensemble libraries, faculty
offices and the music library.

WHITMAN COLLEGE
DEPARTMENT OF MUSIC
345 Boyer Ave.
Walla Walla, WA 99362
Edward Dixon
509-527-4981
Fax: 509-527-4925
E-mail: muzzall@whitman.edu
www.whitman.edu

WASHINGTON D.C

Population: 560,561 (2003 Estimate)

Music Colleges and Universities: American University, Benjamin T. Rome School of Music, Catholic University of America, George Washington University, Georgetown University, Howard University, Levine School of Music, Mount Vernon College, Trinity College, University of the District of Columbia

Marching Bands: Georgetown University

WASHINGTON, D.C.

AMERICAN UNIVERSITY
DEPARTMENT OF PERFORMING ARTS
4400 Massachusetts Ave. N.W
Washington, DC 20016
Daniel E. Abraham
202-885-3420
Fax: 202-885-1092
E-mail: dabrowski@american.edu
www.american.edu

BENJAMIN T. ROME
SCHOOL OF MUSIC
Washington, DC 20064
Mary A. O'Connor
202-319-5834
Fax: 202-319-6533
E-mail: oconnor@cua.edu
www.cua.edu

CATHOLIC UNIVERSITY OF AMERICA
SCHOOL OF MUSIC
Benjamin T. Rome School of Music
620 Michigan Ave. N.E.
Washington, DC 20064
Marilyn Neeley
202-313-5414
Fax: 202-313-6280
E-mail: neeley@cua.edu
http://music.cua.edu

GEORGE WASHINGTON UNIVERSITY
DEPARTMENT OF MUSIC
801 22nd St. N.W.
Phillips Hall, B-144
Washington, DC 20052
Roy Guenther

202-994-6245
Fax: 202-994-9038
E-mail: gwmusic@gwu.edu
www.gwu.edu/~music/index.html

GEORGETOWN UNIVERSITY
DEPARTMENT OF ART, MUSIC AND THEATER
Washington, DC 20057
Jose A. Bowen
202-687-0969
www.georgetown.edu

HOWARD UNIVERSITY
DEPARTMENT OF MUSIC
2455 6th St. N.W.
Washington, DC 20059
Thomas A. Korth
202-806-7082
Fax: 202-806-9673
www.howard.edu

LEVINE SCHOOL OF MUSIC
ADMISSIONS OFFICE
2801 Upton St. N.W.
Washington, DC 20017
Admissions Office
202-686-9772
Fax: 202-686-9773
E-mail: lnarvey@levineschool.org
www.levineschool.org

MOUNT VERNON COLLEGE
DEPARTMENT OF PERFORMING ARTS
2100 Foxhall Rd. N.W.
Washington, DC 20007
Stanley Wood
202-625-4541
E-mail: swood@mvnc.edu
www.mvc.gwu.edu

TRINITY COLLEGE
FINE ARTS PROGRAM - MUSIC
125 Michigan Ave. N.E.
Washington, DC 20017
Sharon Shafer
202-884-9252
Fax: 202-884-9229
E-mail: Shafers@trinitydc.edu
www.trinitydc.edu

UNIVERSITY OF THE DISTRICT OF COLUMBIA
MUSIC PROGRAM
4200 Connecticut Ave. N.W.
MB 4601
Washington, DC 20008
Beverly Anderson
202-274-5802
Fax: 202-274-5589
www.udc.edu

WEST VIRGINIA

Population: 1,808,598 (2003 Estimate)

Capital City: Charleston

Music Colleges and Universities: Alderson-Broaddus College, Fairmont State College, Marshall University, Shepherd College, University of Charleston, West Virginia University

Bird: Cardinal

Motto: Montani semper liberi: Mountaineers are always free

Flower: Rhododendron

Tree: Sugar Maple

Residents Called: West Virginians

Origin of Name: Named after England's Queen Elizabeth I, the "Virgin Queen."

Area: 24,231 square miles (41st largest state)

Statehood: June 20, 1863 (35th state)

Largest Cities: Charleston, Huntington, Parkersburg, Wheeling, Morgantown, Weirton, Fairmont, Beckley, Clarksburg, Martinsburg

College Band Programs: Marshall University

WEST VIRGINIA

ALDERSON-BROADDUS COLLEGE
DEPARTMENT OF MUSIC
College Hill Rd.
Philippi, WV 26416
Kim Klaus
304-457-6200
Fax: 304-457-6239
E-mail: klauskn@mail.ab.edu
www.ab.edu

Approximately 60 music majors are enrolled in the music programs at Alderson-Broaddus College, a four-year liberal arts institution affiliated with the West Virginia and American Baptist Conventions. There are seven full-time persons and a number of adjunct faculty persons. The music department is located in Wilcox Chapel, which houses a concert/recital hall (also used as a worship venue), classrooms, faculty studios and practice rooms. Students use a well-equipped piano/computer electronic music laboratory. Featured ensembles include a regionally recognized concert choir, The West Virginians (a semi-professional show choir), chapel choir, brass choir, concert band, jazz ensemble and hand bell choir. Auditions are required for entrance. Music scholarships are available.

BETHANY COLLEGE
BETHANY, WV 26032
800-922-7611
http://info.bethany.wvnet.edu
Degrees: B.A. and minor in music.

CONCORD COLLEGE
MUSIC DEPARTMENT
P.O. Box 1000
Athens, WV 24712
888-384-5249
Fax: 304-384-9044
www.concord.wvnet.edu
Degrees: B.A. in music.

FAIRMONT STATE COLLEGE
FINE ARTS DEPARTMENT
1201 Locust Ave.
Fairmont, WV 26554
Dr. Suzanne T Snyder
800-641-5678
Fax: 304-366-4248
E-mail: tsnyder@mail.fscwv.edu
www.fscwv.edu

GLENVILLE STATE COLLEGE
DIVISION OF FINE ARTS
200 High St.
Glenville, WV 26351
800-924-2010
E-mail: visitor@glenville
www.glenville.edu

Degrees: Music Education (K-12) major as well as music minor

MARSHALL UNIVERSITY
DEPARTMENT OF MUSIC
Huntington, WV 25701
Dr. Vicki Stroeher
304-696-3117
Fax: 304-696-4379
E-mail: stroeherv@marshall.edu
www.marshall.edu/music

OHIO VALLEY COLLEGE

Parkersburg, WV 26101
304-485-7384
www.ovc.edu

Degrees: Minor in music, Associate of Arts Degree.

SHEPHERD COLLEGE
MUSIC DEPARTMENT

Shepherdstown, WV 25443
Mark McCoy
304-876-5223
Fax: 304-876-0955
E-mail: mccoy@shepherd.edu
www.shepherd.edu/musicweb

UNIVERSITY OF CHARLESTON
DEPARTMENT OF MUSIC

2300 MacCorkle Ave. S.E.
Charleston, WV 25304
Joseph Janisch
304-357-4905
Fax: 304-357-4715
E-mail: jjanisch@uchaswv
www.uchaswv.edu/music

WEST VIRGINIA UNIVERSITY
DIVISION OF MUSIC

Evansdale Dr.
P.O. Box 6111
Morgantown, WV 26506
Jodie Marie Lewis
304-293-4617
Fax: 304-293-7491
www.wvu.edu/music

WEST VIRGINIA WESLEYAN COLLEGE
MUSIC DEPARTMENT

59 College Ave.
Buckhannon, WV 26201
www.wvwc.edu

Degrees: The Bachelor of Music Education degree serves those who are preparing for the teaching profession, and the Bachelor of Arts degree accommodates those pursuing a liberal arts degree or wishing to emphasize a particular aspect of music, such as performance or theory in their study. Various options for a contract major combining music with other disciplines, such as business or Christian education, are possible. All curricula offered provide a strong foundation for graduate study. Minor in music also offered.

WISCONSIN

Population: 5,501,052 (2003 Estimate)

Capital City: Madison

Music Colleges and Universities: Alverno College, Cardinal Stritch University, Carroll College, International Fine Arts Institute, Lawrence University, Mount Mary College, Ripon College, Silver Lake College, St. Norbert College, University of Wisconsin at Eau Claire, University of Wisconsin at Green Bay, University of Wisconsin at La Crosse, University of Wisconsin at Madison, University of Wisconsin at Milwaukee, University of Wisconsin at Oshkosh, University of Wisconsin at Parkside, University of Wisconsin at Platteville, University of Wisconsin at River Falls, University of Wisconsin at Stevens Point, University of Wisconsin at Superior, University of Wisconsin at Whitewater, Waukesha County Conservatory of Music, Wisconsin Conservatory of Music

Bird: Robin

Motto: Forward

Flower: Wood Violet

Tree: Sugar Maple

Residents Called: Wisconsinites

Origin of Name: Based on an Indian word "Ouisconsin" believed to mean "grassy place" in the Cheppewa tongue.

Area: 65,503 square miles (23rd largest state)

Statehood: May 29, 1848 (30th state)

Largest Cities: Milwaukee, Madison, Green Bay, Kenosha, Racine, Appleton, Waukesha, Oshkosh, Eau Claire, West Allis

College Band Programs: University of Wisconsin-Eau Claire, University of Wisconsin-Madison

WISCONSIN

ALVERNO COLLEGE
DEPARTMENT OF MUSIC
3400 South 43rd St.
Milwaukee, WI 53234
Diane Knight
414-382-6130
E-mail: admissions@alverno.edu
www.alverno.edu

CARDINAL STRITCH UNIVERSITY
MUSIC DEPARTMENT
6801 N. Yates Rd.
Milwaukee, WI 53217
Dennis King
414-410-4349
Fax: 414-410-4239
www.stritch.edu

CARROLL COLLEGE
MUSIC DEPARTMENT
100 N.E. Ave.
Waukesha, WI 53186
Dr. Larry Harper
262-547-1211
Fax: 414-524-7139
E-mail: lharper@cc.edu
www.cc.edu

INTERNATIONAL FINE ARTS INSTITUTE
1453 Norridge Trail
Port Washington, WI 53074
George Gordon
414-284-4221
www.aii.edu

LAWRENCE UNIVERSITY
MUSIC CONSERVATORY
420 E. College Ave.
Appleton, WI 54911
Ellen Mitala
920-832-7000
E-mail: ellen.m.mitala@lawrence.edu
www.lawrence.edu/conservatory

MOUNT MARY COLLEGE
DEPARTMENT OF MUSIC
2900 N. Menomonee River Pkwy.
Milwaukee, WI 53222
Sister Rita Schweitzer
414-258-4810
Fax: 414-256-0180
E-mail: schweitr@mtmary.edu
www.mtmary.edu

Mount Mary is a liberal arts college located on a beautiful 80-acre campus. The Music Department has spacious studios and practice facilities. It is known for its annual Christmas Madrigal Dinner concert, which features madrigal singers, hand bells, string ensemble and recorder consort.

RIPON COLLEGE
DEPARTMENT OF MUSIC
300 Seward St.
Ripon, WI 54971
Kurt Dietrich
920-748-8115
Fax: 920-748-8181
E-mail: dietrichk@ripon.edu
www.ripon.edu/academics/music

SILVER LAKE COLLEGE
PUBLIC INFORMATION OFFICE
2406 South Alberno Rd.
Manitowoc, WI 54220
Candice Griffith
920-686-6173
Fax: 920-864-7082
E-mail: cgriff@silver.sl.edu
www.sl.edu

ST. NORBERT COLLEGE
OFFICE OF ADMISSION
100 Grant St.
De Pere, WI 54115
Daniel L. Mayer
920-403-3007
Fax: 920-403-4072
E-mail: daniel.meyer@snc.edu
www.snc.edu/admit

St. Norbert College is a small liberal arts college located on the scenic banks of the Fox River. One of the hallmarks of the college is an opportunity for the students to form strong, lasting relationships with the members of the faculty. Since we have developed a remarkably successful placement rate, our graduates have achieved recognition statewide and beyond. Our four-year certification program attracts a growing number of students. St. Norbert College is one of only a few liberal art schools its size, which offers a large number of quality performing ensembles for all students. Our ensembles have toured the U.S., Europe and the South Pacific.

UNIVERSITY OF WISCONSIN AT EAU CLAIRE
DEPT OF MUSIC AND THEATRE ARTS
Eau Claire, WI 54702
Dr. David Baker
715-836-2284
Fax: 715-836-3952
E-mail: bakerda@uwec.edu
www.uwec.edu

UNIVERSITY OF WISCONSIN AT GREEN BAY
GREEN BAY SUMMER MUSIC CAMPS
Office of Outreach and Extension
WH-480, 2420 Nicolet Dr.
Green Bay, WI 54311
Cheryl Grosso
414-465-2267
Fax: 414-465-2890
www.uwgb.edu

UNIVERSITY OF WISCONSIN AT LA CROSSE
DEPARTMENT OF MUSIC
1725 State St.
La Crosse, WI 54601
Gary Walth
608-785-8414
Fax: 608-785-6719
E-mail: walth@mail.uwlax.edu
www.uwlax.edu

UNIVERSITY OF WISCONSIN AT MADISON

DEPARTMENT OF MUSIC

720 Lowell Hall
Madison, WI 53703
608-263-5615
Fax: 608-262-8876
E-mail: music@mhub.music.wisc.edu
www.wisc.edu/music

UNIVERSITY OF WISCONSIN AT MILWAUKEE

FINE ARTS AND MUSIC

3223 N. Downer Ave.
Milwaukee, WI 53211
Michael Alexander
414-229-4393
Fax: 414-229-2776
E-mail: semm@aol.com
www.uwm.edu/sfa

UNIVERSITY OF WISCONSIN AT OSHKOSH

DEPARTMENT OF MUSIC

800 Algoma Blvd.
Oshkosh, WI 54901
Dr. Andre Gullickson
920-424-4224
Fax: 920-424-1266
www.uwosh.edu

The University of Wisconsin-Oshkosh
Department of Music offers programs which
are designed to prepare students for a variety
of professional opportunities. These programs
lead to degrees in music education, music therapy, music business, recording technology and
performance. All programs are accredited by
the National Association of Schools of Music.
Our music staff consists of 22 full-time and 10
part-time professional musicians and teachers,
a number that allows for a high degree of individual attention to our almost 200 music

majors and minors. The music facilities at UW-
Oshkosh are among the finest in the nation. In
addition to spacious rehearsal rooms and
numerous practice facilities, there is a state-of-
the-art recording studio and a highly-
acclaimed performance hall. The music department is part of the College of Letters and
Science's Division of Fine and Performing Arts,
which makes possible interdisciplinary activities with the art and theater areas.

UNIVERSITY OF WISCONSIN AT PARKSIDE

DEPARTMENT OF MUSIC

P.O. Box 200
Kenosha, WI 53141
Roberta Odegaard
262-595-2355
Fax: 262-595-2271
E-mail: roberta.odegaard@uwp.edu
www.uwp.edu/academic/music

The UW-Parkside Music Department offers the
bachelor of arts in music with degree options
in instrumental, choral or general music education, jazz studies, arts management and piano
pedagogy and literature. Eight full-time and 15
part-time instructors, who are all active as professional performers or composers, staff the
department. Over 200 participate in UW-
Parkside Bands, Choirs, Jazz Ensembles,
Orchestra and Chamber Ensembles. About 65
concerts are presented annually by students,
faculty and guest artists in the Communication
Arts Theater and the Union Cinema-Theater.
Music major enrollment has risen every year
for the past eight years. Seventy-five majors
are currently enrolled.

University of Wisconsin at Platteville
Department of Fine Arts and Music
1 University Plaza
Platteville, WI 53818
Daniel Fairchild
608-342-1151
E-mail: fairchig@uwplatt.edu
www.uwplatt.edu

UNIVERSITY OF WISCONSIN AT RIVER FALLS

MUSIC DEPARTMENT

410 S. 3rd St.
River Falls, WI 54022
J. Michael Roy
715-425-3183
Fax: 715-425-0668
E-mail: music@uwf.edu
www.uwrf.edu/music/welcome.html

UNIVERSITY OF WISCONSIN AT STEVENS POINT

DEPARTMENT OF MUSIC

2100 Main St.
Stevens Point, WI 54481
Barbara Bartkowiak
715-346-3107
Fax: 715-346-3163
http://music2.uwsp.edu

UNIVERSITY OF WISCONSIN AT SUPERIOR

DEPARTMENT OF MUSIC

Belknap and Caitlin
P.O. Box 2000Superior, WI 54880
Dr. T. A. Bumgardner
715-394-8115
Fax: 715-394-8578
http://staff.uwsuper.edu/music

This is a NASM-accredited, quality music program at Wisconsin's Public Liberal Arts College. A highly qualified faculty, excellent facilities and ample performing opportunities are the hallmarks of this program.

UNIVERSITY OF WISCONSIN AT WHITEWATER

DIRECTOR OF PUBLIC EVENTS

800 W. Main St.
Whitewater, WI 53190
Janet Barrett
414-472-1310
Fax: 414-472-2808
E-mail: music@mail.uww.edu
www.uww.edu

WAUKESHA COUNTY CONSERVATORY OF MUSIC

1125 James Dr.
Hartland, WI 53029
Ellen McDonald
262-367-5333
Fax: 262-367-4468
E-mail: emcdonald@hartlandmusic.com
www.hartlandmusic.com

WISCONSIN CONSERVATORY OF MUSIC

1584 N. Prospect Ave.
Milwaukee, WI 53202
Alice Brovan
414-276-5760
Fax: 414-276-6076
E-mail: joycea@aol.com
www.wcmusic.org

WYOMING

Population: 506,085

Capital City: Cheyenne

Music Colleges and Universities: Casper College, Central Wyoming College, Eastern Wyoming College, Northwest College, Sheridan College, University of Wyoming

Bird: Western Meadowlark

Motto: Equal rights

Flower: Indian Paintbrush

Tree: Cottonwood

Residents Called: Wyomingites

Origin of Name: Based on an Algonquin or Delaware Indian word meaning "large prairie place."

Area: 97,818 square miles (10th largest state)

Statehood: July 10, 1890 (44th state)

Largest Cities: Cheyenne, Casper, Laramie, Gillette, Rock Springs, Sheridan, Green River, Evanston, Riverton, Cody

College Band Programs: University of Wyoming

WYOMING

CASPER COLLEGE
MUSIC DEPARTMENT
125 College Dr.
Casper, WY 82601
307-268-2100 or 800-442-2963
www.cc.whecn.edu
Degrees: Associate of Arts Degree Music,
Associate of Fine Arts Degree
Instrumental Music Performance,
Associate of Fine Arts Degree Music
Education, Associate of Fine Arts Degree
Vocal Music Performance.

CENTRAL WYOMING COLLEGE
2660 Peck Ave.
Riverton, WY 82501
307-855-2000
www.cwc.wy.us

EASTERN WYOMING COLLEGE
3200 West C St.
Torrington, WY 82240
307-532-8200
ewcweb.ewc.cc.wy.us

NORTHWEST COLLEGE
231 W. 6th St.
Powell, WY 82435
307-754-6000
E-mail: admissions@nwc.cc.wy.us
www.nwc.cc.wy.us

SHERIDAN COLLEGE
3059 Coffeen Ave.
P.O. Box 1500
Sheridan, WY 82801
307-674-6446
www.sc.cc.wy.us

UNIVERSITY OF WYOMING
DEPARTMENT OF MUSIC
P.O. Box 3037
Universal Station
Laramie, WY 82071
Dr. Julia C. Combs
307-766-5242
Fax: 307-766-5326
E-mail: jccoboe@uwyo.edu
http://uwadmnweb.uwyo.edu/Music

Conservatory or College of Music?

BY ROB ROGERS

You've studied, practiced, performed, and prepared. You know you're ready to take your career in music to the next level. So which direction do you choose – a college of music, or a conservatory?

"In title, there's little difference. It's not like the huge difference between a university and a college," said Todd Krohne, administrative assistant to the assistant vice president for student affairs and enrollment at Berklee College of Music in Boston, Mass. "If you look at all of the aspects – location, curriculum, faculty – each has the same weight and merit."

Your choice is likely to depend on what you want out of both your music and your environment, as well as your answers to the following questions.

What Do You Want to Study?

This might seem like a simple question – you want to study music, right? However, no two schools are likely to approach this goal in the same way. Conservatories emphasize performance, encouraging and demanding excellence in an instrument or voice. Individual conservatories are known

for their strength in the areas of music theory, analysis, and composition.

"Performance is the focus of what students do here," said Allison Scola, associate director of admissions at Mannes College of Music, a New York City conservatory. "The students take some humanities classes, like writing, Western civilization, and art history, that accentuate their music education, but 85 percent of what they do is music-related, including private lessons and chamber music. We want students to leave here with their ear so trained, their dictation skills and analytical techniques so well developed, that 25 years from now, they'll be able to look at a piece of music and be able to say what it's all about, what art and political history influenced it, what the writer was thinking when making key changes. That's the kind of thing we focus on here."

Music colleges – especially those located within a university – often combine a rigorous music program with a liberal arts education. This can be particularly helpful for students considering careers that require both an understanding of music and a background in business, psychology or another discipline. Many colleges offer degrees in areas such as music management, music education, instrument design, and music therapy.

"Our students study music management, production technology, and music education," said Amy Becher, director of admissions of the Hartt School in Hartford, Conn. "We also have the only undergraduate program that I am aware of in acoustics and music. Our students receive a solid conservatory training, with a strong performance background, but they also have the job security that comes with having a marketable degree."

Described as "a conservatory setting within a university," the Hartt School, which became one-third of the University of Hartford in 1957, maintains a unique middle ground between the college and conservatory experiences.

"We're still a conservatory, with a strong performing faculty," Becher said. "But we can also offer students some of the benefits of being part of a university – athletics, Greek life, opportunities to take on projects that go beyond a strictly musical focus. We invite students to incorporate music into every level of their lives, not just the performing level."

In addition, music colleges are often a choice for those students primarily interested in contemporary, rather than classical, music.

"We foster the learning of contemporary music, and it makes such a radical difference," said Krohne, a 1996 Berklee graduate. "There's an excite-

ment, a passion about this place. The subject matter is so up-to-date, so cutting edge, that you graduate knowing what they've taught you is what the industry is doing at that time."

How Much Time Should You Devote to Your Music?

Many colleges follow the National Association of Schools of Music curriculum guidelines, which require students to spend 60 percent of their studies in music, and 40 percent on the liberal arts – creating what Amy Becher of the Hartt School calls "a well-rounded student."

However, some students may find it difficult to devote themselves to a performing career while juggling a liberal arts course load. Others may decide they simply want to spend more time practicing and studying music. For them, a conservatory might be a better choice.

"It can be a problem when, because of the amount of studies and papers you have to write, you don't have time to practice five or six hours a day," said Scola, who graduated from a music college before coming to work for a conservatory. "At my school, the English and history classes I was taking weren't related to the music curriculum at all, and things like the orchestra and chamber music were considered 'extra.' Classmates of mine who wanted to go on to master's programs had to take a year off to practice and get their chops ready before they could play at the same level as someone who had been to a conservatory."

"It's a demanding program," said Haim Avitsur, a 1999 Mannes graduate who now works in the admissions office. "It asked things of me that I never thought or dreamed I could do. I'm a trombone player, so I never thought I would have to learn the piano. But I needed to do that to be able to graduate, and it proved to be a good thing. Now I can read scores that others cannot."

What Resources Should Your School Have?

Music colleges, especially those associated with universities, offer all the advantages of a large school – a wide range of academic subjects, an active campus life, and often significant financial resources. They may also provide musical instruction for students with a wide range of abilities, and emphasize community involvement.

Depending on its size, a conservatory may have fewer resources than a university music college – but the resources at its disposal are focused on a music education.

"As an undergraduate, if I wanted to play in a woodwind quintet, I always had to make sure there were enough players," Scola said. "You don't have to worry about that in a conservatory. Also, my school had a single master class program that I knew of that took place once a year. Conservatories offer master classes on a routine basis."

Some students choose schools based on the opportunity to study with particular faculty members.

"I'm a trombone player, and I wanted to study with Per Brevig, the former principal with the Metropolitan Opera," said Avitsur, who came from Israel to study at Mannes. "He's a legend among trombone players."

Colleges and conservatories also differ in the number and kind of degree programs available. The Hartt School offers eight different bachelor of music programs, two bachelor of arts programs, and a bachelor of science in engineering in acoustics and music, as well as double majors, minors, and honors programs. Berklee offers its degree candidates a bachelor of music in 12 areas, including film scoring, music therapy, and professional music, in which a student creates a major based upon his/her professional objectives. Mannes graduates bachelors of music and science majoring in orchestral and other instruments, voice and opera, composition, theory and conducting.

Are You Ready for the Audition?

The admissions process varies greatly for music colleges and conservatories. Most music colleges require separate applications for the school of music and the university with which the school is associated. Some require live auditions, while others will accept recordings.

Berklee College of Music offers students two options: the chance to become a degree student, incorporating liberal arts and music studies, or a diploma student, studying only music.

"There's no audition process to be admitted, only to receive scholarships," Krohne said. "The application provides us with information about how the student has done in the past, recommendations from teachers, and personal essays. We encourage students to send music along to give us a better idea about them, but it's by no means necessary for admission."

In addition, students applying to a music college may not be limited by the performance needs of a particular school.

"It's the opposite of the conservatory mode," Krohne said. "Students might apply to a conservatory that only needs a certain number of string players or oboe seats. We don't have the mindset that we need more of this or that. We accept students as musicians."

Auditions are standard for applicants to conservatories. Some schools – such as Juilliard, Mannes, and Manhattan School of Music – hold their auditions during the same time period, so students traveling to the New York area can visit all three at once. Some schools accept common applications, like that of the National Arts Learning Foundation. Mannes, for example, accepts the NALF as part one of its application, with part two including a personal statement and an assessment of the applicant's writing skills. Students at Mannes also take a placement test based on their dictation, ear training, and theory skills.

How Competitive Do You Want Your Environment to Be?

Getting into a college or conservatory is only half the battle. In addition to the long hours of practice and strict musical discipline, some students expect a competitive atmosphere when attending a top school of music – and they may be right. However, school representatives say that sense of competition often comes from the students themselves, and not their peers or institutions.

"It depends on the conservatory, but it's definitely more intensive [than a music college]," Scola said. "For one thing, there's more at stake. At least with a B.A. program, there's something to fall back on – there's more of a wide range in the job market."

However, Scola adds that the pressure to succeed tends to bring conservatory students together, rather than set them against each other.

"We rotate our players through the principal chair, second, back section and so on," Scola said. "There are other places where whatever position you end up in, you stay there, unless you're willing to challenge the first chair. That sets up a competitive atmosphere."

"You hear horror stories, but for the most part, they don't happen here," Avitsur said. "You know where you are, and you try to be a little bit better than your colleagues, but when a friend of mine gets a position with an orchestra, I smile and say congratulations. There's no talking behind someone's back, no backstabbing here. New York City is a rough city to live in, and this school is more like a home, a family." ♪

Rob Rogers is a freelance writer based in Massachusetts and has written for School Band and Orchestra *in the past.*

Guidelines for a College Audition

BY MARK THOMAS

Once you decide to pursue a career in music, the first hurdle to overcome is gaining acceptance to a college, university, or conservatory. This may seem to be a monumental challenge, but with careful planning, guidance, and preparation, it need not be a terrifying ordeal. Years ago, it was generally thought that one had to attend a major conservatory of music to receive the best instruction and to pursue study of his/her chosen instrument by an artist-teacher. Conservatories had the stature and legitimacy that young, aspiring students sought. Indeed, in the past, there was some truth to that perception. Symphony orchestras, for instance, were more likely to audition and accept a conservatory-trained player who had studied with a "name" teacher than a college or university student.

Today, though conservatories remain outstanding institutions for instruction in music, there have been many changes in post-secondary music education. In recent years, numerous colleges and universities have recruited and hired nationally and internationally acclaimed artists who were previously only found at the conservatory level. At times, schools even compete among themselves in the effort to gain the services of a specific artist, similar to efforts to find top-flight football or basketball coaches. The thinking is that a well-known artist will attract outstanding music students to the school, just as a popular football coach will attract outstanding high school gridiron stars. Today, aspiring musicians can now gain a first-rate musical education at a number of schools, including many state universities and colleges.

Where to Apply

Most important, plan to apply to at least three to four schools. Never apply to only one institution, since rejection will leave you with no alternative options. When in the selection process, focus on schools that have recognized artists in residence teaching your major instrument. Such teachers can impart firsthand knowledge and experience regarding the requirements of being a successful orchestral player, chamber artist, or soloist — their instruction can be invaluable. If your state has state-supported colleges or universities with good music programs and artist-teachers, check them out. In-state tuition levels can be a real bargain.

Begin to narrow your school choices during your junior year in high school; write the admissions departments early for information. Your high school counselor can provide advice and brochures. Your high school band or orchestra director, your private instrument instructor, or the conductor of your city's youth orchestra can assist you as well. They should be able to answer many of your questions and may personally know some of the music professors at the schools you are considering. Asking one or more of these professionals for a letter of recommendation on your behalf is not inappropriate. Be sure to provide them with the contact person's name, title, and address, along with a stamped, pre-addressed envelope if the letter is to go directly to the school.

What Do Universities Look For in a Student?

Relax. Institutions of higher education do not expect to enroll a finished musician. A school looks for potential in an applicant: one who possesses musical ability that can be shaped, molded, and polished during the academic years. A student with musical sensitivity, however raw, can be guided into a well-focused, mature player with practice and time. A student must come with a willingness to learn by listening and watching. Remember, students with large egos and closed minds are rarely successful.

Of course, an applying instrumentalist must meet certain levels of technical ability, musicality, intonation, and a good start on the repertoire for his or her instrument. Do not expect to be accepted as a performance major if you have been playing for a short time and have relatively little facility on your instrument.

Preparing for the Audition

All schools will require a performance audition, either by tape and/or in person. Most schools will require a live audition. Such auditions are usually held at the school, although some institutions will schedule audition dates in selected cities throughout the country. School auditions are usually preferable because you will have an opportunity of seeing the campus, talking with other students, and meeting the faculty audition committee. Face-to-face meetings can give you a much better "feel" for the school than those slick brochures the school's marketing department sends out.

If your audition application is accepted, you will receive a letter with information as to the audition date and time. If you've started this process early enough, you should have sufficient time to prepare your audition material. Many schools will send a prepared list of pieces that are required for the audition, and most will also ask you to prepare an etude and/or solo of your choice that will display your musical abilities.

Always be prepared to play your major and minor scales, the chromatic scale, and various combinations, such as arpeggios, thirds, and octaves in a variety of articulations, as this is usually a minimum requirement. Most schools will ask you to sight-read something as well. Though it sounds like an oxymoron, you can "prepare" for sight-reading. Simply do it every chance you get, either alone or with another person or in a group. Do not consider coming unprepared in any of the above areas. A nicely played solo coupled with weak fundamentals (scales, etc.) can easily cause your application to be soundly rejected, just as a well-written essay combined with a poor SAT score can cause the aspiring fiction writer to be rejected.

Your solo choice should include a slow section that highlights tone and expression and a contrasting section that focuses on technical abilities. Your private teacher can offer repertoire suggestions if no set required piece or pieces are mandated. It does not have to be a work written for your instrument and piano; many etudes will work quite well. A word of caution: if you are required to play a work for oboe and piano, for instance, you should know the piano part as well as your own, even if you cannot read all of the piano part. Remember that many schools require their piano majors to spend time learning to accompany others, so you will need to know what to expect and be able to tell the other person exactly what you want in order to perform well under those conditions.

Practicing for an Audition

Once your audition material has been determined, carefully analyze the piece(s) for style, tempo, and expression markings. Ask your private teacher for assistance in this area. If the piece is fast and technical, play it slowly and carefully under tempo for many days. Believe it or not, the quickest way to master any fast piece is by steady, rhythmic, slow practice. If in doubt about this, ask any professional musician. Gradually increase the tempo, and never play at a tempo the fingers cannot control. By using this method, your fingers will be on auto-pilot — making stressful performances, such as auditions, possible.

A slow, expressive solo requires very careful preparation — there's literally no place to hide. Play with expression, observing dynamics, and attempt to bring to life the composer's work. Listen carefully for tone quality and intonation, and play between the notes. In other words, play from your soul. Avoid a common mistake of young players, which is thinking about the next passage before you've finished the last one. Remember that a slow solo, well played, will garner positive points at your audition. When you feel you have your audition pieces properly prepared, ask your band or orchestra director to allow you to play during class — there is no substitute for a live audience.

Ask for feedback, both positive and negative, after your performance, and then make corrections in your playing and stage presence as suggested by your teachers and peers. Find pre-audition playing venues, such as your church or a nursing home. The more you play in front of others, the more "in control" you will feel when you play your audition. Remember, too, that daily practice of 30 minutes a day will not prepare you for a successful audition or a career in music. If you have to be told to practice, you'd probably be well-advised to choose another career!

The Instrument

A surprising number of high school students arrive to play a college audition armed with a student model or step-up instrument. While it isn't necessary to have a violin that only Itzhak Perlman would play, or a trumpet worthy of Wynton Marsalis, any student entering college as a music performance major must have a professional-quality instrument. When spending thousands of dollars on a college education, don't invite failure by playing on a marginal instrument. Consult your private teacher for suggestions about brands and models, and buy the best instrument you can afford.

Audition Jitters

Everyone becomes nervous before a performance — professionals often refer to jitters as "heightened awareness." Most players begin to feel nervous a few days before a scheduled performance or audition. Symptoms can include nausea or "butterflies in the stomach," sleeplessness, headache, dry mouth, loss of appetite, diaphoresis (sweating), shivering, and cold hands. Becoming aware of your particular pre-performance feelings can help you overcome them. The truth is, a little "heightened awareness" can keep you alert and even enhance your performance.

Overactive nerves during a performance are often caused by an underlying, subconscious desire to please — to be liked — or to receive approval. In our attempt to please our audience, we become tense and uneasy. The harder we try to please, the worse the symptoms become.

Remember that it is not possible for you to make your audience like you or your performance. Only your listener can make that choice. As a performer, you must learn to adopt an attitude of "If the audience likes my playing, that's okay, but if they don't, that's okay, too." This may at first appear to be arrogant, but it is not. This attitude simply enables you to stop worrying about things over which you have no control.

Audition Day

A few days before leaving on your trip, be certain to get plenty of rest and nourishing food. Attending good-luck parties, eating junk food, and staying up late watching videos will leave you tired and unable to play your best.

Try to schedule your arrival at the school the day before your audition. This will give you ample time to locate your accommodations, visit the campus, and locate the rehearsal room and stage, and if necessary, meet with your accompanist.

Arrive for your audition in plenty of time to secure a warm-up room, but do not over-practice prior to your performance. Remember that your practicing should have been completed long before this point. It is acceptable, too, for you to rehearse with your accompanist on the day of the audition. Don't forget to bring along a book or magazine to read while you wait to be called, as this can offer a needed distraction.

If you are an instrumentalist, you're probably already aware that certain foods, especially greasy ones, can spell disaster to your embouchure. (Have those McDonald's fries after you play.) Also, be aware that the audition is a public performance, so it does matter how you dress. Jeans, T-shirts, or a short skirt if you're female, and dirty or inappropriate shoes (such as running shoes) have no place on stage. Your demeanor is just as important as your playing, and you make a good impression by paying attention to details. If you are unclear about something, ask politely for the question to be repeated. Do not forget to bow after your performance and acknowledge your accompanist if you have one. Then wait on-stage until the committee chairperson releases you.

An audition is nothing to fear if you've prepared carefully. Remember that every member of the audition committee has taken an audition at one time or another. Committee members are, first and foremost, teachers of musicians — they know exactly how you feel and understand the stress a performance causes. Most will be kind and fair.

Your time in high school is nearly over. College is a new world for you to explore, musically and academically. It is an exciting time — go for it. We'll see (and hear) you in Carnegie Hall some day. ♩

Mark Thomas is founder and honorary life president of The National Flute Association (NFA), is professor of flute at the University of North Carolina at Charlotte, where he also directs the university flute choir. A recitalist, soloist, conductor, and clinician, he has appeared in 20 foreign countries and 49 states. He has been on the faculties of The American University, George Washington University, The University of Notre Dame, Indiana University at South Bend, National Music Camp at Interlochen, and Sewanee Summer Music Center, and has lectured at many universities and conservatories. Thomas has numerous published flute works, including the Mark Thomas Flute Method series. He has served as board member of National Public Radio, board President of the Elkhart County Symphony Association, and as artistic design consultant to several leading flute manufacturers. Thomas can be heard on Golden Crest and Columbia Records.

How to Record Your Audition

By Thomas Kikta

The grades are solid and the SAT scores are as good as they are going to get. The final hurdle in attending the school of music or conservatory of your choice is the audition – the performance of a lifetime that will decide the direction of your next level of musical education. Almost every music school requires auditions for the purpose of acceptance, for scholarship consideration and teacher assignment. The best way to audition is to physically go to the school, meet the teachers, see the campus and audition in person. But many people – due to their location, time considerations or expense account – are unable to audition in person and are forced to go the route of the audition tape. If just the mention of this event has not caused you to slam this book shut, then read on, for I hope to not only enlighten you on how to prepare an audition tape but to supply strategies in preparing an audition in general, whether taped or live.

Some Points to Remember

The first thing to remember when preparing your audition is to maintain a positive attitude toward the whole process. The audition is a performance opportunity, a chance to share your music with others and any negative distortion of such an honor is counterproductive. If we have worked to the point where we are set on making music our life's work then an opportunity to share our art with others is a gift. Too many students lose sight of this. The professors on the panel have been in your shoes and are simply using this opportunity to benchmark where you are and estimate your potential.

The second thing to remember is that this audition, whether live or recorded, is a representation of you. All details of professionalism should be considered. If you audition live, then dress and act accordingly. If you are sending in a tape, then make it as professional a product as possible. Better yet, don't send in a tape, speak with the department chair and see if a CD is acceptable. A CD professionally printed and packaged will send a stronger message that your act is together – more so than a hissy, awkward cassette tape. We will get into this deeper, but let's start at the beginning.

389

In the Beginning

After choosing three or four schools for auditions – a decision that should be based on teacher or department reputation – call the school's admission department and request the audition requirements for your instrument. This list will suggest the number and types of pieces to be performed as well as scales and technical studies to be executed. After review, give the teacher or department chair a call and discuss your audition with them. Discuss your current repertoire and how you are studying. This is a great opportunity to take their temperature and get a feel for what they might be looking for. Be sure to ask whether scales and technical studies should be included on your recording and whether a CD could be submitted instead of a cassette. Based on the results, discuss with your teacher an audition repertoire that will meet the requirements. Generally three pieces of contrasting styles, five two- or three-octave scales and arpeggios will be adequate, but go by the requirements for your specific instrument.

This article would not be complete unless I comment on the possibility of the school asking for a video tape. By nature, a professional video production is very expensive. It will look and sound great, but will be out of the financial range of most students. Using a home video system will solve the financial problem but quality will suffer. Though this format will show your posture, technique and stage presence, it will fall very short in audio quality.

Practice Performance

Your preparatory skills are still developing but you, along with your teacher, should have a feel as to how long it is going to take for you to develop all of this material. If this is the beginning of your junior year, then relax and slowly hone your audition. However, if Christmas carols are playing on the radio and you are a senior – wake up!

As you prepare for your recording date, be sure to stress in your practice what many overlook – continuity. Have you noticed yourself playing a selection only to fumble, work on the mistake, then go on in the piece, never really playing it without pausing? Don't mix practice and performance. Practice your rough spots separately and when you play through the piece, do just that: play through the piece in continuity. Use slower tempos to maintain control. It may seem odd that I call this step "Practice Performance," but what I want you to do is to make a section of your daily practice time a "Practice Performance" – a dry run, if you will, of your selections by yourself but as if you're performing for an audience or audition. Stress continuity in your playing. Always try to move on; don't dwell on the errors and definitely don't back up and try to take another whack at an error. Music doesn't go backwards. Think to yourself, "Is this what I want to happen on stage?" If not, then fix it in your next practice section. Try doing your performances with a small cassette recorder. Not only does it log your progress, it also creates a performance stimulus to simulate a real performance. As you develop, you might invite a friend or family member to your practice performance for a more realistic performance opportunity. But remember in these performances continuity.

Let's Record

Deciding how you are going to record is your next step. The most obvious is to buy time at a professional recording studio. If you look in your local Yellow Pages under "Recording Services," you will find a list of businesses that can help you. Give them a call and tell them you're recording an audition tape. Ask what type of equipment they have and what their rates are. You are making a stereo recording, so equipment-wise your needs are simple. A DAT (Digital Audio Tape) machine is common and should be available at most facilities. Another option is to record directly to hard disc on a computer system. High quality standard condenser or electret condenser microphones should be used. A pair of AKG 414, Neumann U87, Audio-Technica AT4050 or equivalent mics will work great for all instruments. Since this is an audition tape, you will not need a lot of signal processing or sound effects. A simple stereo reverb wash will be adequate. Most professional studios will have all of this and will charge anywhere from $30 to $75 dollars per hour, plus materials. When you are finished with your recording, this facility should be able to "burn" you a CD master for your final product.

A special note for pianists or anyone needing a piano accompanist: Ask what type of piano is available and if it has been tuned. A grand piano is preferred and the tuning should be checked before your session.

If your teacher or high school has the above-mentioned equipment, then a money-saver could be to do it with them. Just be sure that the quality is not going to suffer. A favorable recording can be made in your school auditorium, but be sure once your takes are done that you have the resources to sequence your best takes for a final master.

Take This

On the issue of takes, it is imperative that no editing be done on any of your takes. Perform the selection two or three times and move on. A few days later, after the dust settles, sit down and listen with your teacher to choose the best ones. That's it – don't select the best "A" section or "B" section and start pasting them together. It's not fair and any pro studio will object to such a practice for an audition tape. If you want to maximize the likelihood for good takes, then spread your sessions out over a number of days. Do short sessions focusing on specific pieces over numerous days. You might even consider placing them weeks apart.

Minimize your use of effects processing. Heavily used reverb will be a distraction from the real issue at hand, which is your tone. The listening perspective should be as if the performance is happening in a recital hall, not in St. Patrick's Cathedral.

Shortly before you record, make sure your instrument is in the best shape that it can be. Change strings, reeds, pads or anything that is going to get in the way of giving you the best sound. It doesn't matter how state-of-the-art a studio is, it will not make a bad instrument sound like a good one.

A nice touch for your recording is to give a short introduction to your selections. Take some time to go to the library or get on the Internet and do a little research on the composers and pieces. Just a few statements of interest, whether spoken or written, will show that you not only perform on your instrument but have speaking, writing and research skills, too.

The Final Product

With your best takes selected, a final master will be burned. If the studio gives you a DAT, then request an additional CD. You won't be able to play a DAT at home. In either case, keep your master digital and do not send your master materials anywhere. I even recommend a back-up that is never played just in case something happens to your other copies. Have the studio make enough copies to send to all of your schools. These copies should be inexpensive; CDs or cassettes will be $5 to $8 dollars apiece, so don't forget the aunts and uncles.

The CD or tape should be printed on by a computer printer. Do not hand-write your information on the product. Remember the professional appearance. The studio should have some form of a printing system to print up your CD, tray card or cassette label so that it is neat and professional. Try to make it look like a product you would buy off the shelf —no shrink-wrap please.

The suggestions that I have given you are intended to make your

efforts stand out. The competition is fierce and any way to make yourself shine above the others is going to help leave a positive impression with the panel. All the best toward your success. ♪

Thomas Kikta is Director of Classic Guitar at Duquesne University in Pittsburgh Pa. and is President of Digital Dynamics Audio Inc., a compact disc and cassette replication facility.